To Mary

Best Wishes!

Jeffrey H. Jones
October, 2007

Marching to Save a Nation: The 123rd New York Infantry

Chancellorsville
Gettysburg
Tennessee Guerrilla Warfare
Atlanta Campaign
March to the Sea
Carolinas Campaign

Jeffrey H. Jones

Copyright © 2007 by Jeffrey H. Jones

All rights reserved. No part of this book shall be reproduced or transmitted in any form or by any means, electronic, mechanical, magnetic, photographic including photocopying, recording or by any information storage and retrieval system, without prior written permission of the publisher. No patent liability is assumed with respect to the use of the information contained herein. Although every precaution has been taken in the preparation of this book, the publisher and author assume no responsibility for errors or omissions. Neither is any liability assumed for damages resulting from the use of the information contained herein.

ISBN 0-7414-4107-1

Published by:

1094 New DeHaven Street, Suite 100
West Conshohocken, PA 19428-2713
Info@buybooksontheweb.com
www.buybooksontheweb.com
Toll-free (877) BUY BOOK
Local Phone (610) 941-9999
Fax (610) 941-9959

Printed in the United States of America

Printed on Recycled Paper

Published August 2007

*To the men of the 123rd New York Infantry and
all the soldiers that wore the Union blue,
whose efforts ended the scourge of slavery and
saved a Young Nation in the Nineteenth Century;
thereby allowing it to arise a Great Nation and defeat
fascism and communism
in the Twentieth Century.*

CONTENTS

Chapter 1	Washington County 1850-1860	1
Chapter 2	1862: Lincoln's Call for 300,000 Volunteers	15
Chapter 3	Chancellorsville: Rebel Shock & Awe	52
Chapter 4	Nursing Wounds and Pondering Hell	82
Chapter 5	Doubletime to Gettysburg	101
Chapter 6	Letters, Paperwork and Camps by the Rapidan	148
Chapter 7	Railroading West: Guerrillas and Blockhouses	163
Chapter 8	The Running Fight to Atlanta	202
Chapter 9	Marching to the Sea	251
Chapter 10	Finale: South Carolina Burns	277
Appendix A: Muster Roll		323
Appendix B: Personnel Totals		385
Appendix C: Prices for Clothing and Weapons		387
Bibliography		388
Notes		392

Acknowledgments

This work culminates several years of off and on research, reading and study. During that time I have been very impressed by the professionalism and high standards of the institutions I have visited for access to period newspapers and the letters, diaries and photos of the 123rd NewYork soldiers.

I would like to thank: New York State Library, Manuscript and Special Collections, Albany, NY; the U.S. Army Military History Institute, Carlisle, PA; Gettysburg National Military Park Library, Gettysburg, PA; Washington County Archives, Fort Edward, NY; Washington County Historian's Office, Fort Edward, NY; Washington County Historical Society, Fort Edward, NY; Rensselaer County Historical Society, Troy, NY; Hartford Enlistment Center Museum, Hartford, NY; Pember Library, Granville, NY; Cambridge Library, Cambridge, NY; Adirondack Community College Library, Queensbury, NY; Falvey Library, Villanova University, Villanova, PA; Hamilton College Library, Clinton, NY; History Department, Ohio State University; Bridgeport Area Historical Association, Bridgeport, AL; Old Jail Museum, Winchester, TN; Stevenson Railroad Museum, Stevenson, AL; and Historical Data Systems' American Civil War Research Database Website.

I greatly appreciate the encouragement I received from friends during my research and work. To Lisa Marie Buoncuore my thanks for her suggestions on the initial chapters. Finally, my thanks to my father, Harold Jones, sister, Judy Jones and aunt Doris Harrington for their support during this endeavor.

Chapter 1
Washington County 1850-1860

They ran through fields laughing, spent summer days swimming in the Battenkill, Hoosic and Hudson, playing "Red Rover" and chasing loose livestock barefoot back to the barnyard. Among the rolling hills and pastures of Washington County they spent their childhood, a scenic local in Upstate New York northeast of the state capital, Albany, and nestled between Lake George, Lake Champlain and Vermont. They were six, seven, eight and nine years old in 1850, the future backbone of a Union regiment, all volunteers, that would join in the crusade to save a nation. The idea of such a war, a Civil War, to arrive upon them must have never entered their minds as they admired sunsets over the Adirondacks, the brilliant Milky Way above or the Northern Lights on a crisp winter night.

A crossroads for warpaths and army trails, Washington County saw minimal development until after the French and Indian War (1755-1763). Although a few families had settled in the Fort Edward area and the Salem section, the constant skirmishes and dangers rendered the forests of pine, maple and hemlock a no-man's land. British soldiers were given land in the region for services rendered and a flow of families began in the 1760's. This development was rudely overrun by the American Revolution, and, literally, the British Army in 1777. General Bourgoyne marched his Redcoats and Indian allies through the future Washington County on the way to defeat at Saratoga. The murder of Jane McCrea at Fort Edward and the Allen family in Argyle hardened the locals' resolve to remove the threat the British and Indians posed. The American army swelled with militia both at Saratoga and Bennington. A Hessian supply column went down to defeat at Bennington while Bourgoyne tendered his sword a few weeks later.

All this history would have been told to the Washington County youths of 1850: the warriors in paint, the green-clad rangers of Robert Rogers, the remains of fortifications about the county (many taken apart for the stone and wood over the years) and the start of the U.S. Navy at Whitehall on Lake Champlain. Even in their homes they would have lived it as a common wallpaper for the houses of the 1840's and 1850's showed scenes of George Washington at the siege of Yorktown.[1] The vast majority of children had the ability to read about George chopping down the cherry tree, by 1850 there were a total of 229 one-room schoolhouses for the 17 townships of Washington County. During that year 10,798 students kept 244 teachers busy, of those students 47.6% were females. The student total includes 62 blacks: 29 males and 33 females. There were also 12 academies in the county with 700 students enrolled. School days could vary according to community but they often ran 9 a.m. to 5 p.m. with roughly a five-month school term. Besides teaching math, reading and writing, schools of the era were expected to inculcate good morals to the students. Towards that end the children might have had access to readers with such titles as "Effects of Evil Company" and "Dialogue Between Mr. Punctual and Mr. Tardy." The typical day would start out with a Bible reading and a patriotic song.[2]

Every Sunday would see horses trotting buggies and wagons along the dirt roads. Churches were another feature of the county landscape with 84 preaching the gospel by 1850; predominant ones being protestant such as Methodist, Friends, Presbyterian, Congregational, Episcopal, Adventist and Baptist. Two Roman Catholic churches were in Washington County by the 1850 census. Albany had the one synagogue in the region. Activity in the churches didn't mean "activity" outside of them stopped. The county supervisor's minutes for 1857 mention two cases of bonds put on men for bastardies; the 1858 minutes note nine cases of bastardies being cared for in the county Poor House with the fathers being billed. The Poor House had a number of people coming and going each year. During 1856 a total of 228 people entered the establishment, 1857 saw 236 and in 1858 a total of 280 were "relieved and supported" over the year. Supervisor's minutes for 1857 proudly announce that "a new Lunatic House has been erected" next to the Poor House.[3]

It was a dynamic, vibrant time in Washington County during the 1850's. Farming was the main driver of the economy but towns and villages were seeing active growth. Saw, grist and flax mills were active. Carriage factories, tanneries, harness shops, general stores, millinery stores, post offices, cobblers and blacksmith shops could be found from Salem in the south to Dresden in the north. In the Fort Ann area iron ore was mined and smelt at Mount Hope Furnace. Fort Edward had two paper mills by 1850 and the "Fort Edward Collegiate Institute" opened in 1854 to prepare students for college. Lime kilns were active in Greenwich. Welsh immigrants were working Granville's first slate quarry by 1853 and entertaining the locals with their singing going to and from the mine.[4]

Inns and taverns populated the major travel routes. Thirsty travelers would shout for oysters to dip in their whiskey, then chow down on steak with peaches or salt fish and onions. Coffee was becoming very popular. Foreigners were aghast at the amount of food Americans consumed and the speed which they wolfed down their meals. A common slang phrase for eating at this time being, "Gobble, gulp and go."[5] The Champlain Canal was active with shipping going to and fro from the Hudson River at Fort Edward and Lake Champlain at Whitehall. Railroads had arrived with branches along the eastern and western sides of the county. The towns and villages throughout the region were connected by dirt roads for wagon, horse and foot traffic. Toll roads, improved with grading and three inch plank wood surfaces, also existed but often the locals would steer off onto a "shunpike" which was a dirt side road before the tollhouse was reached.

Railroads and canals offered outlets to markets in New York City and Boston as the local farms switched from subsistence to market oriented farming. In 1860 there were over 800,000 people living in New York City while the rest of the state swarmed with an extremely mobile population of rural people.[6] By and large they were people in their 20's and 30's, Americans and immigrants working on farms or in shops to earn money before heading west. The physical demands of farming required young men and women to help in the fields and home. Federal census records of 1850 and 1860 note many Irish immigrants, men and women in their 20's, on Washington County farms as hired help. Besides the Irish, many Germans, English and Canadians found work in the county. Relatives often helped support those just starting out.

Census records show Washington County's 1850 population of 44,750 had grown to 45,904 by 1860. While the county was thriving, the population was generally stable as locals tended to stay put while hired hands would save some money then move on. Farms were prosperous and the beginnings of intergenerational transfers of wealth were starting. A study of property values in the federal census shows that between 1850 and 1860 Washington County real estate increased in value by 56.8%. Generally, the Hudson River Valley (of which Washington County is a part) had a stable population while the areas in Western New York saw migration westward via the Erie Canal and the Great Lakes.[7]

The rapid spread of the surplus market economy saw people embracing a consumer mentality as they moved into cities and towns across New York. Subsistence agriculture wasn't attractive, it was hard, physical daily work with little in the way of comfort. Hunting and fishing often supplemented the root cellar. In the beginning of the 1800's needs were few for a New York farm family; an unpainted hand hewn home with a table, some chairs and two beds in the loft. Luxury items such as carpets or grandfather clocks were mainly confined to the merchant class. By 1840 to 1850 former "luxury" goods such as a wall clock, buggy or store-bought dress were within reach of a farm family. From 1843 to 1861 farmers saw their products increase 33.9% in value while consumer good prices remained unchanged. Factory manufacturing in the United States was starting to fulfill the desires of the farm family. Instead of English, French or German made items the average citizen now had U.S. made goods competing in the marketplace with lower manufacturing costs, transport costs and lack of tariffs compared to the foreign items.[8]

 The grandfather clock that cost $50 in 1810 could be substituted with a wall clock for $3 in 1850. An 1811 wool mattress cost $50 but a family could buy a cotton mattress for $5 by mid-century. Stoves in the same time dropped from $20 to below $10. These items were coming to the farmer's door via peddlers. Roads and lanes were filled by the wagons and carts of these traveling salesmen. New York State licensed 302 peddlers in 1841 for the entire state. In 1855 the state issued 4,131 licenses. Barter was in decline as cash became king. From 1830 to 1850 cash transactions increased in neighboring New England from 43% to 63%. The basic daily wage for a construction laborer at this time period was a dollar per day.[9]

 As the household items expanded so too the items in the fields. Agricultural journals proliferated to advise the farmer how to properly use the cultivators, mowers and seed sowers coming out of factories. Articles emphasized the proper methods of crop rotation, soil enrichment and selective livestock breeding. Just like the "tech bubble" in the 1990's there were "livestock bubbles" in the mid-1800's. A sheep craze in the 1840's saw Merino sheep going for steep prices. Cattle such as the Shorthorn were the next animal to gamble on, imports of the beasts commanding top bids. Then the early 1850's saw hen fever with poultry imported from China, Spain and Italy going for $80 to $100 a breeding pair. By 1855 speculation dried up and prices collapsed.[10] Yet the craze had seen much valuable breeding stock imported to lay the future basis for better yields in meat, milk and eggs. (If you weren't literally forced to eat your investment.)

"Scientific farming" was being embraced, fertilizer such as guano from Peru making it to New York fields. Of those fields, about 90% were owned by the farmer working the plow. In 1855 New York market farmers averaged just over 80 acres of improved land with 11 cows and 15 sheep while subsistence farmers averaged 28 acres, 4 cows and 3 sheep. By 1860 New York farmers had the highest total value of farm equipment in the nation at $29,166,695, for an average farm machinery value of $148. (Metal plows cost $7 in 1860.)[11]

Embracing market agricultural set the future for Washington County farmers during the 1850's. The completion of the railroads into the Mid-West saw cheap transport of vast quantities of grains and beef to the eastern cities. In 1860 New York City consumed 264,000 cattle, 504,000 sheep and 400,000 pigs of which two-thirds came from the Mid-West.[12] Farmers in Washington County could not compete with the Ohio Valley's cheaper production costs of these items so they turned to an area they could excel in and where prices remained strong: dairy. Distance to market still remained critical for milk, cheese and butter products. Churns and cheese presses became common on Washington County farms as the dairy output increased. By 1859 New York State farmers produced 22% of the nation's butter. In 1860, New York farmers produced 46% of the nation's cheese.[13] Besides the dairy products, Washington County farmers added to family income by cutting cordwood, barrel staves and wooden containers called firkins. There was a great demand for firkins as they were used to transport butter. Carved from a tree trunk, the firkin would be loaded with 112 pounds of butter for shipment. A farmer could make three firkins a day and sell them for $1 each. Hemlock bark was another product of the farmer's woodlot as it was used for tanning leather. Each fall saw the men producing cordwood, with 10 to 12 cords for home use and the rest sold. It was not unusual to spend five to eight weeks on cordwood production. Agricultural journals of the time felt that a hard working farmer could cut a cord of wood per day. Maple syrup, apples, honey and beeswax were also valuable additions to the farm family's income. Daily caloric needs for adult male farmers at this time have been estimated to be in the range of 5,200 calories. (Recommended caloric intake for the average U.S. citizen today is 2,000.)[14]

With recent immigrants as farm hands Washington County children would have spent lunch (called dinner then) and suppers listening to discussions of conditions in Europe. The potato famine, the upheavals of 1848, lives set at birth, the attitude of the aristocracy to the workers. If you were born a shoemaker's son you became a shoemaker, if a lord's son you became a lord. The elite of Europe saw that as the proper ordering of a stable society. In 1850 royalty sat on a throne in most of the countries in Europe. America offered opportunity, a chance to break out of one's "class" and make a better life.

Yet America had one class if born into you stayed, the slave. In 1850 the slave population was 3,204,313, it would grow to 3,953,760 by 1860.[15] New York had originally allowed slavery; some of the people massacred in Washington County at the Allen farm in 1777 were slaves. Calls for it to be abolished resulted in two acts, one in 1799 offering gradual emancipation. The second act abolished slavery in the state on July 4th, 1827.[16] By 1850 there were 13,815 free blacks living in New York City. The 1850 census gives the population of Washington County as 44,750 with 44,400 white and 350 black.

Generally speaking, many northern whites had racist attitudes towards blacks. What was different in the North was that there were so few blacks. For Washington County, the total black population didn't even reach one percent of the population. With their own farms, businesses or jobs on the canal, they went about their lives. Some whites were indifferent, some were overt racists and others were staunch abolitionists.

That being said, Washington County did have a role in the Underground Railroad in the effort to get escaped slaves to freedom in Canada. While the main routes through New York for those seeking freedom went through central and western parts of the state, there was a path that used Washington County as an access to routes along Lake Champlain and Vermont. Often the freedom seekers would find their way to the Albany area and then work their way in stages through Washington County. In Easton the De Ridder house was a possible stop, Fort Ann saw the Wray-Goodman farm and in Granville the Chandler-Dougan house. Slaves would be given food and a place to remain hidden and rest. Directions for the next part of their journey would be given; such instructions might have included looking for the sign at Vaughn's Corners in Kingsbury with the black hand pointing north.[17] During warm weather when the Champlain Canal was operating escaped slaves could travel via the canal to Whitehall. From that location they could take a ship down Lake Champlain and into Canada. It might seem strange that runaways could board a vessel in daylight but forged, rented or borrowed papers were often used and questions might not be asked for paying passengers. As early as 1841 a British traveler met a "fugitive couple" on a steamboat from New York City to Albany, they were using forged passes. They were making the effort alone as they didn't realize there were people in the North that would help them to Canada.[18] It should not be thought that Canada was a pure panacea for the escaped slaves; there still was racism to contend with at times but once across the St. Lawrence or Lake Erie they had no fear of the hound, whip and slave hunter following.

Yet even free blacks in Washington County that had only known goodness from their community had to be on guard. Solomon Northup was a black man raised in Washington County. He lived for many years with his wife Anne and children in the Fort Edward and Kingsbury area working on the canal or farming his own land. His wife supplemented their income by cooking for the local court house. In 1841, while in Saratoga Springs, two white men talked him into traveling to Washington, D.C. for a job. Once there he was drugged, chained and sold into slavery in New Orleans. It was several years before Solomon got a message with his location back to people in Washington County. The governor of New York appointed an agent to go to Louisiana and after legal issues he was freed in 1853 to return to the Washington County area and rejoin his family. The book of his experience and suffering, *Twelve Years a Slave: Narrative of Solomon Northup* was published on the heels of Harriet Beecher Stowe's *Uncle Tom's Cabin*.

Stowe's book was a phenomenal seller that electrified the North while infuriating the South. Sectional baiters took to podium and pulpit to denounce or support her. Northup's work brought facts to back up Stowe's fiction. The future soldiers of the 123rd New York could not have avoided the debates and discussions among family, neighbors and townspeople as to freedom and bondage. Not that every supper saw such a topic, not that every neighbor brought it up daily. But it was front and center for discussion during 1853, it was on one's thoughts now and then, something to ponder. Just how did the "peculiar institution" fit with the idea of the Republic? Did it strengthen the United States or weaken it? And just what did the South want anyway?

Southerners wanted the right of slavery extended throughout all territories on the continent. Yankees were adamant against that, wanting new lands for *white* settlement under the rubric of "free labor." If it had been just one incident, one or two books blasting slavery, the matter might have drifted another decade until cooler heads could find a new compromise. But several issues combined over the 1850's to drive a wedge between North and South that resulted in war.

One was the makeup of the U.S. Congress. Due to population growth in the North the South watched its power in the House of Representatives decline over the 1840's and 1850's. They turned to the U.S. Senate to maintain power, to make sure no legislature became law threatening their culture based on slavery. Yet with the admission of

California into the Union in 1850 as a free state they lost controlling power in the Senate.

To placate the South, The Compromise of 1850 that admitted California also contained the "Fugitive Slave Act" which required Northerners to help arrest and return runaways to slaveholders in the South. The act also denied a jury trial to a black accused of being a runaway, made paperwork easier for filing a claim on a person and added federal agents to enforce the law. Northerners were very upset with it.

Cracks were starting to appear in the political parties by the 1852 national elections; the Whig party breaking along the issue of slavery exacerbated by the Compromise of 1850. Northern Whigs saw the compromise as a sop to the slaveholders, southern Whigs seeing it as a successful solution for the nation. The Whig candidate, General Winfield Scott, was chosen on sectional lines at their convention with the northern bloc winning. The Democrats nominated Franklin Pierce and the Free Soil Party's candidate was John Parker Hale. Washington County, New York voters (white males 21 years and older) voted 4,230 Scott; 3,174 Pierce; and 451 Hale.[19] Although Washington County went for the Whig Party candidate, Scott was a losing horse. Democrat Franklin Pierce won 27 of 31 states. The Whig Party stood for business growth and internal improvements (roads, canals, railroads) that attracted market-oriented farmers and the business classes. But the sectional issues racked it from 1852 onwards. The election of that year was seen by many as the end of the Whig Party. Their Illinois leader, a man named Abraham Lincoln, threw up his hands and went back to his law practice.

Stowe's book lit the fires of contention for 1853. For many Northerners it opened their eyes to just what chattel ownership of another human being really meant. In 1854 the Kansas/Nebraska Act was passed, this allowed territories to decide the issue of slavery within their boarders. This destroyed the "Missouri Compromise" of 1820 which limited slavery to below the latitude of 36 degrees 30 minutes and thereby unchained the fissures in Kansas. "Bleeding Kansas" became a common term in the nation as anti-slavery and pro-slavery forces joined battle to decide that territories fate. The *Washington County Post* of May 5th, 1854 discussed the upcoming vote on the Kansas/Nebraska Act with a large U.S. map showing slave states, free states and territories. The page two article warns readers that the Act will probably be passed due to "Dough Heads of the North" favoring it in Congress. "That this bill will still pass," the editors wrote, "is from latest accounts, quite probable, and we have therefore called the particular attention of our readers and friends in Old Washington County to this subject, trusting that their eyes may be opened to the importance of it, and that they may no longer dream that all's well in this matter." The paper ran the same map-Maryland to Missouri to Texas and south in solid black ink for the slave states-the next week. To the west of the blackened area were the territories of Nebraska, Kansas and New Mexico. "Should these territories become slaveholding States, the people will be represented in Congress for their slave property; and a few thousand slaveholders, as is seen in the cases of Florida and Arkansas, would equal in political power a free population five times as numerous." The Act was passed on May 30th 1854. In the June 9th 1854 *Washington County Post* editors Crocker and Gardner blasted the "Dough-faces of the North" that voted for it then stated, "The man who will promulgate doctrines like these to the people of the Northern states, and himself a citizen of a free state, ought in our opinion immediately to become an occupant of an insane asylum, or Penitentiary."[20]

    Passage of the Kansas/Nebraska Act also dealt the death blow to the Whig Party as it tore itself apart on the slavery issue. Many northern Whigs joined the newly formed Republican Party. Others joined the American Party, also called the "Know-Nothing Party." This semi-secret party was for strict immigration control and came about in response to the large Irish influx to the cities. When a member was asked about the party's activities they were supposed to reply, "I know nothing."

The 1856 elections saw the first Republican presidential candidate, John Fremont. The Republican Party had grown with many Free Soil Party members (former Democrats opposed to the expansion of slavery) joining their ranks. Washington County voters went big for Fremont, giving him 5,174 votes; American Party candidate Millard Fillmore 1,848; and Democrat Party candidate James Buchanan 1,632.[21] Buchanan won overall, getting 45% of the popular vote as opposed to Fremont's 33% and Fillmore's 22%.

As tensions increased even the U.S. Senate wasn't immune. On May 22nd, 1856 Massachusetts Senator Charles Sumner, a staunch anti-slavery man, was beaten senseless on the senate floor by South Carolina Representative Preston Brooks. As the legislative branch pummeled one another the judiciary hammered down a decision in 1857 that stunned the North. The case that came before the U.S. Supreme Court, *Scott v. Sandford*, was watched by both sides. The slave in the case, Dred Scott, had been taken into free territory by his owner for a few years then returned to a slave state. Scott sued for his freedom as he had lived in free territory. The Supreme Court declared Scott property and as such he didn't have a right to bring a lawsuit for his freedom. Even worse as the North saw it, the court ruling also said that Congress had no power to regulate slavery in the territories. Slavery could be taken wherever the slave owner wanted it to go. The North exploded in indignation seeing the Southern slave aristocracy on the march.

Coming out of this pot of Northern anger was John Brown. In October of 1859 he attempted to start a slave insurrection in Virginia by attacking Harper's Ferry. Captured by U.S. Marines under the command of Colonel Robert E. Lee, Brown was promptly tried and hanged. But his actions only fed the idea in the South that the North was filled with abolitionists seeking the South's destruction. Southerners discussed the former slave revolts of 1800, 1822 and 1831 in light of Brown's actions. For whites in the South an insurrection wasn't a light matter, of South Carolina's total 1860 population 57.2% were slaves; in Mississippi slaves made up 55.2% of the population.[22]

It's not that people saw the train wreck coming at the nation. Incidents and debates were spread out and people felt common sense would prevail. By the late 1850's Washington County teenagers were taking their guns down off the wall but it was to go hunting raccoon, squirrel or deer, not Southerners.

Lincoln's election in 1860 was the final breaking point for the South. The Republican platform that Lincoln was elected on specifically stated that expansion of slavery would be forbidden. As to how the Republicans would go about restricting slavery after the *Scott v. Sandford* decision was open to debate, but it was going to be pursued. Lincoln and other Republicans had been elected on that issue and they could not compromise on it. As Southerners saw it this was a life or death issue for their way of life, the plantation culture. They would not compromise as to it being restricted. During the run-up to the firing on Fort Sumter, Lincoln and many others in the North overestimated the numbers and strength of unionists in the South. It was expected that southern unionists would curtail secession. Southerners did not expect the North to fight, or, if they did, to make short work of the "Yankees." After that they could turn to the proper expansion of slavery, polite supper discussions pointing to Cuba and Mexico as future areas to conquer with Southern arms.

The 1860 presidential election saw four candidates vying for the office: Abraham Lincoln, Republican Party; Stephen Douglas, Democrat Party; John Bell, Constitutional Party; and John Breckinridge, Southern Democrat Party. There was an 81% voter turnout rate.[23] In New York State the ballot offered Republican Abraham Lincoln and Democrat Stephen Douglas as a "fusion" candidate of the other parties. On November 6th, 1860 Washington County availed themselves of the suffrage: Republican Abraham Lincoln 6,173 votes; Democrat Stephen Douglas 3,482 votes.[24] Lincoln took 40% of the popular vote and 180 electoral votes to win the Oval Office. The *Washington County Post* of November 25th 1859 titled their editorial commentary "The Irrepressible Conflict" stating, "The truth cannot be concealed that while the election of a Republican President would neither show 'hostility' to the South or provoke the least danger to her rights, yet there is and will continue to be an 'irrepressible conflict' between freedom and slavery, that will have its end as we firmly believe in the triumph of the former, and that too through 'peaceful means;' and nothing is more indicative of such a result than the trembling and fears of those who stand as it were upon a volcano of their own igniting and which is likely to burst at any moment as the result of its own combustible material overwhelming all who are thus exposed."[25]

The hopes for "peaceful means" were about to be dashed. South Carolina seceded December 20th 1860. Mississippi followed January 9th 1861, then Florida January 10th, Alabama January 11th, Georgia January 18th, Louisiana January 26th and Texas February 1st. Fort Sumter was fired upon April 12th and President Lincoln on April 15th issued a call for volunteers to put down the rebellion. Thereupon Virginia seceded April 17th, Arkansas May 6th, North Carolina May 20th and Tennessee June 8th.

Chapter 2
1862: Lincoln's Call for 300,000 Volunteers

When the war began in April 1861 many men in Washington County volunteered in the first rush of enlistment. The 2nd New York Infantry, the "Troy Regiment," and the 3rd New York Infantry, the "Albany Regiment," had men enlist from the county. When the 22nd New York Regiment was formed it had entire companies from the townships of Fort Edward, Cambridge, Whitehall and Sandy Hill (today's Hudson Falls). More recruiting as the war marched on and more volunteers from Washington County joined: the 43rd New York having a company from Sandy Hill, the 87th men from Dresden and Whitehall, the 93rd companies from Fort Edward, Cambridge and Argyle; and the 96th a company from Fort Edward. Cavalry units also drew their share of men, such as the New York 2nd, 6th and 7th. These units were filled out with men from a region or all parts of the state. Washington County volunteers found themselves with men from Troy, Oneonta, Waterford, Cooperstown, Brooklyn, Albany, Canajoharie, Poughkeepsie, Schnectady and Chateaugay, among other communities. In this fashion the people of Washington County during the first year of the war saw roughly 1,000 men depart, the equivalent of a Union infantry regiment. Below Washington, D.C. Union troops fought the Secessionists in the battles of Bull Run, Balls Bluff, Jackson's Valley Campaign and the Seven Days battles on the Yorktown Peninsula.

A year into the war teenagers in Washington County were keeping track of the fighting and going about their lives. William Clark McLean, 19, was apprenticed to a dentist in Cambridge. Besides mentioning farm work and church meetings, his diary accounts of that spring show late nights visiting girlfriends, cruising about town in the buggy with his friends and parties. "Had a good time of course and got home at 1 o'clock." But days were dragging for him at times. April 11th he noted, "Everything goes on as usual. Jeff Davis is the same old chap and Abe Lincoln sagasiates just as common, and I myself am traveling the same road as I always have." His entry for May 15th reads, "Nothing of any importance but a dog fight at Porter's between his dog and Clark's and Doc. Norton. It raised quite the excitement."[26]

The boom of a cannon from Whitehall or Glens Falls would echo across the Washington County landscape whenever major news of the war arrived. Papers told of lost battles, of dilatory Union generals, of some Confederate named Robert E. Lee that seemed to understand how to conduct a battle. The realization sank in that it was going to be a long war, not a 90-day adventure, not one great fight and home.

Union victory wasn't a sure thing. The South had good interior lines for movement, good generals (some poor ones to be sure), fighting spirit and, most important, they could sit and wait the North out. Northern armies had to attack, drive into and seize the Southern States to win. The Rebels just had to rebuff advances and let time with its casualty lists and growing cost in money drain the North of the will for the contest. If Northern opinion turned against the war the South could cut its own terms. The South even had supporters in the North, called Copperheads, seeking to undermine the war effort. As the war dragged on, Democrats running against Republicans in the northern elections would become more vocal in the idea of negotiating a settlement with the South, of ending the war even if it meant slavery being expanded.

First Bull Run in July of 1861 saw the Union driven from the field with a loss of 1,500 killed and wounded, 1,200 missing. At the time people were shocked at the numbers of casualties. In April 1862 Shiloh's 13,000 Union casualties flabbergasted them. Two months later the Seven Days Battles in the Eastern Theatre rolled another 16,000 Union casualties onto the lists. It was at this time, beginning of July 1862, that President Lincoln issued a call for an additional 300,000 volunteers for three years service. "The war news is rather bad," Clark McLean noted July 7th, "The president has called for 300,000 more men, but I don't know where they are going to come from. 600 are to be taken from this county."[27]

It was to be almost double that amount. The citizens of Washington County decided to field an entire regiment, approximately 1,000 men. A "mass convention" for the raising was held in Argyle on July 22nd. Several veterans of the War of 1812 were present on the platform, speeches were made to great applause, the Fort Edward band played "Dixie" (popular tune for both sides) and it was resolved to group the 17 townships of the county to form ten companies of 100 men each. Archibald McDougall was selected Colonel, James Rogers as Major and Reverend Henry Gordon named Chaplain. "I went to Argyle today to attend the great war meeting. There was a big turnout," Clark McLean writes, "They had speeches, etc. The supervisors appropriated ten thousand dollars to aid volunteering, offering a bounty of $50.00 to each volunteer in the county."[28] Recruiting committees fanned out into the townships with the recruits to report to "Camp Washington" in Salem at the County Fair Grounds.

War fever was hot for a couple weeks after the meeting. "Lots of boys are going and perhaps I will go myself," McLean notes in the days after the thumping bands and patriotic bunting. "Everyone that talks about enlisting wants to be Captain. It is a pity that the government could not call a regiment of captains."[29]

The *Salem Press* reported on one meeting in Hartford Township that saw a speaker loudly cheered when he said, "Republicanism was on trial, if it failed now, it was the last trial and no more republics would be formed. It was a war of races and if the domineering slave-driving aristocrats of the south could overpower the free north, then we deserved to be slaves."[30] Along the main street in Hartford a cabinet maker's shop was used as a recruiting center. The little white clapboard building saw 65 men signing papers for national service in Company E. (The shop still stands and is a museum open on summer weekends.)

By early August martial spirit had cooled. "The opinion is that we shall have to draft the men that are wanted. Enlisting goes on very slowly." It appears many were giving it serious thought before signing the papers. Then the recruiting offices became busy. On August 7th McLean made the simple notation, "I have a strong notion to enlist."[31] The very next day he stood with two of his friends and took the oath. They went into Company G, formed from the White Creek and Jackson townships.

For the married men it was rough to depart from wives and children. "I will here say that I went into the service wholly from patriotism-that I had a happy home, a dear wife and one child (Ella) who was then fifteen months old…I thought it my duty to go," Company H 1st Sergeant Robert Cruikshank writes.[32] He was 26 at time of enlistment and had a successful contractor and building business. Not all the recruits were from the county, a few men enlisted from Vermont. One, Andrew Benson, was only 17 but went on the muster roll as 18.[33] Although legal recruiting age began at 18, the 123rd had a couple on the roll at 17 plus one, Private John Graham of Company E, at 16 years old.

Muster rolls show the average age of the enlisted men of the 123rd New York as 24.6 years old, with the largest cohort at 134 being 18 years old. The ages 18 to 21 comprised 40% of the regiment. The oldest enlisted soldier was 46, there being a total of 42 men in their 40's. Education wise, out of the 81 enlisted personnel in Company H signing the papers 12 could not sign their name. Projecting that 15% illiteracy across the regiment would total about 144 soldiers. As for size, the average height on a stack of Company H enlistment slips shows the soldiers standing five feet eight inches.[34]

Until the men reached their majority at 21 they needed a signature of a parent or guardian on the enlistment form. The printed forms were just over seven by nine inches with "Volunteer Enlistment" in bold letters along the top, below it an eagle spreading its wings with talons grasping arrows and an olive branch, clasped in its beak is a banner reading "E Pluribus Unum" (Out of Many, One). Spaces were left open for the state, town of enlistment, name, place of birth, occupation and date of enlistment. To make sure the signer grasped the point of the contract the words "soldier" and "three years" were in bold capital letters. The volunteer had to sign before a notary or justice of the peace who also signs. Then the "Examining Surgeon" signs. Below that the recruiting officer then lists the volunteer's height, color of eyes, hair and complexion (light, dark, fair, etc.). The officer then signs stating that the recruit is of legal age, able bodied and "entirely sober when enlisted..." Flipping the form over, the volunteer then has to fill out the "Declaration of Recruit" where he restates age and sees term of service again, "THREE YEARS," and signs again that he has no legal "impediments" as to him serving. At the bottom of the reverse side is the "Consent in Case of Minor" section that was also witnessed.

  The flowing ink script in a stack of 123rd New York enlistment papers is steady from the officer recruiting, the doctor observing and the notary witnessing. The signing hand seems a bit unsteady for some of the parents signing the consent. Levi Gray, father of recruit Levi Jr., signed the consent area for his 18 year old son. Matilda Johnson, mother of Archibald Johnson, 18, signed for her son to go to war. Caroline Parker signed for her son, Calvin, also 18. Vermonter Grandison Sherman must have ridden to the recruiting office in Salem, New York with his 20 year old son Charles to sign his son's enlistment paper. One enlistee, 19 year old David Barker, was "discharged for minority" as no parent or guardian would consent. A few parents could not sign their name so they made an "X" on the paper with the recruiting officer filling the name in and writing "his mark" or "her mark."[35]

"I had often thought of enlisting, believing it to be my duty to assist the cause of our country," Hartford farm boy Rice Bull wrote, "My parents were at first loath to give their consent, but they realized it was a call to duty that could not be disregarded. After grave consideration of the matter they tearfully consented to my going."[36]

Bull was 20 years old when he sought his parent's permission to enlist. A friend of his, Phineas Spencer, had already joined Company D at Fort Ann. They had agreed "that we would go together and stand by one another." The morning of August 13th Rice worked alongside his father in the hay field, in the afternoon he went to Fort Ann and signed papers for three years service.[37] He stayed overnight in the town and the next morning rode a wagon with several other recruits down to Salem, New York. They arrived that afternoon to find many Sibley tents erected at Camp Washington. Eighty men of Company D had already reported with several other recruits still to arrive. McLean arrived that day also with the Company G, White Creek and Jackson, volunteers. There was straw spread for sleeping in all the tents but no equipment or uniforms had been issued. Blankets were available but weren't really needed due to the heat. As the Sibley tent resembles the classic Indian teepee, the area looked like an Indian encampment out west.

The Fair Grounds was a flat field adjoining the railroad station just on the outskirts of the Village of Salem. Friends and relatives of the recruits poured into the village while the men gathered. Bull notes that "they visited the camp in great numbers, they swarmed on the grounds and any order or discipline was next to impossible." Adding to the confusion and milling about, others were in town for the 50th anniversary meeting of the Washington County Bible Society. During this time Bull was sent back to Fort Ann to recruit more men, he returned after a week with 14 additions. Selection of officers having been done by the county War Committee, the non-commissioned officers (corporals and sergeants) were now elected by the men of each company subject to final approval by Colonel McDougall. By

September 1st all the companies were to strength and physicals were given. Out of the 900 plus enlisted personnel it appears that only one, George Edgerly of Company C, was rejected on medical grounds. It should not be deduced from this that Washington County was home to a breed of robust supermen but that the medical examinations were generally kept simple and perfunctory. There was a war on, men were needed for the ranks. Uniforms were now issued, Enfield rifles plus knapsacks and other gear. The men were puzzled as to how they were to fit all the extra items given to them by friends into the knapsacks. Bull had to spend time sorting and discarding, "could I have packed them all up, it would have required the strength of a Samson to carry them." He finally sent home a large bundle of items. "Even after the discarding my knapsack bulged on every side and to any old soldiers who had seen service would have been an object of derision."[38]

They were mustered into U.S. service on September 4th, 1862. Nearly a thousand men from a prosperous county with loving people caring for them, educated, with good economic opportunity at home, not misled as to the dangers, not lied to, not drafted. They volunteered to save the Union as they saw it as their duty. This time-period being an age of masculinity, some must have felt peer pressure to join or were afraid of being the butt of female comments if they didn't but the vast majority signed the papers as it was the right, the necessary, thing to do. Perhaps for a few the 50 dollar county enlistment bounty, 50 dollar state bounty, 38 dollar federal bounty and 2 dollar premium was inducement enough, but after the casualty reports from Shiloh and Seven Days it is hard to think men would sell themselves for $140 or six months of a laborer's wages. They did have other options beyond Washington County and the war zone. Canada was literally a quick boat trip away. Mark Twain gave Southern service a try but dropped out after two weeks and went west to Nevada. One could avoid the war if one sought too. During the gathering at Salem the results of Second Bull Run, August 30th, arrived with 16,000 Union casualties and another defeat. This might have had some affect as by September 5th four of the men had deserted. During the month of September a few more men would have second thoughts with an additional six deserting. But even after the desertions of ten men there were 960 men shouldering arms, taking the oath and standing by their commitment. The men of the 123rd New York went to war, saw it in all its horror and terror yet three years later emerged ragged and blackened from blazing Carolina pine forests with the rebellion tramped out, the Union saved and slavery crushed.

For the enlisted personnel signing the papers it is not that slavery was center-stage at this time. The danger to the Union, the Republic, was foremost in the men's minds. Slavery was the hidden foundation of the war that few Northerners acknowledged. This was a war among whites, some saying they had the right to leave the relationship of Union, the others retorting, "Treason!" Southerners felt they were justified and legal in going their own way, to decide their future without Northern interference. It was one of *their rights.* Northerners would also argue that they fought for *their rights*, the concept of a freely elected government. The South's action was seen as a direct threat to the form of republican government, for its future growth and strengthening. Aristocracy in the South was no different than the aristocracy in Europe smothering the working man's freedom. The United States Constitution was still young, barely 75 years old, and would become worthless if the South was allowed to break apart the nation. The United States would go from a beacon of future opportunity to a shell of a nation, something to be laughed at by the kings and queens of Europe.

There are arguments that even if there was no slavery the southern states still would have seceded. It is hard to conceive of another emotional issue that could have matched slavery to ignite such a conflagration. South Carolina tried to push tariffs as a reason for breaking from the Union in the 1830's but when President Andrew Jackson stood up to stare them down they blinked. No other state sided with South Carolina; no other state deemed tariffs worth fighting about. The actual secession documents from Confederate states clearly point out that they were leaving the Union to preserve their "Peculiar Institution." Abraham Lincoln had been elected on a party platform dedicated to restricting the expansion of slavery. The Republican National Platform adopted in 1860 at Chicago has seventeen declarations. Besides dealing with improving commerce and stopping wasteful federal spending three of the declarations deal with slavery: #7 *"That the new dogma, that the Constitution, of its own force, carries Slavery into any or all of the Territories of the United States, is a dangerous political heresy..."*; #8 *"...we deny the authority of Congress, of a territorial legislature, or of any individuals, to give legal existence to Slavery in any Territory of the United States."*; #9 *"That we brand the recent re-opening of the African slave-trade, under the cover of our national flag, aided by perversions of judicial power, as a crime against humanity and a burning shame to our country and age; and we call upon Congress to take prompt and efficient measures for the total and final suppression of that execrable traffic."*[39]

The vast majority of white Southerners would not be dictated to regarding their culture and institutions, the monster Lincoln could lord over the North but not the South. Among many justifications for South Carolina's secession their declaration states; *"We affirm that these ends for which this [Federal] Government was instituted have been defeated, and the Government itself has been made destructive of them by the action of the non-slaveholding States. Those States have assumed the right of deciding upon the propriety of our domestic institutions; and have denied the rights of property established in fifteen of the States and recognized by the Constitution; they have denounced as sinful the institution of slavery; they have permitted open establishment among them of societies, whose avowed object is to disturb the peace and to eloign the property of the citizens of other States. They have encouraged and assisted thousands of our slaves to leave their homes; and those who remain, have been incited by emissaries, books and pictures to servile insurrection."*[40]

Mississippi's declaration of secession had the following section justifying their leaving the United States: *"Our position is thoroughly identified with the institution of slavery-the greatest material interest of the world. Its labor supplies the product, which constitutes by far the largest and most important portions of commerce of the earth. These products are peculiar to the climate verging on the tropical regions, and by an imperious law of nature, none but the black race can bear exposure to the tropical sun. These products have become necessities of the world, and a blow at slavery is a blow at commerce and civilization. That blow has long been aimed at the institution, and was at the point of reaching its consummation. There was no choice left us but submission to the mandates of abolition, or a dissolution of the Union, whose principles had been subverted to work out our ruin."*[41]

The South understood from the very beginning of the conflict that it revolved around the bedrock of their way of life and culture. The antebellum South embraced slavery and felt it had to be able to expand for future survival. Northerners didn't see it that way. Why did it need expansion to survive? Just stay where you are and we'll leave you alone. When the war began it was the Northern desire to bring the South back into the Union slaves and all. Hard core Republicans and abolitionists wanted slavery dead, stamped out, extinguished, purgatories blight upon the land gone but the majority of Northern whites just wanted the South back in the Union and the slave owners to stop whining. Northerners weren't going to fight for blacks; but as their soldiers marched through hundreds of miles of slave territory, as they saw the stocks, shackles and baying bloodhounds of the plantations, they began to sense that it was an institution anathema to a free republic. It would take many months of sitting around campfires, poking coals with sticks, chatting, discussing the whole question. Slowly it would dawn on the men in blue. To break the South they had to break slavery. There would be no going back to the old ways. That total epiphany would be on the road to Atlanta and the torch and scorched earth was not long in following.

Word spread that the 123rd New York Infantry was to leave on the fifth. There was a resulting crush of "thousands" of well-wishers the next day that brought camp action to a standstill. The men basically packed and spent the time saying goodbye to family and friends. It wasn't until 10 o'clock that night that they were loaded on the train and it pulled away for New York City. Sergeant Morhous (Co. C) recorded that they left amidst "the shouts and cheers of the immense throng of people…" As did Sergeant Cruikshank (Co. H), "cheer after cheer went up from those left behind and was responded to by the regiment again and again…" But for Corporal Bull (Co. D) it was a different scene. "The people lining the track were so wrought with their emotions they could scarcely find to cheer but silently they waved their hankerchefs and we could see tears upon their cheeks."[42]

It was probably a blend of both, some cheers upon loading, then the jerk of the cars as the engine built steam. The men were looking out at the upturned faces, the special few in the crowd taking each mind totally, everything falling away. Bull was more than likely centered upon his parents.

The men were relieved to be on their way as the emotions had been pressing. Bull notes that the departure was tough on all but once underway, "The boys were themselves again, and the joke and the song could be heard in every part of the train."[43] In 24 hours they were in New York City, took a steamer over to Amboy, New Jersey and then entrained for Camden. Another boat across the Delaware River to Philadelphia where the entire regiment was served breakfast at the Cooper Shop Volunteer Refreshment Saloon. Rumors were already afloat as to where they were going, Confederate General "Stonewall" Jackson was raising havoc in the Shenandoah Valley and the thought was they would go to Baltimore to protect it against attack. Boarding cars again they traveled to Havre De Grace,

Maryland where the men were amazed to see the train pull onto a large ferry boat to cross the Susquehanna River. They arrived in Baltimore the evening of September 7th and marched through the streets to the train station that would allow them to depart to Washington, D.C.

They had already suffered casualties. Several men fell sick at Amboy, New Jersey when water contaminated with cholera was issued. Private Evander Burtis became the first casualty of regiment when he died from it. Another took sick in Philadelphia and now one fell out sick in Bull's own company in Baltimore. They also got their first taste of military travel when they reached Camden Station, the final leg of the train journey would be in cattle cars, not the passenger cars they had been riding. Packed in, the train moved off into the night. The men awoke to find the train idled at Annapolis Junction, they had gone all of 18 miles. New rumors swirled that the conductor was a secessionist and some treasonous act had occurred.

The train began to move and the raw recruits noted the many military camps along the tracks. As the train rolled into Washington the men marveled at the ranks and rows of tents surrounding the city. The Army of the Potomac knew how to set up camp but the men now found out that the food situation in the military could leave a lot to be desired. "Oh, what a breakfast!" Sergeant Cruikshank wrote home to his wife, "Nothing but bread and coffee. The tables were wet with coffee and the bread was thrown into it. The coffee was brought in tin cups which I think were never washed. Coffee was running on the floor and most of the men threw what was brought to them there also."[44] Bull adds that salt pork was also available but the men's main conversation centered on whatever the liquid was in the tin cups, some thought tea, some coffee. Bull reasoned a mixture of both.

They then formed up in the street and were marched up past the Capital, going to the south of it and into the Camp Chase area to set up their regimental camp. The men looked over the unfinished dome of the Capital as they marched along. Once at the regimental camp area, officers laid out "streets" and the men were issued tent cloths for their shelters.

Regiments were made up of ten companies of men, each company lettered A, B, C, D, E, F, G, H, I and K respectively ("J" not used as it might be confused during battle for an "I" in hurried written orders). The term "street" as the Union soldiers used it referred to the layout of the camp each company having an alley, or street, for its tents to face out on. Officer and non-commissioned officers tents were at the front and centered facing the rest of the regiment. It was a large rectangular area once completed. As for the tents, the enlisted personnel didn't think much of them. The men referred to them as "dog tents." Each man was issued one tent cloth or "shelter half" which, when buttoned together with another, could be used to construct an "A" type tent. The cotton or light canvas was approximately 66 inches long and 63 inches wide. Wooden sticks of about an inch diameter would be used for support, the ridge pole 6 feet long while both forked end poles would be roughly 50 inches in length. Straw or pine boughs would be spread over the ground to give some cushion for sleeping. For the floor of the tent the men would spread a rubber blanket out, put a woolen blanket on top of that then use the remaining blankets for sleeping. While it was quite normal for two men to make a tent, Bull states that often three men would join together as this allowed the third shelter half to be used to seal off one of the ends. Even so, they left a lot to be desired. "During fair, warm weather these tents made very comfortable sleeping apartments but when it was wet and cold they were anything but comfortable. The tents would shed the rain when it came gently but if the storm was severe the rain would come through the cloth at first like a heavy mist and after the cloth was well soaked would run through in big drops like a leaking roof and we would soon be wet through. In rainy weather we had either to stand out and take the full force of the storm or lie wet in our tents."[45]

The new camp with all the fresh tents arranged properly looked really nice. Then Mother Nature taught the rookies a lesson. "We did not ditch our tents and within 48 hours we were washed out of house and home by a severe thunder shower that struck us...This experience taught us to never again neglect the drainage of our camp."[46] The next lesson for the regiment was in proper weapon handling. On Sept. 11th Charles Lapoint of Co. A was shot in the side accidentally by Benjamin Rodier of the same company. Rodier was sitting three feet away from Lapoint while turning the cylinder of a loaded Colt revolver. It went off, the ball entering Lapoints side. The regimental doctor was able to extract the round and Lapoint recovered.

Lack of knowledge on camps and weapons plagued the men but the utter inability of the enlisted personnel to conform to military routine must have been irritating the officers of the 123rd New York to no end. A strong guard was posted around the camp with no soldier allowed out unless they had a pass from the colonel. "The men know little of discipline yet and a whole company ran the guard yesterday [Sept. 15th] and went into the city and some were brought back under guard," Cruikshank noted.[47] Efforts at drill were meant to instill some of the discipline needed for the regiment and the men of the 123rd were now drilling every day. At Camp Chase the opportunity for the men to watch more experienced regiments snap and wheel on the parade ground was helpful but the person critical to their understanding and improvement was Lt. Colonel Frank Norton. Formerly a captain in the 77th New York Infantry he transferred into the 123rd on its formation. "We had chiefly company drill," Bull notes, "but during the afternoon Lt. Colonel Norton would give the boys a lively regimental drill for an hour or two."[48]

Drill has been critical for infantry since the first professional armies right through to today. During battlefield operations it allows an organized movement of units while bedlam reigns and then rapid division into combat formations. For recruits new to the military it trains enlisted personnel to respond quickly to shouted commands, creates company and regimental spirit, familiarizes the men with their rifles and allows new officers and non-commissioned officers to gain confidence in giving orders and proper commands. On paper Union armies were composed of regiments (1000 men), brigades (three or four regiments), divisions (three or four brigades), corps (two or three divisions) with two or more corps forming an army. A proper method of movement and control had to be instilled among the tens of thousands of men in such an organization. Regimental movements such as forming on the right into line, column into line of battle from half distance, deploying column at a halt, deploying at a march, oblique march in line of battle and changing direction when in line of battle were just the beginning of 400 to 500 page manuals for the soldiers to learn. The men would grow to hate the long hours on the parade ground drilling but it was to pay off once Johnny Reb had the chance to rip a fusillade at them.

On September 16th the regiment broke camp, marched through D.C. and across the Potomac via the Long Bridge to Fort Albany on Arlington Heights, Virginia. It was hot and several of the men dropped out during the six miles Morhous writing "every soldier was loaded down with many things then considered indispensable, but which experience taught them they could not carry."[49] A new camp was laid out and arranged then it was back to drill. As it was a major training area the men participated in regimental plus brigade drills led by General Silas Casey, the officer who wrote *Casey's Tactics*, a Union training manual. Bull recounts of one extra large review where several regiments were drilled by Casey. "As all were new regiments, with full ranks and in bright new uniforms we thought we made a fine appearance but I am sure our marching was not quite up to standard."[50] Cruikshank didn't notice any problems. "I saw a grand sight yesterday [20th]…There were about six thousand infantry in line besides the artillery. We were reviewed by General Casey who is a very old and gray-headed man."[51] Esprit de corps was starting to be instilled in the recruits.

As a form of training, the men were sent on picket two miles from camp. "This was not very dangerous duty as there was probably no enemy nearer than 20 miles of us," Bull relates. Picket duty was relished as it meant they could purchase a meal from a local home while away from camp. The army food, or "stuff," as the men called it, was taking some getting used too. Standard fare while in camp consisted of beef or salt pork, rice, beans, bread, coffee, sugar, salt and vinegar. There was also an item called "hardtack" which really confused the men at first; it was a three-inch square by half-inch thick wheat cracker that was rock solid. "The hardtack was absolutely tasteless and so hard and tough one could hardly chew it. To us at that time it was like eating a shingle and had not much more taste it was almost unbelievable that one could eat enough of it to sustain life," Bull noted. The problem as he saw it was that the men of the 123rd had to reach a "starvation point" before they could readily accept the army chow, "it was at this camp we passed this childhood period of soldiering and in a measure became inured to our food as well as to the other unpleasant conditions."[52]

Private vendors, called sutlers, were near the camps offering food items but the soldiers felt abused from the high prices charged. In retaliation for what was seen as gouging, men often stole from them. Bull lifted some muskmelons off one vendor, telling his brother Gurdon, "The stealing malida seems to pervade the whole camp." Crops in the region were also fair game, "we have had all the Green Corn that we could steal I guess I have roasted a dozen ears to day that makes good living."[53] Corporal McLean explained to his parents, "We have to buy some things to eat or we would most starve...I wish you would send me five dollars as soon as you write any new york money is good send a 2 & a 3 dollar bill I just as leave have Cambridge money as anything though treasury notes are the best."[54]

About this time Captain John Barron, the Company D commander, disappeared. This was strange to the men as an officer, unlike an enlisted soldier, could resign his position and leave. "He did not return to Fort Ann and no one so far as I know ever heard from him, it was supposed he went to the far west," Corporal Bull writes.[55] Some suspected foul play as Washington was a rough town with a lot of unsavory types prowling about. Barron went into the city one evening and was never seen again. He was finally discharged for absence without leave. First Lieutenant Alexander Anderson was promoted to replace him.

Lucifer's followers in town didn't mean all of the men in the 123rd New York would readily take that route. Sitting down on a Sunday to write his wife, Sergeant Cruikshank of Co. H made note that "all have time this morning for thought, prayer and reading their Bibles." As for his comrades in his tent, "They read their Bibles every day, and have resolved with themselves that they will use no profane language. There shall be no whiskey used as a beverage, and no gambling of any sort in our tent, and whoever breaks over will have to leave the tent. I trust none will have to leave." His brother William, a private in Co. H, was joking that "It is time to catch the horses and drive to church."[56]

Private Henry Welch in Co. K also had tent mates committed to clean living but he didn't see many others in the unit taking the vow. "you can hardly imagine the evels and temptations of camp life....there is very few in our camp any but what burn out their piece of candle playing cards. there is not another tent in our company but what they play cards in. The Captains not excepted."[57]

Christian religion was a major factor for Civil War soldiers of both sides. The lamentations of those against drinking, swearing and card playing had practical basis as they saw it for God would not reward the wicked with victory. Immoral men were also thought to be incapable of courage, of the élan needed for battle. Moral rectitude was the hovel of the weak and fearful, not the soldier imbued with the righteous cause carrying the colors forward towards the enemy. The 123rd would have plenty of sinners but also plenty of Sabbath followers, men that felt sure of Christ's divinity and of his protection. Prayer meetings for the regiment, individual companies or even gatherings of a few men of the 123rd outside a tent would be common throughout their service.

At this time Private Smith Hewitt (Co. E) received a letter from a friend and fellow church goer, Lysander Smith, back in Washington County. "I went to meeting to day at our place Elder Barker preached – all are jogging along as usual I often think of you & the hard-ships you have to endure & we have here all of our wants supplied...I never thought I should see such a war in these United States, but it is here and God only knows how it will be stopped...I wish you <u>great</u> <u>success</u> and victories follow untill this <u>cursed</u> <u>Rebellion</u> is quelled – I send Philo the Granville papers & will send you one next week – Please give a discription of the country you pass through your fare, rations, camp life and duties & what they say about the war..."[58]

Camp life fell into a routine of drill, picket, washing clothes and waiting for the mail. "You cannot imagine the pleasure it gives me to hear from home," Cruikshank replied to his wife, "I enjoyed your first letter with Ella's scrawls trying to write Papa." Corporal Sylvester McMurray (Co. F) sent off a letter to his friend Hulbert Snyder back in Argyle with a comment on army life so far, "if you want to see cuntrey joyn the army if you dont get the worth of your money i will by the rum for you and me." Private William Hills (Co. K) had to write his gal back home and calm her fears. "Elln you need not be a frade of my loosing hart down here for i have not sene anney galls since i came here i have seene plenty of dam black wenches down here"[59]

Marching orders saw them break camp around sundown on September 29th and proceed back into D.C. to the train station. It must have been a warm day, Corporal Clark McLean saying, "I fell out of rank and took some ice cream and Lager which revived me very much."[60] The military being a huge lesson in "hurry up and wait" the train was not ready so the men made the best of it, most wrapping their blankets around them and sleeping on the sidewalk. Others went exploring the city, the sound of music drawing several to a nearby building. Joining in, a bouncing dance step was kept until the floor gave way and fell three feet to the ground. No one was hurt and the men went back to the depot area. At dawn the men were loaded into freight cars, 30 to 40 per car, and the train departed for Frederick, Maryland.

After a couple days camped outside of Frederick the men climbed aboard the cars again and rode south to Sandy Hook, Maryland just outside of Harper's Ferry, West Virginia (at that time part of Virginia). A short march found them setting up camp in Pleasant Valley, Maryland. It was here that the 123rd New York was assigned to the 2nd Brigade (Brig. General Thomas Kane); 1st Division (Brig. General Alpheus S. Williams); 12th Corps (Major General Henry W. Slocum); Army of the Potomac, General George McClellan commanding. Kane's Brigade consisted of the 20th Connecticut, 124th Pennsylvania and 125th Pennsylvania besides the 123rd New York. Both the Pennsylvania regiments had nine-month terms of service while the 20th Connecticut had enlisted for three years. The Pennsylvania regiments had already been bloodied at Antietam (September 17th) the 125th losing in killed and wounded 145 men.

"General Kane is a very small man with one wooden leg, has large full eyes and heavy black mustache," Sergeant Cruikshank, always one for a satisfying description, wrote his wife. "We are kept very busy all of the time…Our men are improving in the drills and are complimented by commanding officers." Yet all wasn't rosy. The 123rd New York had been ordered to march light so their knapsacks had been left behind in Washington to be shipped forward later. Cold nights now afflicted the men as they waited for the extra clothes with their packs. Decent food was also a problem. "Our rations are bad. The crackers [hardtack] are wormy the same kind of worms as we find in decayed wood. We break the crackers into small pieces and boil them so we cannot see the worms. We find worms in our bacon and our salt beef has soured in the brine. Were it not that we could buy some food we would go hungry." The packs finally arrived October 23rd yet items had been stolen from them, Cruikshank losing an overcoat and gloves.[61]

General Kane had been irritated by the men of the 123rd during this time as each evening as the cold came on a chorus of "Knapsacks, knapsacks, knapsacks" was started up from the regiment's camp and continued for an hour or more. Kane threatened to post a guard on the entire regiment to pull out and arrest the men making the noise. The general wasn't a martinet. A lawyer from Western Pennsylvania, he was a strong abolitionist and during the 1850's had set up an underground railroad to help move runaways north to Canada. As the commander of the 42nd Pennsylvania "Bucktails" he had seen quite a bit of action, being wounded in the face with his lower right leg shattered fighting Stonewall Jackson's troops in the Shenandoah Valley. He was in poor health by this time and probably didn't need the aggravation. What is important is that he was a fighting general, believed in firing practice, drill and instilling discipline. He was the type of leader a young regiment needed to get them ready for combat.

Why didn't the officers of the 123rd stop the men? It was probably seen as a legitimate grievance and, as no action had come through channels, maybe it was felt this tactic might get better results. There was also the veiled threat of mass enlistment in the army's regular infantry for Colonel McDougall to deal with. "there is a good deal talk about enlisting in the regular army they give $100 and [60?] days furlough quite a number of our boys say that they will enlist about fifty enlisted to day [October 11th] from a regement just north of us for 5 years," Private Welch wrote his aunt and uncle. It all came to a head a few days later. "there was about three hundred of our regiment marched up to the colonels tent and wanted passes to go and enlist in the regular servis he talked with them quite a while and tried to get them to stay I don't know whether they will go or not" But Welch wasn't interested, "I don't think I shall enlist in the regular army just yet I think this is about regular enough to suit me."[62] Private Noah Hill (Co. K) explained in a letter to his mother how the issue was defused by Lt. Colonel Norton, "I will tell you aboute going into the reglars our lutenant colenel told us how it was going to be so will give it up so you must not worey enny more aboute that"[63]

No doubt the food, knapsack and housing situation fostered the talk of enlisting in the regular army. Private Orville Robinson (Co. F) wrote at the time, "I wish that we had comfortable quarters it would not seem so hard. I think if I ever live to see home that I can appreciate a House much more than I did six months ago." Robinson's legs were bothering him due to crawling in and out of the tents. "Our tents are not over three feet high in the highest part...George takes most all the room in our tent, he is so long that I cant stir unless he coils himself up like a snake. We have to back out the door for it is not big enough to turn around in."[64]

McDougall and Norton must have shown some leadership with their talks as no men left the 123rd New York to enlist with the U.S. Army. This was a true citizen army the officers had to deal with; officers could not go overboard with their men with discipline when the men felt they had the moral high ground on an issue. Courage was the defining mark of an officer and at this time none of the 123rd's officers except Lt. Colonel Norton and Major Rogers had seen battle. Officers had to walk a fine line until they had proved themselves. Officers were expected to stride manfully forward, put themselves in harm's way, not flinch, duck or cower. When a regiment or company was told to lie down to avoid shellfire the officers remained standing. If one could light a cigar or walk along filling one's pipe while telling the men to remain steady all the better. It was a high standard. Many couldn't live up to it but even worse for the Union's aspect, those officers that did live up to it often perished. As the war progressed the standard became a tad less rigid and line officers could lie down or take cover from fire. But in a charge or movement towards the enemy they had to be in front directing if they were to maintain their moral authority with the men.

What about a higher moral calling for the war? President Lincoln had issued his Emancipation Proclamation in September and a month later the 123rd New York gathered to discuss the issue. Corporal Bull was in the audience. "We had a war meeting addresses were made by Col. McD Liet Col Norton Capt Willey &c. Capt W. came out square for the Emancipation policy and was loudly cheered. it takes first rate in the army and I haven't seen an old soldier yet who has any scrubles about gutting the 'sacred institution' if it will help put down the rebellion."[65] There were those in the army that opposed freeing the slaves arguing that the war should be just about reunion. But many of the fighting men of the North were realizing that a new day was dawning. From now on any Southern areas taken by battle would see freedom from bondage for the slaves. It struck a direct blow at the entire Southern infrastructure.

But there wasn't any battlefield for the proving of the men or the officers of the 123rd. There had been fighting up the Shenandoah Valley. "We expected that by this time that we would of been fighting the Rebels at Winchester, but we are sadly disappointed," Private Orville Robinson said, "I think their was but few that would not of liked to of went." Robinson did see the results of combat in the nearby hospitals and wrote to a friend at home. "Hulbert, you dont know any thing about the war up north. You cant realize it untill you come right in amongst it...to see poor felows lying with their legs shot off at their knees others with arms. some have had Balls pass right through their heads yet live. there is one fellow that had a ball shot right through his Stomach and yet he lives."[66]

Monotony set in as the month wore on. Haircuts became a point of discussion. Welch had his trimmed close to the skull. "Horace thinks I had better get a file and have the rest of it filed off…but you know I d'ont care as there's no girls down here its in a fare way to grow out again before we get back." Newspapers helped to fill the time, Private Horace Tooley (Co. K) writing, "we have Baltimore and New York dayly Papers here every day which is Better than I expected for five cents we can buy all the lies in the market cheap enough." Yet for all the inaction at least one soldier in the 123rd New York was having a good time, Private Robinson noting, "Joe Laport Enjoys himself first rate. he would not go home I guess if he could. I cant say that I would unless I had my discharge or furlough." Sickness arrived with several of the men falling to "childhood" disease that the farm boys never had been exposed too. Men were also finding visitors in their uniforms. "Small numbers are beginning to be lousy already, but only the dirty ones," Corporal McLean noted.[67]

Desertions continued with two more in October. A questionable "accident" also occurred on October 10th when Private John McCoy shot his thumb off while on guard. His rifle slipped off a stump and when he went to catch it the rifle discharged. "some think he done it aperpose to get a discharge," Private Welch wrote, "the sump was not over six inches high I d'ont see how he could have done it." Even with the boredom and problems, Corporal Bull struck a pretty standard note when he told his brother Gurdon, "I hav'ent seen the hour yet that I was sorry that I enlisted. I am bound to see this war through and I dont believe that we have got to stay three years for that either."[68]

For those putting their time in it was a learning experience. "We have to drill nine hours a day which keeps us busy most of the time," Corporal McLean says, "We are learning the Battallion Drill now and have gained in it a great deal. The Lieut. Col. is liked by all his command first rate." Private Welch discovered he liked scouting and volunteered for it as often as he could, "it seemed like some old coon hunts I used to have [in Washington County]" Six scouts were sent out every day from the brigade to go five miles beyond the pickets and reconnoiter for any Rebel movements. The men also had ulterior motives in that they found freedom to scrounge food, especially fresh meat, during their roaming. As Welch puts it, "we did'ent mean to steal but to confiscate a little."[69]

November 1ˢᵗ the regiment struck camp and marched into Virginia to begin scouting and support activities in the Shenandoah Valley. Camp was made just south of Harper's Ferry with Rebel pickets within a mile and the sound of random rifle cracks echoing among the hills. The men rapidly shifted to finding better food taking pigs and fowl from the locals. "I went oute night before last & got two nice hens & a shanhigh ruster & wee cooked them verry nice," Private Noah Hill told his mother, "wee put in some buttar & some pepper & they most dam good wee have hunney the most of the time wee seal [steal] enny thing wee get our hans on hogs or enny things elce"[70]

"our Regt has a very good reputation for taking things," Corporal John Gourlie wrote his brother, "Genl Kane said if he could only get the 123ʳᵈ N.Y. boys within 3 miles of Richmond they would steal it in less than a week."[71]

Private William Cruikshank (Co. H) was on picket the night of the 4ᵗʰ when Captain Warren (Co. B) approached with several men and giving the password "Sheep" disappeared into the darkness. They returned in two hours with several sheep carcasses, leaving a quarter of mutton at the picket post. The next day Sergeant Cruikshank, his brother Will and several others had just cooked up some of the mutton in pig fat when Captain Warren marched up, announced that some of the locals had complained that they had lost some sheep and he had orders to inspect the camp for mutton. Looking over the meat he declared it pork and moved on. Colonel McDougall ordered the inspection but also enjoyed some of the meat as did other officers and men of the regiment. "When the men can get good fresh meat to go with their army rations, they fare very well," Sergeant Cruikshank explained to his wife.[72] Fresh, raw meat has some antiscorbutic properties. Vitamin C not being discovered or understood until 1928 the lack of fresh fruit or vegetables in the standard Union Army diet created serious danger of scurvy in the men unless fresh meat was supplied or they bought better food on their own. What is so strange about this issue is that the British Navy had been issuing lime juice to fend off scurvy since 1795. For the Union Army, doctors understood that vegetables were needed in the diet and were working on it. At times lemons would be issued to troops once scurvy hit, but they weren't standard fare in the diet. Desiccated vegetables were available but the soldiers rarely ate them as they didn't like the taste. For now the men mainly resorted to supplementing their food via purchases or the chance to "confiscate a little."

There was a third option, food from home. Express mail was available for boxes and the soldiers began to make use of them. Private Smith Hewitt wrote his parents in mid-November asking that they send a box of apples plus "some butter and a chunk of cheese and fride cakes cookes and sutch stuf...you need not send mutch cake let the most of it be in cheese an butter put the butter into an old coffee pot so that I can have the pot to make coffee in..." There was a learning curve for items to ship in the boxes. Although the transit time was often just over a week, some items were not meant to be shipped. Corporal McLean received a box from home and noted, "The provisions were all right except the chicken. It was rather blue." Corporal Bull commented on one shipment, "Newt got his box the other day. It had been so long on the road that the chickens and sausages had spoiled but the cakes, butter & cheese etc was in as good condition as ever." Fruit and chicken were dropped while dried meats and dried apples were substituted. Items of clothing were often included with the food, knitted socks and scarves popular. For the 123rd New York troops, the express box from home was a standard issue during the war.[73]

A snowstorm melted off leaving the roads mud with the men slopping through them on scouting and picket missions every day. One night Colonel McDougall rode out beyond the camp picket during an inspection of the line. As he returned to camp Private John Snyder (Co. H) challenged him to dismount, advance on foot and give the countersign. Colonel McDougall, not wanting to dismount into the mud, attempted to talk the guard into letting him pass but Snyder refused with, "I don't know Colonel McDougall when I am on picket and he is outside the line. Dismount, advance and give the countersign." The colonel complied having to wade through the mud leading his horse up to the picket. Next day when Snyder came off duty he was told to report to the colonel's tent where he was complimented for proper performance of his duties.[74]

The colonel wasn't the only officer having issues when on the picket line. On November 14th Major Rogers of the 123rd was Officer of the Picket and, as such, was on the outskirts of the line after posting the detail. He tied his horse off to a tree and entered a house only to look back out a moment later to see a Reb leaping astride the beast. Bolting back outside, an exchange of pistol shots was followed by hoof beats and Rogers was out a horse plus saddle. Some of the men hearing of the incident went in search of the Rebel, after no luck, the soldiers went to a Secesh house. They selected a horse and "returned to camp and presented it to the Major."[75]

For Private Welch (Co. K) a couple nights later the thought for him was not to be out his life. It was pitch dark as he took his turn on picket at 10 p.m. He noticed something about 100 feet away, "it was so dark I could hardly make out whether it was anything or not but I thought at first it was a man I drawd up my gun to halt him when thinking that it might be a tall stump or something of the kind and if I halted it the boys would laugh at me for halting a stump so I thought I would watch it awhile I kept an eye on it about half an hour but it did not stir…" so he went back to walking his post. The moon finally came out and he checked the spot only to find "no man stump or anything else to be seen."[76]

Guard duty was more than just camp picket. If a local civilian requested protection they might be assigned a guard at their home. Corporal McLean spent a couple days at one house. "I am guarding, writing by the light of the fireplace, have been here for 24 hours and expect to stay here all night. Don't feel right smart this eve, have had no sleep for 3 nights." His food situation also could have been contributing to his mental state. "Have had nothing but crackers to eat for a day or two except what we stole."[77]

For the enlisted personnel the meals hadn't improved much by Thanksgiving. McLean had a simple meal of salt pork and crackers. "The officers had a turkey supper and all got pretty drunk."[78]

Even with all the hassles of camp life it still beat the torture of being in a medical bed. Several of the 123[rds] men fell sick at this time from typhoid and dysentery. Corporal McLean fell to a bad bout of dysentery and fought it off over five days only to have a frantic letter arrive from his mother. It seems a comrade had written home about it. "Leroy was always good at getting up sensation stories & he beat himself writing about my being sick...don't get scared about me again when there is nothing the matter." It wasn't just letters going home alerting parents about loved ones. The weekly papers in Washington County published lists of those in hospitals and those that died. As December moved on the listings were growing and so were local concerns. At the end of the month the *Salem Press* even reported on a suicide, Private Richard West (Co. H) having cut his throat. Sergeant Cruikshank noted that, "At times he had been deranged and was very homesick." He had "repeated declarations to members of our company that there was no impropriety in suicide." People expected combat casualties but the losses to disease began to create discussion in the community.[79]

Back in camp, soldiers sought to help each other. Corporal Rice Bull, upon learning of a comrade being seriously sick, went to Colonel McDougall and got a pass to care for him in the local military hospital. Private Phineas Spencer, whom Rice enlisted with, had fought off a bout of typhoid but now his feet had taken with gangrene. Rice found the hospital, a four-story former cotton mill along the Shenandoah River, all in confusion. The hospital only handled disease cases. There was a triage system, those expected to die on one floor graduating to the better cases on the other floors. When the men were brought in they were stripped, cleaned (somewhat) and given fresh underwear.

Spencer was in the "death ward" and Bull spent a few days sleeping on the floor by his friend's cot attending to his needs. "His feet were swollen nearly to twice their normal size and his toes were nearly black," Bull notes.[80]

Bedlam was the proper way to describe the establishment. Many of the 200 men in the ward were in fever and raving. As he slept one night Bull was startled awake when a patient punched his head through a glass window in an attempt to throw himself out. The man, delirious from typhoid, died within hours. "Every morning from ten to fifteen of these poor men were carried out, having died during the night," Bull writes, "This was all very depressing to me…and much more so to my patient." The one decent aspect he noted was an "old Quaker woman who was almost constantly in the ward." She wrote letters for the men, helped care for them and said prayers for them. Bull must have faithfully followed the doctor's instructions in caring for Spencer, for, after some toes were amputated, Phineas improved and was discharged for home.[81]

Also heading home to recover was Sergeant Robert Cruikshank. He had battled fever and diarrhea for two months in camp and hospital along with several other soldiers of the 123rd New York. Besides the typical typhoid the men were knocked down with scurvy, chronic diarrhea and "congestion of the lungs." From his bed Cruikshank was glad to hear the remaining, healthy, men of the unit were building better quarters. They had been forced to endure cold, wet weather in tents; the men having "no place where we could get warm or dry our clothing when wet." That, with the poor food, put many men on the sick list. Cruikshank was first in a ward with plenty of bed rest and "decent" food, bread and soup, and improved. Once shifted to the convalescent ward he had to walk to a dining hall for meals of regular army fare: coffee with molasses, bread and hash (bread crumbs, remains of the soup, potatoes and whatever meat scraps were available). The soldiers greatly resented the table at the end of the dining hall set aside for the nurses, hospital wardens and attendants. Boxes of food sent by families to the soldiers would be confiscated only to wind up on this table, to be eaten by the staff. This was justified in the idea that patients should not have unfettered access to food. Germ theory was lacking on the operating slab as was dietary understanding in the recovery ward.[82]

Cruikshank did use some of the money his wife sent him to clandestinely purchase some butter. Hiding it under his bed by tying it to a slat, he would slip his piece of bread (they got *one* slice) under his coat at dinner, toast it over the coal stove back in his ward and spread the butter on it. He shared the butter with his 123rd comrades Abel Baker (Co. E) and George Beebe (Co. H). The bed also hid some strawberry preserves that had gotten through from his wife. But Cruikshank knew it was a losing battle and understood the cause, "it is my food that is pulling me back." He deteriorated again. He tried to keep his wife's spirits up in his letters. "You said a year ago when all or nearly all of the babes born were boys that it was a sign of war, and now you write that they all are girls so that must be a sign of peace. And if that is so this war will soon be over, so you should cheer up." The doctor sent for Cruikshank's wife, Mary, to come for him. Two months of army hospital care had nearly put him in his grave. Two months of his wife's care had him reporting back for duty for the nation.[83]

For those healthy enough to be in camp, drums were beating reville at 6 a.m. Forming in their street the soldiers responded to their names for roll call. Breakfast was at 7 a.m. with guard mount at 8 a.m. Drilling would occupy their time from 9 to 12:30 with all the regiments of the brigade using a large open field at the same time. "Our regiment is getting so it can drill with any of them," Corporal Bull proudly told his brother. For the first week of December the men spent the afternoons building better winter quarters. Bull shared a seven foot by fourteen foot log hut with five others. The men bought a stove for $4 and got good results, "it makes the house as warm as an oven. Our beds are built up off from the ground and I can sleep just as warm and comfortable as if I had a feather bed."[84]

An inspection of Company H by Colonel McDougall saw him rating discipline and instruction "Tolerable," clothing "Middling," and military appearance "Good." The men still had the Enfield rifles. A total of 54 men were in the ranks for the company, with an additional 15 sick, 2 on detached service, 1 on leave, 1 under arrest and 6 absent without leave. Five men had died from disease.[85]

At this time the 123rd New York was performing action as part of the right flank of the Army of the Potomac. The main part of the army was stationed south of Washington, with a new commander as of November 5th when President Lincoln replaced General George McClellan with General Ambrose Burnside. With orders from the President for action Burnside moved the Army of the Potomac forward towards Fredericksburg, Virginia. What started as a rapid movement that caught Confederate General Robert E. Lee off guard lost its value when pontoon bridges necessary to cross the Rappahannock River were delayed an entire week. By the time Burnside crossed Lee was ensconced upon the little knolls beyond the town with an excellent half-mile sloped killing field before the Southern rifles and artillery. On December 13th when General Burnside ordered frontal assaults on Lee's line many Union soldiers pinned their names on themselves so they could be identified later. It was that obvious what was about to happen. By the end of the day nearly 13,000 Federals lay casualties versus 5,000 Confederates. Both Burnside and Lincoln came under severe criticism for the disaster.

"They also serve who stand and wait" was the byline for the 123rd New York at this time, or maybe better, "they also serve who march through mud." December 11th the 123rd began a march towards Leesburg, Virginia that was in support of the broader movements of the Army of the Potomac towards Fredericksburg. They marched and countermarched back and forth with few breaks over several days "we did not stop long enough to eat our rations but eat them as we were walking along our rations consisted of eight hard crackers per day with a small allowance of coffee it was rather hard but then its honest" Private Welch wrote his father. "We have traveled about 100 miles in 7 days which considering the time of year and state of the roads is heavy marching," Corporal Bull told his brother Gurdon, "the boys stood the march first rate only 3 of our company of 70 men gave out...We get bad news from the south Burnside has been driven back across the river. there is no use of denying fact these 'Graybacks' are game at fighting."[86]

The regiment, along with the brigade and other units of the 12th Corps, was at Fairfax Station, Virginia. Assigned to guard the railroad station, the 123rd laid out a camp and built log huts for better protection from the winter. The standard huts soldiers built held four men and were roughly 14 feet by 14 feet with a chimney at one end for heating and cooking. Mud plastered around a stick lattice was used to create the chimney while their shelter halves were often used for the roof. One had to be alert while cooking at the fire as a common joke was for a passerby to toss a couple black-powder cartridges down a smoking chimney.

Christmas dinner wasn't much for the enlisted men. Corporal Bull was acting as a clerk for Colonel McDougall at this time and, as the colonel had ridden off for a proper Christmas meal, spent the 25th alone in the headquarters tent penning some thoughts to his brother Gurdon. "It is about 3 o'clock and I can imagine that you have just had a dinner of turkey and its accompanyments, and are having a gay time generally. With us Christmas is like all other days only there is no drill." Bull mentions he had munched some salt pork and hardtack for his holiday meal then turns to more serious concerns as to the war. "The southerners are in <u>earnest</u> while the north just <u>playing</u> fight. Experience ought to teach us by this time that they are dangerous play things and just so long as we conduct this war in such a <u>civil</u> way we need not expect to be successful. What do the people think of the war as it is now conducted? Do the Democrats have much to say against it now that they are in power?"[87] (Fall 1862 elections had seen Democrats pick up seats in Congress and state legislatures, New York particularly.)

December 27th firing was heard in the direction of Dumfries, Virginia where some Union regiments and artillery tangled with Confederate cavalry led by Rebel General James Ewell Brown (J.E.B.) Stuart. The 123rd was issued three days rations and marched to the Occoquan River to support the action. They stayed two days at the river and "suffered severely" from the cold as they only had blankets to wrap around themselves at night. Marching back to the station they found a Rebel cavalry unit had made a raid and taken prisoner one of the telegraph operators during their absence. "It is curious how they will dodge in & get by our men & plunder & destroy our stores & get back without getting caught," Corporal McLean pondered. Over the next couple of weeks several of the sick left behind at Harper's Ferry reported back for duty. A steady routine of picket, guard, drill and inspection filled the days. Cold weather and harsh marching convinced another three men to desert at this time. Corporal McLean saw desertions becoming a greater problem in the near future, in a letter to his mother stating, "We hear that the people are getting sick of the war & are in favor of peace on most any conditions. Every one here soldiers and citizens are for giving it up & making peace some way. After pay-day I guess there will be a good many deserters. I have heard lots of soldiers say they are going home before long."[88]

Union General Burnside decided a quick movement in mid-January was what was needed to break open the Eastern Theatre of the war. The weather clear and the roads in good shape, Burnside ordered the Army of the Potomac to march to the right with the goal of crossing the Rappahannock River and falling on Lee's flank. The 123rd New York was part of the movement, the 1st Division of the 12th Corps beginning route step January 19th toward Dumfries, Virginia. The first day saw good weather and steady marching, by the second day they went into camp outside of Dumfries having made about twenty miles in two days. Midnight of the 20th the heavens opened up flooding the men out of camp as the temperature dropped. The men spent the night standing about bonfires shivering and getting soaked. Says Bull in understatement, "Our breakfast in the rain and it was not a cheerful repast."[89]

The bottom fell out of the dirt roads. Corporal Bull writes, "There was only one road over which to move the trains and no headway could be made. The movement of the trains and artillery soon made the road a quagmire and it was soon blocked with stalled wagons that had settled in the mud up to their wheel hubs." Men sank to their knees and needed help getting free, horses and mules had to be helped, to move an empty wagon required a six-mule team. The 12th Corps, the entire Army of the Potomac, was floundering in the mud. "We only went two miles one day & the wagons could not keep up so we had nothing to eat at night," Corporal McLean told his mother, "The road was marked with dead mules and broken wagons...We were in the rain all night & all day and we got pretty wet."[90]

The rain with intermittent snow squalls continued another day as the men struggled to free themselves. Across the Rappahannock River Southern pickets watched and laughed, some even held up signs saying, "This way to Richmond." Pioneer units, engineering troops assigned for road and bridge building, cut trees and laid them across the mud and slop to corduroy the roads. Even then it was a struggle as the trees sank into the mud. The march "tested to the utmost the endurance of all," Bull writes. All the men of the 123rd were smeared and caked in red clay, water dripping off caps, panting, cussing and tugging one another free. The rain and torture of movement continued for another day, on the 22nd General Burnside called off the march. By that time the 123rd had made it to Stafford Court House, twelve miles for two days effort. The area around Stafford had been the winter quarters of the 11th Corps and, as they were literally stuck at the front, the 12th Corps was assigned the area for camp. As Corporal McLean moved into his quarters he noted, "I have just heard that Burnside has been superceded. I wonder who they will try next."[91]

The morale of the Army of the Potomac crashed from this debacle. One hundred soldiers per day started deserting. During January even the 123rd New York had ten men go over the hill. Prompt decisions were called for, Lincoln had a meeting with Burnside, he was out as commander and General Joseph Hooker was next for the post. Some were aghast that General Hooker was chosen due to his known proclivities for dice and women. The area of Washington where prostitutes plied money from customers was known as "Hooker's Division." But the 1837 West Point graduate took steps that quickly boosted morale. He improved the food situation establishing bakeries plus adding vegetables to the issue, new uniforms and equipment gave the men a better image on parade and drill, and what was really something, General Hooker ordered each Corps to have its own insignia. Before this time one could not look at a Union soldier and tell what Corps or division of a Corps he was in, other than rank soldiers often had nothing else identifying them as to a unit on their uniform. Hooker assigned symbols to each Corps of the army, the 12th Corps having a star emblem, each division of the 12th having a different color: 1st red; 2nd white; 3rd blue. The men of the 123rd New York being in the 1st Division 12th Corps they stitched red stars onto their caps.

Morale was also boosted by local visits and imbibing. On a Sunday afternoon Private Horace Mathews (Co. H) strolled "down to Acqua Creek Landing and see George Frost and had plenty of whiskey and had a good time with him." It seems quite a few of the men were tipping the flask and stories of excess drinking were making their way back to Washington County. Corporal Gourlie wrote his sister that concerning Colonel McDougall, "he loves his drop bitters the same as ever and once in a great while he gets over full. but you must not say any thing about that."[92]

Well, things were being said. In late January Colonel McDougall had a letter dropped onto his desk from the Washington County War Committee wanting some clarification. McDougall in his reply says he had been aware of such comments back home, "That those false rumors &

scandalous stories about us, of which you speak, should have been cut afloat by wicked and mischievous persons does not surprise me or move me so much, as that they should increase in volume and continue for a long time with unabated viralence and such unmitigated malice... Intemperance is one charge. A charge more false could not have been uttered. That ardent spirits have been used to a very small extent is true but I have not seen since I left Salem an officer in this Regiment in <u>the least</u> inebriated with liquor and not over two or three men in the whole Regiment." McDougall claims any drunk soldiers are immediately confined under guard. "I do not believe there is a pint of liquor in this camp altho it is doubtless the best preventive of the diseases which most attack the soldiers. The most universally essential medicine when afflicted. Any Sensible man would use it here, to a moderate extent, at times..."[93]

It seems the alcohol criticism was mainly directed to two of the 123rd New York doctors, Moneypenny and Connolly. The doctors were also being questioned as to ability. Colonel McDougall defended both of the men, saying he has never seen them "drink a drop of liquor" and then puts down the competency complaints to personnel not being given sick leave by the doctors. Soldiers of the 123rd are "from all classes of society, rich & poor, industrious and indolent, thriving & shiftless embracing men of all shades of character, good, bad, and indifferent." With enlistment fever over and bounty money all spent, McDougall says the griping starts.[94]

Concerning the doctors, it might have been a combination of both imbibing and being tough with slackers. Corporal McLean noted in his diary back in October that, "The privates have done their amount of drilling and the Doctors have drunk their usual quantity of sherry and we have given Uncle Sam the benefit of our services one day more."[95]

Every doctor was going to be needed. The location of the 123rd's camp was a disaster for the men. The stream water used for drinking was contaminated from poorly sited latrines. Typhoid broke out, many of the men fell sick and several died. Prayer helped in dealing with the sickness and burial details. "Mr. Gorden preched today," Mathews noted in his diary on February 8th along with, "George H. Sweat [Co. H] was beared." Also buried that day was Chauncey Parker, Co. G. Sergeant Morhous made a list of some of the men that perished due to disease at this time: Jacob Stover, Co. A; Henry Reed, Co. F; Daniel Carmody, Co. K; Martin Dunlap, Co. H; Darwin Easton, Co. D; Andrew Coon, Co. G; Roswell Jones, Co. A. The scythe of disease would claim 27 men over two months.[96]

"Tell Tet Barah it is well that he did not list for if he had he would got a wooden over coat [coffin] before now," Private Levi Eaton wrote his wife. The frustration of the mud, cold and watching comrades die due to disease roars forth in his next statement, "if they would leave it to me I would settle it dam soon they might keep the nigers."[97]

Camp was moved onto a hill never occupied by troops. "During that winter we had already constructed winter camps at Harper's Ferry, Fairfax Station, and Stafford we felt we were getting expert in that business," Bull relates, "In this new camp the health of the men improved at once and the depression that had prevailed in the Regiment passed away." Also helping were ten-day furloughs that many of the men used for visits home. But at least one didn't return from furlough, Sergeant George Clapp (Co. I). His desertion was a surprise to many of the men. "The reports here is that he got as far as Troy & then went to Canada," Corporal McLean told his mother, "If he has got away he is one of the smart ones. I suppose it is all Debby's doings. No one supposed that he would leave but I guess he was pretty tired of soldiering."[98]

For those that stayed it was picket duty, drill and writing letters home. Corporal Bull took another light day at the headquarters tent to write Gurdon, "You want to know what I think of this war now. I think the war is all right but the way it is being carried on is enough to discourage any one our officers seem to work as though they calculate to be about 20 years finishing the job...I am in hopes Hooker will do something when the <u>mud</u> (our worst foe) dries up."[99]

    Private Welch also sent some thoughts home, "Mother I have often heard you say that we had always ought to do to others as we would have others do to us I am most afraid that plan won't work with a soldier if we go into battle I shall try and shoot some body and I cant say that I would have them try to shoot me...all I ask is that the rebels may soon be whiped out and I am willing to do my part in fighting them untill they are whiped for I have soldiered about long enough without doing anything and now I want something done...."[100]

Chapter 3
Chancellorsville: Rebel Shock & Awe

General "Fightin' Joe" Hooker would get something done. "It's not a question of *whether* I take Richmond but *when*," he told President Lincoln. To which Lincoln wryly noted, "The hen is the wisest of all animal creation because she never cackles until the egg is laid."[101]

Robert E. Lee and the Army of Northern Virginia, 53,000 men, sat south of the Rappahannock River by Fredericksburg. Hooker intended to attack and created a good plan, rapid movement to the right with crossings at fords to get onto Lee's flank. This would force Lee to come out from the entrenchments of Fredericksburg and fight in the open. During March and into April the weather improved, the parade grounds drying out as the roads. In camp the 123rd drilled every day in company, regiment and brigade movements. To this was added skirmish drill, where the men spread out and used cover while testing for the enemy's location. "We are kept doing something all of the time and sometimes I think it is only to keep our minds occupied and to give us plenty of exercise so we do not get too much flesh and be thinking too much of home, and get discontented here," Sergeant Cruikshank wrote his wife, "I wish you would get your and Ella's pictures taken and send them to me that I may have them to look at when I do not get letters..." By early April better weather, food and activity had a salubrious effect on the 123rd New York. "Our Regiment is now in a better condition as regards Health & Appearance then it ever was before," Corporal McLean writes, "The Boys feel in good spirits and are anxious to move. General Hooker is a great favorate in the army now...McClellen is not very popular now. He has gone in with the Copperheads most to much to suit the soldiers."[102]

At the beginning of April President Lincoln paid an inspection visit. The 12th Corps was reviewed on April 10th 1863. It was a proud day for Private Orville Robinson (Co. F) of the 123rd New York. "Our Regiment looked first rate...Abe looks just like his Photographs. he came on to the field with a stove pipe Hat with his little boy on a fine pony on his left side and Hooker on the right and officers without number trailing after. theay had hard work to keep up, for old Abe's Horse went like split...Mrs. Lincoln and little ones came in in a carriage. I couldent get a sight of her as their was such a crowd and his body guard and Staff so thick that you couldent get within ten Rod of him." (A rod is 16 feet.)[103]

Corporal McLean was also impressed by it all. "It was the Grandest Military display I have yet seen. The troops marched splendidly. Old Abe came guarded by a company of lancers (Cavalry that carry long spears or lances)...Abe Lincoln dressed in citizens clothes and wearing a tall stove pipe hat. He looked homely and comical enough. He looked as if he was tired most out."[104]

Express boxes becoming so popular, at this time new orders were put in place. "All boxes that come by express now are examined at Corps Headquarters to see if they contain contraband goods such as citizens clothes, whiskey etc.," Corporal Bull relates, "Mine was opened and they drank about half of the wine." But Bull was happy to tell his brother that the boots in the box fit great while the ham and butter came through in "first-rate condition."[105]

By April 17th boxes were also going out from the camp. "We sent our spare clothing to Washington to stay until next fall. I turned in my overcoat and dress coat," Corporal McLean writes, adding, "Our boys beat the 12th boys at baseball today in several games."[106]

In mid-April the men of the 123rd New York, along with the rest of the army, were issued eight days rations (hardtack, salted pork, sugar and coffee) plus 60 rounds of ammo. This was seen among the men as a possible sign of movement and rumors started once again. Private Welch was rather astute in his assessment, "it is thought by some that we are to march to Culpepper courthouse but there's nothing certain about it, I think that we are going to some ford to cross the rappahannock and then try to flank the rebels on the right while Hooker engage's them on the front..." For the soldiers of the 123rd this meant a chance at a real battle with the men favoring the opportunity. As combat loomed, Corporal Bull noted that as the regiment was new with "as yet no practical army experience, this knowledge brought no fear or dread. We were as yet ignorant of the meaning of real war." As the days passed the food was replenished to maintain the eight-day window plus the wagons were reduced to the minimum. Excess equipment was ordered turned in, as was clothing beyond an extra change of underwear. "The roads are hard & dry & the army is in a good condition & I think we will give the Rebs a hard one if we come across them which we will," Corporal McLean told his brother.[107]

Movement in the machinery of the army was being seen about them but for Private Robinson there wasn't movement where it really mattered. His brother, Sergeant George Robinson, was very sick and waiting for papers to be cut for him to go home. "George S. is still here," Orville wrote on April 12th. The discharges were being held up to send all of them in at once "as their is some dozen that are agoing to be sent in. he is quite comfortable, but he ought to be sent home four weeks ago, but they are so slow and reckless in the army about such a thing of that kind that they dont appear to care whether a man lives or dies."[108]

On April 27th the 12th Corps, 11th Corps and 5th Corps, 42,000 men, began marching northwesterly towards Warrenton, Virginia. The 3rd Corps, 19,000 men under Brig. General Daniel Sickles, was left in reserve with orders to follow at a moment's notice. The 2nd Corps, 12,000 men under Major General Darius Couch, went into concealed positions along the Rappahannock opposite Bank's Ford. Hooker left Union Major General Sedgewick in command of the 1st and 6th Corps, 40,000 men, at Fredericksburg to pin the Army of Northern Virginia in place.[109]

Long days of marching were on order with dawn starts and 6 p.m. stops, the soldiers making 12 to 15 miles per day. Many of the men didn't obey the order to travel light and, the weather being hot, the first day saw the roadside littered with extra blankets and overcoats. Meals were of coffee, hardtack and pork. They crossed the Rappahannock at Kelly's Ford and pushed onto the Rapidan River at Germanna Ford. At this location the water was armpit deep and several men were swept downstream while attempting to cross. "I saw our Division Genl Williams rescue one or two from a watery grave," Corporal Albert Cook (Co. A) wrote, "their heavy knapsacks weighed them down and bound their arms so it was impossible to swim."[110] Cavalrymen were stationed in the river to rescue the soldiers that were carried away. The men of the 123rd were watching the commotion and not looking forward to trying the crossing when Colonel McDougall ordered them to span the river with some materials the Rebs had abandoned at the location. In two hours the men created a floating bridge by bracing and nailing timbers against some existing abutments. It was good enough for men and pack mules to cross, the men two by two with six to eight feet between in route step.

Southern cavalry reported movement on the Union side but the question was where the Yanks were going. General Lee waited for better information. As a precaution he sent Confederate General Anderson with three brigades towards Chancellorsville with orders to dig in on the farmland just outside the beginning of the scrub forest. The Union troops marched swiftly and by April 30th they were in the area of Chancellorsville beginning to probe east to come in behind Lee's position. It looked very, very good for the Federals.

But General Lee wasn't one to sit still and let the fight be brought to him. Leaving 10,000 men to hold Fredericksburg, he marched 43,000 men right at Hooker's main force. While the immediate area around the Chancellor

House were open-fields, the region it was in was referred to by locals as "The Wilderness." This was due to the scrub trees-oak and pine-plus heavy vines and thorn bushes throughout the woods. Iron mining and smelting since the 1830's had seen the woodlands stripped for fuel resulting in stunted second growth forest upon the poor soil. It was not the ideal place to position an army as the underbrush prevented proper command and control of units, hampered movement and restricted fields of fire for artillery.

At this time the 2nd Brigade, 1st Division, 12th Corps consisted of the 123rd New York, 145th New York, 20th Connecticut and 3rd Maryland under the overall command of Colonel Samuel Ross. The 145th NY and 20th CT had been organized, like the 123rd NY, in September 1862. The 3rd Maryland was organized in June of 1861, had suffered from battle and desertions and in January 1863 had gotten an allotment of nine-month men from the militia draft.[111]

The morning of April 30th saw the 123rd New York marching from Germanna Ford towards Chancellorsville with the brigade when their initiation to "Seeing the Elephant"-a phrase of the time for something new and unique-came crashing through the woods. A rebel cavalry battery was using a small break among the trees to target the road and shells started screaming and crashing about the area. "Our eyes opened very wide to this introduction to cannonading," Bull says of the moment. The 123rd was ordered to charge and silence the guns sitting on a little knoll. One shell exploded close to Company C as the men formed but the regiment was lucky as the Rebs didn't have the range. "To be sure they did dodge a little when the shells went whizzing over their heads, but they silenced the guns and drove the enemy," Morhous relates. The regiment stayed on the knoll until the wagon train had passed and then rejoined the brigade.[112]

About 4 p.m. of April 30th the 123rd New York was at rest with other Federal troops in the field just south of the Chancellor House at the crossroads. While given the name "Chancellorsville" there was only the two-story brick tavern/hotel of the Chancellor family, the log cabin of their slave overseer and a few smaller shacks. With five roads merging at the location and some open fields among the thicket of surrounding forest it was a natural concentration point. Some of the Chancellor family were on their second floor porch and took to ribbing the troops as they marched by, the soldiers finding the women especially surly. Hooker, his corps commanders and their staffs held discussions on the porch of the Chancellor House then the units filed off into the woods to build breastworks. The 123rd with the 2nd Brigade went in a southern direction about a half-mile into the woods; engineers laid out a line then with shovels and axes distributed everyone set to work. Bull and the men needed some instruction as to what was required of them, "To most of us this was a new occupation but before our service was to end it was one in which we were to become proficient."[113] The men gathered fallen logs in the woods and laid them lengthwise along the marked trench line. Then they dug a trench, throwing the soil atop the logs. When done they had a five foot depth of embankment and trench to protect them, adequate to stop bullets.

    That evening the regiments were called into line and an order of congratulations from General Hooker was read to the army around Chancellorsville. It told the men that they had created the conditions for a great success and now the Rebels must flee or face destruction. Being new to it all the 123rd soldiers took this at face value. Corporal Bull cheered the address with the others "little realizing then what a short step there is between seeming success and utter failure." Sergeant Morhous relates that many in the 123rd New York were afraid no battle would take place. The men "had known only camp life and all were anxious for an engagement."[114] The desire to test their mettle was upon the regiment and the idea of just ending the war and going home wasn't their idea of the proper path. As the men laid down by their trenches for a good night's sleep tramping towards them from Fredericksburg were North Carolinians and Georgians that would shatter the Upstate New Yorker's naiveté.

Early on May 1st the men were up cutting trees and forming an abatis in front of their trenches. An abatis is simply an intertwining of cut trees with the branches pointing towards the direction of the enemy. Sometimes the branches would even be sharpened, the idea being to tangle up, delay and impale any assaulting force right before the trench line where the defenders had clear shots. Around 10 a.m. the order came for the brigade to fall in for marching as the 1st Division of 12th Corps was to push towards Fredericksburg on a reconnaissance. This was to be in coordination with other divisions of the army.

After about a mile along the Plank Road the men heard firing and cannonading to their front. Union troops ahead of them had engaged the Confederates dug in just beyond The Wilderness. The units formed into line of battle but it was at once obvious the problems the thickets posed for combat organization. On an open field the 123rd New York would have formed ranks two deep of each company, the unit stretching along the grass 330 yards for a new regiment of 1,000 men (two ranks with two feet per man in line). The unit flag, the colors, were carried by a color guard of sergeants to the left of the fifth company to give reference to the soldiers. If skirmishers were sent forward they were the two end companies, often deployed about 300 yards out. There was no way the standard formation could be applied this day. "We at once entered the forest in our front but found the scrub pine so close together with their branches so interlocked that it was not only impossible to advance the line in company front but it was with the greatest difficulty a single person could penetrate the thicket," Corporal Bull states, "So we went through the tangle breaking our way through the pine branches, many of them were dead and sharp as spears."[115] Now the shooting was much closer, the 123rd and the 1st Division were just inside the tree line. This was a benefit, as the Southerners could not locate them properly for their artillery to do damage. Still, it was disconcerting to stand there with shells shattering treetops above one and the resulting rain of plant parts.

Finally the 123rd New York broke out onto a large field, the men were scattered but all looked for the colors and gathered for proper regimental formation, company front two ranks deep with companies aligned from left to right: B, G, K, E, H, C, I, D, F, A. The regimental flag was posted on the left of Company C. It took a half-hour to form properly then the regiment moved forward marching up a slope to stop atop a hill. They came into a scene where the Rebel entrenchments were roughly a half-mile away over ravine cut fields, other Union troops ahead of them skirmishing lively. Now in plain sight, the Rebel artillery redoubled their efforts towards the New Yorkers. As the 123rd could not engage the men were ordered to lie down to avoid the shelling and random bullets whizzing along. As the men dropped down the thunder of hoofs behind them announced Union artillery arriving, a 1st Division battery wheeling behind the men and setting up to the regiment's left. Now the Rebs had Yankee artillery to engage so shifted their fire off the 123rd. It was an exciting moment for the 123rd soldiers. "We could see where the solid shot struck the earth by the dirt and dust that was thrown in the air," Corporal Bull says, "The shells were more terrifying than solid shot as they burst in the air the pieces singing and shrieking in every direction."[116]

Orders came for the Union troops to withdraw back to Chancellorsville. The 123rd New York was back at the crossroads around 6 p.m. where they halted for orders. Meanwhile, several Union generals were livid that they had gotten orders to fall back from the open ground. The idea was to get out of The Wilderness, get the full might of the Union forces into open ground and attacking the Rebels in the open, the open! Where numbers could tell for the Nation! What in the world were they back in the woods for?

Hooker had lost his nerve. While the 123rd had been atop the hill watching the artillery duel other Union troops were advancing, Union Major General George Meade with his 5th Corps moving to a location to entirely flank the Confederate's position. At that moment Hooker's orders arrived for a retreat giving the initative over to General Robert E. Lee and the Army of Northern Virginia with devastating results for the Army of the Potomac. Some argue that Hooker lost his nerve when Lee came at him rather than run away; others that Hooker was now too overwhelmed to make sense out of what was happening, the Union army was just too big, sheer size of forces under his control made him feel loss of control.[117] He dropped back rather than risk all, not comprehending the larger danger that entailed as Lee was an opponent that *would* risk all.

The day wasn't over yet for the 123rd New York as it was broken away from their brigade for support duties. They marched along the fields of the Chancellorsville area and up onto an open knoll called Hazel Grove. An advancement of the picket line to the southeast, down into the marshy ground below the hillock was planned. Company "A" and "I" of the 123rd New York were detailed as picket and went off down the hill and into the woods. The picket line was just being established when Rebel cavalry opened on the right driving in four pickets. Captain Orrin Hall (Co. I) was resetting the line when Wright's Brigade-Confederate Georgia infantry- was seen advancing in battle line through the woods. The men exchanged shots with the Rebels but they had to retreat. Company I was ordered by Captain Hall to file to the right away from the firing but Company A turned and sought to return back up the slope thereby losing some men. At the sound of the firing the rest of the 123rd New York advanced to the edge of the open hill overlooking the forest. They heard the firing but no enemy could be seen.

Suddenly the woods erupted on the regiment. "By me stood Jerry Finch," Corporal Bull writes, "At the first volley his gun dropped from his hands, he staggered and fell to the ground at my side. I bent over him thinking I could do something for him but he did not move or speak and his face was ashey white, he was shot through the body and instantly killed." The men dropped down. They had to hold their fire as Companies "A" and "I" were in the sight line. Bullets were whizzing among the ranks, men were being hit while the picket detail was trying to skadaddle out of the way. "I stood by a rail fence with my gun resting on the top trying to get sight of a reb," Private Henry Welch said of the action, "I saw two standing by a bush I took aim and fired and was just raising my gun from the fence when a ball struck my finger took off the nail and struck my arm! it did not hit fair or it would have broke it the ball passed out my sleeve I could not load my gun so went off the field with [Lt.] Col Norten who was severely wounded at the same time!"[118]

Lt. Colonel Norton was waving his sword and directing the men when he was hit in the hip and carried from the field. Corporal Bull also had a couple close calls, "One bullet hit my gun and an other went through the coffee pail hanging by my side." At this point Rebel artillery came into play shelling the $123^{rd's}$ position. It was too hot, too exposed, the regiment was ordered to fall back into a woods line as Union artillery came forward and commenced firing. An artillery duel continued for an hour with the Union gunners getting the upper hand. Exploding shells among the trees brought large limbs crashing down among the men of the 123rd and some began to drop back from the assigned position. Sergeant Cruikshank saw Major James Rogers deal promptly with the situation. The shirkers were "observed by Major Rogers who started for them with drawn sword (he is quite a small man but carried a very large cavalry sabre), calling out to them saying, 'The first man who leaves his post, I'll run him through.' This declaration astonished the men..." And held them in place. By 11 p.m. the men were back to their entrenchments the regiment having suffered 3 killed and 5 wounded. They looked forward to some rest but other obligations came first. As a chaplain offered a prayer Bull and fellow soldiers buried 21 year old Private Finch behind their line. "Jerry was a fine young man, a good soldier." For the men of the 123rd, they had begun to understand the seriousness of their situation.[119]

Colonel Samuel Ross, commanding the 2nd Brigade, reported of the action "the One-hundred and twenty-third New York Volunteers became hotly engaged with the enemy, who appeared in force, driving in the scouts and pickets. Overwhelmed by superior numbers, and nearly surrounded, this regiment gallantly maintained its ground until ordered to fall back, when it retired at about sundown in good order. Lieutenant-Colonel Norton fell, severely wounded, while bravely discharging his duty."[120]

Sheer exhaustion made for a solid night's sleep. The morning of May 2nd was another sunny one. Many of the 123rd's men having run out of food, those with some hardtack and pork left split it with their comrades for a sparse regimental breakfast as bugle calls and drum rolls sounded throughout the camps. Some firing could be heard in the distance towards the left wing of the army but rumors began that the Confederates were retreating.

The Confederates were definitely *moving* the morning of May 2nd. The night before, as the men of the 123rd New York sank to sleep at their entrenchments, two Virginians sat talking by a campfire just two miles away. Generals Robert E. Lee and Thomas "Stonewall" Jackson discussed their options and retreat wasn't one of them. The Army of Northern Virginia would attack. But in what way? Locals had supplied information as to the road network. Rebel cavalry General J.E.B. Stuart relayed information that the Federal's right wing, the 11th Corps, was exposed, open for a strike. Lee, who had already split his smaller army in the face of a superior force once-a serious faux pas in military doctrine-now decided to split it again. Jackson would march 26,000 men the morning of May 2nd across the front of the Union army and position himself for a flank attack on the Union right. Lee would remain with the rest of the army, 17,000 men, in their current location keeping up steady attacks to rivet Hooker's attention. There was real danger to this plan. Jackson would be observable at times by the Federals during portions of the march. If the Yankees charged forth with shot and bayonet there was a good chance either section of Lee's army could be surrounded and cut to pieces before the other section could respond in support. But with that uncanny ability to understand his opponent, Lee had Hooker's card hand. Jackson was ordered to move, move fast, and not worry about any Federal response.

As they munched their scant hardtack and pork breakfasts on May 2nd the men of the 123rd were listening to Lee's plan in action, both in the firing off to their left and the rumors of a retreat. Union scouts had seen Confederate troops marching along the Furnace Road across their front, this only confirmed to General Hooker that the Rebs were whipped and retreating. But the roads Jackson had to use for his march around the Union army took him southwest until he could connect with other traces the locals had told him about, whereupon he pivoted northwest and the far right of the Union army.

Several reports were coming into Union headquarters of this movement. One soldier from the 123rd even climbed a tall pine and watched the Rebels, this was also relayed up the ladder of command. During the afternoon Hooker sent a message to the commander of the 11th Corps, General Oliver Howard, to be alert for any Rebel advance onto his right. Unfortunately Hooker did not personally ride out and inspect the 11th Corps entrenchments and discuss the situation with Howard.[121]

But Hooker did finally order the Union 3rd Corps and 12th Corps forward to make contact and engage any enemy to the south. Hooker pulled the center section of his army out of position to fall upon the fleeing Rebels. But it was a slow response, the men of the 123rd left their entrenchments at 1 p.m. and the entire force didn't make the Furnace Road until 4 p.m. They made contact and some sharp skirmishing ensued but it was with the Confederate rear-guard, the main force was already gone and closing on the Union right flank. During all this fighting the 123rd New York was in reserve. A couple hundred Rebel prisoners were marched by and the Union men taunted them only to be told, "Wait until you hear from old Jack then you wont laugh."[122]

At this moment, an eagle circling over the battlefield would have seen a mass of men in the woods around the 123rd, the blue uniforms facing south/southwest with scattered pockets of gray soldiers moving away from the Catherine Furnace area. Behind the 123rd, back up the hill and among the woods and fields south of Chancellorsville were entrenchments, empty entrenchments of the 3rd and 12th Corps. Beyond the open area, an area with no Union forces of any strength, was the 11th Corps sitting alone, the far right flank of the Army of the Potomac. The 11th were also mainly facing south along the Plank Road, the camp quiet. Snaking towards them along dirt traces of roads, piling up now into the woods to their west, were the gray uniforms of Jackson's army, a huge snake-head forming as regiments, brigades and divisions arrived to be ordered into line. Dashing along on "Little Sorrel" was General "Stonewall" Jackson, completing a personal reconnaissance to ensure his troops would deliver a deathblow once released. To the east flashes, reports and smoke rising from the woods as Southern units kept pressure to Hooker's left flank. Then a massive yell rises up and below to the west the forest screams in fire and a mass of gray pours out of the woods.

The men of the 123rd New York heard it. "Coming suddenly and unexpectedly cannonading at our right, seemingly far away," Corporal Bull writes, "It began slowly but rapidly increased and soon was a continuous roar. With it also came the sound of musketry firing, beginning with volleys then settling into the continuous rattle and roar that comes when firing at will." The men of the 3rd Corps and 12th Corps heard it, the entire Union army heard this low growl of flame that grew and grew on the horizon. Howard's 11th Corps was hit so fast and without warning that it broke within minutes. Little pockets of resistance were offered but the onslaught was too quick and the flanking maneuver too deep on the Union forces that position after position was rapidly lost.[123]

It was imperative that the 3rd and 12th Corps interpose themselves on the charging Rebels before a total disaster befell the Army of the Potomac. Riders atop lathered horses began galloping up to the generals of the 3rd and 12th Corps and a massive return to their entrenchments was ordered post-haste. It was a two-mile run for everyone on the double-quick.

"There was much confusion as all were striving to get back as quickly as possible," Bull says.[124] Halts had to be made as other units came running into the 123rd's front, then the double-quick began again. It took forty-five minutes for the men to be back atop Hazel Grove. They were passed behind batteries of Union artillery rapidly firing towards the west as the cacophony grew and grew before them. Forming line of battle, the 123rd New York marched off Hazel Grove and across the field towards the Orange Plank Road. With other units of the 12th Corps they began to form a line with their right flank anchored on the Plank Road and the left running up to Hazel Grove. It was anything but easy to create as soldiers of the 11th Corps in full flight now stampeded through the 12th Corps!

It was an unbelievable sight to Corporal Bull and the men of the 123rd. "These panic stricken men were coming from the woods in front and fleeing across the open field. Their retreat was headlong and reckless. Everything loose they had thrown away, guns, equipment, knapsacks, caps and many had thrown coat or blouse and were in their shirt sleeves…We were ordered to stop these men…We might as well have tried to stop a cyclone. They would dive through our line regardless of our guns or bayonets. One can hardly conceive the terror that seemed to possess them." There is always the danger of panic becoming contagious, the soldiers were glad when the last of the crazed men cleared their line as they could get back to business.[125]

Night was coming on, to the Union artillery belonged the day's battle. From Hazel Grove and lines of batteries stretching beyond the Plank Road they had thundered the Rebel charge into abeyance. Soldiers had done their part too, but for shear stopping power double-canister, shot and shell rapidly placed among the enemy broke the charge. As the Rebels were charging from the woods they could not bring their artillery to play for most of their front due to the forest thickness. The Yankee gunners therefore had free play upon the Confederate infantry. As long as the Union held the open grounds around the Chancellor House and the very critical high, open ground of Hazel Grove they stood a chance of turning this action to their favor. Lee's army was in two parts separated by Hooker's larger and unbroken army. The next day would be a slugging match for the upper hand.

As the Confederates had taken possession of the western entrenchments first constructed by the 12th Corps the Union soldiers spent the night making new earth works. The men of the 123rd New York were positioned near the Orange Plank Road along the edge of forest. The layout of the 2nd Brigade was as follows: the 3rd Maryland was adjacent to the Plank Road with their line coming off perpendicularly to it; next was the 123rd New York; then the 5th Connecticut and the rest of General Knipe's 1st Brigade; General Ruger's 3rd Brigade; then the 145th New York and 20th Connecticut of the 2nd Brigade (Colonel Ross of the 20th CT commanding). Some of the confusion during the evening of May 2nd can be seen in that the 2nd Brigade was separated, the 123rd New York and 3rd Maryland up by the Plank Road while their brother regiments the 20th Connecticut and 145th New York were a half-mile away entrenching below Hazel Grove. After the 20th CT the line started northeast, the Second Division of the 12th Corps having their backs to the soldiers of the First Division, 12th Corps. The Army of the Potomac now had an entrenchment line like a "V" with the base of the "V" on Hazel Grove. Also showing the confusion of the night before, the 12th Corps had the center of the Union line, intermingled with the 3rd Corps. To the north of the Plank Road, holding the right flank of the 3rd MD, was the Second Division of the 3rd Corps, while the rest of the 3rd Corps were at Hazel Grove outside the entrenchments. For Confederate General Robert E. Lee it was upsetting to have his army separated by this "V" and he resolved to reunite the wings of his army. The obvious solution was to crush the Union center.[126]

Sweaty, dirty and hungry the men of the 123rd New York worked on their entrenchments until 3 a.m. They dropped trees out to fifty feet and formed an abatis, then stacked the larger logs and shoveled dirt over them for their trench. Ammunition and three-days rations of food-hardtack and pork-were issued to them as they finished. They slouched down to munch their fare in the moonlight while watching Battery E, 1st Rhode Island and Battery M, 1st New York flail away building revetments for their cannons 400 yards behind them. The artillery was positioned to shoot over the line by making use of the upward slope of ground to Fairview, the log cabin on the Chancellor property. Reinforcements were readily available as General Mott's Brigade of the 3rd Corps was positioned between them and the artillery. More cannon arrived during the night building up to 34 guns facing west. Veteran soldiers would have seen the firepower being arranged as a clue to the morrow. The men of the 123rd New York tried to get some sleep.

As soon as the sun hit the east the Rebels hit the Union lines. Sergeant Cruikshank and the men of the 123rd New York were ready for them. "They appeared in one solid mass of living grey. The whole woods in front of us seemed to be full of them…The enemy charged on us in solid column again and again, their battle cry sounding above the roll of musketry, the roar of cannon and bursting and crashing of shell. The enemy would come so far, when their ranks would become so thinned that they would fall back a little to fill them up again. When our men would see them giving way cheer after cheer would then be heard. It would be only for a moment as the empty places in the enemy's ranks would be filled and on they would come again." Corporal Bull was in the thick if it, "It was now load and fire at will as rapidly as possible and in the excitement of this work we soon found that the nervousness and fear with which we begun the fight had passed away and a feeling of fearlessness and rage had taken its place."[127]

For three hours General Lane's Brigade of North Carolinians hammered on the area of the 123rd New York's entrenchment. Like Vikings slamming a metallized log against a Frankish castle door, the Union line began to splinter, cave in and falter. "During this time we loaded and fired our guns as fast as was possible but on they came and while the smoke was so dense we could only occasionally see their forms, we could see the flash from their guns," Bull wrote of the pandemonium. Dead were dropping into the dust, wounded crawling away from the line, smoke swirling among those seeking more ammunition, shirtsleeves wiping sweat from brows, Rebs leaping upon the works pitching dead into them, screams, officers yelling, bullets snapping, shells cracking scant feet above their heads the men of the 123rd fought on. "Ed Tanner a fellow that taught school at your district a few day's hd both his leg's shot off above the knees Al Done had one leg shot off…Bryon Briggs was shot dead." "He was wounded by a musket ball which passed close by my head passing entirely through one of his thighs, entering the other until it struck the bone, then it passed down lodging near the knee on the opposite side." "Second Lieut. J. C. Corbett, of Co. C, was left on the field dead, and first Lieut. Beadle and second Lieut. Albert Shiland of Co. I, were badly wounded…." "…I saw a bullet strike him in the head…." "…two dead men were lying close to me, one lying across my feet…." "…I found William H. Dennison (Sergeant) who had been shot through the body, mortally wounded; William E. Stewart (Corporal) shot through the arm; Garrett W. Briggs (Corporal) wounded in the hip and gone to the rear; John S. Dory shot through the face with tongue nearly cut off; Archibald Johnson mortally wounded…."[128]

Almost from the first volley of the Confederates the 3rd Maryland broke and fled. "The rebs charged on the 3rd Maryland to our right, and they like cowards, ran [S]ome of our boys also ran then [T]he rebs then had a cross fire on us but our Regt. did not flinch," Corporal Albert Cook (Co. A) of the 123rd New York notes with disgust.[129] Although elements of Union General Mott's Brigade rushed to fill the gap Confederate forces broke through the front line pouring flanking fire into the 123rd and Federal troops to the north of the Plank Road. A great melee began with charges and counter-charges of regiments. The artillery along Fairview ridge roared shell into the Rebel ranks doing horrible carnage but could not use canister due to their comrades desperately fighting at the barricades before them.

Compounding the problems for the Federals in the area of the 123rd New York, enfilading artillery fire now entered their midst from Hazel Grove. Major General Sickles and units of his 3rd Corps had held the small hill the night before, even making a night attack into the Rebels from it. But in the early dawn before the battle renewed on May 3rd General Hooker had ridden up to Hazel Grove and ordered Sickles back into the trenches towards Chancellorsville. It was a grievous mistake. There was a channel of open field (like a modern power-line trail down a slope) running from Hazel Grove right towards the Chancellor House not quite a mile away. The entire left flank of the Union 12th Corps was in range and could be enfiladed by artillery. Within an hour Confederates had massed 30 cannons atop Hazel Grove and commenced pounding everything that moved, ducked or prayed below them. Union artillery behind the 123rd New York had to swing several guns off the Confederate infantry attack to deal with the Rebel artillery. Still, the Union soldiers were taking a toll on their attackers. By 8 a.m. Lane's Brigade of North Carolinians had broken and fallen to the rear. They had suffered 805 casualties in killed, wounded and missing. The 33rd North Carolina alone losing 41% of their men they took into the fray. Replacing them in a headlong rush at this section of line were O'Neal's Alabamians, Perrin's South Carolinians, Pender's North Carolinians and Paxton's Virginians.[130]

The entire Union center fought, expecting the reserves to be put in, for additional help from their commanding officer, General Joseph Hooker. Atop the "V" formation of the Union position sat the 1st and 5th Corps of the Union Army, over 20,000 fresh troops that were never ordered into the fray. Hooker seems to have been figuratively stunned by Lee's flanking movement of May 2nd and now as the battle reached a climax on the 3rd he literally was stunned. The Confederate artillery line atop Hazel Grove was ripping the Union center apart, one of the shells hit a pillar on the Chancellor House as Hooker was on the porch. He was knocked senseless. It was at this moment that requests from Generals Slocum (12th Corps) and General Sickles (3rd Corps) for reinforcements and ammunition arrived to have no one in authority, in top command, of the army. "At 8 a.m. I informed the commanding general that our small-arm ammunition was nearly exhausted, and that a new supply was necessary or that my troops must be relieved," Major General Slocum, commanding 12th Corps, noted. The battle continued in the entrenchments before Fairview with no support, men or ammo, ordered forward.[131]

Colonel Ross of the 20th Connecticut being wounded, command of the 2nd Brigade fell to Colonel McDougall during the battle and Major Rogers took command of the 123rd New York. This was fortuitous as General Knipe commanding the 1st Brigade ordered, between Confederate charges, Colonel McDougall to advance the 123rd as support for a counterattack by the 1st Brigade. The men of the 123rd New York scrambled out of their entrenchments and started forward. Major Rogers caught up to Colonel McDougall asking what he was doing. Major Rogers pointed out to the Colonel that, as the commander of the 2nd Brigade, he did not take orders from General Knipe. McDougall ordered Major Rogers to return the men to the entrenchments. It was just in time as coming through the woods was another charge of the enemy, the bear claws of the Confederates ready to slash into the exposed regiment. "We had only commenced to move back when the enemy made a charge on us, firing into our backs and yelling like so many demons," Cruikshank says of the maneuver, "Charles Marshall and John A. Mains were, I think, shot down in this charge as I saw them both and spoke to John after we commenced to advance, but they were never seen or heard of afterward. They were both good soldiers."[132]

General Knipe ordered the 123rd New York forward after seeing Union regiments obloquy attacking across his front from left to right. "I at once ordered the One-hundred and twenty-third New York Volunteers to advance over our barricades, and, throwing their left wing forward, it delivered some well-directed volleys into the enemy's flank, immediately in front of the left of [Union] General Berry's line." General Knipe had heard that Colonel Ross, commander of the 2nd Brigade, had been wounded so took it upon himself to assume command of both the 1st and 2nd Brigades of the 1st Division, 12th Corps. With so many officers falling, the confusion of battle led to confusion of command structure.[133]

The 123rd New York officers withdrew the men beyond their works then reformed the regiment and charged back to retake their entrenchments as the Confederates began to enter them. It was getting obvious the tide was going to the Rebs. "Our line had become so weakened we were not much more than a skirmish line and on the right of the road [3rd Corps] they had suffered as much as we had…We gained our works and held them for a few minutes." Sergeant Cruikshank now had his epiphany it was time to leave. "I was so engaged that I did not notice what was going on at my right. It was the hottest time of the fight. Every piece of artillery behind us was worked as rapidly as possible and their shell seemed to graze our heads and I suppose that they came as close as they could and not hit us as the enemy were but a few feet in front of us. I looked to the right and what did I see! All were in grey uniforms, close to me. The right of the regiment were gone; the Colors were gone and Lieutenant Culver with the right half of the Company were gone. I ordered my men to move backward and to the left, the left of the Regiment giving away at the same time. We fought the enemy until we got back to the Creek, then broke ranks and went back up the hill…" As soon as the regiment had cleared their front the Union batteries at Fairview opened with canister that stopped the Rebels in the captured entrenchments.[134]

Colonel McDougall states "we never left until the regiment on our right & the Brigade on our left had retired and the rebs had pressed both of our flanks and were giving us a terrible enfilading fire with musketry on our right & the same with artillery on our left. One solid shot from [their] battery on our left, took a leg from one man, 2 legs from another and a head from another man, of different companies before the order was given to retire...towards the latter end of the fight, our gunners depressed their guns as to just shoot over our heads, our boys actually dodging from our own shells."[135]

It was about 8 a.m. Other Union regiments of the 12th Corps also were withdrawing, many of the commanders reporting they were out of ammunition. Brigadier General Thomas Ruger, commanding the 3rd Brigade, 1st Division, 12th Corps, reported his men out of ammo after "two hours" of fighting. Between 7 a.m. and 8 a.m. Ruger's command was relieved by elements of the 3rd Corps coming forward. These were the units drawn up in reserve behind the 12th Corps entrenchments and as such they still had ammunition. The 123rd New York also would have been facing an ammunition shortage by the time they retreated. Colonel McDougall of the 123rd New York in his after action report does state his troops were out of ammunition after the charge upon the enemy beyond the entrenchments. It appears once generally engaged the 12th Corps units along the fighting line had enough cartridges positioned along their lines to last roughly between two to three hours (5 a.m. to 8 a.m.). This is about the length of time the 3rd Corps lasted with their ammunition also once solidly engaged (7:00 a.m. to 10:00 a.m.). As there was no ammunition readily at hand to bring forward, replenishment became impossible and the units first engaged that morning, mainly 12th Corps, retreated.[136]

It was a surreal scene beyond the artillery. Smoke roiling along the ground with shadows of men marching forward through it, rider-less horses galloping about, knapsacks and rifles littering the ground, wounded staggering or crawling to the rear over ground churned up like a farm field from the exploding shells. "From where we were all the way back the ground was strewn with the dead, dying and wounded." Cruikshank, like the rest of the men of the 123rd New York, was exhausted. "In going back I was so worn out that I could not quicken my pace although solid shot and shell were flying all around. One shell struck a caisson and exploded it, killing several men and stripping the clothes entirely off of one, burning him terribly and blinding both eyes. He was crying for some one to kill him and put him out of his misery."[137]

Yet in the midst of the horror Cruikshank saw an incident that made him laugh. In front of him Private Merrick Knapp (Co. K) was loaded down with his knapsack and rifle walking to the rear when a "solid shot struck the ground several feet behind him, bounded into the air and struck him under the knapsack, raised him several feet from the ground turning him completely over, seating him heavily on the ground." Cruikshank thought Knapp was dead but he leapt up, glanced behind him then started on a run for the Chancellor House.[138]

Also running for the Chancellor House was the 123rd Color Sergeant and to lighten his load he tossed aside the regimental flag. A unit's flag was sacrosanct; it represented the honor and fighting élan of the men. Battles and dates of fighting were added to it showing the veteran status of the regiment. It was a tremendous disgrace to the 123rd New York to lose their colors but, fortunately, a regiment in Union General Mott's Brigade recovered it and it was returned after the battle. "No one regretted the occurrence more than he, and probably he would have given his life if he could have recalled this one dark spot in his otherwise brilliant record as a soldier. He received a public reprimand from the Colonel after reaching camp at Stafford, but received it as a true soldier-with meekness and humility," Sergeant Morhous says, adding, "that in all the fights in which the Regiment was afterwards engaged, he showed himself a cool, brave man."[139]

Bravery and fighting spirit earned a Congressional Medal of Honor for a soldier of the 123rd New York, Sergeant Henry Sartwell (Co. D). "Citation: Was severely wounded by a gunshot in his left arm, went a half a mile to the rear but insisted on returning to his company and continue to fight bravely until he became exhausted from the loss of blood and was compelled to retire from the field." As he couldn't handle a rifle Sartwell returned to the lines with a revolver.[140]

It was now about 8:30 a.m., the remnants of the 12th Corps with the 3rd Corps fought on, forming a new line along the artillery redoubts near Fairview. Artillery at Fairview ran out of shot around 9 a.m. and were dragged off or disabled. Reuniting both wings of his army, Robert E. Lee now threw from the east, west and south a huge maw of Floridians, Georgians, Alabamians, Virginians, Tennesseans, Mississippians, North Carolinians and South Carolinians at the remaining Northern brigades around Fairview. For the next hour they gamely held on as their rifle ammunition ran out and the artillery fell silent. In this melee were the brother regiments of the 123rd New York: the 20th Connecticut and 145th New York. Having been at the other end of the field they were caught in the pincer movement. Along with regiments from New Hampshire, New Jersey, Pennsylvania, Ohio, Delaware, New York, Connecticut and Massachusetts they fought until retreat had to be ordered. By 10 a.m. the remains of the Union 3rd Corps and 12th Corps were falling back to new entrenchments north of the Chancellor House. It was at this point Lee heard of the advancement towards his right flank of Union General Sedgwick from Fredericksburg. He shifted his plan of attack from Hooker to this new threat and the firing died out around Chancellorsville.

Yet there were soldiers that had noticed a quiet, a stillness, earlier that morning upon the same battlefield. They were the wounded of the 123rd New York, scattered along their entrenchment line. Corporal Rice Bull had been hit twice soon after the battle commenced, once along the right side of the face by buckshot and then a ball punched into him just above his left hip, coming out by his backbone. He was carried a little to the rear and laid in a little depression among some bushes where a small stream ran. Bull lay there, blood covering his face and clothes, as bullets clipped leaves and the artillery shells screamed just feet above him. He tried to sit-up once but only opened his wounds again, he laid back down. More and more wounded filled the area. As no bandages or compresses were issued to the fighting men, many of the soldiers bled to death needlessly.

Then the firing ceased. Smoke obscured the view back towards the entrenchments but then Bull realized the 123rd New York was gone. It was quiet, firing was going on other places but…then the sound of voices, officers giving orders from beyond the line. The wounded that could move their heads strained to see who was coming. Suddenly armed men appeared near where they lay. "They were not dressed in Union Blue but gray. The made a soldierly though not a handsome appearance, as no two uniforms were exactly alike either in style or color or material. The officers were much better dressed then the privates having uniforms of light gray, well fitted…The men were well armed and equipped and so far as I could observe were under good discipline." They dressed their lines and moved forward, their officers cautioning the men not to step on or disturb the Union wounded. As the infantry moved off a Confederate artillery battery galloped up to cross the stream. "Some of our wounded men were alarmed fearing they might cross over regardless of them." The Rebel officer in charge said not to worry and he had his men move the wounded from the horses' path. As the afternoon came on the men laid there, some crying out now and then in pain and desperation.[141]

They were helpless. Weak. And, unfortunately, in a zone of lawlessness once the combat soldiers had moved through. Into this zone came predators: the shirkers and cowards of an army. Bull and the others saw another group of Rebels come towards them and begin to pick through the wounded. "Stragglers and skulkers, 'coffee coolers' the boys used to call them, who are found in the rear of every army Union or Confederate and are the cause of most of the disreputable things that happen in both armies came down through the woods…They began operations by using abusive language to the prisoners…they began to rob both the dead and living." Cussing at the prostrated men, they shoved them about to rifle their pockets. "One poor fellow lying near me, who was so weak he could hardly lift his hand, was robbed of his watch and money." It was beginning to look bad.[142]

Yet decent men are not ignorant of this problem. Both the Union and Confederate armies assign troops, cavalry and infantry, to the "Provost Guard," a type of military police. It was their job to deal with the low lifes slithering around the rear areas. Coming onto the scene was a Confederate cavalry unit performing such a duty. "When the Provost Captain came on the ground and saw what the skulkers were doing he was very indignant and went for them with a will. With his drawn sword he struck some of them good hard blows using the flat side of the blade and called them as bad names, almost, as they had us. He at once stopped their dirty work and hustled them off to the front."[143]

Back across the battlefield, at the far left of the new Union entrenchments the remains of the 123rd New York gathered to the rear of the Chancellor House with other units of the 12th Corps. The Army of the Potomac was not beaten, it was roughed up, but the 11th Corps had regrouped and the 3rd and 12th Corps had withdrawn with some order into the entrenchments now north of Chancellorsville. Hooker had over 70,000 effectives in a very strong defensive position with his left on the Rappahannock and his right on the Rapidan. The operative word here is "defensive." Robert E. Lee saw the Federals heavily entrenching and gauged that Hooker wouldn't come out. He left 25,000 men under Stuart to hold Hooker and took 21,000 against Union General Sedgwick's 19,000 at Salem Church. Sedgwick held Lee at arm's length and withdrew across the Rappahannock the night of May 4th. Hooker ordered the rest of the Army of the Potomac across the river on May 6th. Confederate losses for the battle were around 13,000 with Federal losses approximately 17,000. The Army of Northern Virginia started with 53,000 so suffered 24% losses while the Army of the Potomac suffered 15% on their strength of 113,000 soldiers. General Joseph Hooker had been defeated but not the men of the Army of the Potomac. Speaking of the retreat of the army, Private Samuel Atwood (Co. H) penned, "Why we do not know as we did not think we were beaten."[144]

The 123rd New York had fought from 5 a.m. to 8 a.m. the morning of May 3rd then retreated to the rear while losing their colors. Remaining Union troops continued the battle until past 10 a.m. when they had to withdraw or be annihilated. Other regiments and an entire brigade, Greene's, had also been shattered during this time. What were the casualties for the 123rd and how do they compare to the other units in their brigade and adjacent Union regiments during the battle of that day?

On May 3rd the 123rd New York suffered 22 killed, 103 wounded, 20 captured or missing. The regiment to their immediate right, the Maryland 3rd Infantry, suffered 2 killed, 45 wounded, 1 captured or missing. To their left in the entrenchment line was the 5th Connecticut (1st Brigade, 1st Division, 12th Corps) with loses of 1 killed, 16 wounded, 6 captured or missing. Noteworthy is that the 123rd New York suffered much larger numbers of killed, wounded or missing than either of the regiments to their flanks. This can be attributed to the fleeing of the 3rd Maryland. Its right flank was on the Plank Road, the natural avenue (literally) for the Rebel attack, when the 3rd broke it allowed Confederate regiments to flank the 123rd New York and pour a heavy fire down their entrenchment until beaten back. The 123rd New York shielded the 5th Connecticut from this flanking fire thereby reducing their casualties.[145]

Those much higher in rank than the footsloggers of the 123rd New York noted the retreat of the 3rd Maryland. "At this time my second line was about to engage the enemy, my first line being compelled to fall back in consequence of the injudicious retreat of a Maryland regiment..." Brigadier General Joseph Carr of the 3rd Corps, 2nd Division stated in his after-action report. "The Third (Mott's) Brigade, Second Division, after the retreat of the Third Maryland Regiment, moved forward to the breastwork..." Major General Daniel Sickles, commander of the 3rd Corps, noted in his after-action report.[146] (It takes a lot of effort for a regiment to be mentioned in a Major General's report, but this wasn't the type of citation a regiment sought.)

Why did the 3rd Maryland retreat? After the battle of Antietam the 3rd Maryland only had about 200 effectives. The unit was never up to full strength to begin with and they had over 220 desertions in the year leading up to Chancellorsville. During January and February of 1863 the unit received 200 substitutes and draftees. This was under the *militia* draft quota system put into place at the same time President Lincoln called for the 300,000 volunteers that the men of the 123rd New York answered. This was a back-door way of drafting men that wouldn't volunteer by calling the militia up for nine-months service. Major Samuel Kramer of the 3rd Maryland speaks of the new recruits arriving via train at Harper's Ferry. "On the way to the Ferry, many of these men being 'bounty jumpers' tried to desert; but I took the precaution to have the cars doors guarded, with orders to shoot any that should attempt it. On arriving at the Ferry they fought with the guards and several were wounded, and they had us nearly overpowered when the provost guard came to our assistance. We succeeded in marching them to the regiment, and several of the leaders were placed in confinement." The 3rd Maryland was at a strength of around 400 men at Chancellorsville, roughly half of whom were draftees from Baltimore and the Eastern Shore of Maryland, strong secessionist areas with no love of the North. The western counties of Maryland were strongly Unionist but it truly fit the title "Boarder State" in that it was sending troops to both sides. The 3rd Maryland would serve the entire war and perform better at later battles but at Chancellorsville half of the unit didn't want to be there and for quite a few of them they probably felt they were on the wrong side of the lines. When the Confederates ran at them they broke, they had no dog in the fight.[147]

Standing throughout the battle were the 20th Connecticut and 145th New York. Separated from the 123rd New York and 3rd Maryland, they dropped back again and again during the five hours of fighting as the Union center withdrew upon itself from the sledge hammering of the Confederates. The 20th Connecticut suffered 24 killed, 70 wounded and 96 captured or missing; the 145th New York 12 killed, 16 wounded and 14 captured or missing. Large numbers of the 20th Connecticut became captives as the pincers came shut the morning of May 3rd.[148]

Perhaps the large number of wounded reflect the 123rd New York's leaving their position to retreat? If so that would mean their wounded would have been scattered along the retreat route towards Fairview. Some must have been hit crossing that area as Confederate artillery was actively targeting the region (indeed, one was even helped along by a solid shot). But two men of the 123rd stayed behind at the entrenchments to tend for the regiment's wounded, Musician John Larmon (Co. I) and Private Hiram Blanchard (Co. C). It would appear that they felt there were a large enough number of their comrades in one area to warrant such action. Upon the breaking of the 3rd Maryland the 123rd New York's right wing (the five companies to the right of the colors) would have received orders to change front as a way of protecting their flank. Sergeant Morhous mentions that this occurred during the battle. Captain John Poland, 2nd U.S. Infantry and Acting Assistant Inspector-General of the 2nd Division, 3rd Corps, gives the breaking of the Maryland regiment as between 6:30 and 7 a.m. He reports that Mott's Brigade had retaken the entrenchments of the 3rd Maryland by 7:30 a.m. This indicates that the 123rd New York had about 45 minutes of flanking fire upon them with no protection from entrenchments for those companies. A study of the right wing casualties (Companies C, I, D, F, A) shows they suffered 60% of the wounded and 65% of the deaths for the 123rd New York on May 3rd.[149]

The Confederate Provost Guard took away both Privates Larmon and Blanchard. As the latter was in civilian clothes it seems the Confederates held him for questioning but Larmon was allowed to return later that afternoon to care for the men. "Larmon had a busy afternoon, he did all that any one could do and I wondered at his ability to keep on as he did," Bull writes, "Every wounded man within call wanted something and he responded to every call." Towards evening Confederate soldiers came through the area and several helped Larmon move wounded Union soldiers onto spread blankets and rubber ponchos as an aid to comforting. Ultimately the Union wounded in the area, about 500 men, were gathered around the log cabin at Fairview. The men suffered for eight days as the dead mortified around them. On May 12th a truce allowed Union ambulance wagons to arrive and load the men for transport to hospitals.[150]

For the soldiers of the 123rd New York back in camp at Stafford it was time to send letters home. "I tell you things looked rather discourageing when we crossed the river to see so large an army on the retreat," Private Welch wrote to his aunt and uncle, "the boy's say now that the rebels will never be whiped as for my self I think our army can whip them very easy but their Generals are to much for ours at manageing an army!"[151]

"The officers behaved well. Col McDougall was with the men all the time," Corporal Mclean wrote his brother Henry. McLean was guarding the regimental baggage so was to the rear of the battle. "I was lucky enough not to have to be in the fight & I was glad of it...I was in sight & hearing of the battle. The firing was so fast you could not count the guns but it was one roar all the time just like a hard clap of thunder. The 12th Corps fought first rate & has the praise of the whole army. Our Regt also fought well & was the last regt to fall back."[152]

"I came out with just what I had on my back," Private Levi Eaton told his wife, adding that many of the men lost their knapsacks when their position was overrun, "as for me I do not want to see another such battle they did not lick us but we were obliged to retreat the 123rd done very well they fought like men we was the last to leave the trenches."[153]

"They are devils to fight we were there 3 hours & never relieved then were ordered to leave & retreat, shells were bursting on every side...you could see men with arms, legs & heads shot off," Corporal Ransom Fisher (Co. D) wrote his father, "We have got a great name the rebel prisoners said if the rest had fought like us that there would have been no chance for them to live."[154]

"Let. Shaw has stood by us well through all he is a good fellow," Corporal Albert Cook informed his father, "Col. McDougall and Major Rogers done well all through. Most of the Regt Officers done first rate…The prisoners that we took say that the N.Y.REgt was the D--- to fight or in words some thing like their, they also think those fellow with the stars on their caps are tough fellows to fight (the 12th Corps) but those with the crescent (11th Corps which didnt fight very well) on their caps better go home…Father I am proud to say I have done some thing for my country. I never want to go into another battle but if I do with the help of God I shall fight harder then before. The rebels fight hard and make no mistake they are brave men what a pity they are on the wrong side."[155]

Chapter 4
Nursing Wounds and Pondering Hell

In the dawn of May 20th, 1937 Lieutenant George Orwell peered above the trench line toward Spanish General Franco's lines. A sniper rifle cracked, the round cut through Orwell's throat and he collapsed to the ground. It was the end of Orwell's experience in the 1930's Spanish Civil War. He was lucky in that the bullet was a metal jacketed, sharp-pointed, high velocity round that cleanly sliced through his neck. It missed an artery by a millimeter. He lived and went on to write such classics as *Animal Farm* and *1984*.[156]

American Civil War soldiers were not so lucky with the type of bullet finding their bodies upon the battlefields. They had to deal with a different beast altogether.

In the 1860's the half-inch diameter soft lead rounds came on at low velocity (950 feet per second as compared to the 2,000+ feet per second of the Mauser round that hit Orwell) and when they found human flesh they deformed and transferred energy throughout the area of impact. Bones were shattered into several pieces, flesh ripped and torn hideously, pieces of the bullet separating at times and lodging in chunks among the wound. If no bone was hit the bullet might pass through the leg, abdomen or arm but the lead often carried torn cloth from the soldier's uniform as it penetrated adding a high risk of infection. The vast majority of wounds in the war, 94%, came from the bullet. Of the bullet wounds close to three-quarters were in the arms, legs, hands or feet while 18% of wounds were in the torso and 10% in the head and neck area. For the soldiers killed in battle outright, it was found on one field that 82% of the dead were hit in the head, neck or chest area. Whereas a modern round would leave a small hole through the throat, a

Civil War bullet would flail open an entire side of one's neck with massive bleeding from the severed arteries.[157]

That so many of the Union wounded at Chancellorsville had to await a truce before they were transferred to Northern army hospitals meant that such wounds took their toll. When Federal ambulance wagons arrived at Chancellorsville on May 12th many of the surviving men had infected, maggot-laden wounds. The excitement of rescue turned to dismay once the trip started as the wagons traveled the 25 miles to Aquia Creek Hospital over corduroyed roads. The men suffered terribly as the wagons lurched, bounced and shuddered forward over the makeshift road surface. Many wounds opened again, at the end of the first day of travel two of the wounded men in a wagon near Corporal Rice Bull had died. The journey had gotten the wounded men to the Rappahannock River and when they approached it crowds of civilians were there searching for news of their loved ones in blue. "As each ambulance arrived they would visit it to learn whom it contained, anxiously looking for their friends. They would not, however, remain long at the entrance of an ambulance after making inquiry as the stench from the wounds was very offensive. I saw men after visiting some of the ambulances turn from them very quickly, the conditions were so loathsome their stomachs could not stand the pressure." Bull lay in the wagon as people kept popping their heads in to glance over the emaciated, dirty, blood stained soldiers. He dwelt upon the stories the civilians would tell once back home up North. "They would probably think they knew something of the horrors of war, yet how little did they really know."[158]

For the wounded men, ridden with lice and ticks outside their bodies, maggots and infection inside their bodies, the meals consisted of hardtack and coffee. Bull was happy to at least get the coffee but he couldn't eat solid food due to his face wound. The journey continued all day on the 13th, the jerks and starts sheer hell for those with broken limbs, the banging against the wagons threatening amputated stumps. During the travel 2nd Lt. Willis Swift, Co. D 123rd New York, appeared at Bull's wagon. He had heard that 12th Corps wounded were being brought in and ridden out to see if any of his soldiers were among them. He couldn't even recognize Bull and the others of his company due to their wretched appearance. Swift informed them that no one expected them to still be alive and that such had been reported to their families.

The wagons arrived at Aquia Creek Hospital around 5 p.m. The men were stripped, washed and surgeons tended to their wounds. The hospital was among a grove of large pines, the expansive tents having cots, mattresses and blankets for each patient. Decent food flowed to the men; comrades from the 123rd New York began to visit from the regiment's camp three miles away. For Bull, "We felt that again we were in God's country." But it was too late for some of the 123rd soldiers. Sergeant Horace Howard (Co. K) was struck by a shell fragment that shattered a thigh bone. Prompt attention the day of his wounding, the removal of the leg, would probably have saved his life. At the hospital a doctor removed over a pint of maggots from the leg. Howard, 23 years old, died fifteen days later.[159]

"I have been out today moving some wounded fellows from Stonemans Station to Acqui Creek," Private Orville Robinson wrote friends back in Washington County, "their was some pretty hard cases I tell you. One poor fellow had his right shoulder taken off arm with it by a solid shot...there is a fellow in our Regt. that had both legs shot off by a shell. Of all the sights I ever saw this is the worst. I have been in several of the Corps Hospitals and the suffering their is to much for pen to describe. their was five hundred four wounded that layed on the battlefield ten days without anything to eat, you might say."[160]

The 123rd New York returned to their original camp at Stafford Court House on May 6th. For the three days of fighting they had suffered 25 killed, 109 wounded and 20 taken prisoner, a total of 154 men. Of the 109 wounded it appears that 60 soldiers (56%) returned to the ranks over the next few months while 34 men (31%) never returned being discharged or held in hospitals until the war's end. Some of these transferred into the Veteran Reserve Corps, an army corps consisting of injured men not able to do regular field duty but with wounds allowing them to perform garrison and guarding of prisoners in the rear areas. Fourteen (13%) of the wounded died of their wounds. The 13% figure matches closely the 14% that died in hospitals from gunshot wounds for the entire Union army during the Civil War.[161]

Private Milo Shaw (Co. K) has been added to the killed in action grouping as he was MIA as of the end of May 3rd and never seen or found afterwards. Of the 20 prisoners all were paroled (as were the wounded on the field still alive on May 12th) and 16 returned to the regiment. Two of the men deserted at Camp Parole, Maryland while awaiting clearance to return to the 123rd and two of the wounded also deserted, one from a hospital, the other while on furlough to recover from his wounds. Yet one of the wounded, Private George Horton (Co. C), followed the opposite direction. He transferred to the Veteran Reserve Corps in September 1863 because of his wounds but then must have recovered fully as he transferred back into the 123rd New York, Company C, in November of 1864 and was mustered out with the regiment at the end of the war.[162]

While the Union medical corps had improved from the beginning of the war in the removal of wounded and better hospitals, the lack of proper sanitary methods during surgery and treating of wounds during recovery created a high mortality rate. Most of the time doctors had ether or chloroform to knock out a soldier during amputation. This advancement in comfort for the wounded was overridden by contamination of wounds during the sawing itself. Doctors were seen holding cutting saws in their teeth while moving patients, or wiping the saw on their blood stained apron before cutting. Bandages were often reused from patient to patient. The 123rd New York suffered 109 wounded and lost 44% of them from future service. Proper understanding of germ theory was close but it wouldn't arrive to help the men of the Civil War. Dr. Joseph Lister published his paper on bacteria in 1867. Understanding grew among doctors on treating wounds and the need for cleanliness. The American Civil War saw a 14% death rate in hospitals for the wounded. By World War I American wound fatalities in hospitals had fallen to 8.1%; World War II 3.4%; Korea 2.1%.

Although a military unit, trained to fight as one, the loss of certain individuals of the 123rd cut deep for the soldiers at Stafford. "The news reached us yesterday [May 13th] that Colonel Norton was dead," Sergeant Cruikshank lamented, "I saw him when he fell. He was a good officer and we miss him much." For Private Henry Welch it was a really hard blow. "I miss Col Norton very much he was a friend to me. when I was sick with the fever he came often to see me and when I got better he was ever cautioning me to be careful and not get down again on our last march he often went on foot and let me ride. he alway's spoke very pleasantly to the boy's and he would as soon speak to a private as to an oficer." There was also concern for those back at home learning of the loss of loved ones. Sergeant William Harrison, 29 years old, was killed. He left a wife and two children behind. "How Mrs. Harrison will feel I am afraid that it will break her down may she have sympathy and comfort from you all," Corporal Cook wrote his father. "Billy Wood is dead. he was killed instantly by a ball through the Heart. It is a sad thing on Billys mother. she will miss him very much," Private Robinson noted. Billy was twenty-one.[163]

Traumatic experience, the tumult of combat and loss of comrades brings anguish even to the victor. As for Chancellorsville, Private Robinson found a way to deal with the scenes of carnage. He wrote a friend, "to see such a sight as a battle field exhibits, it creates a feeling in a person or in me at least, that it seems that I cant realize anything about the suffering that the poor fellows has to endure. it is better to feel so when you are among them. Such a sight as that was, for a person to have it come upon them without knowing anything about it before hand would make them feel rather faint, I guess, but to work into it by degrees, it don't look so bad."[164]

But for families of MIA's it was bad. Private George Taylor (Co. F) had gone missing at Chancellorsville. His parent's sent a representative to the 123rd New York's camp to find out about their 21 year old son. Company F Corporal Sylvestor McMurray wrote his "Respected Friend Louisa" that, "Mr. Mairs is in camp with us he is in seerch of the remains of G. L. Taylor he cannot find oute eney thing more than has already ben wrote home to his father he was last seen laying on the ground his face downward bleading frealey one of the boyes spoke to him but reiceved no answer..." Taylor was never found. The New York Adjutant General's report states, "supposed to be dead at muster out of company..."[165]

Sergeant Robert Cruikshank of Company H could have sat Chancellorsville out. He was going to be promoted to 2nd Lieutenant and to be done properly he was first honorably discharged before the commission papers were cut. This was done back on March 30th but Cruikshank kept mum about it. He included a copy of the discharge notice in a letter to his wife and explained, "You can see by the above that I am not a soldier now. I do not say anything about it as perhaps some of the men might think I had no authority." He had to wait for a mustering officer to arrive in the area to issue his commission but none arrived before the battle. "Captain Crary and Lieutenant Culver both advised me not to go into battle…It was my duty to go with those men who went out into the service with me and I should look after them. The men of the Regiment knew nothing of my not being mustered in but I would have been thought a coward by all of them. I went into the service because I thought it my duty, and it was no time to shirk it when danger came…I would rather have lost a limb than not have taken part in the battle. I know of three officers who did not and now their men do not respect them and what would people at home have said?" Cruikshank was mustered on May 12th with the commission dated back to April 1st 1863. The battle created opportunity for advancement with five 1st Sergeants being promoted to lieutenants.[166]

Not everyone was happy with who was being considered for promotion to officer. Private Welch and others of Company K were outright hostile to one candidate, Private Dave Rogers. "if the reports prove's true there are over thirty of us boy's are going to enlist in the regular army for we never will serve with Dave Rogers over us the boy's all hate him worse than they do the reb's!…they say that they had rather serve five year's in the regular army than serve the rest of our time under such an idiot as Dave Rogers is…I would as soon serve under a mule!"[167] To be fair to Rogers, whenever a group of people gather some will have ill will, obviously Welch and Rogers did not hit it off. Rogers would ultimately be promoted to 2nd Lieutenant in January, 1864 but he would do an intra-regimental transfer to take the position in Company I. Colonel McDougall seems to have handled such promotions with a deft touch, certainly it was discussed with the commander of Company I, Captain Orrin Hall. Both officers must have felt Rogers capable.

The issue of promotions was a constant thorn in the side of Colonel McDougall. Arriving on his field desk were single page letters of recommendation from citizens and parents writing for their sons. The War Committee of Washington County would also weigh in on promotions and then McDougall had to be alert to the political aspects of conferring officer bars. With every resignation of an officer letters would flood his desk as to the proper replacement. "You will please your friends by aiding him up," is one letter McDougall received pushing Private Charlie Vaughn. Friends of Lt. Josiah Culver also were alert to opportunities of advancement and sent letters. Perhaps the most egregious efforts concerned attempts to get an officer's commission for men not even in the unit. McDougall politely responded to one letter by pointing out he didn't have such power plus, "It would be generally regarded here by both officers & men as an act of the grossest injustice, too hard to be borne." The men in the 123rd New York had all seen "hardship & perils" together. "My Dear friend I would much sooner be shot then rob my comrades in battle of a single thing which belongs to them."[168]

As the 123rd NewYork was a state regiment raised for federal service, it was New York Governor Horatio Seymour that held the final say as to promotions. This was where the political aspects came into play for Colonel McDougall. Seymour was a Democrat while McDougall, and most men in the 123rd New York, were Republicans. When Lt. Colonel Norton fell it was no issue for Major James Rogers to move into the vacated position. The issue was what captain was going to be promoted to major. A series of letters arrived on McDougall's desk pushing Company C Captain Adolphus Tanner. McDougall thought highly of Tanner and wanted to promote him but there were issues. Captain Abram Reynolds of Company A was the senior captain and by rights should have been offered the position. Second in seniority was Captain George Warren of Company B. Yet McDougall felt Tanner deserved the promotion as Reynolds had been away from the regiment as brigade quartermaster while Warren had been sick quite a bit and away from daily interaction with the men. Adding to McDougall's concerns, Reynolds had already mentioned he intended to resign. That would open up the position to Captain Warren, a Democrat, and McDougall readily understood that New York Governor Seymour would not look kindly to promoting Tanner over Warren. Plus McDougall does not want to be seen promoting officers due to political affiliation. So….

McDougall heard that Warren was seeking a promotion into another regiment. The colonel needed time for that to happen so asked Reynolds to stay on longer. Reynolds agreed. Warren received the promotion into another regiment and resigned from the 123rd June 10th 1863. When Reynolds then brought up the open staff position McDougall said he was open to it but that Reynolds needed to study more for the position. Reynolds then decides to resign, leaving July 18th 1863. Major Tanner takes his commission on July 31st 1863, with rank from May 12th 1863. McDougall wrote his friend Edward Dodd, "I have, so far, conducted the promotions of the Regiment without causing any complaints or making the least jar."[169]

It was back into regular camp routine. For picket duty the soldiers were marched out to the line and detailed by the "Officer of the Picket." Lt. Cruikshank drew the duty twice a week at the Stafford camp, each time for a twenty-four hour period. He would divide the detail of men into three reliefs with the first relief on duty for two hours then the second would replace them for two hours and then the third would rotate through and the two hours on, four off, would be maintained for the twenty-four hours. Cruikshank would visit the picket line during every change of the relief and make sure the men were posted behind a tree, brush or rock for cover. The two reliefs not on line were the reserve to be brought forward if shooting started. Private Welch seemed to enjoy the work. "Dowd and I are going to try and get permission to go beyond our lines as scouts if we get the chance we will just be in our element for no business would suit us better!" Even with the four hour rotation of the pickets Welch writes of the men getting little sleep, he totaled all of forty-five minutes one night. The men did face danger on the picket line with Private Arthur Whitlock (Co. E) being shot through the arm one night, the wound resulting in the transferring of Whitlock to the Veterans Reserve Corps.[170]

A regimental review of the 123rd New York was conducted on May 9th by 12th Corps Commander Major General Slocum and 1st Division Brigadier General Williams. The men were complimented by Major General Slocum for their conduct during the recent battle. Besides refitting with equipment the men spent the time building a new camp, even going so far as to "turnpike" (wooden walkways) the streets and erect evergreen entranceways to each of them. Cruikshank spent three days with Captain Crary cutting pines and slabbing them for their hut. The officer's twelve by fourteen foot cabin had a lower bunk for

Crary and Cruikshank and an upper bunk for Lt. Culver. Behind the hut was a mess tent for six officers of the 123rd New York: Captain Tanner, Captain Hall, Captain Crary, Lt. Anderson, Lt. Culver and Lt. Cruikshank. The men employed a cook and split costs six ways for the employee and food. The food situation was much better with dried apples, raisins, eggs, tea, coffee, flour, meat and lemons available. "We are having the best food that I have had since I came into the service and I enjoy it very much as I have a good appetite now," Cruikshank reported to his wife. Good food with a decent camp improved everyone's spirits but the soldiers must have had a haggered look due to the swarming insects. "It was almost impossible to sleep on account of the woodticks and mosquitoes," Sergeant Morhous writes.[171]

It wouldn't just have been those two denizens of the woods seeing the humans as opportunity. Body lice was prevalent in the camps, the men referring to them as "graybacks," plus fleas and chiggers. Fleas, lice, ticks and mosquitoes bite humans for blood while chiggers consume minute sections of flesh leading to irritating rashes across the infected areas. These issues are topped by the disease factor as typhus is often transmitted by lice. It appears the men of the 123rd had already been dealing with typhus as one of its unique calling signs is gangrene of the fingers and toes. Private Spencer was discharged after getting gangrene toes cut off during a bout of "typhoid fever." These two diseases are unrelated but very deadly with 10% to 30% of untreated cases dying in typhoid, 10% to 40% for typhus. With large numbers of ticks crawling their way onto the soldiers one also has to wonder how many of the men suffered from Lyme disease. The spirochete that causes that disease was not discovered until 1982. Another spirochete was also probably present in some of the men, the trichina worm that causes Trichinosis. It arrives in the human body by consuming undercooked meat, often pork.

All the above diseases cause fatigue, fevers, weakness, muscle and joint pain, chills and rashes. Add diarrhea for typhus, typhoid and Trichinosis. The doctors would not have been able to differentiate among the signs or test for the exact disease. The men probably suffered from more than one at a time considering the living conditions and the occasional contaminated water or food.

Northern Virginia wasn't clean due to having armies marching back and forth over the area for two years. Confederate General Robert E. Lee decided to change that; he would take his army into Pennsylvania and live off the Yankees. An avid reader of Northern newspapers, Lee was alert to the growing peace party in the North and felt a win on Northern soil might encourage talks for a settlement. In early June he wrote President Jefferson Davis that "we should neglect no Honorable means of dividing and weakening our enemies, that they may feel some of the difficulties experienced by ourselves. It seems to me that the most effectual mode of accomplishing this object, now within our reach, is to give all the encouragement we can, consistently with truth, to the rising peace party of the North…Should the belief that peace will bring back the Union become general, the war will no longer be supported, and that, after all, is what we are interested in bringing about. When peace is proposed to us, it will be time enough to discuss its terms, and it is not the part of prudence to spurn the proposition in advance, merely because those who wish to make it believe, or affect to believe, that it will result in bringing us back to the Union. We entertain no such apprehensions, nor doubt that the desire of our people for a distinct and independent national existence will prove as steadfast under the influence of peaceful measures as it has shown itself in the midst of war."[172]

Additional inducement to going above the Mason-Dixon Line was possible foreign recognition of the Confederacy if they won a great victory in the North. Both sides understood that the Founding Fathers won independence due to France siding with the Patriots during the American Revolution. The South was hoping for a repeat, to bring Britain in on her side and get help in loans and material from France. Lincoln and his administration were well aware of this angle to the South's efforts and kept up steady pressure on the diplomatic front to avoid such a result.

Lee began his movement June 3rd by shifting his army towards the Shenandoah Valley. Union Cavalry General John Buford's command noted the movement but it was not sure where the Rebels were headed. While all this was going on at the top echelons the 123rd New York soldiers concerned themselves with more mundane matters. "Where are you planting corn," Corporal McLean asked his brother, "How does them grape vines look that we set out last summer. How does the gray trotter get along...I want you to send me some newspapers once in a while some story papers as we get plenty of newspapers." Meanwhile a letter arrived on Colonel McDougall's desk from a lawyer representing Corporal Frank McFarland's family back in Washington County. McFarland's father had died and the lawyer was seeking Frank's discharge to go home to help his mother. The Colonel took a hard line and frankly stated, "There is no provision for <u>vo</u>lunteers to <u>un</u>volunteer."[173]

Union commander Hooker stayed along the Rappahannock River waiting to see what developed. He was considering a dash upon Richmond as it seemed that Lee was opening a path by pulling away to the west. President Lincoln pointed out to Hooker that even if he got to Richmond he couldn't take it without a long seige and Lee coming back to fall upon Union supply lines. "I think Lee's army, and not Richmond, is your sure objective point," the President advised, "If he come towards the Upper Potomac follow on his flank and on his inside track, shortening your lines while he lengthens his. Fight him too, when opportunity offers." On June 12th Hooker told the War Department that, "It is reported to me from the balloon that several new rebel camps have made their appearance this morning. There can be no doubt but that the enemy has been greatly re-enforced." By the 13th it was obvious the Rebels were entering the Shenandoah Valley. Orders were given to the Army of the Potomac to march north, keeping to the east side of the Blue Ridge Mountains to be between the Confederates and Washington.[174]

The men of the 123rd New York broke camp on June 13th and arrived at Dumfries, Virginia on the 14th with the rest of their brigade. They had been eating raw pork and hardtack while on the march as no stops had taken place and they had kept moving through the night. Deciding that some pack animals would help the men rounded up several of the locals' horses. An irate farmer approached 12th Corps commander General Slocum and complained as to his loss of property. Slocum asked if he was a "Union man?" No, he wasn't. "Did they burn your house and barn and kill all your cattle?" No. "Well sir, you ought to thank God and consider yourself fortunate." Slocum shrugged his shoulders at the secessionist and rode off.[175]

Yet the addition of horse power didn't help many on the 15th when the march was resumed. It was a very hot day and many fell out with sunstroke. Sergeant Beattie (Co. H) was pale and starting to stagger when Lieutenant Cruikshank noticed it and got some whiskey for Beattie. After a while Beattie was back on the march but then Cruikshank fell to a bad attack of dysentery. Not wanting to drop out on the march he found the doctor. "He gave me three opium pills and told me to take one each hour for three hours. I suffered so much pain I took them all within fifteen minutes. After a while they gave me some relief so I kept with the Company." When the 123rd arrived at Fairfax Courthouse that evening the ranks were light as comrades were strung out along the road behind. "I about made up my mind that Norton or his sunenlaw would have to do thare work hereafter for all of me," Private James Dickenson (Co. E) told his parents, "but amm all right now." By June 17th the regiment was camped outside of Leesburg, Virginia. "We had a pretty hard march from Stafford here, on account of the heat and dust several men from the Corps died on account of Sun Stroke," Sergeant John Gourlie (Co. D) wrote to his sister Marie. He reported the food situation was very good as the men made use of the surrounding farms' larders to supply their cook pots, "it is laughable to see the boys with their Canteens slung over their shoulder and a cup in their hand, traveling out to the Fields 'to do the milking.'" The soldiers spent a week in the area and Gourlie among others noted the strong secessionist sentiments. "they talk secesh openly and the little boys sing songs about how they made us Skedaddale from Bull Run, Fredericksburg &c ask them to sing about Fort Donaldson, Island NO 10, Pitsburg Landing, Antietiam, Fair Oaks &c and they do not know those places. some of the boys asked them to sing the funeral Hymn they sing at Stonewall Jackson Death well they replied, you did not kill him."[176]

"The town was a perfect nest of sneering Rebels," Sergeant Morhous (Co. C) relates, "The ladies were the most outspoken and bitter. They took every possible means to avoid a soldier, and would step into a yard and wait for a soldier to pass, and if there was no gate near for them to pass through, they would go into the middle of the road." Corporal Albert Cook (Co. A) managed to get some opinions from one local citizen. "I had quite the conversation with a deaf and dumb man by means of slate and pencil he was strong Secesh but more candid than most of them." Private Orville Robinson (Co. F) rode through Leesburg one evening and noted the local attitude. "I saw some of the prettiest girls that I ever saw without any exceptions, but Seceshism was to be seen in every countenance...Even the smallest children had their young minds poisoned against our countrys flag." The 12th Corps put a guard around the town to prevent citizens leaving and informing Confederate troops as to strengths and units of the Federals.[177]

It was here on June 19th that the men watched what was akin to murder in many of their eyes-the execution of three deserters. Two of the men were from the 46th Pennsylvania Infantry and the third from the 13th New Jersey Infantry. The 1st Division was formed into a hollow three-sided square with three dug graves on the open side. At noon muffled drum beats brought the 36 soldier firing squad into view. Behind them came a wagon with three wooden coffins rattling, then a tarped ambulance wagon with the condemned men. The coffins were unloaded and placed by each grave. Blindfolded with arms tied the three men were sat each on a coffin. A chaplain said a prayer, the firing squad obeyed the commands. The entire division was marched by the three bodies. Corporal William Shimp of the 46th Pennsylvania was given permission by 1st Division General Williams to visit the two 46th PA men before the executions. "I done some writing for them but my heart was to full, I could not go to see them shot down like dogs…Everyone thinks it was a very unjust case." Private Henry Welch of the 123rd New York felt that way. "I never want to see such a sight again it seemed to much like murder!"[178]

The town might have been full of secesh but it also offered a table, tablecloth and real dishes. Lieutenants Cruikshank (Co. H) and George Hall (Co. E) went into Leesburg on the 20th and purchased dinner at a "Rebel house." Hall had just gotten back from a leave of absence and told Cruikshank all about folks back in Washington County. "We had a good dinner for a Southern dinner," Cruikshank wrote, "A young lady waited on the table. I suppose the young lady did not dare let a colored servant wait on us as she would not watch us closely enough. The people here think we are all thieves."[179]

The locals must have thought of the Yankees as more than thieves when General Slocum threatened to shell and burn the entire town down. Telegraph wires were cut twice on June 24th in the village. Slocum there upon sent a message to the village authorities that if the wires were cut again the harsh measures would be taken. Cruikshank, who just days before had dined at a local house, supported the tough stance. "It would be terrible to resort to such measures. The innocent women and children would suffer along with the guilty…Harsh measures must be resorted to sometimes to keep these people under subjection or they might murder us all. Many of them are so bitter toward us I feel that if it were not for fear of such punishment they might poison us."[180]

Private Robinson at this time received a letter from his father telling him that his brother George, a former sergeant in Company F, was fading from his sickness. Robinson had to sit in camp and deal with losing his brother. "It is a hard thing for a person, that theay cant get home to see a brother when theay dont expect him to live but a short time, but such is life in times of war. A persons life is considered of little value...It is necessary to have a good nerve for to follow Milliatury long."[181]

The entire 123rd New York was ordered out for three days of picket duty. Due to reports of enemy cavalry in the area the men were on alert all night and then they had to stand out in the rain the next two days. Around midnight of the 25th the men could hear orders being given in the camps behind them, tents being struck and then marching of troops. The 123rd New York was told at 3 a.m. to be ready to march, at 6 a.m. they started route step and crossed the Potomac River at Edwards Ferry into Maryland. "The marching was bad, the mud being quite deep, with continuing rain working it up more and more," Lt. Cruikshank noted. Major General Hooker, commander of the Army of the Potomac, rode past the men the next day and was loudly cheered.[182]

Lincoln wasn't cheering. The day after seeing Hooker the men learned they had a new commander of the Army of the Potomac, Major General George Meade. This didn't sit well with the men. "We no sooner get a Genl and have confidence before he is superceded or resigns," Corporal Cook lamented, "Genl Meade we know nothing about, why he is placed in command is very strange."[183]

There had been a series of communications between General Hooker and the War Department as Lee moved north. Hooker was constantly seeking information from Washington as to Lee's location while Washington was pointing out that Hooker had the cavalry to find out and all they had in D.C. were rumors. Lincoln might also have wondered about Hooker being dilatory in pursuit of Lee as the days went by; as to the state of mind of the general Lee had trounced so badly at Chancellorsville. On June 27th it seems General Hooker had had enough of exchanging telegrams, when told he could not abandon Harper's Ferry he asked to be removed from command. "My original instructions require me to cover Harper's Ferry and Washington. I have now imposed upon me, in addition, an enemy in my front of more than my number. I beg to be understood, respectfully, but firmly, that I am unable to comply with this condition with the means at my disposal, and earnestly request that I may at once be relieved from the position I occupy."[184]

By June 28th Lee's army was well into Pennsylvania, his three corps of 62,000 men spread out in a great arc at the towns of Chambersburg, Carlisle and York. The Confederate commander was not fully aware of the Federals advancing towards him due to lack of intelligence gathering. That was the role of Rebel General J.E.B. Stuart's cavalry command, to maintain contact with the Federals and report back movements of the enemy. But Stuart had lost contact with Lee when the Union Army in their movement north interposed themselves between the Confederate Army and Stuart. How could such a thing happen to such a good cavalry general? There are arguments that Stuart was trying to repeat his acclaimed circling around the Union Army that he had performed during the Penninsular Campaign during 1862. Then there was the recent cavalry fight at Brandy Station on June 9th where J.E.B. was surprised. Although a drawn fight, Southern newspapers blasted Stuart for the affair and that grated on him. It would appear that his ego a little raw from that battle and wanting to embarrass the Union cavalry to garner greater fame, he took his cavalry on a raid. Seeking to go around the Union troops he found he was trapped to the east of the Union army as it moved north. No information would be readily available to Lee as there was no access. It was therefore with some shock that Lee learned late on June 28th that the Union Army was across the Potomac and in northern Maryland approaching his separated command. There were other cavalry units in the

Confederate army but it wasn't until June 29th that Lee ordered them up from the Shenanadoah Valley.[185]

There had been some shuffling of units in the 12th Corps after Chancellorsville. The 123rd New York was now in the 1st Brigade (they had been in the 2nd), 1st Division, 12th Corps. Their fellow regiments in the brigade were the 5th Connecticut, 20th Connecticut, 3rd Maryland, 145th New York and 46th Pennsylvania. Colonel Archibald McDougall was in command of the brigade with Lt. Colonel James Rogers commanding the 123rd New York. Total brigade strength was 1,834 with the 123rd New York fielding 495 effectives, 5th CN 221, 20th CN 321, 3rd MD 290, 145th NY 245, and 46th PA 262.[186]

Standing out in the above figures is that the 123rd New York was almost double the strength of their brother regiments in the brigade. Colonel McDougall was proud of this fact. "My camp & hospital arrangements have not been surpassed in the army. The camp I just left at Stafford was the pleasantest, prettiest & best arranged in the army of the Potomac. So I was assured by old officers. These things preserve the health & strength of a regiment & as to fighting the boys won't give up to either new or old troops." This claim has to be taken with some considerations. The 5th CN was an older regiment that had seen hard service, while both the 3rd MD and 145th NY had desertion problems. But still, the commander of the 123rd New York was making an effort for himself and his soldiers. "I have been much embarrassed in coming out in command of the Regiment without preparatory knowledge of tactics. However my time has been constantly devoted to study & it will not be long before I will be far ahead of very many officers much longer in the Service," he wrote to a friend back in Washington County. As for the regiment, "Still we are far below the standard in drill, in discipline & in many other respects which I wish to attain."[187]

By June 30th Union commander Meade was bringing the 1st Corps (10,000), 2nd Corps (13,000), 3rd Corps (12,000), 5th Corps (12,000), 6th Corps (16,000), 11th Corps

(10,000), 12th Corps (9,000 men) and cavalry from Frederick, Maryland into lower Pennsylvania south of Gettysburg feeling for the Rebels. Confederate commander Lee had Longstreet's Corps (20,000), Ewell's Corps (21,000) and A. P. Hill's Corps (21,000) beginning to concentrate at Cashtown about eight miles to the west of the crossroads village of Gettysburg.[188] The main Confederate cavalry under Stuart was to the east in the Hanover, Pennsylvania area clashing with Union cavalry. Stuart then learned from local papers that Rebel General Early had been at York and trotted off in that eastern direction to attempt to find Lee. Meanwhile Union Cavalry General John Buford was pushing west from Gettysburg on reconnaissance and ran into the Rebel brigade of Brigadier General James Pettigrew marching towards Gettysburg in search of supply stockpiles. There was a small skirmish and Pettigrew, not having cavalry to quickly ascertain the force challenging him, fell back to Cashtown. Buford fell back to Gettysburg and sent a message to Meade as to the location of Rebel infantry and that he was preparing to hold the town. Pettigrew discussed the action of the day with his superiors, Major Generals Henry Heth and A.P. Hill. They were certain no Union infantry was anywhere near the town, Pettigrew was ordered to return the next day, brush the Yankee cavalry aside and seize any supplies he found. Meanwhile Union commander Meade ordered the 1st Corps and 11th Corps, 20,000 infantry, to Gettysburg. Lee intended to concentrate his army at Cashtown, PA, locate the enemy and formulate an attack strategy. Meade was looking at an area in northern Maryland along Big Pipe Creek to form a defensive line for the expected battle. Both men were now to find they were helpless to control events. July 1st 1863 would see Union and Confederate units begin to clash with a resulting suction of their comrades into the fray, all around the little town of Gettysburg.

Chapter 5
Doubletime to Gettysburg

When the Army of Northern Virginia began crossing into Maryland in the Williamsport area on June 20th 1863 they entered a strong Union locale. As the soldiers in gray tramped through Hagerstown, Maryland, civilians watched out their windows, peeked out shades and counted. By June 28th Union commander of the Army of the Potomac George Meade forwarded to Washington information from the people of Hagerstown, civilian blacksmith Thomas McCammon having ridden to the Union lines that morning with his report.

"...The [Confederate] cavalry went back and forth out of Pennsylvania, driving horses and cattle, and the first infantry came yesterday a week ago-General Ewell's men...Rebel troops have passed every day, more or less, since; some days only three or four regiments or a brigade, and some days, yesterday, for instance, all of Longstreet's command passed through excepting two brigades...Think A.P. Hill went through last Tuesday. Heard from James D. Roman, prominent lawyer and leading Confederate sympathizer, who was talking in the clerk's office last night; said that their officers reported their whole army, 100,000 strong, now in Maryland or Pennsylvania, excepting the cavalry. Mr. Logan, register of wills, and Mr. Protzman, very fine men in Hagerstown, have taken pains to count the rebels, and could not make them over 80,000. They counted the artillery, made it two hundred and seventy-five guns. Some of the regiments only had 175 men-two that I saw, 150 men. Largest regiment that I saw was a Maryland regiment, and that was about 700. Don't think their regiments would range 400. Great amount of transportation...Ewell rides in a wagon...Pickett's division is in Longstreet's corps...The

Union men in Hagerstown would count them, and meet at night..."[189]

Lee's army numbered 62,000 infantry, so the 80,000 figure was a tad high but a lot better than other inflated estimates. Union General Hooker gave his effectives as 105,000 on June 27th and in his message to be relieved later that day stated he had "an enemy in my front of more than my number." Even with better intelligence as to enemy strength Union General Meade felt heavy weight upon his shoulders. He was losing sleep and trying to formulate some sort of plan to deal with Lee, a man taking on mythic proportions by this time. Robert E. Lee had defeated or stalemated every Union general sent up against him: McClellan, Pope, Burnside and Hooker. One wants to get into their enemy's head, worry him, make him falter or miss opportunities. Lee was in Meade's head. The Union commander was new to his job, struggling to grasp all that was happening and hoping for a set-piece defensive position. Lower ranking Union officers would perform ably and grant Meade the terrain for the defensive line he was seeking. Lee was just the fighter, with a finely honed instrument, to attack such a line.

July 1st at 8 a.m. the battle started with Buford's cavalry fighting a delaying action just to the north and west of Gettysburg. The Union 1st Corps and 11th Corps under Major General John Reynolds arrived in late morning, messages were sent out calling for support from the 12th Corps at Littlestown, PA and the 3rd Corps at Emmitsburg, MD just over the boarder. Before these troops could arrive the Confederate forces had the day, Generals Ewell and A. P. Hill drove the Yankees through the town. Both Union Corps had suffered losses of 50% but they had brought off their artillery and set about creating defensive works upon the slightly higher ground south of Gettysburg.[190] The Union's 12th Corps came onto the field around 5 p.m., the 3rd Corps 6 p.m. Union commander Meade would not arrive until midnight but by then Union Major General Hancock had the army well entrenched using the terrain to the maximum.

It had been two days on the run for the 123rd New York and the 12th Corps. Not away from the pending battle but desperately trying to get there to help their comrades. June 30th saw them break camp at 3 a.m. their steady fast pace taking them through Taneytown, Maryland towards Littlestown, Pennsylvania. They pushed on into the afternoon covering 15 miles with no stops for eating. About two miles south of Littlestown the 123rd New York was halted and told to draw their charges in their guns, reload and prime. Officers and NCO's went through inspecting ammunition. As this was happening the soldiers heard the familiar sound of thundering upon the ground, then the rattle and banging of cassions and cannons as horses galloped by taking the artillery to the front.

"As soon as the artillery had passed we were ordered to move forward on a double quick," Lt. Cruikshank says, "which we kept up for three miles, passing through Littlestown in this way." The citizens were out on their doorsteps encouraging the men, handing them biscuits, cakes and cups of water. "Ladies waved their handkerchiefs and cheered us on. Some were in tears and some in smiles. At the hotel a number had gathered and were singing patriotic songs. If I ever felt I wanted to fight the enemy it was here where those ladies were calling us to drive the Rebels back into Virginia where they belonged." Sergeant Morhous was running through the town when he heard the song "Hail Columbia" filling the air. "The boys appreciated, but did not have much time to enjoy the hospitalities of the people of Littlestown, nor the smiles of the ladies, but some of them did grab a handful of cake as they passed by." Confederate cavalry had engaged Union cavalry beyond the town. The 123rd New York and the rest of the 12th Corps 1st Division were sent as support. They double-timed a mile beyond the town then filed into a large field and formed line of battle. By this time the Federal cavalry had gotten the upper hand and the Rebs were retreating. A strong picket line was thrown put, tents pitched and the men finally had a meal. They were nine miles south of Gettysburg.[191]

Cruikshank worked on company paperwork, muster and payroll, during the night using a cracker box for a desk. He got no sleep and probably several others in the 123rd New York found little nap time as they prepared for the next day expecting battle. July 1st they broke camp at 7 a.m., marched back into Littlestown and swung north on the Baltimore Pike towards Gettysburg. Covering four miles they then stopped at Two Taverns where the men had dinner. Corporal Albert Cook (Co. A) and others watched 600 Rebel prisoners march by in the other direction, "a hard looking set as ever I saw." About 2 p.m. messengers arrived with information for General Slocum, commander of the 12th Corps, that General Reynolds had fallen in battle and that the 1st and 11th Corps were heavily engaged at Gettysburg. Rifles and knapsacks slung the soldiers struck a quickened pace northward. "All was the wildest excitement," 123rd New York Sergeant Lorenzo Coy (Co. K) says of the rush to Gettysburg, "No man seemed to think of speaking out." The sound of cannonading grew louder and louder on the horizon. The 12th Corps halted a mile south of Gettysburg and began to form for battle. The men in the ranks noticed that the musketry and cannon fire was coming closer to them and they understood the cause; the Union forces were being driven back.[192]

The 1st Division of the 12th Corps was ordered off the pike and into the woods just south of Rock Creek while the 2nd Division crossed the creek and deployed along the pike. Working their way east the soldiers of the 123rd New York climbed across fences and crossed fields up onto Wolf Hill, a small prominance to the southeast of Gettysburg. Orders to halt rang out. "In a minute every man was flat on the ground resting while perspiration ran from our bodies in streams," Sergeant Coy writes, "We were allowed to rest a few minutes when we were ordered up and soon found ourselves drawn up in line of battle."[193] The 1st Division deployed through the area to prevent any left flank attempts by the Confederates. Up by Gettysburg fighting sputtered out around 7 p.m. On Wolf Hill the men laid down with their arms in hand, ready to spring up if the enemy attacked. No supper was taken but at least the night was warm and clear so the men could get a little rest. Generals and staff of both armies worked through the night to get an idea of positions and units along the approximate four miles of Union line being created, of the terrain and opportunities, weaknesses or threats. The 12th Corps was becoming the extreme right wing of the Federal army. Meade intended to have Union lines run north from the area of Little Round Top to curl around Cemetery Hill and run back south to finish beyond Culp's Hill upon Rock Creek.

Early on July 2nd the men of the 123rd New York had a breakfast of hardtack and coffee then joined the 1st Division in moving off Wolf Hill, crossing Rock Creek and entrenching on the lower section of Culp's Hill in the Spangler's Spring region. "The boys, remembering Chancellorsville, were determined to have good works this time, and went to work with a will," Sergeant Morhous says. Cruikshank also saw Chancellorsville as a teacher for the regiment. "At Chancellorsville we learned the importance of good works and now put into use this knowledge." The line laid out for the 123rd went through some large timber, this was dropped, trimmed of branches and then stacked three high. Smaller timbers were notched and used to lock them in place. The top log was raised above the second by about three inches to allow the men to fire between the logs. Then the soldiers started digging throwing the dirt on the side towards the enemy to create a soil slope before the wood to absorb shot and shell and reduce splintering. They dug until they had a trench deep enough so they could stand with the top log protecting their heads as they fired. A step ledge was left adjacent to the logs so the shorter men could also draw down on the enemy. Then they trimmed the limbs cut off the logs and intertwined them before the works facing the enemy, creating an abatis. Sergeant Coy managed to pen a few lines to his wife Sarah before pitching in to help, "We expect an engagement soon, in fact our batteries have already opened but as yet elicited no reply. My thoughts are with you but now I must go and help on the breastwork."[194]

All this time the men could hear skirmish firing off to their left and they had to be careful of a sharpshooter's round if they exposed themselves too much. During the morning as they worked the Confederates began to move into position to target the extreme left of the Union line. Southern commander Robert E. Lee had hoped for an early attack on the Little Round Top area but orders were not issued until 11 a.m. It wasn't until 3 p.m. when Confederate General Longstreet's troops hit the Federals. It was a late start but a good one. The Union 3rd Corps had been moved forward by their commander General Sickles contrary to orders, this resulted in an exposed position. After heavy fighting the 3rd Corps began to fall back. Little Round Top lay exposed to seizure by the on-rushing Confederates. Like Hazel Grove at Chancellorsville, Little Round Top was key to the Union line as the cleared prominence would allow artillery to enfilade Federal troop positions running north towards Cemetery Hill. Arriving Federal troops were rushed to its top to meet Confederates climbing its slopes, after intense hand to hand combat the Union troops held the top while the 20th Maine finished the affair with a desperate bayonet charge along the back of the hill. To the right, the tide of Southerners broke through at the Peach Orchard and pushed through the smoke to find a lone regiment, the 1st Minnesota-all of 262 soldiers-holding a gap in the Union line. Major General Hancock personally ordered them to charge Confederate General Cadmus Wilcox's brigade of 1,600 Alabamians in a desperate attempt to buy time. They charged and suffered 82% causalties. It was late afternoon.

The men of the 123rd New York had finished their entrenchments around 6 p.m. when the order, "Fall in!" was heard. Union Commander Meade was pulling troops of the 12th Corps out of their works to reinforce the hard pressed left wing. They double-quicked towards Little Round Top across the Baltimore Pike and farm fields. As they approached the left-center section of the Union lines along

Cemetery Ridge shells began to fall around them, some coming close enough that the men ducked instinctively. But the firing slackened. Fresh units had filled the gap the 1st Minnesota held, the Rebels, having exhausted themselves, began to withdraw back to the Emmittsburg Road. Not needed, the 123rd New York and other units of the 12th Corps were ordered back to their entrenchments as the sun went down.

Confederate commander Lee envisioned a double flanking attack on July 2nd, Longstreet hitting the Union left while Confederate General Ewell's troops hit the Union right, the 12th Corps position. Ewell was supposed to pitch in at the sound of Longstreet's cannons at 3 p.m. but his attack was delayed. This was fortuitous for the Rebels for if he had attacked at that time the 12th Corps would have all been in position to repel them. The advancing Southerners came upon the works shortly before 7 p.m. when only the 3rd Brigade, 2nd Division, 12th Corps was left holding the line running southeast off of Culp's Hill. Union Brigadier General George Greene's troops refused their line to protect themselves from flanking attacks. Greene, at 62, was the oldest Union general on the field but he was a steady fighter, West Point engineering trained and had created stout fortifications on Upper Culp's Hill. Yet he had nowhere near the amount of soldiers required to hold the remaining trench works running from Upper Culp's Hill onto Lower Culp's Hill. As dark fell on July 2nd Confederate forces entered the abandoned 123rd New York's trenches plus other Union works, creating a semi-circle from Rock Creek up along the seized Union lines then back down the slope as Greene's lines were approached. The Confederate units, Major General Edward Johnson's Division, turned to assault Greene's position and take Culp's Hill thereby destroying the right flank of the Union Army. A two and a half-hour fight erupted as the darkness increased and more pressure was brought to bear to break the Union lines. As the Rebels got onto the right flank of Greene's position the units began to be mixed up in the dark. Everyone, Union and

Confederate, were groping forward in the blackened woods trying to tell friend from foe. Greene requested help from the nearby 1st and 11th Corps which responded with three regiments each. One of these, the 84th New York, was pushing south off Culp's Hill through the dark when a mass of men were made out before them. "As I was in doubt as to whether they were friends or enemies," Colonel Fowler of the 84th New York states, "I hesitated in opening fire upon them, but at length gave them a volley, which drove them from their position on our flank."[195]

Greene's Brigade had held and by 10 p.m. the firing had died out along Culp's Hill. At this time Colonel McDougall was bringing his 1st Brigade back into the area with the intention of marching the men right up to their entrenchments. A rider appeared to warn him that Confederates were in the works. McDougall didn't give credence to this report but fortunately Colonel James Selfridge of the 46th Pennsylvania suggested some scouts be sent forward. McDougall ordered Lt. Marcus Beadle and a squad from Company I, 123rd New York, plus a squad from the 5th Connecticut, to ascertain the situation ahead. As Beadle was getting his men ready several 123rd soldiers came back from filling their canteens at Spangler's Spring. This was in the direction Beadle was to advance and they warned him that Rebels had been there filling their canteens as they filled theirs. The canteen encounter wasn't a friendly exchange across a river picket line, no words of greeting, just filling canteens. Whether the Rebels realized the soldiers across from them were Yankees isn't known but the 123rd men backed out quietly to spread the warning. It was nearing midnight, the Company I skirmish line advancing slowly probing forward in the darkness. Beadle doubted Rebels were ahead but at least had enough sense to halt his men once beyond the stream from Spangler's Spring. He advanced by himself and saw figures ahead, "Who is there?"

The Rebs were a savvy lot. They knew Greene's Brigade were the ones holding the hill. "Pickets from the Second Division of the Twelfth Corps. Come on it is all right." Lt. Beadle walked up to find himself a prisoner. He was told to order the rest of his men forward, instead he yelled, "Fall back men!" At that the shooting started.[196]

The soldiers from the 123rd returned the fire as they withdrew, Lt. Beadle's action saving them from capture. The men of the 5th Connecticut also withdrew but not before five were captured. It was dark, figures were running, flashes of guns stabbing through the night, things were suddenly uncertain as to friend or foe. McDougall's Brigade was in regimental front, one regiment behind the other when the skirmishers went out. The 123rd New York was the first regiment, down a slight slope in a corn field about one hundred feet in front of the 145th New York. Exhausted, most of the men of the 145th had laid down to sleep when the brigade had stopped. All of a sudden the firing erupted and the 123rd New York was ordered to withdraw towards the 145th to form a battle line. The rifle cracks had startled the 145th to its feet and now they had a mass of men moving towards them in the darkness. They fired a volley and broke. Most of the rounds went high, fortunately, but Private Nelson Thayer (Co. K) was killed. "the bulet struck his forehead and went through his head killing him instantly he was killed by our own men," Private Henry Welch wrote his aunt and uncle. He was angry over it. "I had a good notion to fire at the coward's I would about as soon shot one as a reb"[197]

After things calmed down the 123rd New York fell back, put out a strong picket line and slept on their arms until morning. During that time Union General Alpheus Williams worked out an early morning attack, moving artillery into position to rake the former Federal lines the Rebels held. The 12th Corps units having returned, soldiers swelled Upper Culp's Hill. The flank running west to the Baltimore Pike was strengthened, units were posted along the pike and then swung east into McAllister's Woods by Rock Creek. The 123rd NewYork was with the 1st Brigade in an open field between the pike and McAllister's Woods. General Williams after getting all in readiness laid down on a flat rock near the pike at 3:30 a.m. and took a thirty minute nap.[198]

On the other side of the entrenchments the Rebels were also planning an attack. Lee had been pleased with the flank attacks on July 2nd, it appeared the Yankees had almost broken on their left and the Rebels had captured some of the Union right flank positions. For the 3rd Lee wanted a repeat with better coordination and an earlier start. With a hard hit the Yankee's flanks would break and the Confederates would have their great victory on Northern soil. Both Longstreet and Ewell were ordered to throw their men forward at daybreak. Major General Edward Johnson's Division was reinforced with an additional three brigades for the Culp's Hill attack. In the dark the Southern troops on the lower section of Culp's Hill could hear teams of horses and vehicles moving along the Baltimore Pike 500 yards away. Rebel Brigadier General George Steuart voiced the opinion that the Yankees were retreating. It was a better thought for the men than the truth, the movements along the road were Union artillery being emplaced. By the time Union General Williams was ready to take his power-nap there were twenty-six cannon trained on lower Culp's Hill spread in an arch from the Spangler House to McAllister's Woods.[199]

At 4:30 a.m. all of the artillery opened upon the lower section of Culp's Hill for fifteen minutes. The Confederates found themselves under a terrific blast of shot and shell, metal careening off the rocks with tree limbs crashing down upon them. Three companies of the 1st Maryland (CSA) were in the open and were quickly pulled back to cover. Fortunately for the Rebels they had the reverse slope of the hill for protection plus the stout Union entrenchments they had captured. Without those two factors the Confederate forces on the lower hill holding the left flank would probably have ceased to exist. By opening fire first the Union troops took the initative away from the Rebs. Union troops followed up the artillery with probes against the Southern lines but these were beaten back. Rebel General Johnson then renewed his attack from the night before, throwing his right flank forward against the Upper Culp's Hill entrenchments of the 2nd Divison 12th Corps. Little progress was made however as the steep slope and log entrenchments gave the Union defenders all the advantages. Union artillery continued to rake the Confederates positions off and on for the next six hours. Meanwhile the infantry embraced in a roar of musketry that forced officers to scream into men's ears so orders could be heard. Thick powder smoke roiled the slopes of the hill, at times forcing the defenders to sight their shots on the Rebel muzzle flashes. The firing was so rapid and noise from the Culp's Hill area so loud that Union commander Meade inquired if the Federal troops were wasting ammunition.[200]

At this time the 123rd New York was with the 1st Brigade, 1st Division, across a wooded area and then open field about 500 yards from the Rebs. As the Confederates wanted the high ground of Culp's Hill they ignored the 123rd and their brother regiments in the open. What developed were a series of Rebel charges across the 123rd New York's front going to the New Yorker's left towards the hill. Also what developed was a change in Lee's plans. The Confederate commander had sought a coordinated attack but that was now out the window, Longstreet was going to need more time to get units into place. Before Ewell could be told to delay the Culp's Hill attacks the Union guns opened then the Rebel troops engaged. Lee would have to let events play out on the Union right. Perhaps a full scale punch to the Union center would provide the breakthrough needed. Lee ordered Longstreet to prepare to attack the center, near a clump of trees, after a heavy artillery bombardment softened the Federal lines. Discussion of units and deployments proceeded as the sounds of the Culp's Hill battle echoed across farm and woodland acres.

As part of the support for the Culp's Hill defenders, Colonel McDougall deployed the 20th Connecticut forward at 5 a.m. as skirmishers. Pushing off across a corn field they entered some woods and deployed a skirmish line forward to harrass the Rebels in the works. There were actually two forms of cover running along Lower Culp's Hill. There was an old stone wall running towards Upper Culp's Hill then the constructed Federal entrenchments about one-hundred feet beyond. The Confederates kept up a steady fire from the stone wall and entrenchments towards the 20th Connecticut. For the next five hours Lieutenant-Colonel Wooster of the 20th rotated his men through the skirmish line for rest, cleaning rifles and replenishing ammo. Wooster sent back messages as to artillery results in an attempt to improve the effects of shot, often he had to pull his regiment back "to save it from being destroyed by our own artillery." Even so, his regiment suffered several casualties between the Rebs in front and cannons to the rear.[201]

Sadly, it was not only the most forward deployed Union regiment from the 1st Brigade to suffer losses from the cannonade. There were more friendly fire casualties for the 123rd New York during this fighting, this time from the artillery firing over their heads in support of the 20th Connecticut. Shells were falling short among the Union soldiers. The 123rd NY lost one man killed and one wounded from this fire. Several of the shells exploded behind the ranks of the 1st Brigade, particularly the 145th New York and the 46th Pennsylvania. Colonel Price of the 145th NY sent word to Colonel McDougall requesting it be corrected. Colonel Selfridge of the 46th PA promptly had enough. "Colonel Selfridge came to Colonel McDougall saying with an oath, at the same time drawing his revolver, that he was going to see the officer in command of that battery and if another shell fell short he would shoot the Rebel gunner," Cruikshank says of the event, "There were no more shell exploded behind us after the Colonel had seen the officer."[202]

Confederate General Johnson had started the early morning battle with a push uphill with his right wing. That failing, the right and center Rebels units then attacked for a second effort on the upper section of Culp's Hill. By 9:30 a.m. this had failed and Johnson decided for a third attack from the lower section of the hill. Earlier efforts had seen the Confederate soldiers walking forward up a tree and boulder studded slope, then going to ground to engage in a tremendous exchange of firing. The third attack would be off the part of the hill the Rebs held going towards a small ravine between upper and lower Culp's Hill. The Union forces had positioned their right flank along this ravine on the Upper Culp's Hill side. Confederate units in the lower entrenchments, Steuart's Brigade, would come forward, face right, deploy into regimental line and straddling the stone wall with their right flank on the captured Union entrenchments *charge*. It was to be a pell-mell dash over two-hundred yards to break the Yankee line to splinters. The 10th Virginia was assigned the task of taking on the 20th Connecticut to protect the left flank of the Southerners as they made the rush.

    Around 10 a.m. the 10th Virginia pushed against the 20th Connecticut as their brother Southern regiments deployed behind them. There was the clicking of bayonets along the line, the orders, "Forward" then "Double-quick" were given. Nine-hundred soldiers broke from the woods into an open field running. They were cut to pieces. The charge rapidly disintegrated as the regiments fell apart under a cross fire of rifle balls and shells. Some of the Confederates made it to within several yards of the Union lines but they tumbled to the earth dead or badly wounded. At this moment a dog dashed forth from the Confederate ranks and leapt into the Union lines. Bullets and shells were flying everywhere, after being hit the canine limped back out front seeking its master among the bodies. Later that day Union troops would give the dog a proper burial.[203]

    Survivors of the charge fell back into the woods and entrenchments. It appeared the moment had come for a counter charge. Union Brigadier General Thomas Ruger recieved orders to push two regiments forward on the extreme right to try the Rebel lines. He sent orders via messenger to throw forward skirmishers and test the enemy's line which was across a wet meadow along a stone wall which ended on Rock Creek. Through some error the order came through as a regimental charge upon the 31st, 49th and

52nd Virginia posted along the stone wall. The 2nd Massachusetts and the 27th Indiana were sent forward and it was the Federal's turn to be cut to pieces. The charge fell apart quickly under the volleys of the Rebels and the Union survivors fell back to cover. (There are two small stone markers on the Gettysburg field today, one for the farthest advance of the Rebels in their charge against Upper Culp's Hill, the second the farthest advance of the 27th Indiana across the meadow.)

Opportunity did exist for the 20th Connecticut though. When the Rebels fell back from their failed attack the 20th CN pushed forward. They took the stone wall, it was now only a few yards to sprint for the entrenchments. Right behind the 20th CN was the 123rd New York moving forward in support and they swept forward over the stone wall with a cheer. The few Confederates in the entrenchments leapt over them and retreated down the hill. Remaining Federal regiments followed and the lost works were recaptured. Sporadic shooting still continued but by 11 a.m. Confederate General Johnson retired his men to the base of the hill by Rock Creek. The Union troops set about reworking the entrenchments, throwing the tree abatis the Confederates had built back over to the other side and then digging out the firing trench again. "There had been hard fighting here," Lt. Cruikshank notes, "the dead lay on the ground all along the line." Confederate General Johnson's Division had suffered high casualties on Culp's Hill. His brigades had suffered in killed, wounded and missing: Steuart's 40%; Nicholl's 34%; Jones' 26%; and Walker's 23%. The brigades sent to reinforce him for the capture of the hill also saw high casualties, Smith's brigade alone losing 18% of its men. Union General Greene's troops at the apex of the attacks on Culp's Hill had suffered 22% casualties. Strong entrenchments and a defensive stance truly benefited the Federals on Culp's Hill.[204]

Rebel snipers firing from up in trees and the steady shooting from the base of the hill were irritating for the men in blue along the retaken works. It was decided to do something about it. So "there were selected from our Regt about 24 of our best marks men to skirmish with the rebs," 123rd New York Corporal Albert Cook (Co. A) relates, "we went over the breast works and had a pretty sharp time...I took position behind a rock and when ever a reb showed himself blazed away, I think we dropped a few." Other Union regiments along the line also sent out skirmishers with orders to "pick out their adversaries and fire deliberately."[205]

The rest of the 123rd New York made the best of it behind the protection of the entrenchments while random rifle cracks rang out in the woods before them. Wounded were tended too, soldiers cleaned their weapons and munched hardtack. Over to the left of the Union line Brigadier General Henry Hunt, Chief of Artillery for the Army of the Potomac, rode along Cemetery Ridge checking on his charges. It was obvious that across the fields the Rebels were planning something. "As the enemy was evidently increasing his artillery force in front of our left, I gave instructions to the batteries and the chiefs of artillery not to fire at small bodies, nor to allow their fire to be drawn without promise of adequate results; to watch the enemy closely, and when he opened to concentrate the fire of their guns on one battery at a time until it was silenced; under all circumstances to fire deliberately, and to husband their ammunition as much as possible." The whole Gettysburg area was in a waiting game for the next move.[206]

At 1 p.m. it came. Two cannons roared in rapid succession from the Confederate line, it was heard distinctly by many of the men on Culp's Hill. Then all Creation went haywire. Union General Hunt was on Little Round Top when the Confederate lanyards cut loose, he estimated about 120 Rebel cannons in action. The shots were arching through the air towards the center section of the Union army along Cemetery Ridge, shells exploding along the Federal line. Many of the rounds were also soaring beyond the ridge to explode or careen along the ground into the 12th Corps area. The men of the 123rd New York all of a sudden found themselves under a terrific bombardment. Soldiers scrambled for cover among the rocks, stone wall and entrenchment. Their position was on a direct line from the clump of trees the Confederates were targeting, plus shots being fired at Cemetery Hill as a form of support. Any rounds going long were going to drop, bounce or explode among them. And many of the rounds seem to have gone long, ripping through trees and shattering rocks. "The air seemed full of iron missiles, and the forest trees were riven, torn and splintered as if struck by lightning," Corporal Morhous writes of the moment, "The shells fell thick and fast around the Regiment." Second Lt. Charles Warner of the 145th New York was astounded by the amount of artillery fire. "I could not distinguish the different reports, but it was one continual roar. I tell you it was perfectly horrible. Many of the rebel shells fell in our works and poor [145th Colonel] Price was nearly frightened to death, and lay behind a large rock shivering & shaking a disgrace to everyone." Brigadier General John Geary, commanding the 2nd Division 12th Corps, was on Upper Culp's Hill when the shelling started. "The terrific cannonading from the batteries of the rebels massed upon the left center subjected my lines from the rear from 1 p.m. to 3:15 p.m. to a galling fire, as the missiles thickly swept over and into the position occupied by us, causing a number of casualties."[207]

If the Confederates were trying to soften up the Federal line in the area of the "Copse of Trees" on Cemetery Ridge and silence Union artillery on Cemetery Hill, why were the rounds dropping on the 12th Corps? The Rebel artillery was good enough, even with the smoke increasing from the cannons they would have had a few shots to correct for range. For the shells, it was probably the fuses. Screwed into the shell, these soft metal discs would be cut to detonate from one to five seconds in flight. The firing of the cannon would ignite the fine powder in the fuse at the cut location. Trouble is, a lot of the fuses were defective, especially so for the Confederates. Union manufacturing standards were able to produce better quality but even so it has been estimated that the fuses only worked 75% of the time. Colonel

McDougall of the 123rd New York in his brigade report for Gettysburg mentions human error but also "imperfect fuse or defective shells, most probably the latter" for the July 3rd morning casualties from Union artillery. At 3 p.m. of the 3rd Captain Frederick Edgell, commanding the 1st New Hampshire Battery, was on Cemetery Hill returning the Confederate fire. "The firing of the enemy's artillery was now very inaccurate, most of the shots being too high..." Edgell noted, but he also was having problems with his ammo. "I expended this day 248 rounds of shell and case shot...The Hotchkiss time shell and the Schenkl percussion worked well, but the Schenkl combination case seldom exploded. From what experience I have had with this fuse, I think it is not reliable."[208]

But the Confederate's problem with fuses were quite often the opposite, they exploded too soon. Often just beyond the muzzle or only a second or two into flight. Southern infantry knew of the poor fuse quality and dreaded being in front of their gunners. Confederate Colonel J. Thompson Brown of the 1st Virginia Artillery was targeting Cemetery Hill as support for the infantry advancing towards the Union center. He was happy with the results at first. Yet, "had we been able to continue our fire with shell, the result would have been entirely satisfactory; but, owing to the proximity of our infantry to the enemy, and the defective character of some of the shell, the batteries were compelled to use solid shot."[209] By this time the smoke over the field would have been tremendous, obscuring their own infantry out in front engaging the Yankees. Perhaps for a safety factor the Rebel gunners added a tad more elevation than normal when they switched to solid shot. A more likely explanation is that some crews were not correcting the elevation screw for their cannons after each shot. With every recoil the gun would force the screw lower thereby raising the muzzle. In the heat of action crews on both sides often forgot to readjust the screw. It might have been a combination of both across the battlefield as the Rebel infantry moved forward. This could explain why Union Captain Edgell stood on Cemetery

Hill watching cannon balls soar overhead. Could those rounds have made it all the way to the Culp's Hill area? And if they could, how many made the trip?

Union General John Gibbon, who wrote an artillery manual for the Northern forces, gave the effective ranges of the guns as 1,000 yards. At that distance troops are seen as just a mass across a field yet the gun commander can still judge the effect of shot or shell on the target. However, actual distance for firing could be much longer, from one to two miles. The problem was one of seeing where the shot landed, what were the results of the round? Cannon ammunition being expensive and hard to transport it was heavily frowned upon, a gun commander could even face an inquiry, if a battery was seen as sending government property downrange for no purpose. At five degrees of elevation Napoleon cannon, smoothbores, had a range of 1,619 yards (just shy a mile) while the three-inch rifled cannon ranged 1,835 yards (just over a mile). Both could shoot much further if the muzzle was raised by lowering the elevation screw at the rear of the gun. At ten-degrees elevation the three-inch rifle would plow the ground with screaming metal a mile and a half away. Fifteen-degrees could send cavalry dashing for cover two miles away. Even the Napoleons offered greater flight time and distance if sought. In 1864 Union ordnance brought out a twelve-second fuse for shells, the five-second fuse having too short a flight time for some shots. Union 1st Lt. Edward Williston commanding a battery of Napoleons was pleased, "I find no difficulty in throwing these shells over 2,000 yards, which distance I consider to be nearly the limit of effective field fire."[210] (Note that a general concerned with waste of ammo sees 1,000 yards as max range while a field gun commander sees 2,000 yards as the maximum for laying down fire.)

Assuming a maximum flight of a mile and a half for the shells hitting the Culp's Hill area from Seminary Ridge, a total of forty-four Confederate guns come into play. Twenty-four of these were Napoleons, the remaining twenty a blend of three-inch rifles and rifled Parrotts. With elevations approaching ten degrees all these weapons could have been throwing shot into the area of the 123rd New York and 12th Corps. The Napoleon rounds might have been bounding into the area but the rifled guns would definitely have been tearing trees apart overhead of the men. Some of these guns were in Confederate Major William Poague's artillery battalion. His units were only engaged on July 3rd, the ten guns involved firing a total of 657 rounds, or about 65 rounds per gun. The artillery unit in the most direct line with the 123rd New York's position, and deployed forward towards the Emmittsburg Road, was Captain E. McCarthy's 1st Richmond Howitzers. This unit consisted of two Napoleons and McCarthy kept them very busy during Pickett's Charge as they fired "over 200 rounds" in two hours, roughly a round per minute per gun.[211]

Taking the lower figure of 65 rounds per gun times forty-four guns results in a total of 2,860 rounds over two hours. Assuming a 25% on-target failure rate-whether through fuses or elevation-a total of 715 rounds could have been whistling into the 12th Corps area, one round every ten seconds for two hours. If one wants to be more conservative and figure a 10% targeting failure then a round enters the region every 25 seconds.

Lanyards were being pulled on over 120 Confederate cannons with Union gunners replying. On the Confederate side alone over seven thousand metal missiles were launched to break the Federal center. An awesome airborne spectacle to the eyes. Add the roiling smoke, cries of horses and men, crashing trees, utter din to the ears, concussion waves dashing forth again and again with battery after battery kicking back to be rolled forward by sweating gun crews. Concerned as to the amount of ammunition being fired and understanding that an infantry attack was forthcoming, Union General Hunt ordered his artillery to cease counter-battery fire. Shortly after, about 3 p.m., the Union troops saw through the smoke across the fields several thousand Rebel troops, regimental flags arrayed in battle formation, stepping forward. Union Brigadier General John Gibbon, commanding 2nd Division 2nd Corps, was in the area of the Copse of Trees watching the Rebel advance. "The [Confederate] line moved steadily to the front in a way to excite the admiration of everyone, and was followed by a second and a third, extending all along our front as far as the eye could reach." Further to the left Union 1st Lt. Edwin Dow, commanding the 6th Maine Battery, also watched the Confederates come forward through the drifting smoke and made ready to receive them. His unit had been exposed during the whole two-hour bombardment but only had five men wounded. "The enemy fired mostly case shot and shell at our position, nearly all of which passed over our line of artillery and supports and exploded in the woods behind, covering the road with their fragments."[212] The center of the Union line by the Copse of Trees was roughed up, especially the artillery units. But more guns were being quickly brought forward and put into battery. The infantry were intact along the stone walls and more were moving forward in support.

Over twelve thousand Confederates were marching forward. Instead of the Union artillery being destroyed it was only waiting for orders. They were given. Cannon shot and shell ripped great holes in the approaching lines then at 200 yards the blue-clad soldiers rose up to fire volley after volley. The Southerners did make the Union position, ran over the first wall, pushed forward and collapsed against fresh troops coming forward. Their flanks during the assault had been hammered by Union gunners under officers like Captain Edgell and Lt. Dow, both of whom had spent the proceeding two hours watching many enemy shells soar over their positions.

"The artillery fire ceased about as suddenly as it began," 123rd New York Lt. Cruikshank writes, "and then there was one continuous roar of musketry along the whole line for two hours longer."[213] This was behind the men of the 123rd, across the Baltimore Pike, across fields and woods, about three-quarters of a mile away the noise was plain to the ears. "Fall in!" rang out at 4 p.m. for the 123rd New York and it was another rapid hump over the fields to the Union center for the soldiers. Soldiers of the 1st Brigade, 12th Corps, were sent as support as Pickett's Charge peaked. They arrived to find Southerners being moved to the rear as prisoners, remnants of regiments fading into the smoke in retreat. Of the roughly 12,500 Confederates that strode forth it is estimated that less than half returned.

Rifle fire was becoming spaced out and sporadic, it was obvious the Southerners had lost the contest at the stone wall and Copse of Trees. Colonel McDougall was ordered to return his brigade to the Lower Culp's Hill entrenchments. The 123rd New York was walking back with the other units of their brigade and approaching Spangler's Spring. They might have been thinking the battle was over, that it hadn't been that bad for them this time...but across Rock Creek snipers lay in an old mill. There was a rifle crack and a scream.

Captain Norman Weer was hit in a knee, the round blowing it apart. "His cry of pain was heard above every other noise," Lt. Cruikshank says. The 123rd New York Company E commander was carried to a nearby hospital where his leg was amputated. "A splendid officer," Sergeant Gourlie commented when writing his sister as to Weer's wounding. Lt. Colonel Rogers in his battle report refers to Weer as a "brave and accomplished officer" while Colonel McDougall in his report calls Weer a "brave and most valuable officer." McDougall also states that several other men in the 123rd were wounded at this time, there must have been a scattering of shots from the woods across the creek into the unit. Once through the open area the regiment was safe, entering the woods they took the time to brew some coffee and then returned to their entrenchments.[214]

Random rifle shots continued through the night. After midnight the Confederates along Rock Creek were ordered to withdraw to a position to the west of Gettysburg. July 4th was a sunlit day, Lee held his army in position along Seminary Ridge but started his wagon trains of wounded and baggage west towards Cashtown, Pennyslvania to be followed by his army that night. On Culp's Hill Federal soldiers poked forward to find no enemy and returned to inform their officers. The 123rd New York was ordered out on a reconnaissance with several other regiments and an artillery unit. They proceeded along the front of the right wing, entered Gettysburg and returned via Cemetery Hill not finding any Confederates. According to Sergeant Gourlie they moved quickly on the scout, "we went Six Miles in one hour, which considering that we had on all of our equipment was very good marching."[215]

Confederate dead and wounded were all along the front of the 12th Corps line, scattered among the rocks and trees on the slope. "I heard a rebel wounded call for help and in company with Don Humphrey [Co.K] I went down and brought him in-he could walk by leaning on my shoulder," Sergeant Lorenzo Coy writes, "In one spot not 12 feet square I saw 8 dead but I cannot describe what I saw it was too horrid..." It wasn't just the sense of sight that recoiled from the scene. Lt. Cruikshank began to notice what everyone else did, "The stench from thousands of dead men and hundreds of horses that lay all around us was sickening. I could neither eat nor drink anything while in our works...I was detailed to take charge of some men and bury the dead. In front of our Regiment I found the ground literally covered with dead bodies. Officers in grey uniforms were there with their men." "The dead rebs lay thick over the ground our men burying them as fast as possible. I saw at least 800 dead bodies in the woods," noted Corporal Clark McLean (Co. G). "The Corps to which the Regiment belonged buried [July 4th] fifteen hundred dead Rebels," Sergeant Morhous relates, "The dead lay in every imaginable shape...Several rebel officers lay there in their handsome gray uniforms, and among others Gen. Ewell's Assistant Adjutant General. He lay partly under his horse, and both were riddled with bullets." "I saw his body lying beside his dead horse," Corporal Cook noted of the Southern officer, "he was a smart looking man." There was at least one blue uniformed body brought into the 123rd New York's line, Private Wesley Huntington of Company C had fallen while skirmishing in front of the breastworks. He was buried by his comrades on the battlefield beneath a large oak.[216]

"we gave them a fine dressing out theis time and I am in hopes that we will whip them again in a few day's" Private Henry Welch wrote his aunt and uncle. Corporal Cook also had high hopes of a rapid follow up telling his brother, "Lee will have a sweet time getting out of this." "They got soundly thrashed this time I think," Company E 2nd Lt. Seth Carey wrote his mother, "We have had long marches, at times little to eat, not much sleep and considerable rain. But God is with us."[217]

Meade's reaction to the Confederate retreat was to sit for two days. He felt the Army of the Potomac needed to rest and resupply before pursuing Lee's army. There were 14,529 Union wounded to care for, many of them still scattered across the battlefield, and another 5,365 soldiers missing or captured. Total killed for the Army of the Potomac amounted to 3,155. General Meade's victory came at a total casualty tally of 23,049 blue-clad soldiers, or 28% of the men he had at Gettysburg. Lee's losses were 20,451 or 32% of his force with 2,592 killed, 12,709 wounded and 5,150 missing.[218]

Twenty-seven year old Captain Norman Weer did not suvive the amputation of his leg. The soldiers of Company E took up a collection and paid to transport their captain's body home for burial. There was a large turn out for the service, the buggies and wagons lining the dirt road at the little grave yard in Hartford Township, Washington County. On a hillside beneath the maples he was laid to rest, the base of his tombstone inscribed "He did his duty well."

For the fighting of July 2nd and 3rd the 123rd New York suffered three killed, eight wounded and one, Lt. Beadle, taken prisoner. Of the wounded, only one, Private Benjamin Pitts (Co. K) returned to the unit. Private William Norton (Co. K) had his left arm amputated and was discharged. Captain Weer died in the hospital. Private Wallace Orton (Co. A) was discharged for disability, Private John Hamilton (Co. B) deserted, while Privates Robert Cronk (Co. F), William Fenton (Co. A) and William Graham

(Co. E) all transferred into the Veteran Reserve Corps after their hospital stays. Of all the regiments in the 1st Brigade it was the 20th Connecticut that suffered the most, on July 3rd losing six killed and twenty-five wounded. For the battle the 5th Connecticut had a total of three wounded, the 145th New York one killed and four wounded, while the 46th Pennsylvania totaled two killed and two wounded.[219]

The people of Gettysburg, population 2,400, stared out at over 7,000 bodies needing proper burial. It was decided within a few days that a cemetery should be created for the Union dead. Land was purchased on Cemetery Hill and a contractor was hired to rebury the Federal soldiers arranged by state. (The Confederate dead would not be taken south for burial until the 1870's.) On November 19, 1863 the still uncompleted Soldiers Cemetery was dedicated, President Lincoln delivering a few words he had penned now known as the "Gettysburg Address." New York State has the largest section in the cemetery with 866 soldiers. All three of the 123rd New York's losses are buried there: Private John Bell (NY Plot A-135); Private Nelson Thayer (NY Plot B-122); and Private Wesley Huntington (NY Plot E-30).

Private Andrew Benson, Company D
Seventeen when he enlisted, Andrew survived the war and went west to homestead in Nebraska, Kansas and Oklahoma afterwards. Photo courtesy of Rush Benson.

Private Oscar B. Nelson, Company E

Nineteen when he enlisted, Oscar served 11 months before being discharged for disability from the hospital in Alexandria, Virginia July 13th, 1863. Photo courtesy of the U.S. Army Military History Institute, Carlisle, PA.

Unidentified Corporal, Company A, 123rd New York
Besides the original eight corporals mustered into service with Company A of the 123rd New York in September, 1862, there were an additional six men promoted to the rank in the company. Photo courtesy of the U.S. Army Military History Institute, Carlisle, PA.

Quarter-Master Sergeant Charles D. Warner
Twenty-two when he enlisted to save the Union, Charles served throughout the war and mustered out with the regiment in Washington, D.C. June 8th, 1865. Photo courtesy of the U.S. Army Military History Institute, Carlisle, PA.

2nd Lieutenant Luke Carrington, Company C
Entering as a 1st Sergeant, the twenty-two year old was promoted after Chancellorsville had thinned the 123rd New York of officers. Once in the Western Theatre of the war, Luke became a Military Railroad Conductor and was discharged at Albany, New York at the end of the conflict. Photo courtesy of the U.S. Army Military History Institute, Carlisle, PA.

2nd Lieutenant Willis Swift, Company D

Signing the papers saw Willis, twenty-one, placed as 1st Sergeant for Company D. After Chancellorsville the officer rode out to the ambulances when he heard 12th Corps wounded were being brought in from the battlefield. Going from wagon to wagon, scanning over the wounded, Willis at first could not recognize his own men due to their emaciated and dirty condition. The duty-bound officer survived the war and was mustered out with the regiment. Photo courtesy of the U.S. Army Military History Institute, Carlisle, PA.

2nd Lieutenant Jerome B. Rice, Company G
Enlisting when he was twenty-one, Jerome was entered on the muster roll as 1st Sergeant. Wounded and taken prisoner at the battle of Chancellorsville, the officer was paroled. He transferred into the Signal Corps and was mustered out at Albany, New York at the end of the war. Photo courtesy of the U.S. Army Military History Institute, Carlisle, PA.

1st Lieutenant Alonzo Mason, Company A
Promoted to Captain in November of 1863, with rank from July of that year, Alonzo showed enough ability that he ended the war as an aid-de-camp to General Williams. Mustered out with regiment, June 8th, 1865 Washington, D.C. Photo courtesy of the U.S. Army Military History Institute, Carlisle, PA.

1st Lieutenant William Brown, Company B

As a twenty-one year old, William entered the regiment as 1st Sergeant of Company K. He was promoted to 1st Lt. of Company B in January of 1863. Wounded in the leg at Pine Hill, Georgia, William spent some time as a Military Railroad Conductor. He was mustered out with the regiment. Prior service is listed with the 42nd Illinois as a sergeant. Photo courtesy of the U.S. Army Military History Institute, Carlisle, PA.

1st Lieutenant Edward Quinn, Company D

The twenty-seven year old Quinn mustered in as a 2nd Lt. when the regiment was formed. He was promoted to 1st Lt. in February of 1863. During the battle of Culp's Farm on June 22nd, 1864 Edward was struck in the face by a rifle ball which shattered his jaw. He was discharged for disability in May of 1865. Photo courtesy of the U.S. Army Military History Institute, Carlisle, PA.

1st Lieutenant Donald Reid, Company F
Twenty-four when he signed the papers, Reid served
throughout the war and was mustered out with the regiment.
Photo courtesy of the U.S. Army Military History Institute, Carlisle, PA.

1st Lieutenant Robert Cruikshank, Company H

As a 1st Sergeant in Company H, the twenty-six year old Cruikshank saw promotion after Chancellorsville. The conscientious officer saw a myriad of positions, serving at times at the brigade level as provost marshal and aid-de-camp. Battling sickness several times during his first year of service, he returned to take part in the major campaigns of the Western Theatre under General Sherman. He mustered out with the regiment June 8th, 1865 at Washington, D.C. Robert returned home to his wife Mary and their four-year old daughter, Ella. Photo courtesy of the U.S. Army Military History Institute, Carlisle, PA.

1st Lieutenant and Adjutant George H. Wallace

After serving on the staff of the regiment, the twenty-six year old Wallace took the promotion to Captain for Company C in May of 1863. In January of 1864 he was discharged so he could enlist in the U.S. Army's 3rd Infantry. Photo courtesy of the U.S. Army Military History Institute, Carlisle, PA.

1st Lieutenant and R.Q.M. Andrew Crawford
As 1st Sergeant of Company F, the twenty-three year old Andrew was chosen to replace John King when he resigned after only a month in service. Promoted to the Regimental Quarter Master position in November of 1862, Crawford served out the war and was mustered out with the regiment. Photo courtesy of the U.S. Army Military History Institute, Carlisle, PA.

Captain Alexander Anderson, Company D

Spoken very highly of by Sergeant Rice Bull in his memoirs, Anderson was thirty-years-old when he put on the officer bars. Entering as the 1st Lieutenant for Company D he was promoted to Captain of the company in February of 1863. He mustered out with the regiment at the end of the war. Photo courtesy of the U.S. Army Military History Institute, Carlisle, PA.

Captain George R. Hall, Company E

Accepting great responsibility at twenty-two years of age, George took rank as 1st Lieutenant of Company E when the regiment was formed. With the death of Captain Weer at Gettysburg, Hall was promoted to command Company E. When 120 guerrillas attacked a train in Tennessee on March 16th, 1864, Captain Hall led 40 men against them, driving the enemy from the field and rescuing the passengers. Hall was mustered out with the regiment at the end of the war. Photo courtesy of the U.S. Army Military History Institute, Carlisle, PA.

Captain Orrin S. Hall, Company I

Orrin was forty-seven when he took command of Company I. He fought throughout the war to preserve the Constitution as he saw it and was mustered out with the regiment June 8th, 1865 at Washington, D.C. Photo courtesy of the U.S. Army Military History Institute, Carlisle, PA.

Captain Henry O. Wiley, Company K

As he was opening an ammunition box for his men, Captain Wiley was shot through the chest during the battle of Peach Tree Creek, July 20th, 1864. Buried upon the field, he had enlisted at thirty-one years of age. "My dear Madam, I address you today for the saddest of purposes, to inform you that your brave husband..."

Photo courtesy of the U.S. Army Military History Institute, Carlisle, PA.

Assistant Surgeon Lysander Kennedy

Lysander enlisted at twenty-nine years of age as the 1st Assistant Surgeon for the 123rd New York. He left the regiment as the war drew to a close in May, 1865 to take promotion to Surgeon of the 119th Infantry.
Photo courtesy of the U.S. Army Military History Institute, Carlisle, PA.

Surgeon James Chapman

The fifty-four year old Chapman signed on with the 123rd New York after their first surgeon, John Moneypenny, resigned in April of 1863. With prior service as an assistant surgeon in the 90th Infantry, James saw a promotion to full surgeon with his transfer. He mustered out with the 123rd New York at the end of the war. Photo courtesy of the U.S. Army Military History Institute, Carlisle, PA.

Lt. Colonel Frank Norton

Highly regarded by the rank and file of the 123rd New York, Lt. Colonel Norton had prior experience in the 77th New York Infantry as a captain. With the formation of the 123rd New York the twenty-eight year old Norton transferred in as the second in command. During his nine months with the regiment he instilled drill and discipline to the new recruits while earning their respect. Hit twice at Chancellorsville while leading and encouraging the men during combat, he died of his wounds eleven days later. Photo courtesy of the U.S. Army Military History Institute, Carlisle, PA.

Lt. Colonel Adolphus Tanner

Entering the regiment as Captain of Company C, the twenty-eight year old Tanner saw promotion to major in May, 1863 then to Lt. Colonel in February of 1865. He was wounded in the legs slightly during the battle of New Hope Church, May 25th, 1864. He was mustered out with the regiment at the end of the war. Photo courtesy of U.S. Army Military History Institute, Carlisle, PA.

Lt. Colonel James C. Rogers

Upon the formation of the 123rd New York, twenty-three year old James took the position of major. He was formally a captain in the 43rd Infantry, so brought experience to the regiment. A respected officer, he rose through the ranks while serving the 123rd New York: Lt. Colonel in May, 1863; Colonel November, 1864; and Brevet Brigadier General in March, 1865. Rogers was esteemed by the soldiers of the 123rd New York. He mustered out with the regiment June 8th, 1865 in Washington, D.C. Photo courtesy of the U.S. Army Military History Institute, Carlisle, PA.

Chapter 6
Letters, Paperwork and Camps by the Rapidan

Lincoln was greatly distressed that Meade didn't follow up rapidly on the retreating Confederates to engage and destroy Lee's army. The opportunity for another battle presented itself as the Potomac River was in flood stage as the Army of Northern Virginia approached it. A raid by Union cavalry on July 3rd had destroyed the only Confederate pontoon bridge in place. By July 7th the Southern army of roughly 35,000 effectives was encamped on the north bank of the river. Lee knew an enemy of twice his army's size would soon be approaching. It was looking very, very bad but being ever the fighter, he turned his army to face his antagonists and dug in around the Williamsport, Maryland area. His troops began stripping warehouses for the wood needed to build pontoon boats and a new bridge.

But Meade did not push the pursuit. The 123rd New York spent July 4th and part of the 5th in burial details along their line. In the afternoon they were ordered to march south and the men were quite ready to leave. "The stench was terrible and we could stand it no longer...," Lt. Cruikshank writes, "Hundreds of dead horses are lying above the ground, bloated as full as the skin will hold." They marched about ten miles and camped outside of Littlestown, PA. On the 6th they only covered about four miles, passed through Littlestown and camped a couple miles south of it. Lt. Cruikshank and the men found their reception in the village quite a surprise. "The town looked deserted as we passed through. Doors were locked and blinds closed and when any of the men were admitted into a kitchen and bought a loaf of bread he was charged fifty cents for it and the same for a bowl of milk. We could hardly believe that these were the same people who sang and cheered us on when the enemy were near and they wanted protection."[220]

Corporal Clark McLean was making the best use of his time in Pennsylvania and a couple easy days of marching gave him opportunities. "I have had a good many meals among the Dutch [Deutsche] farmers around...The people in this part of Penn. are all Germans and talk german altogether to each other. The women smoke and the girls go barefooted. I would be satisfied to have the rest of our fighting in the Union states." (President Lincoln would have spewed his coffee across the Oval Office if he had *that* idea pitched to him.)[221]

The men got a good rest the night of the 6th but then the effort quickened with camp being broke at 4 a.m. and a hard, fast pace kept towards Frederick, Maryland. With no breaks for eating, the soldiers of the 123rd New York were with others of the 12th Corps outside of the city by nightfall. "We marched thirty-two miles today and I am almost used up," Lt. Cruikshank notes. Sergeant Morhous concurs stating the "boys were very weary." Yet Corporal McLean was doing well telling his mother, "I have stood it first rate" and his brother, "Have been on the tramp most every day. Some days we would go 20 or 30 miles but we can do it easier than could [one-half] of distance last fall."[222]

Rain started the early morning of July 8th and continued throughout the day turning the roads to mud. Still, the men of the 123rd made 22 miles, passing through Frederick, then Middletown and camping near Burkittsville. The start of the day was the highlight for as they entered Frederick they saw a man hanging from an oak tree. Some of the men stepped out of line and went to investigate. They recognized the man as having been often at their camp the fall and winter before outside of Harper's Ferry. He was a spy. "He was in our Camp almost every day and had been with us part of the time on this march. He peddled songs and some small wares that he could carry in his pockets. We all thought him to be half-witted," Lt. Cruikshank says of the surprise, "...when taken he had on his person a map of our line of march all the way to Gettysburg and the weak points of our line at the time of battle." Corporal McLean was very pleased to see the hemp necktie used. "I saw a spy hanging to a tree in Frederick City. He had been hanging two days, thats the right way to serve them Rebel spys. We ought to have done so long ago." Corporal Albert Cook learned it was a family affair, "he is one that used to sing songs and sell papers in camp many recognize him his son is also to be hung."[223]

Union General Meade was bringing the 12th Corps towards Williamsport from the east while other corps positioned themselves to the north against the Rebel position. The 123rd New York pushed on, by July 10th they were on the old battlefield of Antietam. The men looked over the "Sunken Lane" and other areas that had seen combat the year before. Lt. Cruikshank probably made use of Antietam Creek for a daily evening ritual, washing his shirt and putting it back on wet to help against the heat. "I have stood the march very well although I have lain down on wet ground and slept all night in my wet clothes. Often I would not dare remove my shoes for fear I could not get them back on again."[224]

At 4 a.m. the unit was moving forward towards Fairplay, Maryland and after passing the town they came upon the Rebel pickets. Deploying with other regiments, the 123rd New York sent forward skirmishers and they began to drive the enemy. They ran upon the Confederate field works near Falling Waters. Here the Union troops entrenched themselves. The 123rd found themselves in an open field so used fence rails and some cut and stacked wheat with earth thrown over them. Lt. Cruikshank says the men worked on them all night and by morning had stout works considering the material. "We had no shovels or picks but used bayonets to loosen the earth and our hands and shingles for spades." Sergeant Morhous relates that the soil worked easily with plenty of fence rails available but that a local citizen had issues with the men. As they continued entrenching the morning of July 12th the farmer that owned the land came into the 123rd New York's line demanding to know who was going to pay him for his rail fence. "The boys had considerable sport with the old fellow, and we are sure he did not get satisfactory answers to his inquiries."[225]

Corporal McLean was coming to the conclusion he wasn't going to get any satisfaction as to bagging Lee and the Rebel army. As skirmishing continued to their front and the little specks of Reb cannon muzzles pointed their way from a half-mile off, McLean penned a letter to his brother Henry. "I think [Lee] will get away all right, some way or other. Our Generals don't seem to be sharp enough for them." The evening of the 12th General Meade held a council of war as to attacking the Confederate works. Meade liked holding councils of war (Union General Grant found them pointless), at Gettysburg the council voted to stay and fight, at Williamsport they voted to hold off attacking. This might have been a good decision as the Confederate works were well placed. Meade even stated he didn't want to fight a Gettysburg in reverse, the Union charging and getting slaughtered. But it meant Corporal McLean and many others in the Army of the Potomac would shake their heads in disgust. Lee had his bridge completed the 13th and started crossing while a rear guard kept up a steady firing from the entrenchments to fool the Union troops. At 3 a.m. on July 14th the 123rd New York was told to be ready to move out at daylight as part of a "reconnaissance." "We formed in line of battle in front of our works expecting to advance and make a charge on the enemy. Several of their guns were yet in position on the hills and it looked as if we had some hard fighting to do," Lt. Cruikshank says of the moment, "We were all in readiness to advance when we saw a colored man coming from the enemy's line, calling that the enemy had crossed the river." The 123rd pushed forward to find no one before them. The only saving grace for the day was that Union Cavalry General Buford had detected the withdrawal and managed to drive Lee's rear guard into the Potomac while taking 500 prisoners. "The enemy cut the bridge in two, when they saw us coming, while it was full of men and teams," Corporal McLean says, "All who were on the bridge were swept away by the current and large numbers of them drowned." Lee had gotten away. As for the cannons the men of the 123rd New York anxiously saw across the fields while waiting to advance, they were "Quaker Guns." The Rebs had cut trees down to cannon size then painted a black hole on one end and stuck them in the entrenchments. From a distance they could fool anyone as the real thing.[226]

By the afternoon of July 16th the 123rd New York was in camp at Sandy Hook, Maryland, near Harper's Ferry. On the 17th the enlisted men made the most of the day in camp. Corporal McLean used a drum as a desk for writing his mother. "A lot of boys have an opposum up a big hollow tree and are cutting it down. Some writing letters good many reading, some playing cards, playing on fifes, etc. etc. not a very quiet place for writing. I hear our 'Bull-Dogs' barking at front, shelling the Rebs. All kinds of noise and doings and Sunday besides."[227]

The noise couldn't have been helping Lt. Cruikshank complete the company paperwork. "I have been writing all day. I have had to make a report of the campaign and the battle. Everything must be accounted for-from the largest to the smallest article belonging to the Government; the number of prisoners taken; the number of dead buried in front of our Company; the number of guns and the amount of ammunition captured; all must be reported."[228]

Paperwork was a major part of Robert Cruikshank's job as a sergeant and then as an officer in Company H. Besides the monthly muster rolls there were several forms relating to the various government property the army owned. The forms were white paper with printed grid lines and column headings with instructions on the reverse side and a location to sign and date. If receipts for property should be in duplicate or triplicate one could read "Suggestions to Officers Issuing Ordnance Property" for proper procedures. There was "Form No. 1-(a.) Quarterly Return of Ordnance Stores," "Form No. 10 & 11-(b.) Unserviceable Ordnance;" "Form No. 7-(a.) (For issues or transfers of Ordnance Stores.)," "Form No. 12" for "damaged, lost or destroyed" ordnance, and even "Form No. 3" for the reimbursement of an officer's private servant. Some were monthly while others were quarterly reports that had to be filled out and sent off to the War Department in Washington. For the quarterly ordnance report Lt. Cruikshank would receive a receipt - "Property Returns Division (Examination Section-Form 1)"- from the bureaucracy after his report was passed for settlement. Writing at the bottom of the receipt explains that the receipt is evidence of acceptance of Cruikshank's report by government auditors. Then it states in bold type, "It should be carefully preserved by the Receiver."[229]

Cruikshank often mentions he is working on paperwork in his letters to his wife. He had to file a company report, those above him filed regimental reports, then brigades, divisions and corps. Considering that the 12th Corps had 28 infantry regiments at the time of Gettysburg it would have meant 280 monthly forms flowing to Washington (this ignores any artillery and cavalry units assigned to 12th Corps). The Union Army had over 2,000 regiments during the war, assuming 1,000 at any one time were doing duty it would result in 10,000 company monthly reports being filed. That's if only *one* monthly report was filed by each company. These were all hand written in ink with scribe pens. When Cruikshank lacked the proper form he used a straight edge and created his own, but as the war progressed the printed forms were the standard.

As the Lieutenant worked away the men in the 123rd New York discussed New York City with muttered oaths. Draft riots had broken out there on July 13th and gone on for four days. While a combination of issues coming to a head for the white laboring males—conscription, emancipation, wages, job conditions, etc.—the riot was also seen to be the result of agitation by New York Governor Seymour in speeches he made just days before the mobs took to the streets. Seymour, a Democrat, was strongly opposed to conscription and emancipation. Killing of blacks, burning of draft offices and sacking of Republican newspapers went on day by day. The police force fought couragously but were totally overwhelmed by the mobs said to number 10,000 at times. New York National Guard units had been pulled from the city and sent south when Lee invaded Pennsylvania so the police were initially on their own.

"It is reported that the rioters have already recommenced their work of destruction," General John Wool, commanding forces in New York City, stated on July 14th to General Harvey Brown, "Today there must be no child's play. Some of the troops under your command should be sent immediately to attack and stop those who have commenced their infernal rascality in Yorkville and Harlem."[230] Soldiers from the Army of the Potomac were rushed north and they had no concerns with firing into the mobs they felt were stabbing them in the back. By the 18th the city was back under control.

"The soldiers here talk very hard against Copperheads north," Corporal McLean wrote his mother, "Would rather fight them than the Rebs. I hope they will hang these rioters Wood and all, if necessary [Governor] Seymour...I should like to have our Regt. in N. Y. City just now." The 123rd men saw the need for a draft not just to replenish their ranks, but as Corporal Cook told his father, to make a clear statement. "I see some of the N.Y. papers Fred [brother] sends, think there is no need of a draft but we know there is for no other reason than to enforce the laws and show other Nations that our government is strong enough to crush rebellion at home as well as abroad."[231]

As the Yankees sat by Harper's Ferry Lee's army wandered slowly up the Shenandoah Valley (the Shenandoah River runs north). Union commander Meade now swung the Army of the Potomac across the rivers at Harper's Ferry and dashed down the east side of the Blue Ridge Mountains to catch up opposite the Southerners. The 123rd New York started the morning of the 19th with their division, crossed over to Harper's Ferry and went four miles beyond. The next day saw them pushing 20 some miles, going through Loudon Valley and all the way to Snicker's Gap. Guerilla activity in the area annoyed 1st Division General Williams so much that he ordered out patrols to search the local houses for any evidence. The 123rd New York did "heavy picket duty" at the gap while this went on for two days. On July 23rd the men covered over 30 miles with a march to Ashby Gap, then back tracking some miles and on through Upperville to make Piedmont Station at 10 p.m. At the stop Corporal McLean managed a few lines in his diary: "Half the men fell out on the way. The weather is very hot and the roads dusty."[232] Supper was finished at midnight, the soldiers fell onto their blankets exhausted to get less than three hours sleep. On the march at 3 a.m. of the 24th they made Manassas Gap, were issued hardtack, went into the Shenandoah Valley to the town of Linden, had a quick meal of coffee and hardtack, then backtracked through the gap to the town of White Plains. Arriving at midnight, the soldiers had covered over 25 total miles. "We were so tired that we did not put up tents, but slept without covering," says Cruikshank. The Lieutenant was exhausted from all the marching and lack of sleep and now he paid for it.[233]

When the 123rd New York began their march on July 25th at 8 a.m. Lt. Cruikshank wasn't one of the footsloggers. "I was so sick this morning I could not march. I had high fever and was so weak that I could not stand on my feet. I could eat nothing." He rode a horse as the regiment moved forward to Fairplain, Virginia. At that location the ambulances caught up with the 123rd and Cruikshank was loaded into one of them. It began to rain, throughly wetting the men as they trudged into Thoroughfare Gap and on to Haymarket, covering 18 miles. A 6 a.m. start the next morning saw the 123rd New York cover 15 miles to make camp near Warrenton Junction. Cruikshank, and no doubt several others, were in ambulances for the trip. Once the tents were up Cruikshank was placed on a blanket in one, he was burning with fever and desperately desired some cold water. Private Peter McNassor of Company H stopped in to check on his officer. Cruikshank made a simple request for water. "The boy went two miles to a spring and got me a canteen of good water," Cruikshank wrote his wife Mary,

"Peter is one of our best soldiers and the youngest. He marched all the way to Gettysburg and back and when so tired went so far to get me the water. I shall never forget the kind act."[234] McNassor had less than a year before combat would take his life.

The Brigade Surgeon put Lt. Cruikshank, Lt. Colonel James Rogers, Lt. Donald Reid (Co. F) and Captain John Crary (Co. H) all on the sick list. The doctor took Rogers, Cruikshank and Reid to Washington to recover. The officers checked into a private boarding house where they were visited by an army physician. The prescribed solution was bed rest and good food for their bodies ravaged by campaigning. During Cruikshank's recovery Captain Crary visited to say goodbye, the commander of Company H having resigned due to poor health. After six days Cruikshank had the strength to send a letter off to his wife. "The quiet does me good. If you and Ella were with me how I would enjoy this day. I wonder if this wicked war will not soon come to a close so that we can return to our friends and enjoy life. We must await God's own time to bring about these things. He is permitting it for some good purpose. It is my opinion the He will not permit slavery longer to exist in this land. When that is done away with then we can go home."[235]

By July 24th Lee had the Army of Northern Virginia entrenched around Culpepper Court House. The Army of the Potomac marched into positions along the Rappahannock River over the next few days. The 123rd New York spent five days at Warrenton Junction. It was a very active location with trains arriving constantly. Army supplies were unloaded into hundreds of four-mule-team wagons and driven off for the camps as over 80,000 soldiers went into assigned positions. Occupying themselves with washing and mending of clothing, the 123rd soldiers also had time to discuss the great news of the west. "We are getting glorious news from the west now. Grant is doing things up there in fine style," McLean noted on the capture of Vicksburg. On July 31st the 123rd New York marched to Kelly's Ford on the

Rappahanock River and established their camp. They were part of the picket line running along the north bank of the river, spending the days watching their Secesh counterparts across the river. But summers in Virginia can be very hot. "The boys suffered terribly from the heat; in fact the weather being so warm but two hours were set apart for drill-from half-past five to half-past six in the morning, and the same hour in the afternoon, so all the boys had to do during the day was keep cool, which was impossible," Sergeant Morhous says. There were a couple plusses. The men all built raised beds a foot off the ground, constructed of cut tree limbs, which helped for sleeping. In addition, the brigade brass band played every evening. Morhous writes that the music "was a source of great enjoyment to the boys, for the band played well. The principal topic of conversation was the paymaster and conscripts, both of whom were anxiously looked for-the paymaster, that they might have money; the conscripts, that they might hear from home."[236]

Private Welch wasn't too keen on the draft prospects for the regiment, telling his aunt and uncle, "I see that we are not going to get many men on this draft it appears that somebody has got it into their head's that we are going to fight down this rebellion with money instead of men." To his mother he penned, "I have been thinking since the draft was made up there that Washington County would be a grand situation for a doctor for I see that the men all complain of general debility."[237]

Prayer meetings rounded out the camp time and Private Welch saw them as needed. "I hope alway's to be found ready to go when my master call's me. we have many temptations here to resist and many evil's to shun...there is a great many young men ruined in this army that had good principles when they come here but here they are left wholly to themselves they are away from the influence of a christian mother and the advice of a kind Father...soon they form bad company bad habits and are fast on the road to ruin."[238]

Speaking of bad habits, some over in the 46th Pennsylvania needed the "Golden Rule" read to them. "Our boys are having some sport," Corporal William Shimp wrote his fiance Annie, "We get the New York Herald and answer advertisements of young ladies wanting husbands. They get some photographs of some young men and use false names. They always get an answer accompanied with a photograph. In my opinion a young lady is very foolish that will corresponde with a young man she had never seen or have a personal acquanitance with him but every one to their fancy."[239]

In mid-August the paymaster arrived and gave the men back pay for the four months of March to June. Money in hand it was time to spiffy up one's look. "I would like to have a pair of shirts made & sent to me," Corporal McLean wrote his brother Henry, "I want woolen. Fancy color & made up in style. If you have no chance to send them send by express. Express boxes are coming here every few days." Draftees also arrived and Morhous relates a joke they pulled on one of the rookie soldiers. He needed his shoes repaired so asked some veterans where he might find a shoemaker. They promptly directed him to the tent of a man named Knipe who was a shoemaker in civilian life. Trouble was, he was now General Knipe the brigade commander. The private walked into the tent and asked the general to repair his boots. Taken aback by the request, Knipe then realized the new soldier was the butt of a joke and told the soldier "to go back to his tent and not let the old soldiers fool him."[240]

Any of the draftees that arrived at this time were not for the 123rd New York. All during the war Washington County upped the bounty as each draft call was made, thereby getting volunteers or substitutes for the county quota. As an example, Putnam Township in Washington County was required to supply 13 men for the summer, 1864 call-up. Out of these 13 men, four were subsitutes, two were listed as "the Albany credits" and the remaining seven volunteers were from the township. Three of the men signed for three years, and the other eight for one year's service (the two Albany credits were not identified as to service time). Six of the men were paid a bounty of $636, two were paid $600 and three were paid $500 for signing the papers. It cost Putnam Township $6,516 to meet that call up plus another $239.90 in expenses run up by the six members of the recruiting committee. Bond sales or tax increases were used to fund the effort. During the entire war Washington County managed to find enough recruits so as to not have any of their citizens drafted for the 123rd New York.[241] For many of the other regiments soldiers were now coming in via the draft. During late summer of 1863 the 46th Pennsylvania received quite a few draftees and it was probably one of them that Morhous spins his tail about.

The men fell into a routine of picket and scouting. Private Welch was seeing picket duty along the river once every eight days, camp guard duty as often and then patrol duty every ten days. Patrol involved going "over the country to pick up our drafted men that are trying to desert." It was easy duty but sometimes it grated on him. "the rebs are in the wood's a short distance from the river on the other side the saucy imp's come out in sight and swing their hat's at us and make all sorts of motion's. I would like to send a bulet among them once and a while but it is against orders to fire at them unless they fire first."[242]

Troops from time immemorial have had to deal with camp scuttlebutt and it was the same for the 123rd. "Their is Rumors in camp that a move is about to made soon, but cant tell how true it is," Private Orville Robinson wrote his friend Hulbert back in Argyle, "In the army you dont know when you are agoing to move untill you hear the order to fall in." Robinson tells "Hub" he hopes his friend will get the hay in before any rain, then the soldier in camp among trees and cloth tents took pen to larger matters. "If my wishes were of any account the War would be over I think by this time, for I have wished oft times for the War to close, but it seems not to be very near at hand yet...I was calculating on the close of the war to come about the first of Jan. but I am afraid that I won't guess right. the South are waiting to see the result of the Elections this fall at the North. I hope what men that is at home will vote every man that is true blue to the Union into office that comes up, so that the South cant have the first bit of encouragement. I should think that the people of the State of New York would rise up en masse and hang that traitor Seymer to the highest tree that can be found. After hearing of all the victories that the Northern veterans have acheived, to have that Northern Dough-face kick up such a stink as he has is a disgrace to all civilized people."[243]

Colonel McDougall took the opportunity at this time to order particular drills he felt the men of the 123rd needed to practice. Company commanders were to see that their charges covered "marching by the flank in column in full, at half-distance and in mass. And forming division in column closed in mass. Changing direction in column at half distance and also closed in mass." Southern cavalry must have been on the colonel's mind as he also cited, "Column against cavalry. Caseys tactics P. 269-271...These movements will be repeated from day to day in connection with other movements."[244]

Across the Rappahanock Southern leaders were debating their next movement to be taken. The summer had been a disaster for the South, defeat at Gettysburg in the east, then at Vicksburg and Port Hudson along the Mississippi. Their Army of Tennessee under General Braxton Bragg had been forced totally out of that state, relinquishing the vital railroad city of Chattanooga, by an army under Union General Rosecrans. After much discussion it was decided to send General Longstreet and his corps to reinforce Bragg in Northern Georgia. They would target Rosecrans's army, destroy it, and regain the inititive. Longstreet's 12,000 troops began loading on trains September 9th, arriving in stages at Bragg's army over the 18th, 19th and 21st.

Union General Meade learned of the transfer of Longstreet and decided to attack the weakened Army of Northern Virginia. Elements of the Army of the Potomac, cavalry and the 2nd Corps, began filing by the 123rd New York on September 13th and splashing across the river. Also on the 13th the paymaster visited the men again. The soldiers of the 123rd New York received two months back pay for

July and August. Private Levi Eaton sent two dollars to his wife to give to their children Willie and Ida, "get them a stick of candy or some peanuts." Sergeant John Gourlie sent $30 home to his parents with the comment, "The draft must have left Uncle Sam with a considerable amount of cash on hand, for he has been very prompt in his payments since."[245] The conscription act allowed men to avoid the call-up by paying a $300 fee to the government. Cash was flowing into Uncle Sam's coffers but the fee option left many angry with the inequality of the system. The Southern draft law didn't have a fee option but did have an allowance for any male owning more than 20 slaves, they were not drafted. That arrangement made for some hard feelings in the gray-clad ranks.

Welch was having problems with blue-clad apparel. Money in hand meant better clothing and now he too was seeking some new shirts from home. "that blue flannel that you wrote about wont hardly do," Welch told his father, "I dont think it would suit at all, I dont like the stile of wearing flannel very much, I think you can find some grey shriting at some of the store's or factorie's up there, if you c'ant you need not send any, for I can buy me some of the sutler for seven dollar's a pair, its a pretty good price but I can get some there that will suit me. we can draw course flannel shirts of the goverment at a cost of one dollar a peice but us boy's have taken a notion to have something a little nice, you can see that us soldiers are pretty proud..."[246]

The Army of Northern Virginia having fallen back to beyond the Rapidan River, September 16th saw the 123rd New York break camp and march the eight miles to Stevensburg. The next day saw another 8 miles to Raccoon Ford on the Rapidan River. Here the men went on picket as Meade tried to find a way to flank Lee's position. On the 18th General Slocum, commander of the 12th Corps, received a message from General Meade's chief-of-staff to scout along the Rapidan at Morton's Ford for a possible flanking maneuver. Meade "desires your views upon the subject as soon as you have made the requisite examinations...He further requests me to say that the examination should be concealed from the enemy, so that the passage, should one be made, may not be anticipated by them."[247] By the 22nd the men had been issued eight days rations and the units were under orders to be ready to march at a moments notice. The soldiers knew what this meant, hard marching with a battle. "I think that we are going to try and flank them," Private Welch wrote his father, "there is some prospects of our going into a fight before long and if the rebs get me I dont want them to get much money so I will enclose ten dollars in this letter you must excuse this wrieting for I am writeing as fast as I can so as not to be to late for to day's mail."[248] The soldiers of the 123rd New York sat along the banks of the Rapidan in Virginia not realizing events had taken a seriously wrong turn for the Union in Northern Georgia.

>Telegram to War Department, Washington, D.C.:
>*Chattanooga, Tenn. September 20, 1863 5 p.m. (Received 8:40 p.m.)*
>*Major General H. W. Halleck, General-In-Chief:*
>*We have met with a serious disaster; extent not yet ascertained. Enemy overwhelmed us, drove our right, pierced our center, and scattered troops there...*
>*W. S. Rosecrans, Major-General Commanding*[249]

Chapter 7
Railroading West: Guerrillas and Blockhouses

Confederate General Braxton Bragg had managed a victory over Union General William Rosecrans' forces at Chickamauga Creek, several miles south of Chattanooga in Northern Georgia. The two day battle of 56,000 Union infantry and 47,500 Confederate infantry culminated on September 20th when an accidental gap in the Union line allowed Longstreet's veterans to pile-drive through shattering the Federal right wing. The blue-clad troops fled along with General Rosecrans all the way back to Chattanooga. A total annihilation of Rosecrans' army was averted when Union General George H. Thomas rallied the remaining forces on Snodgrass Hill and fought into the darkness before withdrawing in good order. The press nicknamed Thomas "The Rock of Chickamauga" for his actions. Yet some 40,000 Federal troops faced starvation in Chattanooga after Bragg invested the city. Rosecrans sought help from Washington...

> Telegram from Washington, D.C.:
> *September 21, 1863 12:35 p.m.*
> *Major General Rosecrans, Chattanooga:*
> *Be of good cheer. We have unabated confidence in you and in your soldiers and officers...We shall do our utmost to assist you. Send us your present posting.*
> *A. Lincoln*
>
> Executive Mansion to War Department:
> *September 21, 1863*
> *Major General Halleck:*

> *I think it very important General Rosecrans hold his position at or about Chattanooga because if held from that place to Cleveland, both inclusive, it keeps all Tennessee clear of the enemy, and also breaks one of his most important railroad lines...If he can only maintain this position without more [movement] , the rebellion can only eke out a short and feeble existence, as an animal sometimes may with a thorn in its vitals.*
> *Yours, truly,*
> *A. Lincoln*

Secretary of War Edwin Stanton immediately put telegrams out to the executives of the Baltimore & Ohio Railroad as to capacities and time tables for transporting 16,000 troops west. Then he began contacting adjoining railroads that would take over the transport once the terminus of the B&O was reached.

> Telegram - War Department to Headquarters, Army of the Cumberland:
> *Washington, September 24, 1863 2:30 a.m.*
> *Major General Rosecrans, Chattanooga, Tenn.:*
> *In addition to the expected assistance to you from Burnside, Hurlbut, and Sherman, 14,000 or 15,000 men from here will be in Nashville in about seven days. The Government deems it very important that Chattanooga be held till re-enforcements arrive.*
> *H. W. Halleck, General in Chief*

> Telegram – War Department to Headquarters, Army of the Potomac:
> *Washington, September 24, 1863 2:30 a.m.*
> *Major General Mead, Army of the Potomac:*
> *Please answer if you have positively determined to make any immediate movement. If not, prepare the Eleventh and Twelfth Corps to be sent to Washington, as soon as cars can be sent to you. The troops should*

have five days' cooked provisions. Cars will probably be there by the morning of the 25th.
H. W. Halleck, General in Chief

Telegram - Army of the Potomac to War Department:
September 24, 1863 3 a.m. (Received 3:40 a.m.)
Major General Halleck:
I contemplate no immediate movement, though until your telegram the decision was not positive-awaiting information to be obtained to-day. The Twelfth Corps is on front on picket, and could not well be withdrawn and got ready in the time you name.
Geo. G. Meade, Major General Commanding

Telegram - B&O President John W. Garrett to Secretary of War Stanton:
Camden Station Baltimore, September 24, 1863 (Received 8:25 a.m.)
Hon. E. M. Stanton:
I am on 8 o'clock train from Baltimore and expect to be at Department at 10 o'clock, with our master of transportation. Have arranged for full information regarding engines and cars.
J. W. Garrett

Telegram - War Department to the Army of the Potomac:
Washington, September 24, 1863 9:30 a.m.
Major General Meade, Army of the Potomac:
Your telegram of this morning has been shown to the President. He directs that the Eleventh and the Twelfth Corps be immediately prepared to be sent to Washington, as conditionally ordered before.
H. W. Halleck General in Chief

Telegram - Headquarters, Army of the Potomac to War Department:
September 24, 1863 10:45 a.m.

(Received 11:30 a.m.)
Major General Halleck:
Your telegram of 9:30 a.m. just received, owing to break in line. Every effort will be made to have the troops designated ready to-morrow. Cars for the Twelfth Corps, 10,600 men, should be sent to Brandy Station. The Eleventh Corps is now on the railroad from Rappahannock Station to Bristoe. General Howard will be directed to designate a point for the cars to be at. His strength is 5,700.
Geo. G. Meade Major General Commanding

Message - Headquarters, Army of Potomac to Headquarters, Twelfth Corps:
September 24, 1863 11 a.m.
Commanding Officer Twelfth Corps:
You will at once be relieved by the 1st Corps. On being relieved you will fall back to Brandy station, and immediately prepare for your whole comand five days' cooked rations, and take transportation by railroad to Alexandria. The utmost promptitude and dispatch must be shown in executing this order, and the troops be kept on the march if necessary all night.
Geo. G. Meade, Major General Commanding

Telegram, Thursday –
War Department, September 24, 1863 2:40 p.m.
General Boyle, Louisville, Ky.:
Colonel Thomas A. Scott, of this Department, will arrive in Louisville Saturday about noon. Have the managers of the Louisville and Nashville, the Kentucky Central, and, if possible, the manager of the Nashville and Chattanooga road at Louisville when he arrives, to meet for consultation and concentration of equipment.
Edwin M. Stanton, Secretary of War[250]

Preparations along the B&O route went forward with messages to Union commanders along the rail line. General-in-Chief Halleck sent forth orders to protect it from Rebel raids and to "close all drinking saloons at the principal stations."[251] General Meade must have alerted General Slocum as to a possible movement after the 3 a.m. telegram from the War Department, as the men of the 123rd New York were breaking camp that morning. In the afternoon they marched back through Stevensburg and on to Brandy Station with their brother regiments. The 11 mile march saw them reaching the railroad depot before nightfall where they went into camp. On the 25th the men witnessed a shooting of a deserter from the 145th New York, this after watching a soldier of the 3rd Maryland be executed just days before. Firing squads were also being used in the Army of Northern Virginia. General Lee unhappily having to resort to executions to keep discipline in the ranks, the loss at Gettysburg putting a crimp in the morale of his army. For the Union ranks some of the flood of draftees sought to wash back out, they were caught and selected examples were made.

Sounds of tooting whistles, bells, escaping steam and banging of cars filled the night of September 24th along the military rail line in Virginia. The 11th Corps was loaded out and started for Tennessee over the 25th and 26th; the 12th Corps taking the cars over the 26th, 27th and 28th. The soldiers rode freight cars up to Washington where they transferred onto the Baltimore & Ohio railroad which provided regular passenger cars for the trip west. Initial estimates projected 420 cars with seats needed for the men but it rapidly became apparent that extra cars were going to be needed. The strength of the 11th Corps being "greatly underestimated" additional cars were located and sent to D.C. For troops with gear the car loading averaged 36 to 45 men per car (depending on model). Each train numbered 22 cars maximum due to power concerns for hill climbing going west. Artillery units needed flat cars, horses had special needs, and generals with their staffs, of course, had to have the best available. General Joseph Hooker was put in overall command of both the 11th and 12th Corps for the train movement and granted broad authority in use of all railroad property for the operation. The troops were going with 40 rounds per man, the artillery 200 rounds per piece. As the trains were formed several cars of forage were attached for the horses.[252]

Thirty trains with close to 600 cars were chugging west on a 1,233 mile journey. Even with scrambling for more rolling stock to correct for the 20% increase in men and 50% increase in horses, the evening of September 28th saw the War Department telegraph click out, "fully 16,000 heavy now passed the Relay westward." By the time all the men were tallied for both corps it would exceed 20,000 soldiers. (Relay, Maryland, was where the tracks turned west to go to Ohio.)[253]

Bridgeport, Alabama, was the destination for all the troops. On the Tennessee River, it was also a railroad terminus several miles west of Chattanooga, Tennessee. This area is where the state lines of Alabama, Georgia and Tennessee all meet. Rugged terrain of the Cumberland Plateau meant access to Chattanooga had to be via the river, railroad or poor mountain roads. With the railroad bridge at Bridgeport burnt and the Rebels having control of the south bank of the river near Chattanooga, wagon trains of food had to detour sixty miles over a mountain road from Bridgeport. This life line was extremely tenuous as proven on October 2nd when Confederate cavalry under General Joseph Wheeler fell upon a large wagon train. As Union General George Thomas reported, it wasn't the best day for the United States forces. "Lieutenant Stiles had 250 wagons in his train, all of which he reported this afternoon as having been destroyed. Cliff thinks there must have been 300 to 400 wagons at the foot and going up the mountain, mostly general supply and ammunition wagons...Cannot tell how many were destroyed or taken away. Heard one ammunition wagon explode while on top of the mountain."[254] Although Union cavalry were able to drive the Rebel cavalry south of the Tennessee River over the next few days, the smoking wagons of the cavalry raid bespoke the critical position of Rosecrans' force in Chattanooga. As artillery horses died of starvation the besieged soldiers eaked out life on a three-day ration of four hard cakes of bread and a quarter-pound of pork.

Supper for the men of the 123rd New York was oyster stew, bread and coffee in Columbus, Ohio. At 6 p.m. on September 29th the steam engine had pulled their train into the station where the soldiers were allowed a break. Daily stops for a meal or coffee had been given the soldiers through Western Maryland, West Virginia and now Ohio. While the countryside and ruggedness of West Virginia had impressed the men as the engine smoked through tunnels and snorted up mountain grades, it was people's attitudes in Southern Ohio that struck the men. The region was sympathetic to the South. "There were a few Union men and women, and they took great pains to manifest their sympathies, but the majority were traitorous," Sergeant Morhous relates, "All through the state the same element was discernable, especially around Columbus." Corporal McLean must have only spoken to the Unionists at the stops as he notes, "The people of Ohio are bully."[255]

Day and night the engines kept their roaring fires, sparks and smoke from the stacks drifting back over the crowded cars full of swaying soldiers. Midnight saw another coffee stop at Dayton, Ohio, then an 11 a.m. stop at Indianapolis, Indiana. After a meal the jerking start of the cars was felt as they started for Louisville, Kentucky. One o'clock the morning of October 1st saw the men at the Ohio River at Jeffersonville, Indiana. Transported by ferry across to Louisville, the 123rd soldiers marched through town to the depot, breakfasted on coffee, bread and pork then boarded cars for the trip to Nashville.

There was a bit of a disruption from within the ranks of their brother regiment the 46th Pennsylvania as they made their way through the town. While in Louisville it seems the brigade got some unique recruits filtering into the ranks. Corporal James Peifer of the 46th PA was on the scene watching the commotion. "We rec'd two recruits-females in soldiers clothes." The women were spotted and pulled from the men, one of the females putting up a scuffle. "She swore she would fight the man that reported her."[256] But she never got the chance as the 1st Brigade moved on. To put it delicately, it appears the ladies were there to search out business opportunities rather than morally called to arms to defend the Union. That the women were spotted is due to someone pointing them out. Actual medical checks of the recruits being so poor, it has been estimated that about 400 women disguised as men did join the Union ranks. They joined from true motives of patriotism and some acquitted themselves well.

Heavy rains swept the train as its pistons churned southward. The lightbox was lit as night came on, Bowling Green being passed at 8 p.m., then Nashville at 4 a.m. Coming into Murfreesboro, Tennessee about noon of October 2nd the 123rd New York soldiers stared out the windows at soldiers totally new to them. "At Murfreesboro the boys for the first time saw colored soldiers, a line being drawn up to salute the train as it passed," Sergeant Morhous writes. Private Horace Mathews was quite impressed with the new Union fighters. "Passed through Murfreesborough. Saw the first Colored Reg't.; they looked nice; I wish that you could see them." Corporal Clark McLean got to see more of Murfreesboro than planned, he hopped off the train when it stopped and missed its leaving. He made the best of the situation while waiting for the next train, "Had a good time while there. Lots of ale and lager."[257]

They reached Bridgeport at 3 a.m. on October 3rd, unloaded and went into camp near the station. It had been a seven day trip for them. Both Morhous and Cruikshank say the men were in "box cars" for the journey. Yet the *Official Records* clearly state that cars with seats were contracted for and these were provided. It probably was a blend of rolling stock and one just had the luck of the draw. But Cruikshank was relying on someone else's notes as to the movement as he was home recovering from sickness. Morhous was writing more than fifteen years after the event and perhaps sought to emphasize the discomfort of the men by using the term "box cars." Even with seats it would have been a crowded, packed journey for the soldiers. Morhous states that a total of 50 men were in the box cars but, again, there were a variety of car types being used. The largest passenger cars would hold 45 men so it is not unreasonable to assume some extra pushing was done at the loading to get five more soldiers on a car. Even if tightly packed and bounced about for seven days, someone must have muttered to the complainers that it was certainly better than walking.

And, being American soldiers, they also took matters in hand to correct the crowding. Many of the men climbed atop the cars for the journey. Even when orders came forth to have it stopped the men persisted. Some fell to their deaths. Major General Hooker just shook his head on the issue, writing after the movement had been completed, "The accidents referred to as having happened on the way were caused by the men falling off the tops of the cars while under way, a luxury they would indulge in whether their officers were with them or not; at all events no orders to the contrary checked it."[258]

Another luxury for the soldiers of the 123rd New York was the chance to see women at the stations and towns they passed through. Sergeant Morhous says the men made good use of the opportunity. "At every station on the road crowds of people gathered, and some of the boys conceived the novel idea of writing their address on a card or piece of paper, attaching the same to a stick and throwing it to some young lady whom they fancied at the stations. By this means many a correspondence was formed which helped while away the tedious hours of camp life."[259]

Messages were also flowing between Washington and Union Major General Ulysses S. Grant. In mid-October Lincoln put Grant in charge of the Western Theatre with specific orders to solve the problem of Chattanooga. As one of his first actions he relieved General Rosecrans of command and replaced him with General George "Rock of

Chickamauga" Thomas. Then he proceeded towards the city via the railroad from Nashville, TN to Bridgeport, AL. This single track line was the main supply route for the Union troops, running from the main supply base of Nashville south for about 120 miles with several bridges and a tunnel at Cowan, TN critical for its operation. Interdiction of this line would force the Federal troops to fall back as food, ammunition and reinforcements would not be readily available to the front lines. A complete stoppage would probably doom the defenders in Chattanooga as the scant rations they mouthed would disappear while they waited for the help of their comrades. Southerners fully understood this and Rebel cavalry targeted bridges in raids while guerrillas removed tracks to plunge engines and cars into ditches. Small groups of tens to larger groups of hundreds swarmed the rail line, dashing in with pistols firing, burning supplies and ripping up rails to gallop off into the countryside and fade away. Not all of these raiders were legitimate soldiers of the Confederacy. Bands of thugs made use of the lawless region that surrounded the army, many of the guerrillas were seen by the Northern troops as no more than criminals to be promptly hanged if caught.

Guarding this lifeline now became the purpose of the 123rd New York. Over a couple weeks the troops were sorted out as the generals got a handle on the influx of 20,000 troops from the Army of the Potomac and incorporated them into the Army of the Cumberland. When all was settled, the 1st Division of the 12th Corps was assigned to guard the rail line from Murfreesboro to Bridgeport. General Alpheus Williams commanded the 1st Division reporting to General Slocum for orders. As a combat move was being planned to open a shorter route to Chattanooga for the supply trains, the 2nd Division, 12th Corps, was ordered to march forward with the 11th Corps to bolster its strength. This attack, under General Hooker with supporting actions by troops from Chattanooga, was a complete success. By October 28th the southern bank of the river towards the city had been seized to a few miles shy of the defenders. This allowed steamboats to travel safely up to Kelly's Ferry where they off-loaded supplies to be hauled by wagon the final eight miles to Chattanooga. By the first week of November the soldiers were back to full rations while Grant pondered the next move against the Confederates south of the city.

For the first three weeks of October the 123rd New York was on the move via train or foot up and down the rail line. The main towns and critical points along the line ran: Murfreesboro, Bell Buckle, Wartrace, Duck River Bridge, Tullahoma, Elk River Bridge, Decherd, Cowan tunnel, Tantalon, Stevenson (Alabama) and Bridgeport. The 1st Division was strung out along these stations and structures, at times the regiments broken up by companies to man all the posts. They were intermingled with units from the Army of the Cumberland and it seems not all was going well in the fellowship of blue. General Williams found it necessary on October 21st to issue General Order #56:

> *The brigadier-general commanding the division has discovered, much to his regret, a decided lack of harmony between the detachments from other commands that he found stationed on the line of railroad now under his command and the troops of his division. Upon several occasions this feeling has nearly resulted in a collision between small parties of the respective commands. It is earnestly hoped that the present state of feeling may immediately give place to a spirit of apparent harmony. There is really no reason why any disagreement should exist between the soldiers of the commands referred to, and nothing is more likely to produce disagreement than little banterings and reflections which oftentimes are playfully commenced, and it is enjoined upon all officers and men of this division, as well as upon those of the detachments serving with it, to abstain from all assertions or demonstrations tending to create ill will, and hereafter any officer or enlisted man indulging in such will be arrested and punished....*[260]

"It is laughable to hear some of the western men talk about the Army of the Potomac," 123rd New York Sergeant John Gourlie wrote his brother, "the most of them think that we dont know anything about fighting that all we have done is Guard Washington and that we had got when we would see some fighting &c. and our boys will tell them, that when we was in the Army of the Potomac we used to draw Sweet Cake, Butter, Cheese, Potatoes, Soft Bread. and that once a week we had a batch of Pies sent to us from Washington."[261]

General Williams must have had his hands full. Especially so as the lack of harmony wasn't just in the enlisted ranks but at the very top of the 12th Corps. Generals Hooker and Slocum despised each other. When told he was to be under Hooker's command for the transfer west, General Slocum immediately tendered his resignation. It was left unanswered for the movement but now tensions between the two men boiled up again. On October 12th Hooker telegramed Lincoln suggesting Slocum be removed to a post in Missouri. Grant would have liked to have found a way to remove both men as he had enough to deal with without two generals going to fisticuffs. He hesitated as he felt higher authorities should deal with such a weighty matter as removing two major-generals; Grant understanding that politics often figured into such decisions. On the scene in Chattanooga was Assistant Secretary of War Charles Dana. He sent a communique to Secretary of War Stanton on October 29th stating, "Hooker has behaved badly ever since his arrival, and Slocum has just sent in a very disorderly communication, stating that when he came here it was under promise that he should not have to serve under Hooker, whom he neither regards with confidence as an officer nor respects as a man."[262] The issue would simmer in the background while the effort had to be saving the troops in Chattanooga and getting the region under control. In a few months General Slocum would be given the command of Vicksburg but for now he stewed whenever he received orders from "Fightin' Joe."

Daily trains of supplies were arriving at Bridgeport then going back north to reload at Nashville. A huge supply base and fortification was built at Murfreesboro, Tennessee with the rail line running right through the battlements. From this point south to basically the tunnel just beyond Cowan the 123rd New York was to find themselves riding trains, marching and camping during most of October. The catalyst to all this movement was Rebel cavalry operating in the area. It was folly to send infantry to catch cavalry but the attempt was going to be made as the available Union cavalry was exhausted and small in number.

The afternoon of October 5th the 123rd New York broke camp and marched from Bridgeport to Stevenson, Alabama, a distance of 10 miles. From here the rail line turns north to wind up an open valley with slopes of hardwoods to each side and limestone outcroppings dotting the ridge line. Boarding the cars the men started up the little valley, after several miles they passed Tantalon Station then the train entered the 2,228 foot tunnel that took them through the Cumberland Plateau. Rolling out upon Cowan, Tennessee, the train chugged northward. It wasn't a fast trip as they finally made Decherd at 6 a.m. They had covered some 27 miles in 15 hours. While 1.8 miles per hour might seem pretty slow, it was a night journey, the tracks were in poor shape, trestles and bridges were being repaired plus there was the fear of guerrillas removing a rail or placing a "torpedo" on the track (today we would call it a mine). During breakfast in Decherd word arrived that enemy cavalry were attacking the rail bridge at Wartrace, another 26 miles north. After an eight hour trip the 123rd soldiers arrived to find the bridge plus log stockade burning. A series of hit and run cavalry raids along the track resulted in good success for the Confederates as Union commands at the bridge near Wartrace and the Cowan Tunnel abandoned their posts. Telegraph lines were cut, the tunnel obstructed and bridges and trestles burnt.

For the night of the sixth it was a wet, poor sleep along the banks of the Duck River for the 123rd soldiers.

They hadn't bothered putting up tents and a rainstorm set in around midnight. October 7th meant marching. Rebels were in Shelbyville about 10 miles away. Moving forward, the 123rd New York was posted to a crossroads to prevent its use by the enemy as other units went into Shelbyville and pitched into the Confederates. It was a good action for the Federals as they captured over 300 prisoners and killed over 100 of the enemy. After the sun went down orders were given the 123rd to tramp back towards Wartrace. The men had to march over a road undergoing improvements which resulted in many stumbles and falls from the large stones lying about plus open ditches. Pushing beyond Wartrace the men finished at Bell Buckle covering 14 miles and leaving almost half behind in the dark to find their way forward at sunrise. "They all came in in the morning, nearly all used up and many of them badly bruised from falling," Lieutenant Cruikshank notes, "Each one had his story to tell."[263]

October 10th saw them via train to Decherd, Tennessee. Other regiments of their brigade were also positioned there and all went into camp. General Williams, commanding 1st Division, now ordered 1st Brigade, commanded by General Knipe, to protect the railroad from Tantalon to Decherd with headquarters at the latter. Knipe ordered the 20th Connecticut to the village of Cowan, the 3rd Maryland to the tunnel a couple miles south of Cowan, and stationed the rest of the brigade at Decherd: 5th Connecticut; 46th Pennsylvania; 123rd New York; 145th New York; Battery F 4th U.S.; and Battery M 1st New York.

Also on the 10th the 123rd New York had their first mail call since leaving the Eastern Theatre. Their camp was bustling with furry movement as many of the men had a kitten or dog, Lt. Colonel Rogers doing everyone one better with his two pet squirrels he had brought along from Virginia. Rogers was acting commander of the 123rd New York as Colonel McDougall was back in Washington County recovering from sickness. Major Tanner took the opportunity to send a letter off to McDougall saying of the first couple weeks in Tennessee, "We have had the usual fortune of infantry who attempt to chase cavalry..."[264]

It didn't take long for the men to notice one of the local female passions, chaw. Sergeant John Gourlie wrote his sister in amazement about the tobacco use by women. "They are <u>plain sensible</u> women, do not trouble their heads about fashions, Chew Tobacco, smoke, dip & are not afraid to talk to a Yankee soldier. about the first salute one gets on going into a house is from one of the younger female branches who wants to know if you have got any tobacco. tell her yes; then give me a chaw. offer her some fine cut she will ask if you haven't got some plug. she likes that best. it is bad enough for an old woman to smoke but the idea of young ladies chewing is disgusting."[265]

Corporal James Peifer of the 46th Pennsylvania also wrote home about the pervasive use of Virginia-leaf. Most of the locals about Decherd Station, Tennessee were "all good Union people as far as that is concerned, men, horse, women and all, and I glory in that; but the tobacco practice! Everybody and everything uses it; men, women, children, and I believe ducks, hens, geese, cats, dogs, horses, and cows use it, by all appearances."[266]

Peifer was correct as to the Union sentiment of the community along the railroad. But Tennessee was a divided land, the eastern section being strongly Union with the western section holding for the Confederacy. Where the soldiers now found themselves, central Tennessee, was a true hodgepodge of hidden anger or outright support for the blue uniform. During the recent Confederate cavalry raid the Southerners had sacked Shelbyville, Tennessee, calling it derisively "Little Boston." That was in Bedford County, a strong Union locale. Below it, and boardering Alabama, was Franklin County full of rabid Stars and Bars supporters. Winchester was the largest city in Franklin County and staunch South. During the lead up to the firing on Fort Sumter the citizens of Winchester voted to join Alabama if Tennessee didn't secede. Their February 1861 secession meeting praised Jefferson Davis while calling Lincoln "a mental dwarf." It was to be in these lands that the soldiers of the 123rd New York were now to find themselves.[267]

Such guerrilla country meant supply movements had to be supported. October 19th three companies of the 123rd New York were assigned to march with an 11th Corps wagon train going over the Cumberland ridge line to Tantalon. The remaining seven companies were also on the march over the mountains going to Bridgeport, Alabama. The topography rises 1,000 to 1,500 feet from Cowan, Tennessee to the ridge line with a very steep ascent. It was hard going for the six-mule teams and the 123rd soldiers had to muscle the wagons along at several points. They spent the night under a pelting rain trying to shelter themselves by crawling underneath the wagons. Another hard day of going down the mountain saw them arrive at Tantalon exhausted. Using an old shed they built fires, dried out and cooked a meal. Several train changes later they arrived at Bridgeport on the 23rd, a day ahead of the other 123rd companies that marched the forty miles from Decherd. Here the regiment took charge of the small fortification atop the hillock right next to the railroad station. "We are in a little fort and have very good quarters," Private Levi Eaton wrote his wife. Corporal McLean was really impressed with the location. "It is the most pleasant place we have been in yet. We have a splendid view of the river which looks a good deal like the Hudson. The whole army is supplied from here. Trains of cars arrive & leave hourly. While there is no end to sutler shops & Bakerys."[268]

Civilian houses at Bridgeport were just burnt foundations but from military activity sprang new structures. Warehouses were being constructed along the river to handle the supplies being forwarded, the 1,500 foot railroad bridge across the Tennessee River was being rebuilt and hulls of steamboats were being laid along the shoreline. Calls went out among the soldiers for mechanics and carpenters: tool workers to get the large steam sawmill captured at the town back into operation, wood workers for the boat building. As the ships began to form engines for them were shipped from Louisville, Kentucky. The U.S. Chattanooga, Chickamauga,

Lookout, Missionary and Kingston rose amid the noise of saws and pounding hammers. "Every carpenter in the Regiment was detailed to work on the flatboats which were being built to place on the river," Sergeant Morhous says.[269] The unit was also split up with six companies staying at the fort under Lt. Colonel Rogers, Major Tanner taking the remaining four companies to the island in the river where Confederate prisoners were being held. Along with other Union regiments the 123rd fell to guarding military stores and POW's.

Influxes of prisoners ebbed and flowed with the skirmishing before Chattanooga. Then there were the daily batches of deserters coming into the Union lines. "we have from one to three hundred prisoners Come in most evry day," Private James Dickenson (Co. E) wrote his parents, "we have a lot of them to guard evry day they look rough and nasty as the devil they are most start naked" Private Horace Tooley (Co. K) was detailed to work on the boat building but took some time to chat with the POW's, "they say that they do not expect to whip us but are going to hold out as long as possible they are all ragged and nasty" One of the prisoners chatted up Sergeant John Gourlie about some new boots Gourlie had received from home, he writing his sister, "A Reb prisoner offered me $150 in Confederate script for them but as I had a sufficient quantity of old newspapers on hand for all necessary use when I wanted to Sh— Shave I declined the offer." As to the war and new duty station, Private Welch told his aunt and uncle, "all the duty we do is to guard prisoner and deserters from the rebel army they come into our lines every day sometimes twenty or thirty together they all say the next battle will decide this war if Bragg gets defeated they say that his entire army will disband if that is true you will hear of Bragg army disbanding one month from now for Gen Grant will whip them just as shure as he did Pemberton's army at Vicksburg. he is a General that fights to whip and we all have confidence that he will whip the rebel army the next time he fight's them"[270]

For that coming battle more troops were brought into the theatre. Union Major General William T. Sherman arrived at Bridgeport with elements of the 15th and 17th Corps, 17,000 men, during the middle of November. The soldiers moved through the rail head marching on to Chattanooga as the 123rd New York soldiers looked on. Corporal Rice Bull was now back with Company D after recovering from his Chancellorsville wounds. He noticed that the eastern and western troops were definitely different in dress and attitude. "[The western soldiers] all wore large army hats instead of caps, they were very carelessly dressed both officers and men and marched in a very irregular way seemingly not caring to keep all closed up or go in any regular order. These were faults we had been especially taught to avoid." As the soldiers passed bantering began with Sherman's veterans joking that the Potomac veterans were too neat and tidy to be soldiers. To Bull the differences between east and west went all the way to the top of command. "In the east our Generals, as a rule, made a great military show. They have large brilliantly dressed staffs who follow after the General, who himself is in full military uniform with sash, sword and all the buttons allowed his rank. The staff is followed by an escort of Cavalrymen varying in number according to the rank and command of the officer they follow...In the Western Army you seldom see anything of this, they seem to avoid show of any kind and the General officers can hardly be discerned by one not knowing them."[271]

Grant made his move to knock Confederate General Bragg's army away from Chattanooga in the latter part of November. On the 23rd forward Rebel units were overrun in the center and on the 24th General Hooker with his former Army of the Potomac veterans (minus the 1st Division 12th Corps) took Lookout Mountain in a battle where the men fought in a heavy fog along the peak. The finale came on the 25th when an assault up the slopes of the center broke the Confederate lines. Bragg didn't get his army back into some semblance of order until he was 30 miles into Georgia.

Over 4,000 prisoners were taken during the assault and resulting chase. These Southerners now flooded back into the Bridgeport area to be processed through the POW camp on Long Island and then shipped north. Lt. Cruikshank walked over the pontoon bridge to the island to see the prisoners. "They are all discouraged and want the War to close. The first question I was asked by them was, 'Has General Bragg stopped running yet?'"[272]

"the battle of Chickamauga has been fought over again the battle come out much different from what it did the other time," Private Welch wrote his brother John, "there is 6500 rebels at this place now and 200 officer's I think that Bragg's army is pretty well played out and I also think that this rebelion is about gone up" Also going up after the combat to relieve Chattanooga were the Westerners' opinion of the Eastern soldiers. Hooker's command had impressed everyone with their taking of Lookout Mountain. This pleased Sergeant John Gourlie a lot. "You do not now hear the western soldiers say that the Eastern Troops cannot fight."[273]

Yet several soldiers in the 123rd New York were sending letters home saying *do not fight*. Younger siblings were writing their brothers about the increased bounty being offered for enlisting or the prospect of the draft and the older, wiser veterans were having none of it. Sergeant Gourlie made his feelings clear to his brother. "I advice you to stay at home if their is a possibility of doing so, because, in the 1st place our family has already one Representative in the field, who, I flatter myself has always and is still doing his duty and you are needed at home it is not the men alone who fight the battles that are doing all in this war. In the 2nd place let some of our Patriotic neighbors who have no Representative here send. If you are drafted pay the $300. if that is Repealed and you cannot get excused on account of your ankle hire a substitute."[274]

Private Horace Tooley was adamant against his brothers Samuel or Eber enlisting. "I hope they will draft 300,000 and send them in to the field as quick as they can but I hope you or Eber will not have to come do not think of the Bounty that is nothing at all you would be sorry if you could get $5,000 to come" Horace followed with another warning to Samuel just a week later, "Sam do not enlist if Eber is not there they can not Draft you and I would stand the draft first"[275]

Of the four Tooley brothers there were two already in the 123rd New York, Horace and William, both in Company K. Now a tag-team of letters started going home from the Bridgeport front to the younger brothers smitten with the far off war. William took his turn to bend Sam's ear. "I would be very sorry to have you enlist but still it would be better than to be drafted...I noticed in the Granville Register that that town lacked but seventeen of having their quota filled so I think there is a fair prospect of their getting them by Volunteering I hope they will & all other towns"[276]

It was not that the soldiers of the 123rd New York did not intend to fight, it was that they did not want to see their younger brothers undergo all that they had already seen, nor their parents suffer the leaving of another son. William Tooley had been captured at Chancellorsville, paroled, and spent some five months in a Union parole camp near Washington waiting to be exchanged. In August of 1863 he wrote his mother, "you seem to think that I am going to desert But you need not have any fears about that for if I dont get out of the service untill I desert you may rest asured that you will have one son in the Service while he lives for I could never endure the many insults and the name of deserter which would be branded upon me all my life I mean to do my duty as a soldier untill my term expires if it ever does." Four days later William wrote to his brother Eber from the parole camp. "if I were up there in your place & were drafted and could raise the money I should give it instead of comeing down here you would be the gainer in the long run for two or three years in virginia would ruin your health even if you lived to return...dont come down here if you can get rid of it tell them you have been sun struck & can not stand the heat that will clear you..."[277]

At Bridgeport Private Welch even penned some thoughts on the draft to his aunt and uncle. Seeing the war as ending soon with Bragg's defeat he didn't think they'd need many new soldiers "but I guess they will fetch out a few this time still I hope not I dont want to see any one forced into this war its bad enough to come volentairly but I suppose if ther is not volenteer's enough they will have to enforce the draft."[278]

The 123rd New York did need new recruits to fill its ranks. In October when Corporal Bull returned to Company D he found about 60 soldiers present. Company H at this time had 61 in its ranks. But these figures do not account for soldiers sick or on detached service. For the quarterly report that ended December 31st, 1863 Company H had 47 effectives (officers & men) as 3 were on detached service and 11 were listed as sick.[279] It can be estimated from these figures that the 123rd New York at Bridgeport was around 500 effectives. They were now to get a supply of veteran soldiers from an unexpected source, the 145th New York.

Shenanigans might be the best way to describe the way the 145th New York was brought into being and run. Raised in New York City in the summer of 1862 the 145th NY had a large amount of quick deserters, men solely there for the bounty money. Actions by the officers did nothing to help instill discipline. It appears 145th Colonel Edward Price obtained his commission in a round-about way after being first refused one. Another strike on the officers came when Lt. Colonel Roswell Van Wagenen took some of the enlisted men out to a saloon. Use of soldiers as servants without reimbursement and absence without leave were just some of the other charges. By October 11th, 1863 General Williams at 1st Division Headquarters at Decherd, Tennessee cut the orders. "Colonel and lieutenant-colonel of the One hundred and forty-fifth will be arrested on their arrival here." Captain Samuel Allen commanded the regiment for the next two months as decisions were made as to its future. There were good men in the unit but it now became a question of keeping the 145th together. In his January report for the 1st

Division, 12th Corps, General Williams states: "Pursuant to orders from the War Department one regiment, the One hundred and forty-fifth New York Volunteers, has been disbanded, the commissioned officers and surplus non-commissioned officers mustered out, and the privates transferred to other New York regiments in the division."[280] Gaining added personnel from the breakup were the 107th, 123rd and 150th.

Forty men transferred into the 123rd NewYork from the 145th New York in late December as follows: Company E, 2; Company F, 8; and Company H, 30. Although forty were listed, one, Private Benjamin Ransom, left the regiment within days as he was transferred into the Veteran Reserve Corps on January 15th, 1864. So there were 29 transfers into Company H.[281] Recruiting back in Washington County was also being pushed, thirteen officers and sergeants of the 123rd New York having gone back home to aid in the process over the winter. Seventeen additional recruits would filter into the unit by spring from Cambridge, Hartford and Whitehall in Washington County, but also from Troy and one recruit from Schenectady. The recruits mainly enlisted in Companies C and E so it appears the 145th transfers were distributed to better balance the command.

Such a large influx into Company H presented issues with intergrating them into the unit. By mid-January Lt. Robert Cruikshank, commanding Company H, had 74 non-commisioned officers and privates to attend too. Ordnance reports for Company H show seven "Springfield Rifled Muskets" issued to the company during December, with another 22 "worn" Springfields issued by January 22nd, 1864. This totals 29, and Cruikshank must have sought permission from Lt. Colonel Rogers for what happened next as the men had target practice. The company's First Quarter Ordnance Report of 1864 shows 1,571 rounds expended "In practice firing." At the end of December the company had on hand 1,318 rounds ".574 calibre" ammunition and 2,360 percussion caps. An additional 800 rounds were issued with the seven muskets. Another 1,023 rounds were issued in

January with the 22 Springfields, for a total of 3,141 rounds on hand.²⁸² It appears they simply divided the total by two to arrive at the amount to expend. Each soldier on the line would have had 21 rounds to fire (74 men). One has to assume it would have been in an organized way with Cruikshank paying attention to unit timing and response to orders as the commands were given. On January 26th Corporal Clark McLean left camp with two comrades to go hunting, on returning that afternoon he "found the regt shooting at a target." McLean also notes that two months later three companies of the 123rd were target practicing again.²⁸³ Being able to hit a target would have been emphasized but also being one with the unit in action. They probably did a few volleys in mass then went into skirmish formation. It was important that the men would all be able to work together once "the elephant" charged.

But warfare seemed far away as Christmas arrived. "Games of [baseball] and hunting and fishing are all the go now," Corporal McLean wrote, "All of us are enjoying ourselves tip top this winter. We have not enough sick in the Regt. to have a hospital while last Christmas our sick list numbered nearly a hundred." Private Horace Tooley was thinking of home life, writing his parents. "I wish I was there to take a Sleigh ride once more...I would like to be there New Years to eat some Oysters with father but hard Bread will have to do me this year and I hope be fore an other to be at home" Horace also had some wishes to his brother as to the holiday meals. "I wish we had some of that fresh pork it would be very nice we get plenty of fresh beef but I can not eat it it is so tough So I am obliged to eat salt pork or stinking Bacon."²⁸⁴ The running joke among the soldiers concerning the beef issue was, since the cattle were herded to the army, it was "dried on the hoof." A search of the letters at this period shows no specific mention as to the enlisted men's meals on Christmas so it was probably their standard fare, salt pork and hardtack.

Christmas meals for the officers were an entirely different affair. Officers paid for their fare while in camp but it still must have rankled an enlisted soldier to look into the officer's mess tent. Cruikshank records their Christmas dinner (lunch) consisted of roast ham, mashed potatoes, tomatoes, pickles, fresh peach sauce, cheese, apple pie, biscuits and three kinds of cake: fruit, gold and pound. Supper was a larger affair with all the 123rd officers present. On the table were roast goose and turkey, potatoes, bread with butter, cakes, pies, grapes and raisins. Cruikshank chose to decline the after meal cordials of champagne and cigars. The gathering broke up at 11 p.m. The Christmas meal might have been catered. At the end of November the 123rd officers that had been recently promoted gave a dinner at Bridgeport for the other officers of the regiment with a Nashville caterer handling all the arrangements.[285]

Uncle Sam was also doing some catering. Since arriving at Bridgeport the Union army had taken on the roll of feeding Southern refugees. They flocked to the railroad stations by the thousands, mainly women and children, for the chance of a meal to prevent starvation. Soldiers of the 123rd New York stood their watches and gazed out at the huddled groups around the Federal fortifications. "Refugees keep pouring in from the front. The poorest looking creatures you ever see. The people North can let the Sandwich Islands alone for awhile and turn their attention to the white heathens here," Corporal McLean wrote his father, adding with some disgust that the whites weren't doing anything but living on government handouts. "The Colored people are a great deal more comportable. They are on the goin continually, find something to do. They are the only ones who make pies & hoecakes for the soldiers. The longer the white women live here the longer & leaner they grow. I don't believe there will be enough left of them by spring to make a shadow."[286]

"Our Government is feeding large numbers of Southern people," Lt. Cruikshank wrote his wife Mary, "not the men, for most of them are in the Southern army, but the wives and children of those who are fighting us...I thank God that our lot was cast in a Northern state where there are no slaves nor poor people. You never saw such poverty, there is none in the country at the North." In a letter to his wife two weeks later the northern Lieutenant ends it, "The curse of slavery shows itself in everything here."[287]

Civilians eating into the rations arriving for the army in Chattanooga could not be tolerated for long. By mid-November railroad passes to Nashville were being issued to those seeking sustenance. They could be supplied much easier in the rear without draining meals from the combat troops. But the trip north over the railroad must have frightened a few. Private Welch went in a squad of four men up to Nashville at this time transporting Rebel prisoners. The 125 mile train ride up and back over five days was quite the experience. "we had very bad luck getting along the cars run off the track every little while the train just ahead of us run off from a bridge and killed six negro soldier's. the train that I was on run off twice but no one was killed. the road is very much out of repair...."[288]

It wasn't just military cargo rolling back south to Bridgeport from Nashville. Yankee entrepreneurial spirit saw business opportunity among the thousands of thirsty, hungry and bored soldiers all along the rail line to Chattanooga. Newspapers, magazines, and photos of scantily-clad women could all bring good prices but also various foodstuffs to brighten a private's palate. One item was a sure-fire seller and could get a peddler top dollar: whiskey. While the military sought to control access to alcohol it still found its way to the front areas. And woe to the Yankee sutler that insulted a 123rd New York soldier walking his post. Sergeant Morhous relates an incident at this time. A civilian arrived at Bridgeport and wheeled an oak barrel full of whiskey onto the steamboat landing platform. The soldier on guard offered to watch it for the peddler but received a curt reply that no one in uniform was to be trusted. Putting the barrel up against a post the man wrapped a blanket around himself and slept the night sitting atop the barrel. When the guard went off duty he returned to camp, mentioned the insult and some of his comrades decided to correct the situation. When the peddler awoke the next morning he got off the barrel and went to move it only to discover it was empty. A one-inch hole had been bored with a hand auger from underneath the wooden platform into the barrel, the soldiers catching what they wanted in pails then letting the rest run out. "He made no inquiries, for he knew it would be useless, but went directly on board the boat amid the laughing and jeering of the soldiers."[289]

A sense of the demand for whiskey can be seen in the opportunity a peddler offered 1st Lt. Robert Cruikshank. Working in the Commissary Department at the rail head, Cruikshank had the authority to purchase all the whiskey he wanted at a dollar a gallon. Cruikshank just had to obtain the alcohol, the peddler offered to do all the work of reducing the whiskey and bottling it. At $2 a bottle the man was certain he could sell everything produced, he'd split the profits 50-50 and estimated Cruikshank's cut would be $410 *a day*. This wasn't a surprise to the 123rd officer, he'd been hearing about clandestine booze operations. One he knew about involved a fireman on the railroad smuggling cases of whiskey in the water tank of the engine. But the officer wasn't biting. "I thought a good name and clear conscience better than a fortune and refused to have anything to do with the business."[290]

Colonel McDougall returned from his home leave to the 123rd New York at this time much to the dismay of Private Welch. "Col. McDougal has got back to the regt. he met with a very poor welcome I do not believe there was a man in the regiment that was glad to see him we all like Col Roger's much better than we do him he is altogether to national to much of an old granny as the boy's style him." Yet Corporal McLean presents a different picture of the commander, saying of the colonel's return, "He was feeling well and in good humor."[291]

There was dismay throughout the unit when word came through they were to relieve a regiment doing duty along the railroad. Bridgeport was a nice posting for the men, good quarters, steady work to keep them active and plenty of food (plus sundry beverages). Yet January 6th, 1864 found them on cars going back towards Nashville about forty-five miles. They encamped at Elk River on the 7th to guard the bridge across the river and the railroad water tower at Estill Springs about a mile and a half further up the rail line. Company E was stationed at the water tank, Company F took command of the stockade guarding the railroad bridge and the rest of the 123rd New York filed into the vacated huts of the former regiment. Not all the soldiers of the 123rd New York were in this movement as several men detailed for boat work at Bridgeport remained behind. Posting to Elk River at first looked dismal as the 123rd soldiers had to spend three days using tents in the cold and undergo a light snow before the 2nd Massachusetts they were to relieve shipped out. "Stormy day, rain and snow" Corporal McLean noted in his diary, "Makes us think of the dead beats at home warming their shins by the stove."[292]

    Dismay quickly turned to nodding approval once the men had better quarters and settled into their routine. The shanties were in good condition with brick fireplaces, the weather, while cold at times, often was fairly warm with only scattered snow showers. "The picket duty here is quite heavy," Corporal McLean writes, "Nothing else to do but watch for guerillas…There is quite the fort here, mans six guns." Private Welch thought it was a great location. "Elk River is the finest stream that I ever saw its water is clear and crystal we are going to get some canoes if we stay here long enough and then we will have great sport. we will live an Indian's life almost complete and if we get hold of any of these guerillas we will try our hands at scalping a little." That was the one hassle with the location, it was hostile and dangerous territory once away from the railroad. "The guerillas are raising the devil, shooting men and burning houses and tearing up railroads," Corporal McLean notes, adding that the region was suffering. "Houses mostly deserted, fences gone, and the marks of war plainly visible."[293]

Brutal reality struck the regiment within days when Private Nathan Lamphier (Co. A) was shot through the heart the night of January 12th while standing picket near Winchester Springs, Tennessee. He was part of a group of 100 soldiers that Lt. Colonel Rogers was taking on an overnight sweep of the area to the west of Elk River Bridge. After the crack of the rifle the guerrilla fled into the dark but tripped, dropping his gun. The Rebel had etched his name on the rifle so the regiment knew who to look for and, not finding him immediately, they brought in the killer's father and brother. The soldiers of the 123rd New York also turned their attention to the little hamlet of Winchester Springs. "I understand that in that vicinity there is not much property that would burn left," Lt. Cruikshank wrote his wife. Private Lamphier was buried at the bridge with Corporal McLean noting, "The boys felt bad in his company as he was liked by them all."[294]

Private Welch was a tad put out that he had missed the expedition under Rogers due to guard duty in camp. So on the 14th he and Private Andrew Harris (Co. K) went out of camp four miles poking around for guerrillas. No action for the soldiers but plenty of talking and debates with the locals. "the citizen's are most all strong sucesh but they are very kind to us and use us very well. the girls are all sucesh and we have some pretty strong and lively arguments with them, but I must own that we cannot get much the start of them and say what we will we can't convince them that the South has done wrong."[295]

A larger expedition, to seek forage as well as guerrillas over fifteen days, was planned to leave camp January 29th for Lincoln County, Tennessee. This was the county due west of Franklin County and meant a march of some 40 miles one way. "They have orders to show no mercy to people who harbor guerrillas & burn all houses where they may be found," Corporal McLean said of the expedition, adding that Lincoln County "has been a nest for guerrillas for a long time."[296] Five companies under Colonel McDougall were issued marching orders while the remaining five would continue guarding the bridge, water tower and railroad. The day before leaving Private William Tooley wrote his brother Eber as to tensions rising in the regiment over the colonel.

"Col McDougall commands the expedition the men are fast looseing their confidence in him his actions are very curious sometimes the other night he dug us out of bed at One Oclock made us fall in under arms and marched us out into the fort and Stacked our arms you can imagine how provoked we were when we found that all he wanted of us was to move camp a few rods his orders were to have our cabins and everything belonging to us cleared before daylight as everything found there at that time would be burned so we went back to our tents and stopped untill day light then done our work which suited him just as well but he was drunk and didnt know what else to do so he got us up so you can see the reason why we are loosing confidence in him as a commander but do not say any thing about it for any sutch thing said up there goes prety fast"[297]

Leaving Elk River Bridge at 7 a.m. Companies A, E, G, H and K of the 123rd New York made 15 miles on the 29th under a warm sun. Rain began the next day as camp was broken at 6 a.m. but the soldiers had ponchos and rubber blankets so the weather was shrugged off. They put another 20 miles on their boots toward Fayetteville, Tennessee. Rolling farmland garnered a few hills as they passed through Fayetteville and moved on another eight miles to Booneshill. Here the 123rd New York set up camp at a brick schoolhouse and surrounding grounds. Swan Creek was nearby to provide water. Rounding up of civilians for questioning and possible arrest began immediately.

A "Dr. Wood" at Booneshill was one of the first shackled. He was arrested for involvement in guerrilla warfare to be forwarded to Nashville for trial. Houses in the area were searched by squads of soldiers with "considerable evidence against guerrillas" being found according to Lt. Cruikshank. On February 3rd several prisoners were taken. One that escaped, McAfee, had his personal property seized and hauled into camp by the wagons the regiment brought along. The radius expanded from the camp with houses three miles out searched. Finding women and bunkloads of children became common but the local men had fled to the woods. Night movements of companies from the 123rd began in an effort to run down guerrillas. Quick skirmishes with fleeing figures became the norm.[298]

February 8th two brothers, 20 and 22 years old, were seen hiding in some woods and brought in by a patrol. The younger man was frightened and told Colonel McDougall all about the criminal activity of the guerrillas. The band would rob a person then tie the victim to a tree and force one of the brothers to shoot him. A nearby planter was given as the ring leader. Lt. Jerome Rice (Co. G) commanded the squad sent to arrest the planter plus search the residence for a specific amount of money in Confederate and United States currency taken from a man murdered weeks before. The money was found and the planter brought in under arrest.[299]

Information filtered into camp concerning a raiding party of mounted guerrillas to be moving through the area the night of February 11th. McDougall ordered Lt. Cruikshank to take forty men and seal off the crossroads where the enemy were to come through. Not certain as to which road the guerrillas would ride in on, Cruikshank split his force with ten soldiers to each road. This could have been a disaster in the making as the enemy force was much larger than thought, numbering seventy. Sounds of cavalry moving in the distance were heard about 1 o'clock by one of the squads but nothing could be seen. In the early morning as they returned to camp they discovered a bridle path crossing the road near a house. Cruikshank enquired of the owners if they had heard any cavalry the night before and was stunned to be told that at least seventy guerrillas had passed. With his force split as it was, the Lieutenant had sobering thoughts as to the result. "Had they come our way there would not have been many of us left to tell the tale."[300]

A wagon train arrived at Booneshill on the 12th bringing mail. On February 13th nine prisoners were shipped out to be forwarded to Nashville for trial. Another two guerrillas came in and surrendered the next day. "there was plenty of corn & guerrillas too," Private William Tooley wrote his brother Sam about Booneshill, "captured quite a number of them there are very few Union men there"[301]

Those few were happy to see a Yankee in the doorway. Families faithful to the United States knew they were in the wrong locale so took advantage of the blue uniformed soldiers. Lt. Cruikshank spent a pleasant day on the 16th with a squad of men and wagons moving two families to the camp as they wished to go north. The soldiers traveled out five miles to be greeted warmly by the civilians. "They said we were the first Union soldiers they had seen and that they were honored by our call." After an ample feast that included beefsteak, chicken pie, corn bread, maple syrup and custard pie the families belongings were loaded and everyone headed back to camp. "These people are of Union sentiment but will not take part in the War," Cruikshank noted, "They keep no slaves, being very much opposed to slavery."[302]

What was supposed to be a fifteen day expedititon turned into twenty-two. The soldiers were not back to Elk River until February 19th. Their excursion resulted in the capture of fourteen guerrillas, many wagon loads of provisions and the seizure of nineteen horses and forty mules. Even after making the effort to pacify the Booneshill region Lt. Cruikshank felt lawlessness would still reign. Watching the 123rd New York soldiers leave was the brother of a man murdered by the guerrillas. "The brother is well armed and says he will shoot them like dogs when he meets any of them. Another man was taken from his home at night, murdered, and his body thrown into the river. It was recovered afterward and identified by his family."[303]

Cruikshank was glad to be back at Elk River "and not to be on the lookout all of the time for some one who we may expect is ready to put a bullet through any of us. That was the way we felt at Boons Hill."[304]

Another incident with Colonel McDougall occurred while the soldiers were at Booneshill with Cruikshank right in the middle of it. After the search of a house under Lt. Cruikshank's personnel direction the owner complained of theft. A search of the soldiers turned up some stolen knives and forks whereupon Colonel McDougall laid into Lt. Cruikshank telling him he was not fit to be an officer. Jaws must have dropped at this. The Lieutenant had a large detachment of soldiers to oversee plus make sure no one fled from the house while it was being searched. As the Colonel had upset the enlisted personnel by dragging them out of bed for foolishness, he now upset the officer ranks in his regiment with what they saw as an unjust accusation. After a couple weeks tempers cooled with Cruikshank writing his wife, "The Colonel is over his passion toward me and is more pleasant than is natural for him. He often lets his temper run away with his judgment. I will not resign if I can in any way get on with him. He has no cause to find fault with me...He has had trouble with three other officers in the Regiment and they are the best, Capt. Geo. R. Hall, Captain H. C. Warren and Lieutenant Geo. Robertson."[305]

Captain George Hall commanded Company E that was stationed at Estill Springs, a mile or two up the railroad from Elk River Bridge. Standard routine would see patrols sent out along the tracks for three miles to meet patrols sent south from Tullahoma. Captain Hall would have had three squads made up with the second squad sent out about the time the first squad reached its turn around point. The patrols would pass one another at one-and-a-half miles with the third squad leaving when the first returned. As Hall only had forty some men in Company E for duty it appears his "squads" were only two or three men. Moving towards his little detachment in mid-March were 110 mounted Rebels. They rode out of the Hillsboro, Tennessee, area, twelve miles to the east of Estill Springs, and train wrecking was their goal. Common policy for Union Military Railroad engineers was to run three trains, one right behind the other separated by several minutes, on the run from Nashville to Bridgeport.

With any luck the raiders would derail all three for good profit and plunder.

At 1 p.m. on March 16th, 1864 a local citizen came into Captain Hall's camp to report a large column of cavalry moving on the railroad just to the north. This also coincided with a patrol not returning at the regular time. Hall could not just set out in pursuit as the water tower had to be protected. He therefore contacted Major Tanner at Elk River Bridge requesting additional soldiers to protect his assigned position. This took time, it wasn't until after 4 p.m. that Hall set out along the tracks marching north with 40 soldiers of Company E. After about a mile and a half the men saw a train in the distance coming from Tullahoma. With loud grinding noises and a thump it went off the tracks about a half-mile in front of the Company E skirmishers. Rapid, distinct rifle fire could then be heard. Captain Hall filed his men into the woods to the right side of the tracks and advanced on the run.

Like a dropped running bison the steaming engine had skidded into the ground to the side of the tracks. Three cars of hay that had flipped were burning. Passengers on the train were standing along the tracks hands in the air as the guerrillas went through their pockets for watches and money. Then they saw the 123rd soldiers advancing. "I came up on their flank," Captain Hall reported, "opening upon them, which was returned by them, but they made no stand of any account; formed line of battle twice, but as soon as we fired upon them they turned and ran. I pursued them about one-and-a-half miles, when my men became so much exhausted that further pursuit would have been useless..." During the skirmish the 123rd soldiers killed two of the raiders and wounded another while losing no men.

Returning to the train the soldiers put out the fire and tried to assist the wounded. One man, the black brakeman on the train, had been murdered, another black and a white passenger seriously wounded. Two soldiers of the 1st Michigan Engineers were wounded. Over the next hour several soldiers that had been captured and driven from the train by the Rebels wandered back in: two officers of the 20th Connecticut, seven soldiers of the 27th Indiana and two of Captain Hall's men that had been on the missing patrol. After taking any valuables or money the guerrillas had turned them loose. As the scene was being cleaned up the following two trains were flagged to a stop behind the wreckage. For the first train only the three burnt cars were a loss as the engine was not badly damaged. Hall reported capturing three saddles and one carbine. Witnesses said that the horses the attackers rode were branded "C.S."[306]

But were the raiders legitimate Confederate calvary or guerrillas out for plunder? Private Welch was of the opinion that they were simply guerrillas, and says that within the week Union cavalry had captured thirty of the raiders. "they were either hung or shot after they were captured. there is no mercy shown a guerilla if he is taken and its not likely they will show us much mercy if they take us. the boy's all say they will never be taken alive by a guerilla for my part I prefer death by shooting instead of hanging so I shall never surrender to one of these low lived cowardly guerilas. I saw a tree when we were out to Boon's Hill where they had hung three [Union soldiers] they threw a rope over a limb and drew them up as they would so many dog's."[307]

Payback was in the offering. Colonel McDougall was at military court proceedings in Nashville deciding whether to hang the Booneshill prisoners the 123rd New York had brought in during their expedition. Lt. Cruikshank heard that the gavel brought the noose for several and was glad. "Those men are not soldiers but a band of robbers and murderers. They don't mind whether a man is a Union or a Confederate, if he has money they will take it. They commit crime on the Confederate people and then the Union soldiers are charged with it. I do not intend ever to fall into their hands."[308]

Spring weather filtered into the region as the soldiers continued guarding the railroad. Every Sunday would see inspection of the men and camp. Falling in at 9 a.m., the officers of the companies went over the uniforms, rifles and gear of their charges. Then the living quarters were inspected, followed by the cleaning of the camp. Lieutenant Cruikshank was generally proud of the soldiers in Company H but he finally had enough of one soldier. "One man kept himself so filthy I made a detail take him to the creek and wash him and put clean clothes on him. When he returned the men pretended they did not know him and when introduced by the men who had washed him, they all shook hands with him, congratulating him on his good appearance. He has not had to be washed the second time. There is no shirking here."[309]

No shirking but a few parties. Corporal McLean plus some other soldiers spent one afternoon touring the local community. "We visited a number of houses. Was treated good. Heard the young ladies play on pianos and sing the 'Bonnie Blue Flag' etc." Such visits got McLean thinking of home, "Warm weather, moonlight evenings which we are losing by not having a chance to improve them by riding out to shindigs, etc." He turned to filling his free time by perusing Victor Hugo's *Les Miserables*. His reading was interrupted one afternoon as a "sutlar brought down some ale and lager and we have had a good load all day. There is considerable amount of noise on account of it. Boys will drink ale as a cat will milk." Within two weeks of the ale fest Colonel McDougall shut down the sutler which didn't sit well with the soldiers. "He thinks officers can roll in whiskey and beer but enlisted men must not be permitted to get a taste of lager. Poor rule that wont work both ways."[310]

At this time new rules arrived from the War Department that must have had soldiers stupified. "Circular No. 10 – Series of 1864" dropped onto field desks ordering the renumbering of blank forms. "Property Accountability" forms change thus: 1(g.) is now 1(a.); 1(a.) is now 1(b.); 1(c-d.) is now 1(e.); 3(a.) is now 7; 5 now 8; 12 now 14. It goes on for 28 forms. Under "Money Accountability" seven forms are renumbered, "Personnel" sees ten forms, "Material" five forms and "Inspection" eight forms. This was to "better adopt [the forms] to the present wants of the service" and adds that all unserviceable ordnance is now to be entered on forms in red ink.³¹¹ Headquarter clerks must have gone out into the woods to bang their heads against trees.

Churning steam pistons began to bring larger amounts of freight south to Chattanooga; more mules and horses, more ordnance and supplies of all sorts. Soldiers were recalled from their furloughs. As April days went by it was clear some sort of movement would begin soon and the scuttlebutt started. Corporal McLean found the talk interesting but not very informative, "all kinds of rumors afloat in regard to our summer travels it is curious and amusing to hear the different stories which circulate through the camp." Sergeant Lorenzo Coy (Co. K) found time to start reading *Nicholas Nickleby* by Charles Dickens. "If this work is a fair specimen of Dickens' works, he will be a favorite author of mine."³¹²

Worries were once again on the minds of older brothers in the 123rd New York concerning their younger brothers and the war. Corporal McLean wrote his father with the perfect solution, as he saw it, to his brother Henry's desire to be a soldier. "We hear that the Militia is to be called out for 100 days. I hope so. Now if Henry has any idea of enlisting let him go for 100 days with the Militia. They wont see fighting & will have a comparitively easy time & he will see enough so he will never enlist again."³¹³

What about reenlisting for the soldiers of the 123rd New York? During the winter the 46th Pennsylvania, 5th Connecticut and 3rd Maryland had reenlisted, getting a bounty, month furlough and "Veteran Volunteer" titles. As spring came on attention turned to getting the 123rd New York to reup for the duration of the war. "there is a good deal said in the regt about reenlisting," Private Henry Welch noted in April, "the bounty offered is some over eleven hundred dollar's, we can reenlist when we have served about one month more I think that a good many of the boy's will go in for another term as for myself I think that I will see my free paper's before I bind myself again. three year's is about all I can afford to soldier it."³¹⁴

The original three year contract was the limit for the men of the 123rd New York. "You need not have any concern about my reenlisting if I live my time out," Private Artemus Harrington told his parents, "I am coming home first and see what I like for a while and if I think it best it will be time enough then." Efforts back in Washington County to raise money as an inducement to veteran the regiment also fell on deaf ears. Private William Tooley states, "We hear the County is raising money for the purpose of renlisting this regiment but they might as well let it alone for Washington Co. is not worth enough to veteran this regiment and I hope they will not try it."[315] The soldiers of the 123rd New York would serve their three years but then it was the duty of others to step forward for the Republic.

As for others wanting to enlist, Private Tooley was having a hard time trying to find a solution for his brother Eber who seems to have fallen into a depression. "I am very sorry to learn that you have allowed sutch ideas a place in your head indeed I cant express with pen & ink the regret that I feel at your getting discouraged there at home surrounded by friends and everything for your comfort...perhaps you will never be satisfied untill you enlist but I wish you might be contented to stay there I cannot advise you to enlist for I know you would regret it after although your choice of enlisting in heavy artillery would be mine if I were going to enlist again..." William suggests his brother find a good gal and marry then rent a farm to work. One can picture the older brother sitting in camp, a quill in one hand, running the other hand over his head again and again in desperation to convey military life. He finally pens, "when you become a soldier you have to dispence with all freedom to act for yourself and know nothing except to Obey Orders and satisfy every whim of all and every low pupy who gets an office in the service and they are many we have officers that when they were at home were the lowest specimens of humanity in the country who would arrest you and have you punished if you did not treat them with all the respect due the president or the king of England."[316]

The men probably learned of the possible calling out of the state militia from the weekly papers sent from Washington County. Other publications also were popular such as the *N.Y. Evangelist* and *Christian Advocate and Journal*. Prayer meetings and sermons filled Sundays and even free time during the week. Sergeant Coy spent one Sunday listening to two sermons, on another Sunday he took to the woods for reflection. "In the morning went out into the woods and finding a chrysalie of the butterfly sat down and asked myself if that was not a type of ressurection of the body of man, or is it a type of the Restoration of all things. In the afternoon I enjoyed myself well in the woods, reading my Savior's works as recorded by St. Mathew, 2nd and 3rd chap., and in prayer."[317]

Private Horace Tooley was praying for some mail from home, writing his brother, "Sam any thing you can write will be interesting to me a letter any time is very acceptable to me from home but I am very lonely when I do not get any I know I write a very poor letter but I do the best I can and I hope that the time is not far distant when I can talk fase to fase to you..." Horace then adds a suggestion for his brother to write back to him about. "where does the prety Baker Girls live this summer..."[318]

Word came to the men that the 11th and 12th Corps were to be consolidated into the 20th Corps under the command of General Hooker. This, naturally, was not viewed favorably by the soldiers of the 123rd New York who felt they and the other regiments of the 12th had earned a good name for the Corps. "The record of the 12th Corps has been a noble one," Sergeant Coy noted in his diary.[319] In early April the 123rd New York found themselves part of the 1st Brigade, 1st Division, 20th Corps. The 12th Corps insignia would be the 20th Corps badge so the soldiers of the 123rd New York maintained their red stars. The 20th Corps would be part of the Army of the Cumberland, commanded by General George Thomas. General William T. Sherman would be overall commander of the armies around Chattanooga and the coming spring movement.

The campaign season of 1864 was beginning to come to the forefront of everyone's mind, North and South. Sergeant Coy articulated to his wife Sarah just what was riding on the coming combat in the woods and heat of a Georgia summer. "The south will hold out as long as they can in order to see the result of the election for President the coming fall. If Lincoln should be re-elected, they will disburse and at once give up the contest as hopeless. If the loyal men of the north and the west could be made to see the case as it really is and act accordingly, the cause of the union would be triumphant. If they knew that every copperhead vote and speach will require the life of a union soldier as assuredly it will, I know that sympathy for the brave men who are standing between them and ruin would rally them as one man to their country's cause...The welfare of the nation and the lives of thousands of brave and true men will be the momentous stake to be decided by the votes of the Free men of the Nation. Oh! That all party strife and animosity might be buried and that all would wish and seek the highest interest of their country instead of place and power."[320]

Chapter 8
The Running Fight to Atlanta

It wasn't the bullet but the ballot box. Whereas Southerners had seen victory on the horizon for the first couple of years via military action, minds were now seeing hope in the coming 1864 presidential election. If they could hold out until Lincoln was tossed out of office it was felt they would be able to negotiate an end to the war. An end where the Confederacy burst forth as a nation and the shackles remained on the slaves.

Local and congressional elections in the North had swung Republican or Democrat with the ebb and flow of military success for the first three years of the war. Weekly papers in Washington County, and newspapers across the nation, were openly partisan as to their politics. The *Salem Press* waxed happy after the fall 1862 elections when Democrats made big gains in Congress and state houses. "Abolitionism Rebuked! Emancipation Condemned!" ran their headlines. They weren't so sanguine after the 1863 elections. New York Governor Horatio Seymour, Democrat, helped to contribute to the Republican take over of the state legislature that year by his veto of a soldiers voting bill. This played to the Republican weeklies in Washington County. "The Democrats say that Soldiers in the Army Have No Right to Vote" was the headline in the October 16th, 1863 *Granville Register*. Republican veto-proof majorities in the New York legislature allowed a bill for soldiers sufferage to be moved. A state constitutional amendment allowing soldiers to vote in the field was put to the electorate in March, 1864, and passed, taking effect immediately. Soldiers of the 123rd New York were well aware of all the political manuvering going on back home concerning their rights. Private Henry Welch gave vent to his thoughts at this time in a letter to his father. "I suppose they think that the soldiers if allowed to vote would not support the copperhead party very strongly I hardly think they would. I would like to ask them if the soldiers who are fighting to sustain the government had not ought to vote who had."[321]

Corporal Clark McLean wanted to carry it a lot further than asking questions, noting in his diary, "The '[Washington] County Post' reached us today with the number of votes that were cast against allowing soldiers to vote. We know about who they are. I wish our regt was at home to put some of them out of the way. I would help hang one of them as quickly as help shoot a rebel soldier. The soldiers have some courage and honor but the copper heads neither."[322]

After the drubbing of the fall 1863 election the *Salem Press* asked, "Is the Democratic party dead?" Not hardly. Northern civilians had high hopes for their armies as the spring sun of 1864 dried the roads. General Grant took the cars for Washington and assumed overall command of the entire Union military machine. Plans were formulated for a coordinated effort against the Southern armies. Grant would drive against Lee in the east while Sherman went against General Joseph Johnston, the man that had filled Bragg's position after the Southern debacle at Chattanooga.

Results were expected but they did not come. Trainloads of wounded rolling north from Virginia and Georgia began to sap the will of Northerners at home for a fight to the finish. The Democrats in the north saw their political chances for taking the White House grow with every new listing of casualties hawked by street vendors. In just under two months of fighting in Virginia, Union casualties were some *60,000* men in killed, wounded and missing.[323] By late June of 1864 Grant finally ground to a halt before Petersburg, Virginia. Lee and Grant entrenched to begin a waiting game across their no-man's land. A month later 15,000 Confederates under General Jubal Early burst out of the Shenandoah Valley marching on Washington. This totally stunned the Northern people, it was supposed to be the reverse: Southern defeats, Southern losses, Southern capitulation!

Civilians wondered what had gone wrong. Newspapers hostile to the Lincoln administration painted a picture of incompetence, of the White House resident being no more than a buffoon. Newspapers supporting Lincoln fell silent. What to say when faced with such losses on the battle field? Within the Democrat Party the peace faction gained greater say as to the party's platform for the fall election. They wanted a halt in the war, peace first, then negotiations to bring the South back into the Union. Lincoln understood what this meant, the South was not going to compromise or come back willingly to the Union. Eleven states meant to leave and there was nothing to negotiate. Stop the war to talk about compromise and the South would win. There would be no restart to the war once the Northern armies laid down their arms. Burnt out on bloodshed it would be all at this moment in time for the North, or nothing. Abraham pondered the future. Victory seemed far away, the war lost, his administration lost. A tremendous victory in the field could change political fortunes overnight for the Lincoln administration. Atlanta, the fall of Atlanta would be such a victory. What of the troops in Georgia? Could Sherman's soldiers take Atlanta?

Back in April of 1864 General William Tecumseh Sherman had formulated his strategy for his advance into Georgia. Confederate forces, 65,000 men under General Joseph Johnston, were entrenched twenty-five miles south of Chattanooga along Rocky Face Ridge. Sherman would be overall commander of three armies against his antagonist: 13,000 men in the Army of the Ohio under General John Schofield; 25,000 men in the Army of the Tennessee under General James McPherson; and 60,000 soldiers in the Army of the Cumberland under General George Thomas. The 123rd New York was under Thomas, in the 20th Corps (Hooker), 1st Division (Williams), 1st Brigade (Knipe).

Alerted to a coming movement on April 5th, the 123rd New York began processing paperwork requests as to soldiers present in the ranks, arms and equipment. "Every man, every company, every regiment, every brigade and every corps in this great army must be looked after to see if they are all present and provided for and it takes time to do it," Lt. Cruikshank noted. Serious shortfalls needed to be corrected for the 123rd before the main movement south began. There were only 13 line officers present out of the required 30. Many were still on recruiting duty back in Washington County. Cruikshank at this time breaks down the command structure of the ten companies thus: two commanded by 2nd Lts.; four by 1st Lts.; and four by Captains. Officers were on their way back to their regiments throughout the Army of the Cumberland, Army of the Tennessee and the Army of the Ohio. Also enroute to the 123rd New York was Chaplain Myron White, a Methodist minister from Whitehall, New York. The soldiers had been attending services given by the Christian Commission, plus various visiting ministers ever since Chaplain Henry Gordon had left a year before to return to Washington County. Lt. Cruikshank looked forward to Chaplain White's ministry to the troops. "I hope he will be the man for the place. We have all sorts of characters here to come in contact with. If he is the right sort of man he can do good that is needed very much. He will find good men here, also very bad men."[324]

An express box for Company H arrived at this time with letters and items for the soldiers from the "Ladies Aid Society" of Salem, New York. The men responded with several letters of appreciation for remembering them. The *Salem Press* printed replies from Lt. Cruikshank, Private Horace Mathews and Private Daniel Foster. As Foster saw it, attention from the feminine side of the race was critical for the well being of men. "The Soldier's life is a rough and unsocial existence at the best. Banished from the two sweetest and purest elements of moral improvement and intellectual development-women and children-he finds but little exercise for his highest and best faculties, while his ruder qualities are continually called into activity...."[325]

Three hours of drill per day, preparing gear and cleaning rifles were now brought to use. At noon on April 27th the 123rd New York received marching orders. The camp at Elk River Bridge was immediately struck. "We know now how to start on a march, that is, to abandon everything we can get along without. The men take but little with them," Lt. Cruikshank said of the activity that afternoon. By 5 p.m. the 123rd was on the road south, covering the five miles to Dechard the men went into camp. The entire 1st Division, 20th Corps, 6,715 men with red stars on their caps, were marching forward to join the 20th Corps at Chattanooga. General Joseph Knipe took the 123rd New York and the 46th Pennsylvania south planning to gather up the other regiments in his 1st Brigade along the railroad. Other main units of the 20th Corps consisted of the 2nd Division, 5,847 men with white stars, the 3rd Division, 6,689 men with blue stars, and the 4th Division, 5,590 soldiers with green stars as their insignia. The 4th Division was to remain behind guarding depots and rail lines. General Hooker would take three 20th Corps divisions totaling just over 19,000 soldiers south towards Atlanta.[326]

Breaking camp at 9 a.m. the next day the 123rd New York marched to the base of the Cumberland Plateau and began the 1,500 foot ascent. It was a hot day, a mistake was made in the route so an extra four miles was tacked onto the journey then a quickened march to make up for lost time. By evening they were encamped up in the mountains at University Place, where a southern college was in the process of being created when the war broke out. The soldiers set their tents up among the scattered stone foundations. (The college was refounded in 1868 and today it is Sewanee: The University of the South.)

What had been an exhausting day before was topped by the mistakes of the next day. Leaving at 7 a.m. the soldiers marched one-and-a-half miles before it was discovered they were on the wrong road. Back to their camp and another road. Three miles then officers realized it was, again, the wrong road. Back to camp, onto another road for two miles. At this point some mounted soldiers were sent to scout the way and they returned after dinner (today's lunch) with the correct direction. After 20 miles the 123rd was off the mountain pitching camp in the dark along the road. That night it rained hard and Company H was flooded out of their tents. In the morning daylight the soldiers realized the plot of ground they were assigned was a pond area for rain water, their tent poles were just visable at the water surface. April 30th saw the monthly ritual of muster and inspection at 8 a.m. for the regiment, then officers made out their monthly reports. At 10 a.m. the were on the march, passing through Bridgeport to make camp on the island for the evening. The 5th Connecticut and a detachment of the 3rd Maryland rejoined the brigade at Bridgeport. Seven miles on May 1st brought them to Shellmound where the 141st New York completed Knipe's brigade, its aggregate strength 2,308 men. Regimental strengths break down thus: the 123rd New York with 523 effectives, 141st New York 456, 46th Pennsylvania 763, and 5th Connecticut some 500. There was a detachment of the 3rd Maryland also with the brigade, the majority of the 3rd having reenlisted they were back in Maryland on furlough and would be reassigned to the 9th Corps. (The detachment of the 3rd Maryland would be mustered out in October.) For the next four days it was a series of easy marches, seven to ten miles per day, as the men passed south of Chattanooga, joined with the 20th Corps, and turned towards the Tennessee-Georgia boarder.

The critical aspect for the coming Georgia combat was the railroad that ran from Chattanooga to Atlanta. Both Johnston and Sherman intended to use it as their supply line. So as the opponents sparred in battle it was always the railroad that they came back too no matter how far they swung away in maneuver. Sherman's goal was to swing around Johnston's army, cut the railroad and force Johnston to come out of his entrenchments in an effort to reopen his supply line. Chomping his cigar, alert to his opportunities, Tecumseh would thereupon seek to utterly destroy the Confederate Army of Tennessee. Johnston intended to destroy Sherman's army but, being outnumbered to such an extent, he would wait behind entrenchments and hope for a mistake on the Northern commander's part. If he saw an opening to cut up the Union forces the Southerners would lash out.

Rifle cracks were audible for the 123rd New York soldiers as they stood picket duty on May 8th near Buzzard Roost, Georgia. This was a pass through the ridge line to Dalton, Georgia. Elements of Sherman's army had engaged Johnston's forces along Rocky Face Ridge to the 123rd New York's front. These were just meant as holding actions as other Union troops marched south to turn Johnston's left flank. Back into combat, Private Horace Tooley (Co. K) sat down to pen his parents some thoughts. Horace expected a lot of marching, "perhaps some hard fighting but I hope not I have a great deal of faith in our Generals that are at the head now or at least in Gen Grant...this Country is very rough & heavy timbered with but very few inhabitints they are poor & Ignorant set as there is in the world I shall be glad if we ever get out of the southern States where there is somebody that knows enough to eat with out breaking their Legs" He wished to see family, to be back home where "I can lay down at night with out being disturbed be fore morning with the role of the drum...We had several new recruits come to our regt from Washington Co last week I pity them I hope Sam or Eber will not enlist."[327]

Confederate entrenchments on Rocky Face Ridge faced west and north protecting the railroad running south to Atlanta. Johnston's engineers had built strong breastworks along the crest of the ridge and probing attacks convinced Sherman it was folly to push at the front door. To the west of the ridge ran two roads, one parallel to the other and separated by several miles, that allowed Union columns to proceed south. Using the far road Union General McPherson's Army of the Tennessee marched south then swung east through Snake Creek Gap. An easy opening through the ridgeline and 18 miles south of Buzzard's Roost and Dalton, it had been left undefended. This was an amazing mistake that offered tremendous opportunity. McPherson had orders to roll through the gap, seize the town of Resaca, Georgia, destroy the railroad then fall back to the gap and take up fortified positions. Their supply line having been cut, the Rebs would have to come out and fight. On May 9th the 24,000 soldiers under McPherson poured from the ridgeline opening to the surprise of the 2,000 Confederates at Resaca. The Rebels manned their entrenchments and put their battle flags up.

McPherson had a 12 to 1 advantage but he didn't know that. McPherson was highly regarded as one of the best generals in the army, respected by all that knew him. McPherson also respected his men. And now he felt the weight, the total weight, of the lives of 24,000 soldiers under his command. He looked at the entrenchments and dwelt upon what committing his men to blade and bullet really meant. He paused, then ordered a retreat back to Snake Creek Gap. Sherman would see it as one of the greatest mistakes of the war. That evening a disappointed Sherman ordered a redeployment of the entire army to Resaca.

Breaking camp at 1 a.m. on May 10th, the 123rd New York joined the 1st Division moving south along the road nearest the ridge. By 8 a.m. they were in Snake Creek Gap, General Williams having been ordered to support General McPherson's movement. Per instructions from McPherson, Williams ordered two of his brigades, Robinson's and Knipe's, to fortify the left side of the gap. Williams' third brigade, Ruger's, was ordered through the gap towards Resaca and positioned as support for McPherson's troops. Fortifying an opening through a ridgeline didn't mean chopping trees at the base of the mountain. One chopped trees along the top, several hundred feet up steep slopes.

"This was a hard task," Lt. Cruikshank says, "the mountain being very steep we could take but a few steps before resting." Forming their battle line once on the ridge the men set about chopping, digging and entrenching. They worked until past dark when all of a sudden around 9 p.m. driving rain hit. "We had the hardest storm I ever witnessed," Lt. Cruikshank wrote, "Everything we had with us was soaking wet. We made out to keep our powder dry as that was at this time the most essential."[328] All during the next morning the soldiers of the 123rd New York continued on the breastworks. Meanwhile, lookouts on Rocky Face Ridge were reporting Union troops marching south, this, combined with frantic despatches from Resaca, alerted General Johnston his left flank was being turned. Having a shorter line to Resaca, Johnston's army reached there before Sherman could bring up the bulk of the Union forces. This time Federal attacks on the fortifications would be ordered. Shoveling for the 123rd New York would now include graves for their comrades.

All the effort atop the ridgeline was left behind as Union forces converged around the Confederates at Resaca. By the 14th Williams' 1st Division was reunited with the 20th Corps along Camp Creek just 2,000 feet to the west of the Confederate entrenchments. Soldiers of the 123rd listened to heavy fighting to their left as elements of the Union's 14th and 23rd Corps hit the center of Johnston's entrenchments. Having to wade Camp Creek and wrestle through heavy underbrush the attacks went off badly with heavy losses to the Yankees. To make matters worse, in the late afternoon the Confederates strongly attacked the 4th Corps, holding the Union left flank, and help was requested. Hooker's 20th Corps was pulled out of line and shifted to the left flank. It took over an hour of steady marching before the 123rd New York was in their assigned area. As they moved through the woods heads started turning to the right as Lt. Cruikshank relates: "We were marching by the flank at the foot of a knoll, coming onto a level piece of ground in the woods when we saw the enemy not twenty rods [320 feet] from us marching parallel with us by the flank, from the other side of the knoll. Our men came to a front at once and ran to the top of the knoll as that was the choice of ground. If the enemy should secure it they would have the advantage over us. Our men were there first and the enemy went back flying."[329]

The left flank of the Union army was in flux, Confederate General John Bell Hood's troops coming out of the entrenchments in an attempt to keep it unhinged. On the 15th the 123rd New York along with its fellow brigade regiments shifted position again and this time their luck went sour. When the 1st Division came to a halt and fronted most of the units were in a woods line offering some protection but the 123rd was in an open field within easy sight of the Confederate works. The soldiers were ordered to lie down in an effort to protect them. Private William Tooley (Co. K) must have been sweating with all his comrades as they watched horses drawing artillery appear. "our co lay on a ridge in fair vieue of the enemy & saw them plant their batterey for our especialy benifit the co behaved bravely rather than to break and run with out orders we lay there huging the ground while ourselves and drunken officers were loocking on...a recruit by the name of Watters had both legs taken off by a solid shot one close to his body the other below the knee" Shells also broke an arm of Private Amos Potter's (Co. K), slashed open Sergeant Charles Cowen's face (Co. K), ripped off one of Private John Pitts'(Co. K) arms while shattering a leg, gave Private William Pierce (Co. H) a head concussion, disemboweled Private William Martin (Co. G), and killed Sergeant Willard Harris (Co. B).[330]

Private Henry Welch was right at ground zero, "we could see them load as plain as could be then the flash and the shell would come screaming through the air sometimes they would just skip over us and again they strike the ground and bound over us covering us with dirt." Union artillery unlimbered behind the regiment to begin counterbattery fire. "This was a trying time," Lt. Cruikshank says of the moment, "holding these men in plain sight of the enemy and they shelling us. The enemy were soon ready to charge and advanced on us down the hill out of the woods into the open field. When within thirty rods [480 feet] of us our men sprang to their feet and gave them volley after volley. They wavered for a moment, then fled into the woods and up the hill to their works. Our men with a cheer followed them to the edge of the woods close under the enemy's works." Sergeant Morhous describes the Confederates withering under the rifle and artillery fire, "At first they tried to face the storm of lead and iron, then, staggering and swaying like a crowd of drunken men, they moved to the left, hoping to find the 2nd Brigade easier to handle, but here again they were severely beaten, and rushed back pell mell into their breastworks. The work was done." The 123rd New York with other Union regiments followed them up to a clear zone under the enemy's breastworks where the canister and grape from the Confederates went over their heads. Firing was continued until dark then the soldiers began entrenching near the Rebel line.[331]

As this battle continued on the Union left, Sherman sent a division of troops marching south to the Union right. These troops crossed the Oostanaula River at Lays Ferry and, once again, threatened Johnston's railroad supply line. At dawn the soldiers of the 123rd New York saw empty entrenchments before them. Johnston had pulled his army out during the night and marched south. He had suffered some 2,800 casualties, the Federal forces 2,747 in killed, wounded and missing.

Within a few days Private William Tooley would hear that Pitts and Private William Waters (Co. K) were dead. "we hope not for Pitts was a good soldier & Watters had been with us but a few days Oh! It is a hard business" When Private Waters was hit he was carried back to the 20th Corps field hospital and tended to by Surgeon J. W. Brock of the 66th Ohio Infantry. Brock reported that, regarding Waters, a "large fragment of shell" had "completely carried away his left thigh" and fractured his right leg bones. Even so, Waters "partially rallied from the shock" was given chloroform and the surgeon amputated his left leg at the hip joint plus most of the soldier's right leg. "The patient survived the double operation but a short period." Odds were almost totally against the soldier as hip operation fatality during the Civil War ran 88%. Waters died that afternoon after a month and three weeks in the service. He had arrived with the returning recruiting party just a couple days before the battle. Other casualties at Resaca for the 123rd New York were Private Charles Tefft (Co. A), Private James Hay (Co. F) and Private Montravill Hartt (Co. G) all wounded. Of the eight wounded four would return to the regiment after treatment: Cowen, Hartt, Pierce and Tefft. Privates Potter and Hay would be discharged from hospitals several months later. Ten casualties and a 60% loss rate to the regiment. Private Welch was of the opinion that it could have been much worse for the regiment, "very few of their shell bursted or they would have killed many of us..."[332]

Rivlets of blue flowed south after Johnston's army. By 8 a.m. of May 16th the 123rd New York was on the march with the rest of the 1st Division. "Hundreds of dead men and horses were along our route," Sergeant Lorenzo Coy (Co. K) noted, "We passed several rebel field hospitals in and around which wounded men were dying. It seems as if they left all their mortally wounded to die uncared for." The regiment made about eight miles and camped by the Coosawatter River. Corporal Rice Bull (Co. D) and several others made use of the stream to bathe. Hygiene was a real problem in the field as Bull notes, "not the least unpleasant has been the impossibility of keeping oneself clean and keeping free from the 'graybacks' that will, do what we may, crawl upon us."[333]

Another eight o'clock start on the 17th saw a gray, rainy day but easy marching as the generals made sense of intelligence reports and formulated strategy. By the 18th the Confederates were entrenched at Cassville. On that day twenty-four miles of marching put the 123rd New York, with other units of the 20th Corps, a few miles north of Cassville. Union forces attacked on the afternoon of May 19th taking the town. "we had another fight yesterday we drove the rebs three miles they made quite a stand at the place about four o'clock," Private Henry Welch wrote his brother, "but we drove them and now have possession of the town it is about the size of Granville cornner's our reg't was very lucky..."[334] The soldiers ran through a burning forest during part of the fight then had to cross before Confederate artillery. One shell wounded Corporal Albert Woodruff (Co. D) as the regiment double-quicked to support a Union battery. The rest of the fight the 123rd lay on the ground near the battery but suffered no other casualties.

Lt. Cruikshank says of the engagement that the Confederates "kept so far from us that they did but little injury." It was just great luck that the 123rd New York, and the entire 20th Corps, had "but little injury." Sherman's army advanced in four separate columns from Resaca and it appeared the opportunity Johnston had been waiting for, he would crush the Federal left wing. On the 19th General Johnston set a trap specifically aimed for the 20th Corps coming towards Cassville. He had Hood's and Polk's Corps positioned to fall on the flank of Hooker's men. But the Rebel yell never rent the air due to Union cavalry suddenly appearing in force behind Hood's Corps. At this, Johnston moved back south of the town to a prepared defensive position.[335] After fighting late into the afternoon the Southerners retreated that night across the Etowah River.

Private William Tooley vented a bit of his frustration at the situation to his brother Eber, "before the morning came we found the Jounies had taken advantage of the darkness & left Although we had them bagged as usual but somebody allways fails to tie the bag so that they allways crall out at the mouth" Yet Tooley saw the Union command structure as good. "we have confidence in Joe Hooker we believe he is a good corps com Although he may not be able to handle a large army" Then the older brother offered some reflection on life to his sibling frustrated at being at home and feeling dismal as to his prospects. "Eber I am sorry to see you write so discouraggeringly of your future prospects both worldly and spiritual I think it is the duty of everyone to try and live as mutch as possible to the glory of God"[336]

At this time Sherman chose to rest his troops a couple days while resupplying via the railroad and countryside. Sergeant Lorenzo Coy found the Cassville area much to his liking. "I cannot restrain my admiration for this country. It is a rich and productive soil with most beautiful scenery and abundance of water." As for the town itself, it also rated high marks. "Cassville was a beautiful little village but a deserted one," Sergeant Henry Morhous (Co. C.) relates, "A few remained but they appeared as much afraid of the boys as if they had been a pack of ravenous hyenas. Those who remained did well, for their property was not destroyed, but where a house was found deserted it did not fare as well." This was the beginning of a trend, a standard way of doing business for the soldiers, if the residents were in their house it wasn't burnt. If a home was abandoned it was fair game for pillage and fire. Not that the officers condoned such actions. Sergeant Coy says that as the first Yankee units entered the town pillaging started. "Gen. Hooker, to his honor be it said, at once put a stop to it. The inhabitants all fled on our approach. Had they remained they and their property would have been respected, excepting pigs and pultry."[337]

Forage and provisions for the soldiers were always considered fair game. Sergeant Morhous watched as the region around Cassville was stripped bare. "Large and thrifty fields of corn, wheat and oats soon disappeared under the hungry mouths of an army of horses. For a width of twenty miles not an acre of any kind of forage was left. Every head of stock was 'confiscated.'" Also coming into the lines were deserters, Morhous puts them at over 400, wanting to take the oath of allegiance to the United States and go back to their homes.[338] On the 22nd the men were issued six days rations, the soldiers knew what this meant and went through their gear tossing out what they didn't want to carry.

May 23rd dawned hot. Most of the 123rd New York soldiers were now down to a haversack (a large satchel, often of rubberized cloth) for their gear plus their rifle. Tents, blankets and knapsacks had been left behind. They covered eight miles in a southwesterly direction during the day. Sherman knew that the Confederates had taken up position at Allatoona Pass, across the Etowah River and to the southeast of Cassville. This was an excellent defensive barrier enhanced with engineered traverses, rifle pits and artillery redoubts. Johnston hoped Sherman would be foolish enough to attack and shatter the Union troops against the fortifications. But Sherman as a younger officer had been stationed in the region and knew quite well how impregnable the pass was naturally, let alone with entrenchments. Ignoring Johnston, he put twenty days provisions in wagons and did a wide flanking manuver to the west with his three armies. His goal was to swing around Johnston and come behind him into Marietta, Georgia. Sherman's one faulty assumption during this maneuver was that Johnston would retreat once the Yankees were on his flank. By the 23rd the Confederate general knew of the marching Federal columns. He didn't retreat but attacked.

Shifting his army west, Johnston arrived just ahead of the 20th Corps on May 25th and dug in along a seven mile line from Dallas, Georgia, through New Hope Church to Pickett's Mill. General Hooker was marching his command in concert with other Union Corps converging on the area. Of Sherman's armies, General McPherson was coming up on Johnston's left at Dallas, General Thomas had the center at New Hope Church and General Schofield the Confederate's right at Pickett's Mill. Hooker's three divisons were marching along, his 2nd Divison, under General Geary, having the lead when it literally ran into the Confederates right at New Hope Church and combat erupted. The Rebels were in battle array through the thick woods and brush having come forward from their entrenchments.

Soldiers in the 123rd New York heard the rifle fire in the distance and then a lathered horse with dispatch rider galloped to the head of the column. "All laughter and joking immediately ceased along the line," Sergeant Morhous says.[339] Quickly came the shouted order "double-quick march" and the soldiers were off on a run in support. Under General Hooker's orders and observation, General Williams formed his 1st Division in three lines of brigade front, moved them forward of Geary's and Butterfield's divisions, sent the 13th New Jersey and 61st Ohio forward as skirmishers and advanced at a rapid pace. The Yankee's fighting spirit was up as Sergeant John Gourlie (Co. D) writes, "Our skirmishers drove the Reb skirmishers before them at a Double Quick and we followed them up so rapidly that the line of battle had to be halted several times to give our Skirmishers time to get a little ways in advance..."[340] The 123rd New York soldiers crashed through the heavy brush on a run, shots cracking around them as they closed on the fleeing enemy. *Then everything changed with a crash of artillery.*

The brush was so thick the men never saw the edge of the woods line until they popped out of it-right before Confederate entrenchments. Southern artillery lanyards flicked with a resulting roar. Sergeant Gourlie hit the ground just in time to not be cut in two, "a terrible fire at short range, we lay down & by doing so saved ourselves a great deal from the effect of their fire. The Grape and Cannister just fairly whistled over us cutting off the leaves in showers but it was much to high to do much execution. We lay on the ground & loaded our pieces & then raise up and fire."[341]

Amazingly, the 123rd New York "had charged to within a few feet of the enemy's cannon," Lt. Cruikshank says, "Being so near, and on the side hill, the enemy could not depress their cannon so as to rake us...Our men would lie on their backs, load their guns, roll over and fire."[342]

Cruikshank didn't lie down but used a tree for cover as he watched to make sure his men stayed low and didn't expose themselves too much. He was grazed in the arm by grapeshot but fortunately suffered only a bad bruise. Private Henry Cleveland (Co. K) did raise his head a little too high and "a canister shot struck the top of his forehead and ran over his head, cutting through the skin. Had he raised his head an inch higher it would have killed him." Sergeant James Cumming (Co. D) tempted fate when he stood up and was not so lucky. "Jim Roy Cumming was struck in the head with a musket ball that entered his right eye and passed out at the back part of his head," Sergeant Gourlie writes, "we all thought he was dead but he lived about 30 hours after he was hit. Poor Jim, I do not think he was in any pain from the wound for he was not sensible & did not speak after he was hit."[343]

The initial artillery blast caught Colonel Archibald McDougall. As Sergeant Gourlie went to ground the first one he saw fall was the colonel, having been hit in the right leg by canister. McDougall called for help and some soldiers carried him to the rear. Major Tanner also fell after a shell exploded near him and injured both of his legs. "As soon as he recovered from the shock [Tanner] returned to the Regiment, for which the men gave him a hearty cheer," Lt. Cruikshank noted. The 123rd New York was fully engaged before the Rebel lines around 4 p.m. and fought into night. A light rain began around 10 p.m. which resulted in slackened firing from the Southerners, the men immediately using the break in action to gather parts of trees and create some rough breastworks. Lt. Cruikshank says that much of the material were tree sections that had fallen from the artillery raking the woodline. "We had to do this without making any noise or the enemy would open fire on us again."[344]

Around midnight a regiment came forward to relieve the 123rd New York so they could go to the rear. In hushed tones the soldiers of the 123rd tried to tell the relief force not to be too loud, that the enemy was very close. Sergeant Morhous says this was ignored and "contrary to the advice given, the officer in command, in a loud, pompous tone, gave the order to 'right dress,' when the enemy opened with grape and canister and nearly swept away the relieving force..." Lt. Cruikshank also writes of this incident, mentioning that the relief unit wore white stars (2nd Division) so as they passed over the men of the 123rd they muttered, "Here goes the white stars over the red." Then the Southern artillery opened up. "Such a getting back I never saw! They paid no attention to orders but ran back over us, trampling on us. Our men lay close to the ground and holloed at the top of their voices, 'Here goes the white stars over the red.'" It turned out to be a decent night for the 123rd New York. "Our men picked up a good supply of tents, blankets, ponchoes and rubber coats that the other regiment had thrown away in their flight."[345]

Properly (quietly) relieved at 4 a.m., the 123rd New York went to the rear to cook some coffee and get some rest. The 1st Division incurred 102 killed, 639 wounded and 4 missing for a total of 745 men on the fight of the 25th called Dallas, or New Hope Church. For the Washington County Regiment, they only had one soldier killed outright, Private Robert Skellie (Co. I) but suffered 19 wounded. The regiment would lose to further service 42% of their wounded. Privates Franklin Woodard (Co. E), Thomas Rogers (Co. F), Lewis Tripp (Co. I) and Benjamin Pitts (Co. K) would spend months in hospitals and be discharged. Privates Peter Crombie (Co. G) and Horace Tooley (Co. K) died of their wounds as did Sergeant James Cumming. "I saw his grave," Sergeant Gourlie wrote his father of Cumming's death, "he is buried near where our Division Hospital stood on the road leading to Dallas...there is a board placed at the head of his grave with his name Company & Regt marked on it."[346]

"I presume before you get this you will hear that Horace was wounded," Private William Tooley wrote his brother Eber, "as I told mother his wound is not very severe the last time I saw him he was doing well...I am very sorry to have Horace wounded & be with out him but if he lives and gets out of the army by it I shall be satisfied." Satisfaction for William was not to be. Horace died June 8th.[347]

His right leg shattered on May 25th, Colonel McDougall underwent surgery on June 4th. Assistant Surgeon Kennedy of the 123rd New York amputated the right leg in the lower section of the thigh. McDougall was then transported to the officer's hospital in Nashville, Tennessee. At this stage of the war military hospital trains had special cars for transporting of wounded. Instead of seats, the cars were equipped to handle stretchers along each side. To minimize vibrations to the wounded, rubberized loops were used to suspend the stretchers. McDougall probably rode one of these trains north to Nashville. The wound was a bad one and his wife soon arrived by his bedside. On June 23rd Colonel Archibald McDougall died. The *Salem Press* reported that the funeral in Washington County was a private, family affair as per their request, but that many citizens attended the church service for the fallen commander. Officers of the 123rd New York had local papers in the county plus Albany print a resolution on McDougall from them, stating that he was "a brave soldier and skillful officer." Brigadier General Alpheus Williams in his 1st Division after action report of the Dallas battle mentions Colonel McDougall. "Among the severly wounded on this occasion (since died) was Colonel Archibald L. McDougall, One hundred and twenty-third New York Volunteers, a most faithful, patriotic, and valuable officer." But perhaps Corporal Clark McLean said it best about the colonel in a letter to his mother a month after his passing. "The regiment feels the loss of the Col. he had his faults, like every one, drinking was the worst one, but he was a true & good soldier never flinching in battle, always in his place no matter how great the danger, never asking the men to go where he would not lead them."[348]

Several hundred yards behind the main line, the 1st Division did reserve duty for the next six days. This didn't mean they were safe and could relax. On the 28th Sergeant Lorenzo Coy was with the regiment near General Hooker's tent when "the enemy had got the range on us for their cannon, one shell exploding in front and breaking some dishes on Gen. Hooker's table at which he was sitting..." Hooker's accomodations and the regiments nearby were immediately moved further to the rear. Moving into the lines on relief duty then rotating back out, the 123rd New York suffered two more casualties as the armies sat facing one another in the New Hope Church area. Sergeant Larned Amidon (Co. H) was hit on May 29th and would be discharged a year later after hospital stays. On the 31st Sergeant Coy noted, "Situation unchanged, brisk skirmishing and some falling artillery has been going on all day. Now and then a bullet whistles over our heads. This is the 7th day since this battle commenced and so far as I know neither side has gained any permanent advantage."[349] Shifted to the left on June 1st the 1st Division took up posts in the Picketts Mill area. Private Hiram Bentley (Co. I) was the last casualty for the 123rd New York in the battles about Dallas. He was hit June 2nd and after medical treatment would transfer into the Veterans Reserve Corps for the rest of the war.

Needing supplies, by June 6th Sherman was shifting troops to the left to reconnect to the railroad at Ackworth, Georgia. Johnston shifted the Confederate forces to the Pine Mountain region. Skirmishes and artillery bombardments were constant along the miles of earthworks as both armies leapfrogged east. Shifting of Union troops would see the New Yorkers moved into the front line then a day later moved back out to continue marching to the left. It was grinding down the soldiers of the 123rd New York. "we have faught enough for this time as a great number of us are worn out & sick of the business," Private William Tooley wrote his parents, "It has been forty two days since we started and twenty five days of that time we have been within close hearing of their guns." Sergeant Coy was so exhausted he began to dwell upon what would be called in World War II the million-dollar wound. "I am tired out, sick and have the blues, and at times almost envy those of my comrades who are suffering from wounds in the hospitals. Heavy skirmishing and cannonading has been going on all day."[350]

Blast concussion, high decibel missiles and just general raw roar of rifles, cannons and mortars wore away one's sanity. "I would give most anything to spend one week where I would not hear a gun or anything about war or Rebelion," William Tooley sighed onto a letter. But Tooley still had some fighting spirit, possibly from nicotine withdrawal. "tell Eber to send me one pound paper of Shields & Adams chewing Tobacco immediately by mail before I knock him down I have not had a chew of Tobacco in a week"[351]

Even during movements the men read newspapers to see what was going on in the nation. Sergeant Coy found a copy of the June 5th *Chattanooga Gazette* which had an article on the coming fall election. He learned "that the Abolition Radical Convention has nominated John C. Fremont and John Cochrane as candidates...If Fremont accepts that nomination he will learn that the people of the north are not radicals - that while they determine the overthrow of the Confederacy, they are equally determined to wage war for that purpose from principle and not from fanaticism. Not that I do not like Fremont, but the party I cannot endorse." Newspapers were also informing the men of the battles back in Virginia. They noted the casualties that Grant was racking up and felt thankful to be with Sherman. "we have great confidence in Gen Sherman," Private William Tooley wrote, "we believe he is carefull of his men and does not rush them in where he thinks they will get all cut up but we think it is not so with Gen Grant he has made a great sacrifice of human life in his late battles we hear that his lines are within a few miles of Richmond" Of course some of the papers they were reading might have had quite a slanted view of Yankees. Corporal Welch says that the men were getting Southern newspapers into the lines via trade, "our picket line is in speaking distance of the rebel pickets we exchange paper's with them every day, they think or did think that Lee was whipping Grant badly they say they are going to drive us out of Georgia of course we are anxious to have them do it. but the thing can't be done easy."[352]

Sherman, and his troops, were "anxious" for Johnston to come out of his works and hit the Union army. During the Dallas battles Johnston had sent forward his soldiers in force to hit the Yankees the night of May 29th plus probing attacks continued over the following days, evenings and nights. Repulsing the Confederates each time, it only convinced the Union soldiers that it was better to be on the defense than to be the ones charging entrenched positions. But Confederate General Johnston was no fool, and he shifted east to keep his army between Sherman and the prize of Atlanta. The Southerners had the luxury of prepared lines of fortifications to fall back into as slave labor had been put to work creating them. By June 10th the Union army was resupplied and began to move south again. Before them the Confederates were ensconced in well prepared fortifications along Pine and Lost Mountains. Larger strategic issues were always in the background as Sherman considered his next movement. There was concern that the Confederates would shift some troops east against Grant if Johnston was not pressed constantly. "One of my chief objects," Sherman telegraphed General Halleck at the War Department, "being to give full employment to Johnston, it makes but little difference where he is, so he is not on his way to Virginia."[353]

By June 12th the 123rd New York was building breastworks a half-mile before the Confederate positions, the men plainly hearing rifle and artillery fire where the 4th and 23rd Corps had engaged. These were dreary days as steady rain, day after day, continued. "Last night I went to bed wet through and cold but slept well," Sergeant Coy noted. Gray days combined with bad news from his wife. "A letter from home brings me the intelligence of my little Mary's ill health. My prayer to God to take her (our first-born) not from us. How my affections cling about that child. She is to me almost a sacred being and daily do I thank God for the precious gift and our little Alice. God bless them each. My heart yearns towards them and I long oh so much to see them."[354]

The regiment got a break the 13th as they didn't move and Coy made the best of it. "We have built a good fire in front of our tent and are trying to keep warm and dry ourselves. The last is a doubtful job as the rain is still falling fast and driving hard." Lt. Cruikshank worried about keeping the ammunition dry. "I never knew of so much rainy weather. The men had just as soon fight as to have so much rain and mud. We have so little to protect us." Finally the sun broke out on the 14th. Cruikshank joined the rest of the men in being happy to see the fiery orb. "The sun is out and it is drying off fast. Our clothes have not been dry for eleven days."[355]

Marching commenced on the 15th to the south. By 4 p.m. the 123rd New York went into combat as Hooker sent the 1st and 2nd Divisions against the Rebel works. "Both bullets and shells flew thick over our heads for more than two hours," Sergeant Coy writes, the 123rd "pushed within four rods [64 feet] of the rebel's main works then under cover of darkness threw up breastworks."[356] Two soldiers were slightly wounded, Private Frank Ames (Co. I) and Private John Cobb (Co. I). Dropping back to new lines over the night of the 16th, the Confederates kept their flanks protected from Sherman's attempts at turning them. Waking to silence, the men of the 123rd New York had their breakfast of hardtack and coffee then swung on gear and started south. After two miles the skirmishers commenced firing. In late afternoon the soldiers started building breastworks while undergoing artillery fire. Union batteries were brought forward and began counterbattery fire. Flashes and cracks of rifles continued heavy all night and rolled on through the day in a driving rain. The night of the 18th Johnston dropped back once again, this time to major fortifications along Kenesaw Mountain.

General Thomas brought his Army of the Cumberland towards Kenesaw Mountain: the 4th Corps, 14th Corps and 20th Corps. Sherman had Thomas taking the center section of his line while McPherson was to the left. After sizing up the Confederate's position, Sherman determined to turn Johnston's left flank. Thomas' and McPherson's armies would hold Johnston in position with strong skirmishing along the Kenesaw Mountain entrenchments while Schofield's army (23rd Corps) along with Hooker's 20th Corps swung to the south. Hooker's corps would be the far right of Thomas' line with Schofield beyond him to the south.

June 19th the 123rd New York moved out at 10 a.m. and was engaged before Kenesaw Mountain by noon. "We charged and gained the top of the range of hills and commenced building breastworks as fast as we could so as to hold our ground," Lt. Cruikshank says, "It was warm work for us, the bullets whizzing past us lively." The 123rd was on a ridge looking across a little valley to the Rebel earthworks along Kenesaw. Other units were before them engaging the enemy up close, Corporal McLean joining the rest of the 123rd in watching. "There is a battle going on now right in front of us. Our Brig. are reserves to day and from the ridge where we are we have a splendid view of the line of battle...The firing is now going on brisk on our left four of five Batteries of our Corps are pouring solid shot & shell in to the woods where they are & they will probaly be getting out of the way tonight or they will get helped out tomorrow."[357]

Relieved by other troops early the next morning, the 123rd New York marched to the right about three miles with the 1st Division and went into camp in a clearing. That afternoon the men heard heavy fighting behind them, by moving as they did they avoided a Confederate attack on the Union lines. "Howard's Corps (4th) is doing some noble fighting today," Sergeant Coy noted. He also watched Generals Thomas, Hooker and Howard "evidently holding a consultation pass up and down the lines."[358] The next day was spent strengthening their breastworks in the rain, alert to any threat to their front.

A sunny morning broke on June 22nd, it must have brightened the soldiers after all the rain. Yet the day was to turn very nasty for the 123rd New York as an unseen cataclysm of combat moved towards them. Confederate General Johnston noted Sherman's turning attempt and had shifted General Hood with 11,000 men to confront Hooker's and Schofield's troops. Getting the order to deploy for the 1st Division as skirmishers, Lt. Colonel James Rogers lead the 123rd New York forward at 9 a.m. to establish a forward line as the divisions of the 20th Corps came behind them through the forest and fields. Moving off at the same time to their far right was the 14th Kentucky, on the same mission for the 23rd Corps. At this time the Union forces were moving towards the property of the Culp's family (proper spelling of the family name is Kolb but as many reports, letters and memoirs of the time period use Culp it is used here). It was thought that only light resistance would be in the area as the shifting of Confederate forces had not been ascertained. Instead, General Hood, on his own initative, decided to come forward and attack the Union forces trying to flank the Confederate position.

Advancing a half-mile the 123rd New York relieved the pickets who returned to their proper commands. Then Lt. Colonel Rogers deployed the entire regiment to the left and right, each man ten feet apart. This took time as the woods were thick and it wasn't until 11 a.m. before the bugle sounded "forward." They stepped off, the three divisions of the 20th Corps following. Within a half-hour the 123rd had run onto a Confederate picket line and steady, but not rapid, firing began. Driving the Rebels slowly backwards the New Yorkers crossed little clearings and more woods. By noon they were at the Culp Farm, coming out of the woods onto a low ridge. Cleared fields were before them sloping down to a small stream, the land then rising easily back into dense forest with the clearing being just over a half-mile. The farmland was cut up by ravines and had large dead trees from girdling dotting the landscape. Moving into the fields, scattered firefights erupted. Sections of the 123rd New York routed out the enemy from little ravines or from piles of brush where they took cover to fire at the Yankees while the New Yorkers used the same techniques to flank each contested point. "One looking lengthwise of our line would have seen men behind trees and stumps, others lying flat upon the ground behind some hummock or obstruction and hiding in the little ravines or gullies," Corporal Bull says of this moment. Still they pushed the Rebels back, steadily moving them from the clearing into the far woods. At this moment the New Yorkers realized rifle pits were running along the woodline, the Rebels quickly dropped into them and gave their yell. There was a ravine running parallel to the pits about 300 yards shy of the woods. Lt. Colonel Rogers ordered the men to make a dash to it. "To get there we had no protection and had to fully expose our persons to their fire and while we went in very quick time we were yet a fair mark for their riflemen and lost several men in the rush," Bull laments.[359]

Firing picked up as Yanks and Rebs blasted at one another. Some of the 123rd New York were in the open using the ravine as cover but to the right the ravine ran into the forest. Getting orders to advance, Rogers ordered the right wing of the regiment to advance further into the woods. Out in the open Lt. Edward Quinn (Co. D) sought to advance from the ravine. He leapt up with pistol calling for men to follow him but was immediately hit in the face by a rifle ball and collapsed to the ground. He lay there several minutes with shattered jaw before managing to crawl back into the gully.

Moving into the woods quietly, the New Yorkers used the brush to screen them and they managed to get within 200 feet of the Confederates. These weren't in rifle pits but moving about, something was going on but the brush was too heavy to make it out clearly. "I could hear men marching through the woods, the giving of orders in a low voice evidently by officers, the neighing of horses, and further back, bugle calls," Corporal Bull writes. Leaving others to watch silently, Bull dropped back to report to Captain Alexander Anderson (Co. D). Finding Anderson and Rogers conferring, Bull related what he had heard. Rogers immediately had Bull take him forward. After listening a few minutes the Lt. Colonel told Bull, "They are massing troops in our front and will probably attack. In case they advance have the men fire their guns and immediately fall back."[360] Rogers sent a message back to 1st Brigade commander General Knipe that the enemy was preparing to attack.

By now it was about 4 p.m., the 1st and 2nd Divisions, 20th Corps, had arrived on the wooded ridge line a half-mile back. Coming across the clearing to their far right the 14th Kentucky was moving forward but was not adjacent to the 123rd New York. There was a large gap between the units but it was not to matter. The enemy force about to step forward would make any attempt at a stand for two regiments suicidal. The 123rd New York soldiers lay silently in the hot Georgia woods, then at 5 p.m. a bugle sounded and they heard feet, thousands of feet, tramping the forest floor.

Major General Carter Stevenson's Division, some 5,000 Alabamians, Georgians, North Carolinians, Virginians and Tennesseans were coming through the woods right at Corporal Bull and his comrades. A second column, Major General Thomas Hindman's Division, was moving forward on Stevenson's right. Hindman's 5,000 Mississippians, Alabamians and South Carolinians were aimed to burst onto the 123rd New York soldiers in the open field. Lt. Colonel Rogers had barely 500 effectives and they were about to be steamrolled. The "Rebel Yell" went up.

"They came down on us fast as they could through the brush, screaching and yelling. Our men gave them one volley then fell back," Lt. Cruikshank says. With three lines of Confederates coming at them, Captain Orrin Hall (Co. I) and Lt. Cruikshank fell back with their men to where some fence rails were piled up. The attempt to make a stand was very short lived as Major Tanner shouted for "every man to take care of himself." A 20 to 1 whirlwind was charging onto them. Rebels were taking 123rd soldiers prisoner within ten feet of Cruikshank, "I could not run to the right and keep under cover of the woods, but to keep from being caught must keep straight ahead through the open fields and run the risk of being shot. I chose the latter as I preferred being shot rather than being taken prisoner. I had a half-mile run to get into our lines."[361]

All the men had a half-mile run across open ground. A major handicap to the 123rd soldiers was that they had their gear on, knapsacks or haversacks, blankets, etc. Stripped for combat, the Southern ranks were covering ground much faster. Tossing equipment aside, the New Yorkers kept their rifles and ran. Private Levi Eaton (Co. D) made for the rear, "I had to scrach gravel to get away the rebs fired at me a number of times but they did not hit me." Many of the New Yorkers were not as lucky. Cruikshank saw one of his best soldiers gasp and tumble, Private Peter

McNassor (Co. H) being shot through the body and calling for help as he fell. "Sam [Corp. Samuel Mahaffy Co. H] ran out to him, picked him up and ran back into the woods. Then Peter told Sam to save himself, that he was dying, and to lay him on the ground. Sam did so and found he was dead. He left him there." Private Joseph Kearsing of Company H also fell at this time. "In these two boys I lost two of my bravest men," Cruikshank says, "They were boys in years, not nineteen and small of their age, but they were men in a fight."[362]

Stevenson's Division brushed the 14th Kentucky aside. Being in regimental formation it made a stand with volleys at the Rebs but then saw the light and fell back to the right rear, out of the developing battle zone. Meanwhile the 1st Division, 20th Corps, had their artillery planted to the flanks, breastworks thrown up and regiments in battle line along the ridge. As the Southerners fully emerged into the open Union artillery cut loose. For the running soldiers of the 123rd New York it was now a nightmare of enemy fire to the rear and "friendly" fire to their front. To avoid death at their comrade's hands many of the men fled down ravines to the right. This sheltered many of them from the metal crisscrossing the field. Sergeant Lorenzo Coy (Co. K) had "the command of the left of our Co. and before we knew that there was anything more than a skirmish line coming upon us, the whole force was upon us. In falling back, which I did as fast as I could, I found myself at one time under the fire of the rebels and our own line of battle..."[363]

Running to the right, to the left, or straight ahead, the 123rd was scattered all over the field. Cruikshank had sprinted halfway to the Union line when, exhausted, he stopped behind a tree stump for cover. Gasping for breath he watched the lines of Confederates moving rapidly forward behind him, then looked before him watching Union officers going along their men on the line giving encouragement and telling them to hold their fire. Getting a deep breath the Lieutenant broke from cover. "As the enemy got sight of me they began to fire, their bullets flying all around me."

Cruikshank leapt over the breastworks where officers immediately inquired if all skirmishers were in, Cruikshank, having seen most of the 123rd men break right and left with no one else behind him, nodded yes. At that the line opened. "When they had got within a few feet of us, we raised a shout, giving them a volley right into their faces," Lt. Cruikshank says, "at the same time the artillery sent their charge of canister nearly lengthwise of their line." Withering before the lead and iron, the Rebels fled back to the ravine, reformed and charged. Again they fell to a wall of shock waves and metal. To the ravine again, reforming of lines, then another charge on the Yankees. After this attack failed they dropped back to the ravine and woods continuing the battle until after dark. That night, safe behind their breastworks, Union troops watched the Confederates search by torchlight for their dead and wounded.[364]

That evening the 123rd New York attempted to regroup but many of the men were scattered about the Union lines. Sergeant Coy sat in the darkness planning to wait until daylight to find his unit, "thanks be to God for His preserving care, I escaped unharmed, but did not know where the reg't is and will be here in the woods to the rear tonight." Several others were unaccounted for, Private Eaton stating, "Oliver Smith from south bay is missing but whether he was killed or taken prisoner we do not know he was on the skirmish line...Walter Martin was taken prisoner the same time..."[365]

For the onslaught that they faced, the 123rd New York could be said to have gotten off easy. They lost three killed, 30 wounded and 14 missing (POW's). Of the wounded, only 14 would return to duty with the regiment, a loss of 53%. For the prisoners, some were seized unhurt but several were lying on the field wounded when captured. Two, Privates John Wright and Joseph Kearsing, died of their wounds while in captivity. Four soldiers would disappear into Andersonville Prison, Privates Oliver Smith (Co. D) and John Decker (Co. A) surviving the notorious camp to be exchanged several months later. Private Patrick

Malone (Co. F) died of disease at Andersonville and is buried in the National Cemetery there: Section H, Grave #9457. Corporal Benjamin Deuel (Co. H) disappears at this time, moved from Andersonville to a new POW camp at Millen, Georgia, he fades from the records and never returned home. Privates James Morrissey (Co. G) and Matthew Monneghan (Co. G) would be paroled and return to the regiment within months. Lt. Walter Martin (Co. F) would manage an escape back to the regiment within two months. It would take Sergeant Benjamin Smith (Co. B) six months to engineer an escape, making a surprising reappearance to the regiment after being given up as lost. Of the POW's only five returned to duty for a loss rate of 64⅔%. Every company in the 123rd New York lost soldiers at the battle of Culp's Farm. Overall the regiment lost 47 soldiers, 19 of whom returned for later duty.[366]

Culp's Farm resulted in 350 Union casualties and some 1,000 Confederate. While claimed a Yankee victory, it had important repercussions in Sherman's planning. Hood's attack squarely stopped any flanking movement of the Kenesaw Mountain position. After considering his options, Sherman decided to assault the center, explaining, "...I perceived the enemy and our own officers had settled down into a conviction that I would not assault fortified lines. All looked to me to outflank. An army to be efficient must not settle down into a single mode of offense, but must be prepared to execute any plan which promises success. I wanted, therefore, for the moral effect to make a successful assault against the enemy behind his breastworks, and resolved to attempt it at the point where success would give the largest fruits of victory."[367] Feeling that Johnston must have weakened his center by moving troops to his flanks, Sherman hoped to punch through the left-center of Johnston's army, separate it into two parts and destroy it piecemeal. He set about planning the assault.

General Hood withdrew his troops back to Mt. Zion Church the day after the Culp's Farm battle. Union forces thereupon moved forward to claim the wooded area where the 123rd New York had made their desperate, albeit quick, stand. "I have recovered the body of Peter McNassor and buried it. I feel his loss very much as I was much attached to him. I also feel the loss of the other men....," Lt. Cruikshank said, "I cannot see how I made my escape when I was so near the enemy." The 123rd got a respite from movement in the hot weather and laid in their breastworks for the next ten days. Chaplain White used the stationary days for preaching. Religious services were well attended but Cruikshank felt turnout could have been better, telling his wife, "[Reverand White] holds prayer meetings three times a week when it is fair. They are strong Methodist prayer meetings. The Regiment turns out to the service very well but not as well as they did to hear Mr. Gordon. Mr. White does not understand the men as well as Mr. Gordon did." Corporal McLean said of the chaplain, "He dont draw a very large crowd, whether by the sickness of the men or lack of smartness is the question." But Corporal Welch had high praise for the new preacher. "Mother we have got a very good Chaplain with us now. we all like him much. we have meeting's nearly every evening that we lay still, they are attended by many and seem to be interesting to all. it would be a scene well worth looking at for our friends away up north to see us sitting together in the moonlight listening to our Chaplain and hear the firing of our pickets some forty rods distance only from us..."[368] New clothing was issued at this time, they were mustered for pay and an inspection was held by the brigade inspector. While not moving directly on the enemy, the soldiers were under rifle fire day and night as skirmishing was constant all along the line.

 Even with all the shooting, mail from home was still on Corporal McLean's mind. "Tell Henry to mail me a letter & when he sends me a newspaper to put a cigar or two in it as we dont get any smoking material now days & tobacco to smoke is as indispensable to a soldier as coffee."[369]

 On June 27th Sherman's attacks went off. The 123rd New York soldiers watched from their entrenchments. "About 6 this morning [Union General] Butterfield opened his guns upon the rebel works, followed at 7 by [Union Generals] Geary, Howard and Palmer," Sergeant Lorenzo Coy writes, "An hour after we saw Howard's Corps (the 4th) moving over Geary's works and cross a large open field in 5 lines of battle...The men of our brigade flocked to and onto our works to witness the sight. The rebels seeing us fired 2 shells at us which flew screaming over our heads to the rear. I guess we got down then."[370]

Sending some 13,000 Federal troops forward in attacks against Pigeon Hill and Cheatham Hill, the Yankees were repulsed. Suffering 2,500 casualties to the Rebels loss of 500, Sherman called off any further attempts to carry the works. It was back to flanking again, blue uniforms of Schofield's army appearing on the far left flank of the Confederate works with back up from McPherson's marching columns. At this Johnston ordered another withdrawal. The morning of July 3rd the soldiers of the 123rd New York broke camp at 4 a.m. and moved forward to find the Confederate entrenchments deserted. "Their works were strong and could not have been carried by assault" was the view of Sergeant Coy and many of the other soldiers. They were an exhausted lot and a new item was included in their daily rations. "Whiskey was issued this evening," Corporal McLean says, "The men are pretty tired of digging and making breastworks." New critters, body lice, also contributed to their misery. "We are troubled with the 'little devils.' It is impossible to keep rid of them on the march."[371]

General Johnston now established his troops in excellently prepared works along the west bank of the Chattahoochee River. While the works were formidable, Johnston's position somewhat surprised Sherman as it was on the same side of the river as the Union army. For diversions Sherman sent cavalry south along the river while at the same time keeping active along the Rebel works. Meanwhile Schofield's army used roads away from the river to march north. Surprising Confederate cavalry at a river crossing, they established a bridgehead. At this Johnston fell back across the river to just outside the defensive works of

Atlanta. Granted a respite, soldiers in the 123rd New York spent a few days near Vining's Station with their camp among some woods. The weather was very hot. Trees offered some shade but not much help, Corporal McLean writing that the men "can not keep cool no way in the middle of the day. dont have Hew Ackley's soda water or Newman's Ice Cream to keep the heat out." Yet a new item was issued for their field rations at this time and was a hit. McLean had the standard lunch of coffee, pork and hardtack but also a new item: potatoes. "they are dried and ground by some operation so they look like corn meal it makes good eating." To occupy time the men climbed trees to view the steeples of Atlanta ten miles away. Soldiers also searched around and hit paydirt. "Some boys in our brigade found eleven thousand dollars in Rebel money at a house out by our picket line day before yesterday. It is against orders for any of our soldiers to have Confed money in our possession and they are trying to find where the money that was found is. but it is like finding out who breaks the teachers ruler at school, no one knows anything about it."[372]

Pickets were along each bank of the river, the enlisted personnel making truces for trading and swimming. Sergeant Gourlie was familiar with all the goings on, saying of the Rebs, "they are very friendly with the boys from our Division on Picket. they go in swimming together in the river & sometimes our boys go over and stay a [half-hour] & talk with the Rebs about the war & the prospects...The Rebel officers are very much opposed to this display of friendship for very often some of their men are missing from Morning Roll Call." Both sides were thrilled to trade coffee, of which the Yankees had plenty, for tobacco, which the Rebs had in abundance. Men would strip and swim the river holding a bag of the trade goods above the water. "It is against orders for the pickets to talk to each other," Corporal McLean notes, "But they do it a great deal."[373]

As part of passing the time, Yankee soldiers walked over the abandoned river fortifications. Sergeant Gourlie spent the time reflecting, "Sherman has seen the folly of charging – where he can compel the enemy to retreat by flanking him & he has done it at every position the Rebs have lately taken – Gen Sherman has displayed more Generalship on this campaign than I have ever seen during my military experience he is terrible on the flank and that is the way he will take Atlanta." Private William Tooley was most impressed with the Confederate works taking time to describe them in a letter to his brother Eber. The abandoned entrenchments were "ten to twelve feet in thickness with two tier of large logs filled between with dirt & about ten feet high then 20 feet infront is a row of sharp sticks three or four inches apart slanting from the works...The rebels build terrible works for us to charge on but we do not always do it"[374]

The retreat across the Chattahoochee was the last straw for Confederate President Jefferson Davis. He removed Johnston from command. Davis wanted a fighter. He had expected Sherman to be kept at bay in Northern Georgia, now the Yankees had breached the last natural barrier before Atlanta and were within eight miles of the city. He put General John Bell Hood in charge of the Confederate forces. Hood graduated from West Point in 1852, had served on the Texas frontier then entered Confederate service when the war broke out. A shell had rendered his left arm useless at Gettysburg and he lost his right leg at Chickamauga. Not for a moment did those injuries keep him from returning to the battlefield. One thing he could be counted upon to do was attack the Yankees. Perhaps Johnston should have attacked Sherman's troops more often but on retrospect it now seems the Southern command went from one extreme to another; a general that delayed action to a general that only understood action. A telling point is that when Sherman was informed of the change he was happy about it, he understood it meant the Rebs would be coming out to fight.

But how many would be charging? Back east, Rebel General Jubal Early at this time was approaching a panic stricken Washington with 15,000 troops. He sparred with the defenses on July 11th, his men even getting a few shots at

President Lincoln when Abe stood up to look over the trench parapet. But after testing the mettle of the defenders for a day Early realized it was folly to attempt to take the city and withdrew back into Virginia. This prompted some quick messages to Sherman in Georgia. On July 16th at 10 a.m. Grant telegraphed Sherman from City Point, Virginia worried as to the next location of Early's troops and warning him that they might show up at Atlanta. General Halleck at the War Department must have seen the message going out, thought on it for a few hours, then also sent a message that day at 4:30 p.m. voicing the same concerns. Was Sherman ready for all aspects of what the Rebels might throw at his army?

    Tecumseh replied to both dispatches that night at 11 p.m. from his Georgia field headquarters near the Chattahoochee River. A War Department telegraph in D.C. clicked out his response the next morning at 10:45. Sherman was well aware of their concerns but "I do not fear Johnston with re-enforcements of 20,000 if he will take the offensive..." A larger issue as Sherman saw it was his long supply line, and to solve that he was moving forward as much material as possible from Nashville to depots at Chattanooga and Allatoona. Cigar smoke, late nights and morse code seemed to go together for Grant and Sherman at this stage of the war.[375]

    Hood took command on July 17th. At this time Union forces were moving forward from the Chattahoochee towards Atlanta in two columns: Schofield and McPherson from the east, Thomas from the north. On the 18th the 123rd New York was in battle formation in support of skirmishers as they moved crosscountry through creeks, hills and swamps. It seemed the enemy had withdrawn into the defenses of Atlanta. But Hood had seen the separation of Sherman's forces and chose to attack Thomas' exposed troops as they attempted to cross Peach Tree Creek. He planned for Hardee's and Stewart's Corps to hit the Union forces when crossing the creek and the blow would mainly land on Hooker's Corps. Lead elements of the 20th Corps were at the creek early on July 20th waiting throughout the morning as engineers laid a pontoon bridge. Confederate forces came out of their entrenchments but delays in forming meant the Rebel attack went off when the first brigades of the 20th Corps were already across.

Being one of the lead regiments, the 123rd New York crossed the waterway around 3 p.m. and then marched onto a small knoll with other regiments of the 1st Brigade. All the units stopped closed in mass, that is, in column, and stacked arms. Cooking fires were started and the smell of coffee permeated the air as officers chatted and the men laid on the ground resting. A line of skirmishers were out in the woods with scattered shots now and then but nothing unusual.

Then rapid firing began, growing and growing. Men began to stand up, scanning through the forest one could see the Yankee skirmishers quickly falling back. The noise rolling closer and closer, blue uniforms of the skirmishers were seen moving quicker and quicker then breaking into a dead run towards them. Bugle calls blared out "Assembly" and almost immediately after, "Advance." Dropping cups of coffee soldiers scrambled for their rifles, men jostling each other as they sprinted into formation. Gun fire grew with bullets clipping among the 123rd New York causing casualties. Joining in the rifle cracks and zinging bullet chorus, then rising above the bedlam of noise, came the familiar Rebel Yell. Calling for the brigade to form, General Knipe positioned it along the top of the knoll, with the 123rd New York on the left, then the 141st New York, 5th Connecticut and 46th Pennsylvania. Several hundred yards to the right of the 46th PA was the Union's 14th Corps, a gap existing between the 14th and 20th Corps.

Dashing into position the 123rd New York "came to a front at once and charged, moving forward about three rods [48 feet], when they saw the enemy not thirty feet away…We were engaged without forming a line as they were onto us before one could be formed," Lt. Cruikshank says. All the men were surprised by the turn of events. "we were lying in the woods massed by regiment when the rebels commenced the charge," Private William Tooley wrote, "so we had to advance on a ridge & form our lines under a heavy fire" Sergeant John Gourlie told his brother, "we had just time to form a kind of a line when the Rebs opned on the right of our Brigade a destructive fire-it was directly on our flank and we had to form our line under fire-which is a hard task-but we soon got in shape and in less time then it has taken me to write this we were hotly engaged."[376]

Somehow the Union forces stopped the first Confederate charge and forced them back. All was activity along the knoll. Galloping up among the 123rd New York were two guns of the 1st New York Light Artillery, wheeling their guns among the regiment the gunners began their loading sequence. Officers of the 123rd New York meanwhile shouted orders. More ammo was needed along the line, details were sent for it. About half the men were ordered back to an old log cabin just behind the regiment and the soldiers with frantic efforts and curses tore it into pieces. Dragging and carrying the chunks of logs to the line the men erected crude breastworks as other comrades loaded rifles. Stench of powder and human sweat mingled with the heat of the summer woods...another charge!

Another Rebel Yell along their front with gray lines running at them through the brush and trees. "We were still busy with our log works when the Johnies again came up this time with more determination," Sergeant Gourlie says of the second attempt.[377]

"The boys loaded and fired with such rapidity that their guns became so heated that they could not hold their hand on the barrel," Sergeant Morhous writes, "Corporal [John C.] Smith's gun went off while he was in the act of ramming home a cartridge, and John had to hunt around and find another ramrod." All the rifle fire plus the cannons unloading canister at close range devastated the Confederate ranks. Gourlie notes that "after a severe trial we had the satisfaction of turning them back with great slaughter."[378]

Regrouping, the Rebels made more charges. "The fight continued until dark," Lt. Cruikshank writes, "Every time the enemy would charge on us I would caution my men not to fire too high but aim at the knee. When the enemy are advancing up a hill, if they should aim at the body they would generally shoot over the head."[379]

Both sides were finding their marks. Captain Henry Wiley (Co. K) was shot through the chest. "I stood within a few feet of the captain & saw him fall & helped to carry him off," Private William Tooley wrote. Also carried to the rear was 2nd Lt. John Daicy (Co. E) shot through the head, 1st Lt. and Adjutant Seth Carey with a shattered leg, and Color Sergeant William Hutton (Co. C). Lt. Cruikshank saw Hutton stagger and drop, shot through the body. "When he fell I was close to him and asked him if he was badly wounded. He said he did not know, that he felt numb all through the body. He stood the Colors against a tree nearby by holding on to the staff to keep them up. He was a brave and true soldier." When a lull occurred Cruikshank had Hutton and Private Henry Danforth (Co. H), shot through the left thigh, removed to the rear. Both would succumb to their wounds.[380]

The 1st New York Light Artillery was a blessing but also a curse to the men of the 123rd New York. Like huge shotguns, they wrecked any Confederate charge that came before them. But in doing so they sent blast waves roaring through the ranks of Union infantry all around them. "The concussion would almost sweep us along the ground, they were so near to us," Lt. Cruikshank writes, "This was no time to think of moving to the right or to the left. To hold our part of the line was enough."[381] There was a tremendous amount of smoke. Often the soldiers of the 123rd New York couldn't fully see the massed Rebel ranks but just aimed at the muzzle flashes stabbing from the fog down the slope. As dusk came on the charges ceased. The enemy withdrew.

"This has been the hardest fight I was ever in. I fired 112 rounds," Sergeant Lorenzo Coy wrote, "I would here ascribe thanks to God for His care over me. Today death has been about me on every side but no harm has come near me." Coy fired over a hundred rounds even though he missed the second charge as he took a detail of three men to the rear for more ammunition. Corporal Rice Bull fired "about 70 rounds" but knew of many men that claimed to have fired over one hundred rounds during the battle. Total losses for the Federal forces: 300 killed; 1,410 wounded. The Confederates: 1,113 killed; 2,500 wounded; and 1,183 captured/missing.[382]

For the 1st Brigade it appears a total of 61 men were killed, 162 wounded and two men captured or missing. The 46th Pennsylvania alone accounts for 41% of those killed in the brigade. On the exposed right, it came under flanking fire during the attacks until the 27th Indiana was rushed forward to plug the hole between the 46th PA and the 14th Corps. Regimental losses break down as follows: 46th PA, 25 killed, 33 wounded, 1 missing; 141st NY 15 killed, 37 wounded; 5th CT 14 killed, 50 wounded, 1 missing; 123rd NY 7 killed, 42 wounded.[383] While it had the lowest casualties, the 123rd New York was right in the center of the battle. How did they keep the casualty numbers low, to what can this be attributed?

One reason is the prompt action to construct some sort of breastworks for protection and the lucky chance of a readily available log structure to provide material just 50 feet behind their initial line. Corporal Bull noted that, "The logs from the old house saved our company from great loss as without the cover they made we would have been greatly exposed."[384]

Topography also played a factor. Sergeant Gourlie specifically attributes terrain for helping the 123rd at Peach Tree Creek. "Our Regt suffered the least of any in our Brigade on account of the situation of the ground we occupied the Rebs shot over our heads." They were on a low ridge line behind crudely constructed breastworks with the Confederates firing up the hill at them.[385]

Intelligent actions by the 123rd soldiers out on the skirmish line just before the battle opened also played a part. A day after the battle, when Lt. Cruikshank asked the pickets for their report on the action they told him a man in a Federal officer's uniform had ridden along the line just before the attack ordering the skirmish line to advance. "Our men did not know him and did not obey. He was a Rebel trying to trap our men."[386]

"Dear Father I will try and write you a line but I am most afraid you cannot read it I have only one hand to write with and I cant hold the paper still...."[387] What Corporal Henry Welch's parents must have thought on reading that opening! Wounded during the battle, he sent a cryptic, short note home as he was about to be shipped back to a hospital in Nashville. Yet the wound was of the million-dollar variety. Amidst the battle, Welch must have raised the ramrod up above his head during loading when a bullet struck off two fingers of his left hand. He was going to the rear to let his hand heal and expected to return to the 123rd ranks soon. But he was not going to see the front lines anymore, the war was over for him. The majority of the 123rd New York wounded were done with fighting. Of the 42 wounded, eight would die of their wounds, 17 would be discharged from hospitals or transferred and only 17 (40%) would return to the regiment's ranks.

"As soon as daylight came the dead were picked up and placed in row for burial. Each company buried its own dead, marking the graves with a head-board with the name, regiment and company to which they belonged. The wounded received every attention that could be given," Lt. Cruikshank says, "The whole day was taken up in looking after the dead and wounded."[388]

Corporal McLean visited the hospital. "The scene defies description. Wounded not yet attended to lay all around groaning and making a most dismal sound. Mangled in every shape, calling for aid. Surgeons hard at work amputating." Sergeant Lorenzo Coy walked over the battlefield the next morning, "The sights were sickening... went to the 1st Division Hospital. Found many a familiar face here and there torn and mangled. Saw Capt. Wiley's corpse. Lt. Hill of Co. I is now in command of Co. K."[389]

"My dear Madam, I address you today for the sadest of purposes, to inform you that your brave husband has lain down his life for his country," Lt. Colonel James Rogers wrote to Jennie Wiley. Rogers tries to comfort the widow by writing of her husband's last minutes, the men having spoken as Wiley passed by with a box of ammo. "I never saw him in better spirits." 1st Lieutenant George Baker of Company K also wrote Wiley's wife in an effort to comfort her. "Capt. was spoken very highly of both by Officers and men and died nobly doing his whole duty which though not making the loss less to you must be a consolation...Permit me in behalf of the Company and myself to tender you our sympathy in your great bereavement."[390]

The loss of Wiley, Daicy and Carey was a blow to the 123rd but for sheer command structure destruction the battle fell heaviest on the 141st New York. Riding forward as the fighting commenced, the 141st staff officers ran right into the Confederate ranks; shot down in rapid sequence were the Colonel, Lt. Colonel, Major and Adjutant. It could have been worse for the entire 20th Corps except for those messages exchanged a few days before between Sherman, Grant and the War Department. In response to concerns as to Rebel reinforcements from Lee's army, Sherman had ordered McPherson's troops to swing far enough south to cut the railroad linking Atlanta with the east. Just as the battle of Peach Tree Creek was about to open, Hood learned of this movement. He pulled one of the best divisions in his army out of line, General Patrick Cleburne's, and sent it southeast to help counter McPherson's advance. The body punch to the Union 20th Corps was still solid, but weaker than it could have been.

After the repulse at Peach Tree Creek Hood ordered his troops into the defenses of Atlanta. Pushing forward on July 22nd with the rest of the Union forces, the 123rd New York came within sight of the city. Fortifications stretched from horizon to horizon, circling the southern citadel on a circumference from a mile to a mile-and-a-half from the city center. Moving forward to seize some high ground near the city, the 123rd New York started digging entrenchments and immediately came under artillery fire. Lt. Cruikshank kept his company at work while he watched for the shells. "...I would watch for the flash of the gun and when I ordered them to lie down they must drop flat on the ground. They did so and when the shell had passed over they would spring up and work as fast as they could until I saw another flash and would call for them to lie down again. In this way we built our works."[391] By nightfall they had a good beginning for entrenchments, ones they felt they could hold if attacked. During the night company officers went forward with details to establish a picket line. Out in an open field, the picket locations were excavated rifle-pits with enough room to hold three to five men. Silently dug that first night and manned, shift changes would only occur at night as snipers would kill anyone showing themselves during daylight.

Sherman did not have enough men to fully invest Atlanta. He would have to cut the final railroad line to the south if he was to succeed. Artillery emplacements, redoubts, traverses and spiked abattis began to work around Atlanta on the east and north as the seige lines were created. Shelling was constant, the sputtering orbs crisscrossing the sky over the 123rd New York's position. Explosions, whining and screaming of metal, dirt flying skyward and splattering down among the troops; it all became routine. "It is strange how fearless men will get of shells," Corporal McLean noted, "The men are all over the fields, shells are skipping along occasionally wounding a man but not much notice or warning is taken from it." Private William Tooley couldn't help but notice one Rebel calling card. "this morning I was lying in my tent reading when a shell came over & burst over our heads a piece of it struck just at the edge of the knapsack that my head was on throwing dirt all over me and the tent I have been very fortunate so far"[392]

Confederate artillery was launching a myriad of 20, 64 and 100 pound shells at the 123rd New York. They made an impressive sight in the air but didn't really dismay the soldiers on the receiving end. "they are either poor artilerests or cannot get range on our breastworks," Sergeant Gourlie noted, "one shot struck the works near the left of our Regt & made the dirt fly in all directions. I believe that is the only one they have succeeded in putting in the 'right place.'" There were some close calls though. "One shell struck the ground, then bounded over the works and struck the ground again where Lieutenant Beattie had stepped from, then bounded into a tent ten feet away and landed in a frying pan," Lt. Cruikshank relates, "It was fortunate for us that it did not explode. How the men laughed when they saw the twenty-pound shell in the pan. They thought they would not cook it as it would be hard to digest."[393]

With Atlanta's railroad communications to the north and east destroyed, the Confederate army depended on the remaining southern line into the city for supplies. Sherman decided to sever it and sent Union General Howard's troops sweeping west around the city on that mission. On July 28th at Ezra Church Howard's troops were attacked. Union casualties were 632 to the Confederates 3,000 but the battle stalled any further advancement towards the remaining rail line into the city. A follow up attempt to send two Union cavalry forces on raids, one against the rail line and the other to rescue POW's at Andersonville, ended disasterously with both virtually destroyed. Sherman sat back in his lines and let artillery work over the city while planning a new maneuver.

On August 4th Sergeant Lorenzo Coy sat in the trenches and penned some thoughts. "My birthday. The 2nd one I have spent in the Army. It becomes me this day to ask myself if I am living as I should. I have placed my mark high, I have strived to take Jesus as my great example – but how far short I fall. I want to be a better man. I have won the name of being a good and brave soldier in my country's service – Let me be the same in my Lord's." He also reflected on joining the military, "I do not regret the step. I then, and do still, consider the cause of the Union a sacred cause."[394]

Lives were being given for it. On August 8th Sergeant Coy noted that Private Alpheus Osborn (Co. K) was shot and killed on the picket line. "He needlessly exposed himself by standing up the bank in view of the enemy." Ten days later Lt. Cruikshank lost one of his Company H men, Private James Beattie, on the picket line. "The enemy got sight of him and shot him through the heart. He did not know what killed him. We buried him near our camp." Cruikshank felt an elevated level of hatred in the Atlanta seige lines. "I never before saw the enemy show such a murderous disposition for so long a time. Sometimes our men will place a hat on top of the works as if someone were looking at them and soon a zip will be heard, a bullet passing close to it. The men must keep out of sight all of the time." By the 16th Cruikshank notes, "The enemy keep a close lookout for our movements and fire on any man they can see. There is no exchanging for tobacco now."[395]

Day and night shells were being fired into Atlanta every ten minutes. Skirmishing was constant as were sniper rounds among the 123rd New York soldiers. Near their position were two 32-pound seige cannon roaring forth on that ten minute schedule whether the men were in the entrenchments or trying to get some sleep. Corporal Clark McLean was within the concussion zone of the big guns puzzling over nothing flitting about in the few trees. "I haven't seen a bird in a number of months. I dont know whether it is common in this climate or whether cannonading that is going on daily is the cause." Even with the steadily timed artillery blasts ringing in their ears, the sound of Rebel bands could be heard each evening. Yankee bands would play in reply. Nights were somewhat cool so, other than the noise, it was decent for sleeping but the days were another story. "The heat is awful," Sergeant Gourlie wrote his sister Marie, "but we have become pretty well accustomed to it. all tanned up. you would not hardly know us." As for Atlanta, he told her the men of the 123rd were looking forward to "walking its aristocratic Streets which have never been tread by the feet of Yanks or the Northern hordes." Gourlie also wrote his brother Henry, "glad to hear your crop of hay is so good wish I could give you a hand at doing the haying but we have a pretty good crop of Rebs here which we will have to take care of first."[396]

Sherman's plan for taking care of the Rebel crop in Atlanta involved a massive movement of his army out of the entrenchments and a westward swing for that final rail line once again. To protect his own railroad communications, he decided to detail the 20th Corps to the bridge at the Chattahoochee River and the nearby fords. By August 24th rumors were going through the 123rd camp that some movement was imminent. At 5 a.m. orders came through the ranks. August 25th saw the 123rd New York break camp at dawn and march with quickened step back to the railroad bridge crossing the Chattahoochee. As it came into view the men saw another regiment was already at work throwing up entrenchments. Engineers laid out a line for the 123rd and the men started shoveling and heaving timbers into place. As evening came on the entire 20th Corps arrived and joined in the fortification building. Sherman evacuated the seige lines overnight and disappeared from the Confederate's front. The 20th Corps' job was to hold the railroad line at all hazards while the rest of the army marched to the west and then south to disrupt Hood's final supply line.

On the 26th skirmishers were sent out from the 20th Corps to make contact with any Rebel forces. Patrols of the enemy were within a mile of the river entrenchments trying to find the Yankees and make some sense of what was going on. Lt. Cruikshank says no firing took place, "The enemy were looking to see what had become of us. Some of them had better look the other way and find where the larger part of Sherman's army is, with Sherman planning for their capture."[397]

The 1st Division of the 20th Corps was guarding the railroad bridge, the other two divisions were along the river guarding nearby fords. For the 123rd New York it was a great location as they were in a wooded area right next to the river. As the men basically just had to rotate through guard duty it was an easy time. "We have strong lines of works built & some very tolerable forts with 20 pounders mounted. The Rebs will have hard times to drive us away," Corporal McLean writes, adding, "the river is full of Yankees all the time, quite a novelty to see a thousand or two in the water at once."[398]

Relaxation for the many at this time found only grief for one. Private William Tooley was still trying to deal with the death of his brother Horace two months earlier when he learned upsetting news. Horace had saved up about $100 and sent it home before he was killed, now there was a risk of it being used for a drinking binge by their father. William wrote his brother Eber to make his feelings clear on this issue. "And now I must speak on a different subject and one that pains me to think of for it does not seem possible that any being having the least claim on humanity could be so depraved and have so small a position of human feelings common to all men as to do as father has done in regards to Horace disposition of his money...But my mind is made up on one thing now That is if one cent of that money goes for liquoir that Father need never look to me for another cents worth of help if I live to return and if not I will have it so arranged that my wishes may be granted in regards to what I may leave...one hundred dol if he gets it will never do the family ten dollars worth of good...but if he & Mother would take 100.00 of it and use it as other men would to by clothing flour &c it would do a great deal of good..." William added in the margins of the letter, "It is at your own Option whether you read this letter to father or not when he is sober but not when he is not sober"[399]

Another top command change for the soldiers occurred at this time, General Hooker having resigned after not getting a promotion he felt he deserved. General Slocum thereupon returned to lead the 20th Corps. "General Slocum rode along our lines today. He met with an enthusiastic reception from the men of the old '12th'," Sergeant Coy notes. One of those cheering was Corporal McLean. "He was received with hearty cheers as he rode along the line the first time. Next to Joe Hooker he is the man for us."[400]

On a much more personal, and hostile level, the soldiers of the 123rd New York where shocked to learn at this time that they had a new colonel. Not their beloved Lt. Colonel Rogers with whom they had shared so much combat and danger but an officer in New York City, one Ambrose Stevens, former Lt. Colonel of the 46th New York. This was not viewed favorably by the men. Corporal McLean probably voiced the thoughts of all his comrades when he wrote, "He is on Gen Dix's staff in New York City. One of the home soldiers, a pretty specimen to place over men who have seen hard service in the front for 2 years. He will meet with a cool reception if he ever comes to the regt." Word of this rapidly got back to Washington County and questions started to be asked as to why the 123rd New York's Lt. Colonel Rogers had been passed over. Republican papers were quick to blame Governor Seymour. An article at the time in the *Salem Press,* which rose to the defense of Seymour, sheds light on the promotion. General Dix, says the *Salem Press*, was seeking to have Stevens appointed a colonel so he would have sufficient rank to be Judge Advocate on Dix's staff. The general had asked the governor to appoint Stevens a colonel at the first opportunity. Colonel McDougall of the 123rd died and it was the first opportunity. Colonel Stevens was never to come out to the field and take command of the regiment. Instead he stayed in New York City while Lt. Colonel Rogers continued commanding the men. As a way of correcting this, Stevens would be appointed the colonel of the 176th New York in November, Rogers would then be promoted to the top command of the 123rd New York.[401]

As to who would command Atlanta, the Southerners in the city were in for a rude surprise. After finding deserted Yankee seige lines General Hood assumed Sherman had retreated. The citizens were thrilled to have survived the dreaded hordes of the North and Hood arranged a victory ball. Then it all came crashing down. August 28th Hood learned the true situation and tried to hurry troops south to protect the remaining railroad line. Battles ensued but it was too late, the bluecoats severed the last supply corridor for the barricaded Secessionists of Atlanta.

About 3 a.m. of August 31st the soldiers of the 123rd New York were awakened by explosions from the direction of Atlanta. Rapid musket firing then continued for an hour. The next morning at 4 a.m. another series of explosions had the soldiers discussing the battle they all felt sure was going on. The explosions were "so heavy that the earth trembled at this distance," Lt. Cruikshank noted.[402] They passed the day standing duty near the river and wondered where their comrades were and what the results of all the fighting had been.

Pickets went out early September 2nd but came back reporting no enemy in the immediate front. The 123rd New York was sent out on a reconnaissance towards the city, with back up from following 1st Brigade regiments. After approaching the outskirts the 123rd commenced light skirmishing but the few defenders fell back through their fortifications and continued on through the city. At this point a courier rode up with a message that Union detachments had entered the city and that Lt. Colonel Rogers was to enter with his command immediately. Atlanta had been abandoned! The men were excited and cheered as they entered the deserted fortifications and marched into Atlanta proper. It was a proud moment for all of the men, Sergeant Gourlie writing, "<u>our</u> Brigade Flag was the <u>first</u> Yankee Flag run up on a flag-staff in Atlanta City."[403]

"How the men did cheer as they passed through the city! They did little plundering," Lt. Cruikshank says, although he notes, "They found a tobacco storehouse and helped themselves to tobacco and cigars." Actually, the soldiers of the 123rd loaded themselves down with a lot of leaf. "Our Regt was in the advance of the Brigade & our boys have got a supply of <u>Tobacco</u> & <u>Segars</u> on hand sufficient to last for some time. some of the boys got as much as 150lbs. of Tobacco," Sergeant Gourlie wrote his brother. Private Levi Eaton partook of the opportunity and felt the men all had "enough now to last us 3 months."[404]

The men marched along looking over the rubble from the burned and blasted out houses. In every yard the soldiers noted little mounds of earth and timbers, forms of underground bombproofs which families ran into whenever the shelling got too near. Locals referred to them as "gopher holes." Smoking wreckage along the railroad tracks in the city settled the question of what all the explosions were a couple nights before, the Rebs had torched an ammunition train. Forty cars of shells, powder and cartridges devastated the region around the depot, even tossing five train engines about. Also fired were several warehouses of supplies. "Talk about Nero fiddling while Rome was burned. We beat that here," Corporal McLean wrote. He also noted a macabre spectacle as he marched through the city. Sitting on the smoking ruins of a machine shop was a Union soldier playing a harp. "He cut quite a grotesque figure."[405]

"As the campaign is over we all feel pretty well used up," Lt. Cruikshank wrote his wife. "From May 14th until August 25th we were not out of the sound of musketry firing. I thank God he has protected me through all these dangers."[406]

Chapter 9
Marching to the Sea

"We certainly have had a great victory," Private Levi Eaton wrote his wife from Atlanta. With much prescience Corporal Clark McLean wrote his father the day after entering Atlanta, "The news of the taking of the place will not be apt to help the Chicago numines. I understand McClellen got the nomination."[407]

One can assume that McLean used "numines" as a play on the Democrat candidates for the 1864 national election. At the end of August the Democrats met in Chicago and nominated Union General George McClellen for president and George Pendleton of Ohio for vice-president. McClellen was counting upon strong support from the soldiers to put him in the White House but he had an uphill battle. The party platform was created by the peace faction of the Democrats. It termed the war a failure while calling for a stop to the war without preconditions. McClellen tried to distance himself from the platform as he wanted reunion but such attempts fell weakly upon many ears, particularly as his running mate was a peace advocate. Soldiers in Atlanta just had to discuss the coming election with the locals to clarify the situation. McLean made the rounds only to note, "Gen McClellen nominated at the Chicago convention for president. The secesh here are all in favor of Mc. and the Union opposed to him."[408]

Not all the Unionists were against McClellan. Over in the 46th Pennsylvania Corporal William Shimp wrote his wife, "Well from present appearances Genl. George B. McClellan will be the Candidate for President and my hopes and prayers are that he may be elected and then I think we may have peace. I have a new way to make Democrats out of Republicans – draft them and they soon oppose the administration and change their politics. I know men that were drafted and sent to the regiment that are now the strongest kind of Democrats."[409]

Surprisingly, there were quite a few Unionists in the city. "The people of the city appear pleased that we have possession of it," Lt. Robert Cruikshank wrote, "There are a number of New York families here. They have made themselves known and ask protection, which is given to all who are of Northern principles." Sergeant John Gourlie also found the locals wanting the blue uniforms around. "the City suffered severely from the shelling which the Yanks gave I should judge about [three-quarters] of the houses have been struck by shot or Shell. a large number of the citizens stayed & some of them appeared might glad to see the Yankees." Many of the 123rd New York soldiers took their rations and knocked on doors in the city to contract for the lady of the house to cook a dinner. Sergeant Henry Morhous says that it was "not that she could prepare the meals better than they could themselves, but the great attraction was in eating from white plates and sitting at a table." With the 20th Corps moving into the city, construction of shanties commenced and there was plenty of building material at hand. Doors, windows and timbers were gathered from the destroyed houses lining the streets. Says Corporal McLean, "We have got the best camp & quarters we ever had, have a good house built with three windows & a good fireplace."[410] The 123rd New York was on the east side of the city with the 1st Division between the last houses and the evacuated Confederate fortifications.

Around this time Private Jeremiah Holbrook must have returned to the regiment. He had deserted in December of 1862. He was arrested May 14th, 1864 in the Albany, New York area for desertion. His trial on June 23, 1864 at Alexandria, Virginia found him guilty of desertion and sentenced him to forfeit all pay and allowances to May 14th, to forfeit $8 a month from his pay since May 14th and to make good time lost by his desertion. The Quartermaster Office of Albany sent a small printed form to the 123rd New

York seeking "authorized reward of $30.00" for capturing a deserter. Holbrook must have had very little, if any, money issued to him on future paydays. On the back of the Quartermaster request is written, "J. Holbrook charged $30.00 for his arrest."[411]

He also would have been billed for transport costs back to his unit. While soldiers could ride the military rail road for no charge, once out of the war zone tickets had to be purchased. Even soldiers given furloughs for home had to cough up the bucks to ride the rails. Private Samuel Atwood (Co. H) at this time had a furlough for home. It cost him $3.80 to go from Nashville to Louisville, then $17.96 for transport from Louisville to Albany. This was charged against his payroll account and, as privates were given $13 a month, the round trip would see just over three months pay docked.[412]

Thirty miles to the southwest of Atlanta Confederate General Hood sat with his army of 40,000 planning his next move. Sherman's supply line stretching some 120 miles from Chattanooga offered opportunity. Hood intended to interdict it, force Sherman to come north from Atlanta to reopen it and then commence battle when a favorable moment arrived. During September 1864 Sherman would dispatch troops piecemeal to protect his railroad lines, beefing up command posts as Southern cavalry began to cause problems. Hood began his movement north on October 1st, two days later Sherman knew of it. Ordering the 20th Corps to guard Atlanta he took 55,000 men north after Hood's army. A series of skirmishes and marches now commenced in Northern Georgia. Always one step ahead of Sherman, Hood by mid-October was in Alabama. While frustrated with trying to pin Hood down, Sherman had received good news from Grant. A march through Georgia to the coast would be allowed. Union General Thomas was stationed in Nashville with sufficient forces to deal with Hood if he moved into Tennessee. Sherman returned to Atlanta to plan the coming March to the Sea.

Tecumseh wasn't bothered by any locals while riding the streets of Atlanta. There weren't any civilians left in the city. When Southern troops disrupted the railroad it became a question of supplying food to the soldiers and civilians in Atlanta. For the commander it was not even a tough call, his troops came first and the civilians would leave. Sergeant John Gourlie wrote his sister Jennie that Sherman ordered the locals to take the oath and go north or "pack up & move south where their rights were to be found." A detail from the 123rd was sent with other Union troops to escort refugees to the town of Rough and Ready, Georgia, several miles south of the city. There, under a flag of truce, they would be turned over to Southern officers. Corporal Bull made the journey as part of the escort. "It was heartrending to witness the distress of these people as they left their homes with the little they were permitted to carry, to go as they said among strangers." Sergeant Morhous felt that it was only the lower strata that had remained in the city, "The wealthier families removed from Atlanta when the firing began, those only remaining who were willing to take the risk of shot and shell, and the possibility of Sherman's army taking the city. Many of those sent into the Rebel lines at Rough and Ready felt very sad at being obliged to leave their homes. They had not felt the war before, except in the cost of the luxuries of life."[413]

Union victories at Mobile, Alabama and in the Shenandoah Valley in Virginia combined with the grand prize of Atlanta to raise Lincoln's chances at reelection. As Sherman's coming campaign called for cutting loose from all communications and disappearing into Georgia, Sherman was under orders not to leave until after the election. President Lincoln did not want rumors and falsehoods of combat disasters dogging his White House chances.

"I suppose there is great excitement about the election there," Private William Tooley wrote his brother Eber in Washington County, "there is great here I shall be glad when it is all over." Abraham Lincoln was quite the political animal. For his running mate in the 1864 election he had Tennessee Governor Andrew Johnson, a former

Democrat. The election ticket would not be "Republican" but ballots would have the title "Union Party" in an effort to pull votes from Democrats wanting to solidly pursue the war. With the Democrats split into pro-war and anti-war wings McClellen was saddled with his pro-war, pro-union statements and an anti-war platform. Nineteen states now allowed their soldier citizens to vote in the field. McClellen expected the soldier vote, it was due him based on the respect and feelings he felt he had earned while leading tens of thousands of troops. He should have done some polling in the camps. "All busy making out our votes," Corporal McLean wrote his mother on October 14th, "I shall send mine to you in a few days. 'Little Mac' will get but few votes from this army."[414]

In order to vote a soldier had to fill out a "Soldier's Power of Attorney" form to authorize a person in Washington County to cast his vote. This was signed by the soldier and witnessed. Then he would fill out the front of an inner envelope which would hold his vote. He states that: he has been a citizen of the United States for ten days, is 21 years old, a resident of New York State for a year, four months a resident of Washington County, with 30 days of town residence, "and am not directly or indirectly interested in any bet or wager depending upon the result of said election...." The ballot would be sealed in the first envelope. Then a larger envelope with "Soldier's Vote" in the upper right corner in bold capital letters would be used for the power of attorney and the sealed ballot. Printed lines in the center of the envelope were used for the address, the soldier being able to send it to the election committee or anyone else in his voting district. To the far left side was printed, "Duties of Elector receiving a Soldier's Vote. Extract from Section 5 of Chapter 253 Laws of 1864." Electors were instructed to open the outer envelope on receiving the letter but not the inner envelope. On the day of election the elector delivers the sealed envelope to inspectors of elections at the proper polling location.[415]

And election committees could be quite one-sided in Washington County. The ballots sent to the 123rd New York from Kingsbury Township had this letter with them dated October 8th, 1864:

The Committee "takes great pleasure in forwarding to you and your noble comrades in arms, the necessary blanks and tickets to enable you to vote in the coming Election. You have heretofore been deprived of the sacred privilege by 'Seymour's veto,' but can no longer be deprived of *killing with the ballots* those enemies in the rear, who are continually giving *aid* and *comfort* to *rebels* in *arms*. We have no fears from the army however, as the soldiers from the front inform us that there are no *Copperheads* there; that the soldiers are all right, and will never do with the ballots what Jeff and his traitorous crue are unable to do with the bullets, to wit: *Drive* PRESIDENT LINCOLN *from Washington.* We have enclosed none but Union tickets as we did not believe that any soldier from Kingsbury would ever honor, with their votes, any 'General' for whom *Peace* men *plead, Copperheads* electioneer, *Rebels* hurrah, and *Traitors* shout...together we will wipe out treason and Copperheads at the North, Traitors and rebels at the South, Foreign enemies all over the earth; and then again, shall that dear old Flag float o'er *all* the land of the free, and the home of the brave."[416]

Democrat ballots were found for the men that wanted to vote for McClellen. "I sent my vote-a good Democrat one too-to Alanso Axtell," Private Levi Eaton told his wife. Private Thomas Dickenson (Co. H) had written his father in August, "well i cant tell you how James [brother] will vote but i shall vote the old ticket that will bee a demacrat one..." Unfortunately for McClellen, Thomas would die of disease within a month so never voted. It reflects the national results. McClellen went down to a 212 to 21 electoral vote loss, carrying only Delaware, Kentucky and New Jersey. Lincoln had taken 55% of the 4,031,887 votes cast. But what stung McClellen the most was the soldiers vote. It is estimated that the military went 70% to 80% for Lincoln. The 123rd New

York would actually top that statistic. Of the 366 votes cast in the regiment, McClellen received 30 votes (8%) to Lincoln's 336 (92%). There were at this time around 420 effectives in the 123rd, those not voting having not yet reached their majority. Over in the 46th Pennsylvania Corporal Shimp wasn't to see much better results for his candidate. The 46th PA went McClellen 131 (35%) and Lincoln 243 (65%). Back in Washington County the votes were McClellen 3,642 (37%) to Lincoln's 6,220 (63%).[417]

Lt. Colonel Rogers in his report for this period states, "The elective franchise, conferred by an act of the New York Legislature at its last session, was here exercised, and it is believed with less of partisan heat and undue influence than ordinarily occurs at elections held in communties free from military authority."[418]

While women could not vote it didn't mean they weren't interested in the election. Mary Cruikshank had written her husband Lt. Robert Cruikshank as to how the men were going to vote. He waited until all the votes were in and on their way to Washington County before replying on October 20th, 1864. "You ask me in your last letter my opinion on the election and the vote of the soldiers. I am sure of Mr. Lincoln's election. I know of the vote of the Regiment for I administered the oath to the officers who filled out the votes for the men in their companies. It was my business as acting adjutant. I have sent my vote to brother Will to cast for me and wrote him if he voted for McClellen he would have to cast one for Mr. Lincoln also. McClellen will get only one soldier's vote to twelve for Lincoln in our Regiment. The army will stand about the same." Lt. Cruikshank gave his wife the tallies for the regiment then adds, "McClellen will have a small soldiers vote. If he is elected it will be the people at home will do it."[419]

It also appears Mary had voiced to her husband some political opinions on larger issues in her recent letters. "I am glad that you feel as you do on the peace question," Lt. Cruikshank wrote his wife, "We had better not have peace until we can have it so that it will be lasting. I would rather stay in the service another year than have it settled as the Copperheads would have it. If it were settled in that way all we have done and suffered, all that has been done so far in putting down the Rebellion both life and property would be thrown away."[420]

With the election over it was time to leave Atlanta and break for open countryside. Sherman began trimming units of weak men, weak animals and excess baggage. Trains started carrying equipment and personnel north that would not be going on the next campaign. While all this was going on in Atlanta Confederate General Hood began an invasion of Tennessee. Northern newspapers fretted over Hood's army running about in the rear areas of the Atlanta troops. Sergeant John Gourlie found the papers sadly deficient as to the Yankee veterans' attitudes on Hood's actions. "the soldiers here are just as unconcerned about Hood being in the rear as though he was in front. we can whip him where ever he is." Due ten months pay, at this time the paymaster arrived and issued eight months currency. The 123rd New York soldiers sent another batch of money home to families, Gourlie sending $160 via a check to his father. Letters had also been going home to younger brothers once again as to the war and the draft. Private William Tooley took time to bend his brother Eber's ear, "I am glad you did not make a fool of your self as Wm T did and run off to canada I was telling Philip about your going out west and a man that heard it says then you mean to get clear from going into the army"[421] William still didn't want his younger brothers Eber or Samuel to join the military but there were ways to avoid service with some honor, running off to Canada wasn't one of them.

Sergeant Gourlie had a few comments for his brother Henry as to the battle for Atlanta and the election. "I have no doubt the citizens of the north were getting impatient about Atlanta. I know a good many that would say – why dont Sherman take Atlanta? what is he waiting for etc etc. one thing that citizens of the north have not got and that is patience..." Gourlie also discusses the return of 2nd Lt.

Walter Martin of Company F who was captured at Culp's Farm. Kept at Charleston, South Carolina he escaped "and a short time since reached our lines about five miles from here. a happier man you never saw than he was when he reached the 123rd. when he was taken prisoner he was strong McClellen man said he would see Old Abe d—d before he would vote for him. while he was a prisoner the Rebs told him several times that little Mac would be next president & that would save the confederacy. pretty plain talk to a Northern McL man that was fighting to put down the Rebs dont you think so? well it was most to strong for the Lieut. it made a Lincoln man to the backbone of him & he voted for Old Abe when we had our election. I wish some of our McClellen Citizens could be placed under the Rebs care for about two months it would cure them."[422]

    Martin's escape and return went around the regiment. "He has had rough times," Corporal McLean noted in his diary, "Got away from them twice and was retaken. Lay in a swamp over night and was bitten by a snake. His wound was so bad that he was obliged to give himself up...He reports much suffering on the part of our prisoners. The rest of our boys are at Andersonville."[423]

    The 123rd New York started the Atlanta Campaign with 523 effectives. A few days after entering Atlanta, Lt. Colonel Rogers gives the total in ranks as 415. As the men were preparing for the next campaign 43 recruits came into camp. Rogers notes that very little drill or training could be completed with them before orders came to march. He also made sure to have all convalescent 123rd soldiers returned to the regiment. Rumors of a movement were bandied about camp in early November but a series of wet days delayed the striking of tents. By November 11th the soldiers expected to be going towards the coast of Georgia and Savannah was understood to be the probable destination. Everyone was in waiting mode for the weather to break. For the movement Sherman had four corps divided into two wings: the left wing comprised of the 14th & 20th Corps under General Slocum; the right wing consisting of the 15th & 17th Corps under General Howard. The army would total some 60,000 men. While Savannah would be a nice prize and seal off another port from blockade runners, Sherman's larger goal was to break the Southerners will to fight by devastating the countryside and demonstrating that Federal power could be projected at will across the land.

The 123rd New York would field 18 officers and 447 men for the march. (The regiment at this time had 14 officers and 73 men on detached duty, total 552.) With Slocum promoted commander of the left wing General Alpheus Williams took command of the 20th Corps (some 13,000 infantry), General Nathaniel Jackson 1st Division (5,363), and Colonel James Selfridge 1st Brigade (1,511). Brother regiments of the 123rd in the 1st brigade consisted of: 5th Connecticut, 141st New York and 46th Pennsylvania. A sign of the severity of the Atlanta Campaign can be seen in that of the four regiments in the 1st Brigade, the 123rd NY and 5th CT were commanded by Lt. Colonels, the 46th PA by a Major and the 141st NY by a Captain.[424]

Rains ending, the columns were put in motion November 15th with the right wing striking towards Macon and the left wing towards Stone Mountain, Georgia. Telegraph wires were cut and Atlanta left in such condition that no use of it could be made by the Confederates. Any building of use to the Southern war effort-machine shop, warehouse, factory-had been set afire. The use of the torch "meant the destruction of the whole city," Corporal Bull writes, "for when once the blaze was started there was nothing to prevent its spread." The 123rd New York soldiers marched out loudly singing "John Brown's Body." Behind them a four square mile area of structures was sparking, crackling and crashing to the ground. "It was yet early morning, there was but little wind and the smoke hung like a great black pall over the doomed city..."[425]

"We left camp at 6. The city is in flames and the buildings falling in," Corporal McLean noted on leaving. After the day's march of fifteen miles, he says, "This evening we could see the fire near Atlanta very plainly."

According to Corporal Bull the regiment was into camp by 6 p.m. That night, "as we looked toward the west the sky was lighted up with the flames of burning Atlanta."[426]

Sherman's two wings had a front of nearly sixty miles as they moved forward. The four corps were marching side by side and within support distance if any of them were attacked. These were hardened veteran troops commanded by officers in whom they had faith. Fall onto one of the columns and expect a slashing snapping strike from the nearest support. But would there be any attacks at all? Did the Rebs have a means of stopping Sherman's soldiers? The only force large enough to seriously challenge the Union columns was Hood's and he was moving into Tennessee away from Sherman's troops. Hood intended to destroy Union forces in Tennessee, move into Central Kentucky, recruit his army up then move through the Cumberland Gap to aid Lee. Georgia was on its own. With Yankee wings in Georgia spread out on such a wide front, the local commanders could not ascertain just where Sherman was going. Most assumed Macon or Augusta as these were major industrial centers for the Southern war effort, then there was the state capital at Milledgeville. Arguments erupted as to the proper action to take, what cities to try and defend, what towns to write off. But other than General Joseph Wheeler's cavalry and some locally raised militia there weren't any troops for defence.

There were plenty of blue-uniformed ones for offense though, and well equipped. "All the troops were provided with good wagon trains, loaded with ammunition and supplies, approximating twenty days' bread, forty days' sugar and coffee, a double allowance of salt for forty days, and beef-cattle equal to forty days' supply. The wagons were also supplied with about three days' forage, in grain," General Sherman wrote of the movement, "All were instructed, by a judicious system of foraging, to maintain this order of things as long as possible, living chiefly, if not solely, upon the country, which I knew to abound in corn, sweet potatoes, and meats."[427]

The area around Atlanta having been stripped bare from the opposing armies, it wasn't until the 20th Corps was beyond Stone Mountain that foraging would return a profit. By the third day of the march the soldiers had entered a highly productive farming region and the foraging began. Every morning an officer from each regiment was put in charge of a foraging detail. Each detail was made up of about 25 volunteers, the men being referred to as "bummers." Starting early, the foragers would advance out to the Union cavalry screen and commence visiting plantations. At first going out on foot, the men rapidly found mules and horses at the plantations for future foraging use. Food was the main item sought but also any property that could be useful for the Confederate war effort was targeted for destruction. This included cotton gins, cotton bales and any fodder not taken for Federal use. Locals knew the Yankees were coming and tried to hide their food and farm animals. Food was often buried in boxes while horses, mules and cattle were driven into swamps. "As the work of concealment was done almost entirely by Negroes and as they knew where every box was buried it did not take long for our 'bummers' to find out where they were hidden," Corporal Bull says, "The Negroes were used, or I may say were forced, to reveal the hiding places." Ham, corn meal, bacon, sweet potatoes and carcasses of pigs or even razorback hogs were nightly trotted into camps to roast over the fires. "Fresh pork, ham and sweet potatoes were the articles most desired," Bull writes, "articles we could cook & carry along with us."[428]

Corporal Bull seems to have had a distaste for the foraging aspect of The March to the Sea. "While I appreciated the necessity of securing supplies from the country over which we were passing, the gathering of these supplies was a service not relished by me. There were those in the Company who were anxious for this detail and anxious to do this work, and having a desire for it would be more efficient and successful."[429]

There also was a system to the marching. Each Corps was to have its own road as a system of parallel highways existed. Then there was a daily rotation within each Corps to be fair and spread out the duties. The 20th Corps consisted of three divisions and the Corps would march thus: cavalry scouts ahead; then two divisions of infantry with the Corps artillery; the baggage train; ambulances; wagons carrying pontoons for bridging; the third division of infantry bringing up the rear with at least one of its brigades assigned to march among the wagon train to protect against cavalry attacks. Further to the rear and to the sides of the column were more Union cavalry. Each division would shift position each day of the march. Therefore if the 1st Division led on Monday it would bring up the rear on Tuesday, be the second in line Wednesday and return to lead the column Thursday. As each division also had three brigades the same rotation occurred on a daily basis within the divisions. Every daily start units assigned to the rear had to wait until everyone else was marching forward. So, every third day the soldiers had a couple hours to relax as the day started. Ideally this is the way the system was supposed to work, in reality it could be a couple days before a rotating of units occurred due to marching conditions or concerns of enemy action.

    For the first five days the weather held and the road surfaces were dry. By the 18th the 123rd New York was marching through Social Circle, Georgia. According to Sergeant Henry Morhous it was here that the first blacks began to follow the 20th Corps column. Slaves would make their escape to the Union troops and find some way to make themselves useful. Morhous relates that each company of the 123rd had two or three pack mules for carrying equipment. Soon the blacks were given the duty of caring for and leading the mules on the march. They also became cooks and general servants for the men.[430] Marching another fifteen miles on the 19th troops passed through Madison. Now more runaways joined the procession; following in the wake of the column with their few belongings and family members, hoping that Confederate cavalry didn't fall on them, that the Federals didn't abandon them, that reaching the coast would also mean reaching opportunity for freedom and a chance at a new life.

"Negroes of all ages and every variety of physical condition, from the infant in its mother's arms to the decrepid old man, joined the column from plantations and from cross-roads, singly and in large groups, on foot, on horseback, and in every description of vehicles. The vehicles were discarded, as obstructing the progress of our very long column. Beyond this no effort was made to drive away the fugitives. The decrepid, the aged, and the feeble were told of the long journey before them, and advised to remain behind. I estimate that at from 6,000 to 8,000 slaves, at different points in the campaign, joined the march of this corps..." reported Brigadier General Alpheus Williams, commanding 20th Corps.[431]

It was sheer luck as to the reaction of a regiment's white troops when the blacks approached. Sherman's army was a hodgepodge of toughened soldiers from the Northeast to across today's Upper Midwest. Abolitionist leanings were present in many of the units from the east while many of the western troops had no love at all for the freedman.

November 20th a cold rain broke upon the marching soldiers. "This days march was a very severe one, owing to the muddy conditions of the roads, more or less rain during the entire day and night," Colonel James Selfridge, 1st Brigade commander, noted.[432] (Selfridge was former commander of the 46th Pennsylvania.) As each day's march was coming to an end, officers would ride ahead and select fields for the encampments. The lead unit would file off first to pitch tents, then the following unit, and then the rear unit going to the front for the next day's march. As soon as guns were stacked the men dashed off for fence rails and wood for fires. Then tents were set up and dinner was made. Singing and dancing might fill the evening until "lights out." Another slog on the 21st saw them make 12 miles as they passed through Eatonton.

The next day the 20th Corps arrived at the Georgia State Capital of Milledgeville. On the 23rd all efforts were directed at the capital and the section of Georgia Central Railroad running through the town. Soldiers of the 123rd New York, along with others, spent the day destroying war material. "The magazines, arsenals, factories of various kinds, with storehouses containing large amounts of Government property, with about seventeen hundred bales of cotton, were burned," Sergeant Morhous writes. Colonel Selfridge reported that the 1st Brigade put their backs to the railroad "five miles of which we completely destroyed by burning and bending the rails." Southern railroads weren't hard to destroy and Corporal Bull puts it down to the lightweight construction and the use of pitch pine ties which burned readily once lit. Some of the men, like Private William Tooley, wondered what comments the home folks would have as to the destruction. "I dont know what people would think up there to see men destroying good solid rail road in a way we done it we would all get at one side and get hold of the ties at one end of a piece of the road and tip it all over whole after it was started it would all be bottom side in a few moments the length of the brigade"[433] Piling the ties for a fire, the men then would lay the rails over the flames. Once red hot in the center the men pulled them out and either put wrenches at each end and twisted the rail into a corkscrew or simply wrapped them around trees. The latter method became known as "Sherman's neckties."

    Since the men were stationary for the day they chose to have an early Thanksgiving. A thousand bushels of buried sweet potatoes were found in a plantation field where the 123rd New York made camp. For meat the foragers brought in fresh pork, geese, hens and turkeys. Bull and ten other 123rd soldiers pooled their food of several hens, a goose, fresh pork and a bag of wheat flour for a feast. They paid two dollars to a woman in the slave quarters of the plantation to cook the meal, the soldiers helping by plucking the fowl and gathering the water and wood. "We felt that we had much to be thankful for," Corporal Bull writes, "I do not believe there were many homes in the North, that Thanksgiving Day, had any thing better or a dinner that was more fully appreciated than the spread we had in the Negro hut at Milledgeville." The soldiers lingered in the quarters for the warmth until night was coming on then said goodbye to the cook, left "a goodly portion" of the food with her and went out into a snow flurry. As for all the sweet potatoes, the entire crop was consumed within twenty-four hours by the army.[434]

The delay in marching wasn't just for destroying the railroad. Southern units on the 22nd had attacked a brigade of the 15th Corps at Griswoldville. Units of Confederate General Joseph Wheeler's cavalry and 3,000 Georgia militia threw themselves upon the Federal right flank as it passed to the east of Macon. An all day affair, it saw three Rebel charges upon the Yankees but to no avail. Nightfall saw the Confederates retreat after suffering over 600 casualties. Union losses were 13 killed, 79 wounded, and 2 missing. This action delayed the march of the right wing of Sherman's army and the left was told to hold a day. As for the town of Griswoldville, much of it was military industry. Union cavalry burned gun shops, mills, factories, the railroad depot and most of the homes. There was nothing left but Griswold's home which had been used as a headquarters. The town ceased to exist.[435]

When the 123rd NewYork marched forward at 7 a.m. on the 24th the Georgia State Capital had been ransacked with many government buildings burned but the private homes of its two thousand some residents still lined the streets. As the rear guard in blue went into the eastern horizon food was the main overriding issue for the remaining civilians. The troops had eaten or loaded out everything they had found. Help came when Confederate cavalry herded 50 captured beef cattle into the city and rations were sent from other areas of Georgia. Yet with the railroad destroyed and the main bridge over the Oconee River burned Milledgeville was totally isolated. In 1868 Georgia moved its capital to Atlanta.[436]

Roads were much better with the weather cold and clear as 14 miles were made to the little town of Hebron. The march was halted at 4 p.m. and the troops went into camp. An early start at six on the 25th ground to a halt at eight before Buffalo Swamp. Rebel cavalry had destroyed nine bridges through the boggy ground and the wagons, let alone the thousand of soldiers, would need a proper roadway to proceed. First some of Wheeler's Cavalry had to be chased away. It was a light skirmish, some 15 Yanks were casualties and some Confederates were captured. Southerners had been amazed and frustrated at the speed at which Northern engineering troops could repair railroad tracks destroyed by raids. They were now to see the abilities honed in bridge and roadway work. "Were detained here until 2PM by which time the bridges were rebuilt and we passed quietly over the Swamp," 1st Brigade commander Colonel Selfridge notes.[437] Pushing on another five miles the column made camp two miles shy of Sandersville.

Sandersville was reached on the 26th with skirmishing all the way to the village. As the 1st Brigade had the lead, one regiment was deployed as skirmishers and the 123rd New York with the remaining regiments were in line of battle to each side of the road as the column moved forward. "The movement was executed in the handsomest manner, and was so effectual as not to impede the march of the column in the slightest degree, although the roll of musketry was unceasing," Sergeant Morhous writes. Although the 123rd did not suffer any casualties the brigade had about twenty. "The loss to the Rebels must have been more than double that number, for many dead Rebels were seen along the streets of the village. Two or three were killed on the steps of the church."[438] Wheeler's Cavalry would now be a constant harassment to the 20th Corps front but the Southerners were in no strength to seriously challenge the Union forces.

Sandersville was a village of about 800 people. "The citizens are all scared to pieces. Think that a lot of savages are coming," Corporal McLean noted in his diary, "The principal buildings in town are burned." With all the 20th Corps up, the 3rd Division was assigned to guard the wagon trains parked just outside of town while the 1st and 2nd

Divisions began the work of destruction. Colonel Selfridge reports the 1st Brigade "destroyed about 2 miles of Rail Road together with large Government Warehouse, the Rail Road Depot and sixty-two bales of cotton." The 2nd Division continued the railroad destruction the next day to Davisboro as the 1st Division marched the 12 miles along the south side of the tracks. Getting their chance on the wrecking crew on the 28th the men of the 123rd New York got a workout. "Moved to Georgia Central Rail Road and assisted in destroying the track from Davisboro to Spear's Station a distance of 12 miles," Colonel Selfridge notes. "The boys were divided into three parties," Sergeant Morhous says, "The first party turning ties, sleepers and rails over...The squad following would pile the ties up and place on top of the pile the iron rails. The third squad followed on with hatchets and matches..." It was the same on the 29th as Colonel Selfridge reports; "Continued destroying the Rail Road at 7AM and reached Bottwick Station about 6PM after having had destroyed eight miles of Rail Road." Targets of opportunity were also sought out, Morhous listing a steam saw mill with stockpiles of railroad and bridge timber being laid waste.[439]

Leaving the hilly upland region the soldiers now were marching onto the Coastal Plain, a landscape featuring flat terrain and sandy soil. Poor for crops, it was used for tree plantations. Cathedral stands of one-hundred foot pine had shafts of sunlight glinting on the rising dust from a five mile long column of blue. For the marching days of November casualties had only amounted to 144 for the entire 20th Corps.[440] There was no one to stop them. Another 14 miles saw the column through Louisville. December 1st and 2nd had the 123rd New York, along with the 1st Brigade, assigned to the 3rd Division for guarding of their wagon train. Heading towards Millen the march followed the railroad. As units assigned for guard duty marched along their comrades to their side swung, heaved and sang. Fires dotted their march as piles of ties were lit and "Sherman's Neckties" fitted the landscape up for a cotillion.

Millen was reached on December 3rd, some of the Yankees taking the time to visit the POW stockade just outside the village. This was Camp Lawton, built to reduce the numbers at the POW camp at Andersonville. It had only begun to receive transfers on September 28th, 1864. A total of 10,299 POW's arrived at the stockade before Sherman's march required the removal of them. Union cavalry swung off from Sherman's column in an attempt to rescue their comrades at Camp Lawton. They arrived on November 27th to find just scattered trash. The last POW's had been removed five days before. As prison camps go, Camp Lawton was thought out much better than Andersonville. There was a large spring pouring forth nine million gallons of fresh water daily, the latrines were sighted properly to reduce disease, camp ovens had been built and, perhaps the true lesson learned at Andersonville, the camp was laid out in an orderly fashion, the POW's were not shoved into the compound to fend for themselves. The 42 acre compound was built to hold 35,000 prisoners. Although in full operation only six weeks, 685 Union soldiers were buried on the site with about 300 of these labled "unknown." As the 123rd New York soldiers walked the compound and looked over the graveyard they might have wondered if any of the unknowns were from their regiment. It is possible. Andersonville records show Corporal Benjamin Deuel was "sent to Millen, GA November 1864." At this point Benjamin disappears, and as Morhous says, "never heard from." (The Union dead were removed to Beaufort, South Carolina, National Cemetery in 1868 and reinterred. Today the site of Camp Lawton is Magnolia Spring State Park with historical markers as to the POW camp. The spring still flows and is home to sundry turtles.)

During the 15 miles on December 4th the men of the 123rd New York noticed a plantation burning. On closer inspection the men discovered several bloodhounds shot dead in the front yard. Sergeant Morhous states that this was now standard operating procedure. "The soldiers were determined that no more flying fugitives, white or colored, should be followed by hounds that came within reach of their powder and ball. Wherever the boys marched everything in the shape of a dog was immediately shot."[441]

An easy day on the 5th as the 123rd was guard for the wagon train. They didn't start to move until near sundown and then only made four miles before a halt was called near midnight. Roads were poor because of the swampy nature of the ground and lots of work had to be done before the wagons could proceed. The column now was swinging to parallel the Savannah River with a straight shot of sixty miles to the target city.

In the upland regions the farms were abundant and croplands yielded good harvests for the soldiers to appropriate. The sandy pine regions saw harder scavenging of food. Low returns from the "bummers" saw a larger effort being made on December 7th as 100 men under an officer and non-commissioned officer were sent out from the 123rd New York. Striking off to the left about three miles towards the river they came across a plantation. As it had not been visited already by other foragers, the men shot the hogs and loaded out the meat plus a crop of sweet potatoes. Sorghum syrup was also found in troughs and several of the men filled their canteens with it. Further on they came across another plantation but this had already been visited and ransacked. Walking into the house, the officer and NCO found three women who weepingly showed "a scene of shocking confusion; articles of furniture, soiled and broken, were strewn about the floor; bureau drawers had been pulled out and their contents scattered around; trunks had been broken into, and household utensils shattered into pieces beyond the mender's art."[442] It was the third time the house had been vandalized according to the women, by men clad in gray and then by men in blue. When the soldiers could be kept under an officer's control, when discipline was tight, such actions generally were rare. But, again, as an army passes through a landscape it has turbulent areas of lawlessness along its flanks and rear. Many bummers volunteered with the hopes of not being under any officer's control, to be given free range of the countryside to do as they pleased. With 60,000 troops moving through Georgia, if only one percent were of criminal intent that is still 600 armed men. Moving along a front of 60 miles would see ten men per mile of front out solely for themselves. Some of the regiments now had large components of draftees. One has to wonder if there might have been less incidents if the army was still all volunteers. The 123rd New York never had any draftees in its ranks as Washington County increased the bounty until it met its quota for every call up by the federal government. Not that the 123rd boys didn't like a plantation in flames, but their orders were to seize food and destroy property that could help the Southern war effort. There cannot be a doubt that some of them lifted an item or two during the war beyond the standing orders. But no records were found charging any of them with rape or murder.

By the end of December 8th Colonel Selfridge noted that the 1st Brigade was "about 20 miles north west" of Savannah. Moving out as the vanguard of the column the next morning the 123rd New York soldiers were joking and laughing. This was certainly easier than the Atlanta Campaign, a lot of marching but other than that....

A cannon cracked, the shell screaming above them and exploding. The 123rd soldiers "halted without the word of command for once," Sergeant Morhous says, "Several shells were thrown over, but no one was injured. Soon Gen. Williams and staff came dashing up."[443] Rebel units were taking advantage of swampy terrain to make a stand. Two redoubts had been constructed with some artillery emplaced and timber dropped across the roadway for about 200 yards. Swamp was to each side of the road so the wagons could not detour. Any attempt by the Union pioneer troops to clear the timber was impossible as they would be under fire. Williams deployed the 1st Division to attack.

The 1st Brigade was arrayed in battle formation to each side of the road, the 2nd Brigade went to the right and the 3rd to the left. When the "forward" signal was given the 123rd New York men were wading through swamp water up to their knees while enemy artillery and small arms fire peppered the area. Sergeant Morhous relates that only one man, Private Isaac Barrett (Co. C), was hit by a Minie-ball that sharply grazed his head knocking off his hat. Barrett seemed stunned then commenced shaking his fist at the Rebs and swearing. "His companions yelled for him to come on, but he did not stir, and kept shaking his fist in the direction of the Rebels...Some of the boys took him by the arm and he went along, swearing vengence on the Rebel who that fired shot. The hit on the head seemed to make him crazy for a little while." While Barrett was shaking his fist the 3rd Brigade managed to flank the enemy position and the Rebs fled posthaste. Colonel Selfridge says that the flanking maneuver "drove the enemy in great confusion from both forts." The only casualties of the action being three men in the 46th Pennsylvania. After pursuing the Confederates for a couple miles the 1st Brigade dropped back to the redoubts and encamped for the night.[444]

Defensive fortifications for Savannah were roughly four miles out from the city. Union troops came up against them on the 10th and dug in. To defend Savannah Rebel General William Hardee had some 10,000 men. Critical for the defense of the city was Fort McAllister which was to the south on the Ogeechee River. On the 13th units of the 15th Corps stormed and captured it. Communications were thereupon opened with the U.S. Navy fleet holding station offshore. As the soldiers in Sherman's army had been reduced to eating rice gathered from the fields around Savannah, the government rations couldn't get ashore fast enough. Corporal McLean notes that on the 15th he had, "Rice for breakfast, dinner and supper." Another item sitting on the ships out at sea was their mail. On the 17th packages and letters were delivered to the men. Lt. Cruikshank rejoiced at six letters from home and one from Washington correcting a pay snafu. "We expect our baggage soon that was sent back from Atlanta...," Cruikshank wrote his wife, "I hear that there are plenty of rations being unloaded from steamers and will be issued to the men as soon as teams can haul them to the Camps." McLean by the 19th had been issued a ration of hardtack and sugar which was "very welcome."[445]

Hardee understood it was only a matter of time before the city would be taken. On the night of December 20th he had the cannons spiked and slipped his troops across the Savannah River into South Carolina. The morning of the 21st the mayor and aldermen of Savannah rode out of the city under a white flag. They happened to be on the road controlled by the 2nd Division of the 20th Corps, 2nd Division commander General Geary assuring the civilian leaders that the city would receive protection. With that Union troops entered and guards were posted throughout Savannah. Soldiers of the 123rd New York were with other units moving into Savannah by 6 a.m. of the 21st. Once Savannah was secure the city was assigned to the first troops to enter, the 2nd Division of the 20th Corps, while the 1st and 3rd Divisions of the 20th Corps erected camps to the west of the city limits. Other Union Corps also formed camps around the outskirts of the city. Savannah was open to visits by the men when off duty and the day after occupation Corporal McLean went into town and knocked on a door. "Took dinner with a secesh family. Had a good dinner and a warm argument."[446]

For the Savannah Campaign the 123rd New York only lost one man, Corporal Albert Nicholson of Company D, who was taken prisoner on November 13th near Madison. He would be paroled in March of 1865. For the 20th Corps total casualties amounted to 12 killed, 88 wounded, and 165 missing.[447] It can be assumed that the majority of the missing were captured during foraging. Percentage of 20th Corps personnel lost while marching through 300 miles of enemy territory amounts to two percent.

"I doubt if the Rail Roads of Georgia will ever be running condition again during the war," Sergeant John Gourlie wrote his brother from Savannah. "We lived off the fat of the land...we also got a supply of splendid Mules & Horses which by the way we could never have got through without as our old Atlanta ones were nearly starved to death."[448]

Private William Tooley wrote his brother Eber, "there is so mutch wood land you can not see but a short distance the pike that we came in to savannah by is so straight and level that we could see a number of miles ahead" To his mother William wrote, "only eight more [months] from this day and my contract with Uncle sam will run out that seems much shorter than two or three years then tell father that we will go and catch some bull heads tell him that I saw some splendid basket timber at Millegeville but could not stop to cut it as we had other business on hand"[449]

"We passed through the principal cities & towns of central Georgia destroying the Rail Roads and all public property. Burned thousands of cotton gins & all the cotton we found, left a desert waste behind us," Corporal Clark McLean wrote his parents, adding, "We had election news to hear & were rejoiece to find that Mc [McClellen] & [New York Governor] Seymour had gone up Salt River."[450]

Sergeant Gourlie was also interested in the election results and wrote his brother Henry, "the defeat of the Copperheads in the late Election is very gratifying to the soldiers & rather a severe blow to our Confederate friends."[451]

Another severe blow was the destruction of Hood's army before Nashville. Over December 15th and 16th an entire Confederate army was annihilated before a Union onslaught. Union General George Thomas' men took 4,500 prisoners and chased the fleeing remnants of Hood's troops back into Mississippi. No Southern army would pose a serious threat in the Western Theatre again. In Nashville observing all the action was Corporal Henry Welch, his left hand having healed from the amputation of two fingers, he was now working as a clerk in the medical department. Welch wandered the hospital wards after the battle. "Last night I was at the hospital and spent the night among our sick wounded and dying soldier's it makes me sad as I sit here writing to look back and think of them, there was quite a number died during the night. I will write a few words about one that I took particular notice of, he was shot through the bowel's and mortaly wounded he was a young married man and as his mind wandered he would talk to his wife thinking she was beside his bed he would tell her how he had thought of her and how glad he was to see her once more, about 1'o clock he died, oh the agony of that poor soldier, as he was carried to the dead house I could not help thinking of the sorrow of his young wife when she hear's the terible news, shurely this war is terible."[452]

During the March to the Sea, the 123rd New York reported seizing "twenty odd beef cattle" and "a number of fine horses and mules." These animals were turned over to the brigade commissary of subsistence and brigade quartermaster, respectively. The men consumed anything else they "bummed" from the land. For the total march, Lt. Colonel Rogers states that "Ten days' rations of hard bread and three and a half days' salt meat were the only issues of those rations brought from Atlanta up to the time of entering Savannah."

The 1st Brigade, 1st Division, 20th Corps, reported seizing 40 horses and mules, 36,094 pounds corn, and 75,231 pounds fodder. During the march the brigade commissary of subsistence took in from foragers excess food and reissued it when needed. This consisted of 100 beef cattle, 100 sheep, 50 hogs and 12 wagon loads of sweet potatoes at 1,600 pounds per wagon (19,200 lbs.).

The 1st Division, 20th Corps, reported seizing 560 cattle, 300 sheep, 500 hogs, 150 horses and 175 mules. Crops gathered, in pounds: corn 298, 472; fodder 399,051; and sweet potatoes 164,200. Fresh meat to the tune of 95,000 pounds was also taken.[453]

The 20th Corps reported marching 305 miles, destroying 71 miles of railroad, and seizing: 600 horses; 1,720 mules; 3,290,452 pounds of corn; 1,229,819 pounds of fodder. General Williams in his 20th Corps report states that the corn and fodder figures are low as, "The waste of this, as with other articles, was enormous...Of the quantities of turkeys, geese, ducks and poultry of all kinds taken no estimate can be made. For at least 200 miles of our route these articles were in great abundance, and were used lavishly and wastefully...it would be safe to say that the amount [of all foodstuffs seized] might be doubled for waste and subsistence of thousands of refugee slaves who followed our march."[454]

"I estimate the damage done to the State of Georgia and its military resources at $100,000,000 at least, $20,000,000 of which inured to our advantage, and the rest is simple waste and destruction," General William Tecumseh Sherman wrote, "This may seem a hard species of warfare, but it brings the sad realities of war home to those who have been directly or indirectly instrumental in involving us in its attendent calamities." In modern value, the $100 million of 1864 would be the equivalent of $1.3 billion in 2007 dollars.[455]

During the March to the Sea a Georgia farmer approached Sherman to vent his frustration and anger over the Yankee pillaging, saying, "Why don't you go over to South Carolina and serve them this way? They started it."[456]

Okay. That can be done.

Chapter 10
Finale: South Carolina Burns

Soldiers on both sides blamed two states for the Civil War: Massachusetts for pushing abolitionism, and South Carolina for pushing slavery. It seemed the moment had arrived for running roughshod over the latter state. Sherman wanted to continue his march through the Carolinas as a way of completing the South's destruction. But first he had to convince Grant. The commander of all the Union armies was planning to transport Sherman's troops via sea up to the Virginia theatre to help destroy Lee at Petersburg.

While messages were exchanged at the highest levels as to the next movements for Sherman's troops, the occupation of Savannah went ahead peacefully. "General Sherman is putting everything in the city to order," Corporal William Shimp of the 46th Pennsylvania wrote his wife Annie, "He is organizing fire companies and the mayor and City Council, having taken the oath of Allegiance, are ordered to go on with their business as they did in time of peace." Shimp had attended some of the 123rd NewYork's prayer meetings and he was now to realize a gift from God. In late January he was informed he was a father. "Annie, now commences the most serious time of our lives. There is one great responsibility resting on us to raise him so he will be a credit to us and community to which he belongs. My duty shall ever be a pleasure to me and that is to try to set him a good example and raise him right."[257]

By the middle of January, 1865, the 123rd New York was encamped about two miles up river from Savannah near a large mansion called Marble Hall. The main house was used for the 1st Brigade's headquarters. Large, stout oaks draped in moss were about the mansion and Private William Tooley was most impressed, noting, "the live oak is a beautiful tree" Fatigue work on new fortifications (with a reduced radius so a smaller Union force could hold the city) and standing guard filled the men's duty hours. Off hours would see boating on the river, horseback riding or walks into the city. On January 12th Private Horace Mathews went into town to see a review of Union cavalry under General Judson "Kill Cavalry" Kilpatrick. "Went down town and saw Kill Patrick's Cavalry review and leaned up against a lamp post all day." There was also a chance for business acumen to shine. "Some of the boys speculated in provisions, etc., to some extent," Sergeant Henry Morhous relates. Sutlers were downriver about sixteen miles at Fort Pulaski. Several of the soldiers in the 123rd would paddle "long dug-outs" with the out going tide in the afternoon. Buying food items from the sutlers they would wait for the incoming tide the next morning to return to camp. Butter went for $1 a pound at Pulaski but they could sell it for $1.50 a pound in camp. Cheese was seventy-five cents a pound from the sutlers, arrival at camp saw a price markup of fifty cents. A barrel of molasses cakes could be had for $14, which the soldiers then sold at camp at 14 cakes a buck. Apples would be bought at $20 a barrel then exchanged at camp for ten, twelve or fifteen cents apiece depending on the size. "The cakes and apples commanded the best sale, although now and then would be found a soldier willing to indulge in butter and cheese." A large oyster bed was near the fort and while waiting for the returning tide the entrepreneurs would gather a bushel or two of oysters then row ashore and "have a feast of raw oysters."[458]

    Church services were also attended, Corporal Clark McLean visiting an Episcopal church one Sunday. "The sermon was good and the preacher smart. The congregation was about half citizens and the other half soldiers."[459]

    Just before the march began into the Carolinas, Sergeant Benjamin Smith (Co. B) made his way into the 123rd New York's camp. He had been six months in captivity after being captured at Culp's Farm. Smith escaped from a train while enroute from Savannah to Thomasville. "About

50 jumped off in a swamp but most of them were recaptured by the blood hounds they were hunted with. Smith with 4 others found a half breed Indian that lived in the swamps away from the road who concealed them from their pursuers and fed them for several weeks and finally helped them to our line," Corporal McLean says, "He has seen hard times & tells hard stories of the cruelties of the Rebels. When Sgt. Smith left us he was a rugged stout man now he is starved to a skeleton."[460] Making the rounds of the regiment, the haggard soldier drove home to the men the hazards of being taken prisoner plus it might have fired some discussion as to the coming march. Maybe some payback was due.

  The opportunity for that arrived within days as pontoon bridges across the Savannah River swayed with marching columns. Confederate newspapers assured their readers that this was folly and certain destruction for Sherman's hordes. Sherman was making the same mistake Napoleon did in invading Russia; Sherman's army would dwindle to its death. Rivers with their swampy lowland boarders flowed east to the Atlantic all across the Yankee's line of march. With the winter rains coming on the rivers, creeks and lowlands would be in flood stage. Roads would be impassable. The swamps of South Carolina would bog down, starve and certainly finish off the invaders.

  General Sherman had his army in two wings once again for the campaign with the same basic command structure throughout. General Oliver Howard would command the right wing, consisting of the 15th and 17th Corps, with General Henry Slocum commanding the 14th and 20th Corps comprising the left wing. About 60,000 Federal troops cutting a 40 mile swath were being unleashed. A Southern army was being gathered in North Carolina to oppose the Yankees, General Joseph Johnston being called out of retirement to lead it. Yet the Confederates needed time to mass plus Johnston had to deal with Union forces on the coast of North Carolina. It appeared South Carolina would find itself alone like Georgia. But there was a difference in that the Union troops had an edge to them, a chip on their shoulder as it were, for South Carolina that they never harbored for Georgia.

"The first house which the boys passed after crossing the river into South Carolina was in flames," Sergeant Morhous says of the 123rd New York's entry into the Palmetto State, "and it was a welcome sight to them, for South Carolina had commenced to pay her debt." January 17th, 18th and 19th the soldiers trudged with the 20th Corps column a few miles from the river in a northwesterly direction. "The country we passed seemed badly wrecked with many houses burned," Sergeant Rice Bull writes, "During the day [19th] passed through Hardeeville, which could, at its best, have been only a poor looking place and now can hardly be described as there is not much left standing that one can see. One of our boys said it looked 'warstruck' and it certainly looked it." Corporal McLean wasn't surprised by the sights. "The boys were determined to raise the devil in S. Carolina as it was the cradle of secession."[461]

Reaching the Purysburg area, the men went into camp on the 19th with a steady rain falling. All ground to a halt for the next six days. "Rained continued for some days making the roads almost impassable," 1st Brigade Commander Colonel Selfridge reports, "Our trains were unable to move and everything looked gloomy." Soldiers and wagons sank into the mud while the Savannah River rose. "The rain fell incessantly for several days and nights," Colonel James Rogers of the 123rd New York says, "and the low ground near the river becoming submerged we moved back on the 23rd instant to higher ground and laid out a regular camp, with log quarters and chimneys." To help the men shake off the poor weather some medicinal liquids were proffered. "A ration of whiskey was issued to the men," Corporal McLean noted, "the first this year and the camp songs and shouts of laughter tell its effects." Marching forward on the 27th the regiment with the brigade went into camp near Robertsville. The goal was to get to the river eight miles away at Sister's Ferry. Steamers were in the river waiting to unload supplies for the army. It was expected that some work on a dock and roads would have to be performed. But when the 123rd New York advanced towards the river with the 5th Connecticut the entire lowlands were found flooded. "On entering Great Black Swamp, at this point more than two miles in width, the causeway that bisects it was found entirely submerged," Colonel Rogers writes. Ordering his men to keep pushing forward, they "waded through for nearly a mile, when reaching Cypress Creek, which flows through the center of the swamp, the bridge that crossed it was found to have been swept away and the stream was too wide and deep to be forded." A working party was assigned the task of rebuilding the bridge and the remaining troops returned to camp. Two days later the 123rd New York was back wading through water for nearly a mile to get to the ferry, Colonel Rogers stating, "This they did without a mumur, although the weather was cold and chilling and the water at the freezing point."[462]

"Yesterday we had to wade about half a mile through water up to our knees so we got pretty wet," Corporal McLean wrote his sister, "over half a million rations have been landed & they are still bringing more here." The entire 1st Brigade having been detached for duty at Sister's Ferry, the men laid out camps then set about unloading ships, corduroying roads and building bridges. For five days the soldiers put their backs into their loads while slopping through wet ground. The 123rd New York headquarters were established in a nice home that had been deserted, McLean noting, "The people in this state have all left their houses & homes with what they could carry with them." Relieved by a brigade from the 14th Corps on February 4th, the 123rd New York left camp with the 1st Brigade. As for the pleasant house with library, piano, melodian and sewing machine used for the 123rd New York headquarters, McLean says it didn't last long; "it was soon in flames every house so far that we have seen is now a pile of ashes...We show no mercy to the people of this state."[463]

Marching eight miles to Robertsville and making camp, Sergeant Morhous and the 123rd soldiers discovered that "the little village had been nearly destroyed by fire." For the next few days the 1st Brigade, 1st Division, would march with the 2nd Division as the rest of the 20th Corps had pushed ahead while the 1st Brigade was at Sister's Ferry. February 6th the smoldering remains of Lawtonville were marched through. Corporal McLean did notice one house that wasn't burnt, "The man living there is an Union Man or pretends to be. He had a Union flag flying over his house." By the 10th Blackville had been reached, Colonel Rogers referring to it as "formerly a thriving village and station on South Carolina Railroad..." Lt. Robert Cruikshank told his wife that concerning South Carolina, "I think the state will suffer some before General Sherman gets through with it. The men will be harder on this state than they were on Georgia as it was the first to secede." A few days later Cruikshank noted, "So far on our march nearly every house and building was burned and other property destroyed."[464]

Assigned as the train guard, it meant more swamp work for the 123rd New York. The men spent a day splashing around in water up to their waists as they corduroyed a road and helped muscle 200 wagons forward. Colonel Selfridge, commanding the 1st Brigade, says the men worked until midnight trying to get the wagons forward. A request was made to 2nd Division commander General Geary for extra help but it was denied and Geary marched the 2nd Division forward telling Selfridge to get along as best he could with the wagon train.

By the 8th the column was coming upon Beaufort's Bridge through swampland. "Wading and stumbling over the narrow road which led a half a mile through the swamp [the 123rd New York] emerged from the dense jungle, and beheld upon its boarder a line of well built works, extending for some distance on either side," Sergeant Morhous says. The men were lucky in that the Confederates had retreated. Not because of the troops coming through the swamp but due to another Union column coming up on a road that threatened to flank them. "Probably if the Rebels had not been flanked, and could have defended this place, many lives would have been sacrificed before its capture."[465] Sherman's marching order of four large columns meant that the Rebels always had to be concerned as to their flanks. Southerners would need to raise a much larger force if they were to throw themselves across the front of any of the columns. Not that Confederate Cavalry General Wheeler didn't try with the means at hand. Skirmishing commenced on the 10th between the 1st Brigade and Wheeler's troopers where Drewens Bridge crossed the Edisto River. The Rebels disengaged once the entire Union force hove into view. There was no loss of life for the Federals.

But there was an easier way to find Yankees to kill. It wasn't just columns of Yankees marching, there were also blue-clad foragers milling about the countryside. Every day each regiment would dispatch about 30 men under an officer to scour the region for food. "The foraging is good. The men have all they can carry, both meat and vegetables," Lt. Cruikshank writes of this time. February 16th the 123rd New York was in the Lexington Court House area and danger became very real for those leaving the column. "The enemy in this section would not take any of the foragers prisoners, but if captured they suffered death. Their bodies were found mutilated, with papers pinned on their breasts on which was written, 'Death to foragers.' The men retaliated by burning everything that they did not want to carry away, that would burn. I have known of them carrying the sick out of the planters houses into a negro shanty so as to burn the houses. I could tell how far the line of march had advanced on the other roads by the fires."[466]

"A forager was in more real danger than the soldier in the ranks," Sergeant Morhous says, "Seldom a day passed but what they had a skirmish with the Rebels. Woe to the forager that fell into their hands. Generally his dead body would be found at the side of the road with his throat cut..."[467]

They were now near the state capital, Columbia, just a few miles to the west of it. Marching had been a miserable affair so far for most of the days in South Carolina, rains making roadways slippery mud surfaces that required manhandling of wagons and animals. Quite often, "hurry up and wait" seemed to be the phrase of the day. Sergeant Bull says of the mud slogging, "We could only stand and wait, hour after hour, while our tired mules creapt along with their burden so slowly the wheels hardly moved. We could not sit or lie down as the ground was drenched with water. So we could only wait, standing with our load upon our shoulders, a load that always seemed heaviest when we were not in active motion."[468]

Disappointment arrived on the 17th when the 20th Corps column turned north and skirted around Columbia. The soldiers of the 123rd New York had hoped to see the city. By that evening they were camping on the north bank of the Saluda River looking back towards the city where there was a glow on the horizon. There wasn't going to be much of Columbia for anyone to see in the coming months. "The sky was lit up in the direction of the city of Columbia, and the boys knew that large fires were raging there," Sergeant Morhous notes.[469] Elements of the 15th and 17th Corps entered Columbia on the morning of February 17th when the mayor surrendered the city. A series of events were now to unfold that doomed over half the city to ashes. Although martial law had been declared by Confederate authorities on the 15th, disorder had grown with some stores looted as the Yankees approached. Large quantities of cotton were stored in the city and before the Confederate military left it was decided to burn the commodity. Huge stacks of the white tinder were removed from warehouses so it could be transported outside of town. Trouble was, there wasn't any transport available. When the first Federals entered the city they found vast piles along the main thoroughfares. The Yanks also found booze. Large amounts of whiskey had been moved to Columbia from Charleston and other cities in South Carolina for safe keeping. It was thought Sherman would sack Charleston but never attack Columbia. As Union troops filtered into the town many locals offered them cups of whiskey as a way to curry favor. Later in the morning barrels of whiskey were rolled into the streets for consumption. Also mingling with Sherman's veterans were some escaped Union POW's, many with a grudge as to their treatment. Marauding convicts that had somehow been released from the city jail were also working their way around town. Then gale force winds began to whip through the city with little tufts of cotton swirling like snow flakes.

Sherman told the mayor not to worry as men would be posted to secure Columbia from destruction. Cotton bales were burning by late afternoon but enough soldiers remained sober to help extinguish the fires. Drunken soldiers, when found, were rounded up and put under guard. During this time Sherman visited several families in the city with the mayor. Although he intended to burn several government warehouses and machine shops, Sherman told the mayor it would not be done until the winds had died down. Yet as the commanding Union officer retired for the evening enlisted personnel put into action other plans. As darkness came over the city three flares shot skyward: one red, one white and one blue. Fires broke out rapidly in several locations throughout the city. Sherman was in bed when the dancing glare on the walls of the room called him out onto the street. People were reporting twenty, thirty, and then one hundred fires having been started all across Columbia. Flames were whipped into a roaring froth by the winds. Cheering the conflagration were roving gangs of soldiers with torches. Looting was widespread, men staggering under their loads of family valuables while dressed in gowns or masonic robes. Some rapes occurred, both black and white women suffering.

Sherman rushed into the street to find General Howard and other officers barking orders. Fresh troops were hurried into the city. While some turned to fighting the fires the rest were put to work against the lawless bands. Sherman ordered the arrest of one drunken private and watched an adjutant shoot the man down when he resisted arrest. Thirty drunken soldiers were wounded and over three hundred placed under arrest as control was wrestled back for the city. But the fire could not be controlled. Only a shift of wind saved the remaining section of the city. At dawn close to 70% of Columbia was gone. Debate would rage for years after the war as to who was responsible for the destruction of South Carolina's capital. Sherman would blame the Confederates for putting all the cotton into the open and then firing it as they left. Any orders to set the cotton afire was denied by Southerners, they fully claimed it was the Yankees that caused the conflagration. Criminal elements, both in uniform or in convict's clothes, were milling about the city with alcohol readily available. If Sherman can be blamed for anything it was in not having enough troops in the city to maintain order and fight any fires that broke out. A larger aspect is that the Union rank and file were quite happy to see Columbia torched and Sherman touches on this in his report, saying that troops not on duty "may have assisted in spreading the fire after it had once begun, and may have indulged in unconcealed joy to see the ruin of the capital of South Carolina."[470]

While the 15th and 17th Corps spent the next two days destroying railroad track and any government stores still to be found in the Columbia area, the 20th Corps was sent in the direction of Winnsboro. This would allow more railroad to be destroyed but also keep the enemy guessing as it was also a feint in the direction of Charlotte, North Carolina. Sherman's goal from the beginning of the Carolinas Campaign was to link up with other Union forces at Goldsboro, North Carolina. As the soldiers of the 123rd New York tramped forward, Union engineers 300 miles away at New Bern, North Carolina laid out plans for a railroad to Goldsboro. When Sherman's 60,000 veterans arrived a rapid supply line would be in operation from the coast.

But it was to be several weeks before the foot sloggers were to hear a train whistle. Drawing wagon guard duty seemed to be the 123rd New York's lot for the next few days. This wasn't sought work as the men had a morning delay for everyone else to march by, then at times manhandling of the wagons and teams had to be performed. Combined with the stops, starts, halts and being the last ones into camp late at night it made for fatiguing work. Yet they certainly could see the muddy roadway on the way to Winnsboro once the sun went down. "Every house along the road was burning or had been burned," Sergeant Morhous says of this time, "In fact the road was lit up all the way by burning buildings." Being at the rear of the 20th Corps the soldiers of the 123rd never had a chance to start fires, but some of the men did help "two old people" escape from a house in flames. Not that the men would have foregone torching an abode. "Had the house been vacant when [the 123rd] came to it," Morhous relates of the rescue incident, "we certainly would not have invested any money in the property with the thought that it would remain unburned."[471]

Winnsboro would be the next city reduced to rubble. On the Charlotte and South Carolina Railroad, it was right in the destruction path. The 123rd New York marched through the town with the 1st Brigade the evening of the 21st. Although a halt was made in the city, the men were not allowed to break ranks. Taken beyond the town a couple miles a camp was made for the night. Sergeant Morhous in his memoirs claims the town was burned by the Rebels but Lt. Cruikshank states that Winnsboro was destroyed by fire the night the Union troops arrived. Sergeant Bull also says it was the Yankees, "There was great quantities of cotton in storehouses and piles of cotton bales around the railroad depot." All was ignited. "I can hardly describe the appearance of Winnsborough but it was certainly deplorable."[472]

Destruction of the railroad was continued another 15 miles to Blackstock Depot by Union troops, then the 20th Corps swung towards Lancaster, South Carolina. Still doing rear guard with the wagon train the men of the 123rd New York stumbled along the cut up clayey roads in the wake of the army. When the wagons stopped it was 4 a.m. and the men had taken fifteen hours to go thirteen miles. During the darkness engineers had laid a pontoon bridge across the Catawba River. Next morning it commenced raining as the column marched northward. Once across the river there was a large clay hill to ascend and with the rain the mud was soon churned into a slippery mess. Mules fell to the ground as they could not get the traction to stand up. General Sherman arrived and commenced ordering a large detail for corduroying and pulling the mules and wagons up the hill. It was a lucky day for the 123rd New York. As they had already been doing wagon detail for two days, they were ordered to march forward a couple miles and make camp. Putting up their tents in the rain they sought some rest.

Moving out next morning the men made three miles but then ground to a halt as the 14th Corps was crossing the 20th Corps line of march. Although the rain continued, the soldiers were glad for a break. Camp was made and the 123rd rested their feet and backs for two days. Hard physical labor combined with no rest took the life of Private Ira Stacy (Co. K) at this time. He "died of disease of the heart" the night of the 24th. Also falling to exhaustion was Private George Osborn (Co. K), he died on the 28th near Hanging Rock, South Carolina. Both of the men were in their late thirties.

March 1st saw the men marching rapidly on a sandy roadbed along a ridge line. With no hinderances from the soils or the Rebs they made fifteen miles. The men of the 123rd New York were happy as the foragers found plenty of food plus they were finally leading the 20th Corps instead of doing wagon guard duty. But their wool uniforms were starting to suffer from all the rain. "Our clothes are getting in a very bad condition having been wet and dried upon our persons so many times they have shrunk out of shape and are creased in every direction and our shoes our nearly done for," Sergeant Bull says. They needed to get to a base of supplies soon or "we will be ragged and shoeless."[473] The ragged band marched forward again in the lead on the 2nd as the other divisions of the 20th Corps were delayed with the trains. Approaching Chesterfield Court House, rifle shots rang out.

Confederate cavalry with some artillery were just south of the town entrenched across the roadway. The 1st Brigade was rapidly deployed with the 5th Connecticut and 141st New York sent forward in a skirmish line, the 46th Pennsylvania and 123rd New York advancing in support. Union artillery also galloped up and the guns unlimbered. Once pressed, the Rebels retreated. "We followed after as fast as they ran driving them through the large open fields around the village," Sergeant Bull notes.[474] It was a three mile chase to the bridge over Thompson's Creek. Smoke roiled up from the bridge as the Union troops approached. Sprinting forward, the 5th Connecticut ran onto the structure and put out the fire. To protect the bridge until the column could come up the 1st Brigade deployed through the swamps around it. The soldiers would spend several miserable hours in the water and muck before being ordered back onto higher ground during the night. Two men were wounded during the action, both from the 5th Connecticut.

While a quick affair, Lt. Cruikshank says the skirmish had caught the local civilians completely by surprise. "The white people had all run away out of the village and the black people all ran into the brick smoke houses and were crowded in as full as they could hold of big and little, young and old. One woman had her ear shot off and was almost frightened to death. The houses looked as if the inhabitants had only stepped out to make a call. The woman's work was lying on the chair or the table as if it had just been thrown down. Fires were burning in the grates, all showing we were not expected."[475]

The next day was spent corduroying about a mile of roadway through the swampland and in repairing the burned section of the bridge. Half of the 123rd worked on the roadway while the other half had the bridge detail. It was six hours of labor before units were marching forward. Sergeant Bull was one of the soldiers slopping around in the swamp. "The bridge repairers had the best of us today," he says, "All the timbers and poles used in the work had to be brought from the swamp and in doing that work we were covered with black mud from our feet to our bodies."[476]

Drawing wagon guard detail the next day, the 1st Division had to wait for the 2nd and 3rd Divisions to pass plus their wagon trains. By noon all the troops had passed. The rear of the wagon train finally went by as dark fell. Falling into line the 123rd soldiers began their march as blackness enveloped the roadway. "This meant for us a night's march as orders required that trains be brought, every night, up in close touch with the troops," Sergeant Bull writes, "It was worth one's life, almost, to walk upon the rough, uneven timbers of the corduroy in the dark. After trying it once we kept off the logs and plowed, in preference, along in the mud." By 4 a.m. they had covered the eight miles to camp. To Bull the tramp seemed like twenty miles. Of these night marches Corporal McLean noted, "The roughest work in soldiering except fighting is wading through a road on a rainy night."[477] They were now near the Great Pee Dee River. Several columns of troops converged on Cheraw, South Carolina where a pontoon bridge had been thrown across. Also at Cheraw were vast stores of Confederate supplies shipped from Charleston for safe keeping. Ordnance, food and much of the city went to the torch while the railroad was destroyed as far as Darlington. Crossing the Great Pee Dee, the soldiers marched on into North Carolina. A new mood struck the men.

"The conduct of Sherman's soldiers perceptively changed during that first day's march into the state," Sergeant Morhous says, "There were no evidences of plundering; the men kept their ranks better, and what was remarkable, not a single column of fire and smoke marked the positions of the different lines of march, as had been the case in South Carolina." After several days in North Carolina, Lt. Cruikshank would note, "So far since we entered the state there has not been a house fired."[478] Orders had gone out from Sherman's headquarters to rein in the destruction once in North Carolina. Better control of the "bummers" was sought with provost guards under orders to arrest any soldier found foraging alone. General Howard, commanding the right wing, even went so far as to restrict foraging details to 60 men under an officer from each division, instead of each regiment. While the left wing was admonished to show more respect to the local citizenry by General Slocum, it appears the regimental foraging details were kept. For the 123rd New York the same method was used that had worked so well in South Carolina; thirty mounted men left every morning under a commissioned officer. During the march through South Carolina the officer in charge was 2nd Lt. Dave Rogers (Co. I), once into North Carolina the foraging party commander was 2nd Lt. Duane Hall (Co. E). Riding out at dawn every morning, the foraging detail would cover at times close to fifty miles visiting homes and plantations seeking forage and food. The band would attack and disperse small Confederate groups while avoiding large units of the enemy.

Although more restraint was being shown towards homes, the soldiers found a new source of tinder. The region the men were marching through now consisted of vast forests of pitch pine with factories scattered throughout for the making of turpentine, tar and rosin. Barrels of the flammable product were stacked throughout the region. As war material, this was considered fair game for destruction. Fires appeared rapidly along the line of march as the factories and products were lit. The soldiers were tramping through tall shafts of pine with smoke spreading out over their heads underneath the tree canopy. All the precipitation hardly dampened the flames. Rains were steady the first three days in North Carolina and foraging poor. The men slogged on towards Fayetteville day after day often with little sleep. Sergeant Bull relates, "It had rained so hard during the night that not many men stayed under their tents until morning as the ground under our 'shelters' was so completely soaked that it was more comfortable to stand around the pine knot fires with our ponchos over our shoulders." Streams were swollen from the rains and the roads just impassable slop so it was heavy labor these days building bridges and corduroying roads. The entire 1st Division cut and laid trees for several miles on the 9th with the 123rd New York wading about in water up to their knees most of the day completing a one-hundred foot bridge. Moving forward on the 10th saw more corduroying of the roadway with several miles having to be worked before the wagons could proceed. "The mud was deep and the streams swollen," Lieutenant Cruikshank says, "The men were as wet as they could be so forded streams without stopping." Foragers came into camp that evening with only some potatoes and cowpeas. The latter item had to be boiled into a thick paste before one could eat it and was not highly thought of but it would have to do.[479]

Sunshine greeted the men the next morning and a quickened step was taken by the 1st and 3rd Divisions of the 20th Corps towards Fayetteville, North Carolina. The 14th Corps was already near the city and it was suspected an enemy force might be in the area. Covering twenty miles, the soldiers went into camp just outside of Fayetteville that evening. Within two days Sherman's entire army would be bivouacked around the city. With the United States flag run up the flagpole in the marketplace, units of the 14th Corps took positions throughout the town. Engineer troops also arrived to begin the destruction of war material. First on the list was the old United States arsenal which had been seized at the start of the war. Much of the gunsmithing equipment from the Harper's Ferry arsenal had been shipped to this location. All machinery found was wrecked and the arsenal walls punched into rubble with battering rams. All four cotton mills in the town were destroyed, plus shops and factories. One grist mill was left in operation for the locals but all others burnt to the ground. Union cavalry rode out and destroyed the railroad up to the Little River. Warehouses were fired while powder and ordnance found were rendered useless. The soldiers also took delight to trash the three newspapers in town. After the drunken melee of Columbia, Sherman made sure to have enough troops in Fayetteville to maintain order. All the above was done per instructions. Quite a bit of pillaging had occurred during the initial occupation as "bummers" had gotten into the city ahead of the 14th Corps troops assigned to police the area. Once troops were stationed throughout the city general order prevailed although smoke, flame and crashing of brick walls into rubble could be seen wherever one turned. Private houses within Fayetteville generally escaped the torch, the soldiers were only interested in destroying buildings used for commerce or the Confederate military. It was the homes and plantations outside of the city that received harsh treatment. The nights of March 11th and 12th saw fires dotting the landscape for miles around the city.[480]

Within a day all food that could be carried off was gone. The citizens of Fayetteville faced starvation and had to apply to the Federal army for sustenance. This was given as long as the army was in the city but Sherman intended to march on within two days of entering. Such harsh measures levied on the local population were due to shooting at soldiers during the Yankees entry and the destruction of the bridge over the Cape Fear River. Sherman had given out word as he approached Fayetteville that if no fighting occurred and the bridge was spared the town could expect decent treatment. Tecumseh was particularly peeved that the bridge had been burnt. Pontoon bridges would now have to be laid across the Cape Fear River.

Yet the delay that entailed brought opportunity to send mail to the folks back home in Washington County. Around noon on Sunday, March 12th, the quiet of the city was broken by the blast of a steam whistle. Out on the river sat the U.S. Army tug *Davidson* having sailed up from Wilmington, North Carolina. Joining her in a few hours was the U.S. Navy gunboat *Eolus*. Sherman sent dispatches downriver giving as his objective Goldsboro and ordering General Schofield at New Bern to promptly move upon that city. As the tug had the room, Sherman let out word that anyone wanting to send a letter home would have the opportunity. When the *Davidson* departed that evening she carried an army captain with dispatches for Washington, some refugees and a huge pile of mail on the deck.

"we have been living on the country for a long time," Private William Tooley wrote his parents, "and I suppose we will have to go fifty miles or more before we get rations we have not drawn an army ration in over one month I am in good health and have stood the march well" Sergeant John Gourlie told his brother, "You cannot form an idea of the treatment <u>South Carolina</u> recd from our Army. there is not a foot of ground within miles of the course that we marched through the state but is striped of everything in the way of food & forage. every <u>unoccupied</u> mansion or building of any description was burnt to the ground."[481] Glad for the chance to contact home, the men of the 123rd New York were also thankful for a complete day of rest. Foraging was good so the men had a solid evening meal of ham, bacon and corn meal.

As there was a large column of refugees, white and black, following the army, Sherman at this time ordered them to Wilmington. A couple hundred soldiers were detailed as guards for the march. Soldiers that were sick were also sent with the column, several of the 123rd New York men being transported. About 6,000 refugees and 1,000 to 2,000 sick soldiers left Fayetteville for Wilmington. Delay was something Sherman wanted to avoid at all cost. His goal was to get to Goldsboro, join with other Union troops, rest and refit then seek out whatever force Confederate General Johnston had gathered. By moving quickly Sherman had been able to place his columns between the scattered Southern units in North Carolina, so far they had not been able to bring together their forces. But Sherman's hopes for a campaign without serious fighting were fading. General Johnston now had approximately 16,000 infantry and 4,000 cavalry gathered and he moved forward hoping to find one of Sherman's Corps alone.

Breaking camp on the 13th, the 123rd New York marched through Fayetteville with the 1st Brigade where they were reviewed by Sherman and his staff. "The General saw a ragged lot of fellows," Lt. Cruikshank writes, "Some had one sleeve in their blouses and others had none. Many of them had pants torn off at the knee or all in rags from the knee down. The most of them had shoes so worn that their feet were almost on the ground, and yet the men appeared happy. The General called them his 'ragamuffins.'"[482] Crossing the Cape Fear River, the men marched about seven miles and camped. The spectacle of the review must have had an impact as the next day some clothing was issued to the men. Fresh ammunition was also distributed. They had another day of rest as the remaining corps of the army crossed the river and moved forward. Sherman understood that Johnston was now concentrated to his front so he arranged for faster marching. The left wing, 14th and 20th Corps, was ordered on the road to Averasboro, North Carolina, with four divisions in light marching order and stripped of most wagons. The majority of the wagons would be escorted by the remaining two divisions on a direct road to Goldsboro. The right wing also adjusted its marching order while taking other roads to the east. Averasboro was on the road to Raleigh, at the village a road branched off to Goldsboro. Sherman was using the four divisions on the left as a feint towards Raleigh in the hopes of pinning Johnston there to defend that city. But the Southern commander would be proactive in finding out just where Sherman was going. Johnston ordered General Hardee to take 7,000 men to Averasboro, engage the enemy, slow the left wing to separate it further from the right wing and discover Sherman's objective-Raleigh or Goldsboro.

Union General Judson Kilpatrick's cavalry taking the lead, the 1st and 3rd Divisions of the 20th Corps marched forward with the 14th Corps' 1st and 2nd Divisions following. About 3 p.m. on March 15th a strong line of Confederates were encountered across the roadway a mile south of the hamlet of Averasboro. Confederate General Hardee actually had three lines of entrenchments back to the town. Rhett's Brigade was deployed in the first line, then Elliott's Brigade was entrenching for the second line (these two brigade's constituted General Taliaferro's Division) and in the last line McLaw's Division. Rifle shots became rapid as the cavalry dismounted and probed forward trying to size up the situation. Word was sent to the rear for support as it became obvious that a sizeable force of "Graybacks" were in front. Sent forward double-quick was 2nd Brigade, 1st Division, 20th Corps. Commanded by Colonel William Hawley, the 2nd Brigade assisted in skirmishing and building breastworks as night fell. By mid-morning of the 16th both the 1st Division and 3rd Division of the 20th Corps, about 12,000 men, were on the field deployed for battle. The 123rd New York was on the far right of the line with the 1st Brigade advancing across the flat terrain of sandy crop fields and scattered stands of pine woods. The brigade was in two lines, the 5th Connecticut and 123rd New York in the lead with support from the 141st New York and 46th Pennsylvania behind them. Colonel Rogers threw Company E of the 123rd forward as skirmishers. As they were advancing Union cavalry was seen falling back towards them and going to the right rear. The 1st Georgia Regulars and 32nd Georgia was following rapidly and seemed ready to turn the Union right flank. Rogers, on his own initiative, shifted the front line further to the right while ordering the 46th PA to fill the gap in the front rank. Everyone had promptly completed the maneuver "when the column of the enemy emerged from a marshy piece of woods in our front not a hundred yards distant, and was met by a simultaneous volley from the whole brigade. This was evidently unexpected, as seeing the cavalry fall back, it is not probable they had looked for a line of infantry there. Our fire threw them into confusion, and after a few volleys they fell back in disorder."[483]

To the left, the 3rd Division managed a flanking maneuver on the first line of Confederate entrenchments. Falling back to their second line, the Confederates were again driven out. As night fell the Union soldiers moved forward to prepare for the next day's attack on the final Confederate line. But Hardee had completed his work, the action had delayed the Yankee's left wing a day plus intelligence gathered showed Goldsboro as Sherman's destination. During the darkness the Confederates retreated. The battle of Averasboro saw 678 Union casualties and 865 casualties for the Confederates. For the 1st Brigade, the 5th Connecticut suffered the worst as they had been deployed forward as skirmishers after the initial action and lost 4 killed, 8 wounded and 8 missing. The 46th Pennsylvania had 1 wounded and 4 missing while the 141st New York suffered 2 wounded and 1 missing.[484] While both Lt. Cruikshank and Sergeant Morhous say the 123rd New York suffered five wounded, Colonel Rogers in his report of the battle puts the wounded at four while the New York State Adjutant General records for the unit only shows three: Sergeant Peter Boushe (Co. E); Private Patrick McKinna (Co. E); and Private John Sherman (Co. K). It appears the proper number is four. Corporal Russell Fullerton (Co. F) was also wounded but the date is March 14th according to the Adjutant-General's report. As the 123rd New York was in camp refitting all that day, it makes more sense that Fullerton was wounded during the March 16th battle. Another factor to consider is that Company F relieved Company E the evening of March 16th as skirmishers, this would have put Fullerton into a more exposed danger zone. After hospital stays three of the 123rd wounded were discharged; Private John Sherman was hospitalized but then deserted. Sherman's "desertion" should be given some consideration. He left the U.S. Hospital in Troy, New York, May 25th when the 123rd New York was in Washington ready to be mustered out. Given hospital food and conditions, the fact that the regiment was about to be discharged, plus being so near home, the temptation probably proved too much.[485]

    Confederate General Johnston was tempted *now*. Going by the maps before him, Sherman's left wing appeared to be alone, too far away from the right wing to be properly supported if attacked. He ordered all his units to concentrate at Bentonville, a little village on the road to Goldsboro. He knew the Yankee units engaged at Averasboro would be marching on that roadway and he intended to strike them. Trouble was, the maps Johnston was using were faulty. The mileage was wrong and distances were off in Sherman's favor, the Yankee wings were closer than Johnston thought. Thinking he had a full day of a killing field, the Southern commander only had a few hours once engaged before other Union forces would be on the field responding to the rolling rumbles to their north.

But Sherman's maps were also faulty. After Rebel cavalry burned the bridge across Mill Creek the Union commander let his guard down as it was the only road from Smithfield shown on his map that Johnston could use to hit the left flank. Confident that Johnston now intended to defend Raleigh, Sherman bid goodbye to General Slocum the morning of March 19th and rode for the right wing with his escort. But there was a second road from Smithfield not shown on the map. Twenty miles up the Goldsboro road Confederate General Johnston had 16,000 infantry and 4,000 cavalry going into position to do battle. The Union 14th Corps moved toward them with the 20th Corps following; General Slocum having about 25,000 infantry in the two corps. They would be in marching order, not battle array, as they made contact with the Confederates.

After the battle of Averasboro the soldiers of the 123rd New York spent two miserable days pulling wagons and mules along in the mud. On the 17th the men broke camp at 7 a.m. and struggled with the wagons until 10:30 p.m. covering just one and a half miles. Making ten miles on the 18th, creeks were waded with water at times up to their waists. When the 20th Corps went into camp that evening it was about eight miles behind the 14th Corps. It had been a busy day for the vanguard of the 14th Corps, Rebel cavalry had been steadily skirmishing and dropping back as they closed towards Bentonville. As there were a series of turpentine stills in the woods along the march route, columns of smoke marked the Federal's progress.

By the 19th road conditions were better for the 20th Corps as it was all corduroyed from the troops going before them. All the way to the rear of the 1st Division guarding the wagons, the 123rd New York made seven miles when cannonading was clearly heard to the front. Back came the lathered horse with dispatch rider. The 1st Brigade started double-quick for the sound of combat.

Action had commenced early that morning when Federal foragers ran onto Johnston's units deployed across the Goldsboro Road. An area of level sandy crop fields and pine thickets, it wasn't obvious at first that the Rebs were there in force. But as the initial 14th Corps brigades came up and moved forward they were pinned down by rapid fire of artillery and musketry. Sending three brigades forward to probe the Confederate lines in the timber resulted in a heavy repulse. By noon Union General Slocum realized he was facing a serious threat and ordered the 20th Corps forward on the double. Slocum also dispatched riders to find Sherman with the right wing. All that had saved the Federals to this point had been the late arrival of Confederate divisions and the time needed by them to deploy. By 1 p.m. word was coming back from Union line officers that a large column of enemy infantry was massing for attack. Federal troops had been put onto the field hodgepodge; there were gaps between brigades, holes ripe for exploitation by a charging enemy. By 2 p.m. part of the 20th Corps was on the field, the brigades of the 1st Division having arrived. The 1st and 2nd Brigades were sent to the left of the road and ordered to entrench at the Morris Farm, the far left of the Union line. After a two mile double-quick, the panting soldiers of the 123rd New York filed into a field, each man ordered to grab a fence rail for constructing breastworks. While considered the left flank of the entire wing, the 1st Brigade was not adjacent to the 14th Corps left, there was about a half-mile of ravine and woodland between them. Meanwhile, the 3rd Brigade was sent a mile further up the road to fill in a gap near the center of the 14th Corps line. It would arrive just in time to be hammered into a retreat by the attacking Confederates.

At 2:45 p.m. the charge came out of the thickets onto the Union regiments and it was time to-run! Overlapping the 14th Corps left flank the gray ranks also punched through a hole in the center. This completely broke the forward units of the 14th Corps on the left of the Union line. Artillery units were overrun so quickly that three guns were captured. Only the Union right had held as the Confederates in that area under General Braxton Bragg had been tardy in attacking. This allowed the Yankees on the right to strengthen their breastworks plus pivot a brigade to challenge the advancing Confederates on the left.

Back at the Morris Farm, Colonel Selfridge was ordered to quickly bring the 1st Brigade to the right and form across the Goldsboro Road. As the 123rd New York formed in regimental line just to the south of the road, the 1st Division of the 14th Corps went streaming to the rear completely broken. The 3rd Brigade of the 1st Division, 20th Corps, retreated in good style and reformed about 250 yards in front of the 1st Brigade. Grabbing more fence rails, the 123rd New York soldiers were issued shovels and created enough breastworks for at least two regiments in line. As the 20th Corps units entrenched back at the Morris Farm, up the road the Union right flank, the 2nd Division, 14th Corps, was now hemmed in on three sides by Rebel rifles blazing. After repulsing an attack to their front, the Union soldiers leapt over their breastworks and fired to their rear. Coming to their rescue were elements of the 20th Corps 3rd Division which were now pouring onto the field. The right flank was saved after hand to hand fighting. With all of the 20th Corps up and a proper battle line forged, muskets and cannons cracking, the Union troops dealt the Confederate assaults severe repulses. Four times the Rebels came across the open fields into ranked artillery and massed infantry fire. They lost heavily. Nightfall saw torches wandering the field searching for the dead and wounded.[486]

For the 123rd New York it was a day with the 1st Brigade in reserve. They were behind the first line arrayed near artillery watching the flashing flames, drifting smoke and carnage. That evening the 46th Pennsylvania came up and moved alongside the New Yorkers. As night came on the 1st Brigade moved forward and relieved the 3rd Brigade to their immediate front. "On reaching this front line [the 123rd New York] at once went to work to rebuild and strengthen the line of breastworks there, which were very poor," Colonel Rogers noted, "We lay on our arms all night ready for a renewal of the attack at any moment."[487] A wagon load of ammunition was distributed along the line as the men worked on their entrenchments. At dawn they waited for the onslaught.

They were surprised when the Confederates didn't renew the attack. Sherman having responded to requests for help, General Johnston had other things on his mind. Colonel Rogers says that on the morning of the 20th, "we were cheered by the sight of reinforcements, the two remaining divisions of the Left Wing and one from the Right Wing coming up in the night." At the same time the rest of the Right Wing made fast time for Johnston's left flank via Cox's Crossroads. Confederate cavalry contested the advance of the 15th Corps and alerted Johnston that 15,000 Yankees were about to emerge onto his rear. It was going to get worse, the 17th Corps, another 11,000 men, were right behind. Johnston drew his forces back into new positions to meet the threat. Over on the Union left, lines were strengthened while patrols were sent out. The 123rd New York sent a reconnaissance party forward, they returned with nine prisoners, two of whom were wounded, plus forty muskets picked up from the field. According to Sergeant Morhous they could have brought in one more prisoner. "One Rebel who was severely wounded would not accept of help. He said he would die rather then accept of a favor from a Yank, and he was as good as his word for he did not accept of even a drink of water and died in the afternoon."[488]

Action would now concentrate on the Union right as the 15th and 17th Corps engaged and tried to break through Johnston's new line. Noon saw cannons flaming and massed ranks with flags whipping crossing fields and woods. The climax came on March 21st when Union troops nearly broke through on the right to the bridge Johnston needed for a retreat. As the Confederates desperately fought on until night would allow a withdrawal, Johnston was informed that telegraph communication with Goldsboro had suddenly ceased. Union General John Schofield, advancing from New Bern with his 23rd Corps, had taken the city. Also closing on Goldsboro was Union General Alfred Terry with his 10th Corps. These two corps marching in from the coast brought another 20,000 soldiers into the theatre. During the night of March 21st the remains of Confederate General Johnston's army, some 17,000 men, withdrew from Bentonville. Sherman thereupon put his 56,000 troops into motion for Goldsboro.

Bentonville had seen in Union casualties 191 killed, 1,168 wounded and 287 captured or missing, for a total of 1,646. Confederate forces lost 239 killed, 1,694 wounded and 673 captured or missing for a total of 2,606. Of Sherman's Left Wing, it was the 14th Corps that had suffered the most with 886 casualties while the 20th Corps had 258. The 1st Brigade, 1st Division, 20th Corps only suffered four casualties. The 46th Pennsylvania had two wounded. The 123rd New York accounted for the other two casualties; Private George Winn (Co. C) was wounded and Private Orville Branch (Co. B) was taken prisoner. Winn would be in hospitals until discharged while Branch would be released at the end of the war from Camp Parole, Maryland.[489]

Covering fourteen miles on the 22nd, the 123rd New York went into camp at 9 p.m. a few miles shy of Cox's Bridge which crosses the Neuse River. Moving out at 8 a.m. the next morning, the soldiers of the 123rd marched in the column of ragged veterans. Uniforms were wore out, hair unkept, many were bearded and all were black. Trudging through miles of burning woods, sitting before sundry campfires, powder smears on their faces, scores of burning houses, days of soot and grime billowing with no soap and no stops for bathing had coated them. Once again trees were crackling all around them. "The forest was filled with stifling, black greasy smoke and in places the heat from the burning trees was so intense that it was almost impassable to march upon the road and at times we had to separate the files, dodge through the burning fires and come together further on," Sergeant Bull says of the day's march.[490]

Approaching Cox's Bridge the men emerged from the burning pine forest to find a division of General Terry's 10th Corps drawn up by the road to honor them.

The divisional honor guard consisted of black troops and they did a double take as Sherman's troops emerged into the sunlight. "This is hardly surprising as we certainly looked quite as black as they," Sergeant Bull says, "While in the matter of complexion we may greatly resemble our new found friends in blue, in many other ways we presented a strange contrast to our colored comrades. Their uniforms were new, well fitted, bright and clean. The shoes they wore were new, black and shining. Their guns were the Springfield latest model and almost sparkled with brightness. The men looked fat and sleek, showing the good care and food they had received and their officers were spendidly dressed, with buttons shining and wearing new unfaded sashes...[Sherman's Army] looked thin and gaunt...the mens hair had not been cut for nearly three months it was long and ragged...clothes were worn threadbare and were in rags, covered in mud...Their shoes were in the last stage of existence, many being held together with strings tied around them...In making this contrast between our men and the new troops we passed today I do not mean to criticize them. I do not doubt they are good soldiers and if they remain long in active service they will soon enough lose their fresh appearance."[491]

Sergeant-Major McLean was also impressed. "Saw division of colored troops and was agreeably surprised to find them making such good appearing soldiers." Just as white eastern troops shipped west had to prove themselves in combat to the white western soldiers, the black soldiers had to prove their mettle on the battlefield. By the spring of 1865 through fighting at Port Hudson, Fort Wagner and many other engagements blacks had proven their fighting ability. Of the total Federal forces of 2,778,304 men, 178,975 were black.[492]

Yet several hundred miles away in Nashville, Tennessee, Corporal Henry Welch wasn't impressed even while wanting slavery to end. "there has been a good deal of talk here lately about the amendment of the constitution abolishing slavery, well I go for doing away with slavery for I think it caused this war, but as for the negro I cant say that I have a very high oppinion of them..."[493] On reading over Corporal Welch's letters one feels that Henry was sliding to this opinion over two years of service. Two reasons come to mind. One, he was dealing with a lot of recently freed slaves and, since it was illegal for a slave to receive schooling, the majority of blacks he came in contact with had no education. The second reason to suggest is what today we call "Blaming the victim."

Entering Goldsboro the afternoon of March 24th the regiment passed in review before General Sherman and other officers, continued two miles beyond the city and went into camp. The Carolinas Campaign was over. Crossing through 500 miles of enemy territory in winter, through terrain regarded as impassable, on a march many regarded as foolhardy and certain to kill them, Sherman's Army instead averaged ten miles a day while fighting two battles and leaving a 40 mile swath of devastation behind them.

For the Carolinas march, it seems the 123rd New York soldiers turned to becoming "bummers" with greater interest than during the March to the Sea. In Georgia only one man was lost foraging while twelve were taken prisoner in the Carolinas. Six were taken in South Carolina: Privates Charles Byrne (Co. E), Henry Carter (Co. F), Harlan Farnum (Co. H), William Smith (Co. H), Henry Johnson (Co. C) and Burnam VanGuilder (Co. E). Once into North Carolina, it appears the men were particularly careless around Fayetteville. Five 123rd soldiers were taken prisoner there over five days. Privates Harry Daniels (Co. F), John Delmore (Co. F) and Charles Dings (Co. F) were taken prisoner March 9th at Fayetteville before Union troops were even near the city. On the 11th it was Private John Grooms (Co. A) turn, then Private Joseph Laport (Co. F) on the 13th. A final forager, Private Joseph Whitten (Co. C), would be taken on March 20th as the troops approached Goldsboro.[494] All would be paroled as the war drew to a close. About half of the foragers taken prisoner were transfers from the 145th New York. Total casualties for the 123rd New York for crossing hundreds of miles of enemy territory: five wounded and thirteen taken prisoner (one taken in combat at Bentonville).

For the entire journey, the 123rd New York reported having been issued only "six and a half days' rations hard bread, nine days' rations coffee, and five days' rations sugar" of U.S. military sustenance. During the march the regiment's foragers brought in 21,280 pounds of meat, 260 bushels of flour, 369 bushels of potatoes, 300 bushels of beans and 500 pounds of rice. Fifty cattle were turned over to the brigade's commissary while 19 horses and 23 mules were turned over to the brigade's quartermaster. The 1st Brigade reported taking 773 beef cattle, 230 sheep and 300,200 pounds salted meat besides bushels of beans, rice and sweet potatoes.[495] It had been many days of feasting but also quite a few of heavy labor with very little to eat. Soldiers prefer to know their meals are pretty much guaranteed. For that, one needed a railroad.

Private William Tooley was happy to hear a train whistle near the 123rd New York's camp. "it seems good to see the cars running once more after living so long without rations some of the time we lived very well and some days we had nothing but now we get full rations and are sure of them every day" Soap was tossed to the men to be followed by new uniforms and equipment. A sense of the hardship of the march can be seen in the wear and tear on equipment. A year before just as the Atlanta Campaign was to start, an equipment inspection for Company H of the 123rd saw 19 knapsacks, 10 haversacks, 14 canteens and 27 shelter halves labled "worthless" and "to be abandoned." The items had seen six to seven months service. Now at Goldsboro another inspection saw 8 knapsacks, 16 haversacks, 5 canteens and 10 shelter halves written off after only three months service.[496]

The 123rd NewYork's camp was regulation, streets laid out by company with mail calls regular. "The country is one immense camp for 5 miles around the river. the entire circuit covered with camps and trains," Sergeant-Major McLean wrote his mother, "The Rebels do not molest us at all now. all quiet & no firing on the picket line."[497]

It might have been quiet on the picket line as the soldiers were making love not war. Clark didn't mention one aspect of camp life to his mother but noted it in his diary: "Plenty of loose women living in the vicinity. They were ordered out of town and have gone in vacant houses near the picket line and live by the generous gifts of escorting men of both armies."[498] An astute business analysis by the working women must have clearly shown they'd maximize their sales opportunities with a proper positioning of their assets. That is, between both armies.

With nice weather the soldiers rested while the sick and wounded were all issued furloughs for home. To liven things up horse flesh was tested. "Horse trot today," McLean noted April 4th, "Some quite heavy betting. All the sporting events of the Long Island Course." Perhaps to clear his conscience of the gambling McLean also made time for Sunday services. "Went to church but such a crowd we could not get a seat, so did not stay long. Saw some of the Southern beauties, out in full regalia looking sweet and fresh as a lilac bush after a spring shower." Grant's actions at Petersburg were being read about as newspapers were once again available. "I hope that Grant will give the Rebs a good dressing out," McLean told his parents.[499]

What about dressing out Johnston? After the battle of Bentonville the Confederates had retreated to Smithfield which put them between Goldsboro and Raleigh. Rebel cavalry were positioned to keep a close eye on Sherman in Goldsboro. But Sherman intended to give his troops a much needed rest and was not planning to move until April 10th. Even then, he was thinking of ignoring Johnston and marching north to join up with Grant to crush Lee. A series of meetings between Lincoln, Grant and Sherman at City Point, Virginia, corrected this line of thought for Sherman. Grant was adamant that the Army of the Potomac should defeat Lee and the Army of Northern Virginia without help. Ulysses saw it as a matter of pride for the Potomac veterans so long on the losing end from their Southern foe. While Sherman's army refitted, Grant sent the Army of the Potomac forward on March 29th, Richmond fell April 3rd and Lee surrendered the Army of Northern Virginia April 9th.

Word of such a great victory had not reached Sherman's army the morning of April 10th as camps were broke and soldiers slung their gear on. Private William Tooley of Company K, 123rd New York, had a few days before written home to his parents. He was glad to hear his brother Eber had returned to the farm, "I hope he will be content now to stay there for if I live to get home I want to see you all." William reflected on the loss of his brother Horace during the Atlanta Campaign, "It makes me very sad indeed to think that we can never spend another sabbath with him."[500] Tooley marched out at 5:30 a.m. with the regiment as the 20th Corps column took the road to Smithfield. Rebel skirmishers were encountered around 9 a.m. and the 123rd New York, having the lead of the 20th Corps column, was deployed forward. Several hundred mounted Confederates of the 1st South Carolina and 6th North Carolina were before them.

Colonel Rogers had the men push the enemy and the soldiers of the 123rd New York did it with alacrity. A running firefight developed as the New Yorker's dashed in groups working the cover across fields and woods. The Southerners fell back across Moccasin Creek taking up most of the boards of two bridges that crossed deep channels in the adjacent swamp. A mill pond dam upstream was also cut by the Rebels resulting in the flooding of the lowlands. Splashing into the water, the New Yorker's waded towards the Confederates. Firing was steady with the enemy attempting to make a stand on the far side of the first channel. "On the edge of this stream the boys stood in the water waist deep and kept up a hot fire on the enemy for an hour," Sergeant Morhous says, "Many of the men had to hold up their cartridge boxes to keep their ammunition from getting wet, and some of the shorter men had to place their cartridge boxes on their shoulders...At last it was decided to charge the enemy, and with a yell, over the boys rushed, crossing on the narrow stringers some thirty feet in length..." Dashing for the remaining timbers of the bridge, Rogers reports the soldiers of the 123rd New York "crossed under a very brisk fire; plunged into the water to the waists of the men, pressed steadily forward and gained a position commanding the bridge over the second channel." Once elements of the brigade were up in support the 123rd New York charged forward again, taking the second bridge and putting the Rebels to flight. The 123rd "had some hard work driving the Rebels out of the swamps. were one afternoon in the water up to our waist for four hours under a brisk fire of the enemys cavalry," Sergeant-Major McLean told his father.[501]

Colonel Selfridge, Commander of the 1st Brigade, reported: "Colonel Rogers advanced with his command, pushing the enemy slowly backward, the latter contesting every inch of ground and showing a determination to hold us at bay...After driving him about a mile our skirmishers reached Moccasin Swamp, which was almost impassable, owing to the depth of water and the thick growth of underbrush, which impeded the advance of our troops and rendered the position of the skirmishers extremely hazardous...Colonel James C. Rogers, commanding One hundred twenty-third New York Volunteers, deserves much credit for the admirable manner in which he handled his regiment, and for the determination evinced in driving the enemy from his strong position on the opposite bank of the swamp."[502]

It had been an impressive feat of combat that even Major General Alpheus Williams felt compelled to mention in his 1st Division report. Describing Moccasin Creek as "a broad swamp, heavily tangled with trees, brambles, and bushes," the 123rd New York "spiritedly dashed into the swamp and, advancing through deep water and strong entanglements, drove back the enemy, so that the bridges were promptly relaid and the whole division placed in camp a mile north on Atkinson's Plantation before nightfall."[503]

Not quite the whole division as there had been some losses in the firefight. The 123rd New York had three men slightly wounded: Corporal Silon Ormsby (Co. B), Private David Irwin (Co. F), and Private William Nelson (Co. F). One soldier was killed. Sometime during the battle a bullet found Private William Tooley. Whether he fell face down onto Carolina soil or collapsed into the flowing waters of Moccasin Creek isn't recorded. He was the last soldier to die in the war for the 123rd New York Volunteer Infantry.

The skirmish at Moccasin Creek put the 123rd New York on display before General Williams and his staff, the 1st Brigade, plus other units arriving in support. It was clear the war was nearly over yet the men plunged into the firefight with great elan. Compliments to the regiment were given by many of the witnesses, Lt. Cruikshank telling his wife that the 123rd "did splendidly and got a great deal of praise from all the officers in the Corps. They say to me that I belong to a Regiment that I may be proud of."[504]

Arriving near Smithfield, the 20th Corps made camp among plantations that the men thought the best they had seen. Foraging brought in plenty of ham and cornmeal for the evening meal. April 12th at 8 a.m. the 123rd New York soldiers were in formation awaiting the order to march when Lt. Harvey Bosworth (Co. A) galloped up to announce-Lee has surrendered! "Hats, caps, cracker boxes, knapsacks and haversacks were thrown high in the air, and small colored boys were tossed high in blankets," Sergeant Morhous writes, "Everybody was glad, everybody rejoiced, and the boys of the 123rd, especially, were in ecstacies, for they knew what the old Potomac army was, by experience, and their old comrades had gained what they had so long and unsuccessfully struggled for."[505]

"As soon as the men heard the news they broke ranks at once and gave cheer after cheer and threw anything and everything they had or could get hold of into the air," Lt. Cruikshank says of the moment. Sergeant-Major McLean told his brother Tom that "roaring cheers & booming guns were heard from all parts of the Army. We think now that that old backbone of the rebellion that has withstood all our efforts to crack it for four years is now really broken." After about a half hour the ranks marched forward with soldiers calling out, "We must have old Johnston now." There was excitement, a real sense of seeing home and family again, of the clock running short for the South. Marching through Smithfield the men crossed the Neuse River and went into camp about 3 p.m. Lt. Cruikshank says it wasn't a quiet night around the campfires. "The bands throughout the army played National airs during the evening. There was rejoicing everywhere. The men indulged in very little sleep. We all sat up late and talked over the prospect of the War coming to a close."[506]

 General Sherman was worried that it might not close for years. What would Johnston do with the remaining Confederate army? Too small to really fight it out with the Yanks, Sherman was concerned Johnston might order it to disperse into guerrilla bands. A vision of a decade of internecine warfare was on his mind. Ordering his lead units to strip for fast marching, Sherman moved into Raleigh on the 13th with the goal of bringing Johnston to heel before a nightmare turned real. As for Johnston, he, along with many others in his army, did not at first believe Lee had really surrendered. After the truth of it sank in, Johnston planned to retreat westward to meet Confederate President Jefferson Davis (fleeing south from Richmond) and discuss options. Twenty-some miles west of Raleigh the last Confederate army in the east sat encamped by the Haw River.

 Skirmishing was steady along the front of the Federal's advance all the way into Raleigh. Most of the city was taken intact but the railroad depot had been fired by retreating Confederate cavalry. Once again, before combat troops could enter and police the town there had been pillaging by Confederates leaving and Union "bummers" arriving ahead of the main column. Frightened citizens had locked themselves in their homes, not peeking out but huddled in parlors and bedrooms listening to the tramping of infantry marching on the streets outside. The only incident of note was when a Rebel cavalry trooper that had stayed too long to plunder bumped into Union troopers escorting Union Cavalry General Kilpatrick. The Texan made the mistake of emptying his pistol at the Yanks, in the resulting pursuit his horse fell. Kilpatrick had him summarily shot. Per standing orders, local newspapers that advocated secession saw their printing presses destroyed. Citizens began to appear outside their homes as guards were posted at major locations throughout the town and squads walked regular patrols of city blocks. Sherman began attempts to bring Johnston to terms.

Late in the day the 123rd New York went into camp on the south side of the city near the State Lunatic Asylum. It "was filled with demented people who seemed rejoiced to see us thinking we had come to liberate them. They filled the windows and shouted to us to let them out," Sergeant Bull says, "One of the inmates made a great plea, saying he was sane, that he had been placed in the asylum by the secessionists for the reason he was a staunch Union man. He was a fine talker and made a great impression upon the soldiers...our officers looked into his case and found he was one of their most violent inmates. So he was left behind the bars but he certainly made a great plea." Lt. Cruikshank was watching all of this and it was a bit much for him. "We can hear the inmates screeching all of the time, night and day. I would rather be a soldier than to be connected with, or be a nurse in an insane asylum."[507]

There was also an institution for the blind and deaf in the city. Cruikshank and others accompanied the brigade band one evening when it serenaded the blind patients. Colonel Selfridge knew some of the teachers at the institution and the officers made time to dine with them.

Not that there was a lot going on at the regimental or brigade level. The soldiers of the 123rd New York made their camp as pleasant as possible and dealt with passing rain storms. Discussion was centered on when, or if, Johnston would surrender. Mail was, as usual, the highlight of their time in camp. "Sherman's Army entered this place yesterday morning a 8 a.m.," Sergeant-Major McLean wrote his father from Raleigh, "Johnston retreated going west. we shall follow him up close...We can use Johnston up in a hurry if we can catch him."[508] Confident, the soldiers looked forward to finishing the conflict. In a good mood, they would fight to whip but not to destroy their enemy.

Then late in the evening of April 14th a pistol shot occurred in Washington. Sherman learned of Lincoln's assassination the morning of April 17th via a coded telegraph message. He promptly ordered the telegraph operator to not say a word of it to anyone. Sherman was leaving on a train to meet Johnston and he understood the reaction the Union soldiers would have to Lincoln's death. Lampooned as an ape, buffoon, idiot and mental incompetent by the opposition papers in the North, President Lincoln was revered by most of the Union army. No president had ever been assassinated before in American history. If John Wilkes Booth thought he was doing the South a favor he was gravely mistaken.

Rumors of Johnston surrendering had been circulating through the Union camps the afternoon of the 16th, when Sherman left the next day for the meeting it was generally assumed the war would be over in a few hours. Sergeant-Major McLean spent the morning of the 17th writing his father, "We are rejoicing over the surrender of Johnston's Army...You cannot imagine the extent of the enthusism & Joy that pervades our Army at present. Last evening when the news reached us the Hills & Valleys around this place shook to the Hurrahs & wild shouts of the victorious Army. the noise was kept up most all night & now although everything is quiet a deep excitement prevails...Three cheers for the 'Universal Yankee Nation' and let the <u>British Lion Lookout</u> & <u>Maximillian tremble</u>."[509]

At a little farmhouse outside of Durham's Station Johnston was told by Sherman of the President's death. Beads of sweat were seen on Johnston's face as it sank in. Surrender now or face annihilation. Johnston disavowed any knowledge of, or involvement in, the assassination by the Confederate Government. Yet it wasn't the single general sitting across from him that needed convincing but the 80,000 Yankee horde back in Raleigh that was ready to be turned loose. After a discussion of a couple hours the two generals parted with nothing settled. Sherman was now going back to a mass of men he would not only disappoint with no peace terms, but then shock with the news that their beloved "Father Abraham" was dead. Before letting the news out to his command, Sherman increased the guards on the roads into Raleigh and ordered all personnel into their camps.

"The camp is quiet as a graveyard," Lt. Cruikshank wrote his wife Mary, "The report has just reached us that President Lincoln has been assassinated...The men threaten that if they have to follow Johnston's army they will show no pity. I know it will be hard to hold them in check. Every town will have to suffer as towns had to on former campaigns where the soldiers have found slave pens where they have been sold at auction, where there would be whipping posts and stocks. Plantations and towns where these were found were soon reduced to ashes. I feel so badly I cannot write, to think that this War has nearly come to a close so that Mr. Lincoln could see the end and yet not be permitted to rejoice with us. It is sad. It is my opinion that Johnston will surrender, that he will understand the result if he does not and we have to march after him through the country."[510]

"We have recd notice that Abraham Lincoln has been assassinated at Washington," Sergeant-Major McLean noted, "had a glorious time until it was quenched by the sad news of the Presidents death. That spread a gloom over us and no one has had the heart to rejoice much since. The citizens were mighty mum and they would have been served the same way if they had shown any pleasure about it."[511]

"President Lincoln was the idol of the army," Sergeant Bull wrote, "every man reverenced him and they could not have suffered greater grief had the notice been of the death of their nearest friend or relative." For Sergeant Morhous "over all there brooded a sorrow as if the most revered had fallen, as if the shock of personal bereavement had smitten separately every soldier, and embittered every heart toward the Rebels, to whom they attributed the murder."[512]

Sherman and Johnston cut surrender terms April 18th and they were promptly carried by an officer to Washington for approval. General Grant promptly arrived at 6 a.m. April 24th. He informed Sherman that his terms to Johnston were unacceptable to Washington, they were too lenient and to prepare to move upon the Confederate army to engage it in battle. Sherman was shocked by this, but he really did not comprehend the mood in the North especially after the death of Lincoln. His terms had also touched upon political matters that were out of bounds for a commander in the field. The terms given to Lee at Appomattox were to be offered as was the required forty-eight hour notice regarding the ending of the truce between Sherman's and Johnston's armies. That afternoon all Union commands around Raleigh were put on marching order status.

"We move on the enemy tomorrow morning at daylight. I do not know the cause of this movement, all I know is that General Grant is here in the city and we are to move," Lt. Cruikshank wrote his wife, "It would be madness for Johnston to bring on a battle. We can annililate his army. The men say if they have to fight again it will be the last battle for the Johnston army. They are desperate over the assassination of Mr. Lincoln. They know the Army of the Potomac have finished their work, and now if they take this army, the War will be over."[513]

"Lincoln will be terribly avenged if we go through the country on another campaign," McLean noted. "All sorts of rumors were in circulation," Sergeant Morhous says of the camp of the 123rd New York, "the most of them being to the effect that they had to go and fight Johnston. They knew Gen. Grant was in the city with Sherman, but whether his presence meant fight they did not know."[514]

For sure it meant marching. Breaking camp on the 25th the soldiers tramped twelve miles to Holly Spring. Confederate General Johnston's army was to their front, some 30,000 men. The truce would end on April 26th at noon. The Southern commander was struggling with orders he had received from Confederate President Jefferson Davis. Davis had ordered Johnston to do what Sherman feared, disperse the infantry into groups across the countryside and send the remaining mounted troops as an escort for Davis as he fled to Texas to continue the war. Johnston disobeyed Davis' orders and asked Sherman for a meeting to discuss new terms of surrender.

It was quiet all along the front lines, no skirmishing or rifle fire broke the afternoon stillness. Meeting on April 26th terms were arranged and Johnston surrendered all remaining Confederate forces. Sherman took the terms back to Raleigh and asked Grant, who had waited behind and let Sherman act as the field commander and accept the surrender of the enemy, to endorse them. Ulysses signed his name to the document while saying all he would have changed was to have Sherman's signature atop Johnston's. The soldiers shook hands, Grant left for Washington and Sherman set about closing down the war in his department. Forty Confederate generals and 39,012 officers and enlisted personnel were paroled over the next few days in North Carolina. Union officers in charge of the paperwork felt that probably 50,000 was the true total but the remaining Rebels had left ranks and started walking for home without seeking their parole.[515] All weapons were to be turned in but many of the Southern soldiers smashed their rifles to splinters and tossed them aside. About 800 cavalry under Confederate Generals Wheeler and Hampton rode south refusing to surrender. Isolated incidents would still occur as the news made its way west. But throughout the Confederacy riders in gray with flags of truce approached Union outposts to arrange surrender and parole. The war was over.

The Republicans in Washington seeking to trim the cost of the war put many units on the fast track to discharge.

The 123rd New York spent another day at Holly Springs then on the 28th marched back to Raleigh. There was rejoicing over Johnston's surrender but it was tempered with the thought of Lincoln's death. At camp in the city they wondered how long it would be before they would be discharged. Sergeant-Major McLean was anxious to get up to date as to the local doings back home in Washington County, writing his sister, "I want you to tell me all the gossip there is among the 'Old Women' and all the news concerning the young people."[516]

Her reply was going to have to be forwarded. The 123rd New York was told to be ready to march north for Washington at 7 a.m. April 30th. Sherman's Army of Georgia and the Carolinas was going home. New units like the 10th & 23rd Corps would take over the region as reconstruction began to be formalized.

"A lovelier day never dawned than April 30th," Sergeant Morhous writes. The men were on the road at 5 a.m., crossing the Neuse River and making fifteen miles they went into camp about two o'clock. It was going to be hard to hold the soldiers back as the thought of home had many wanting to push on, complaints were now heard when they went into camp with hours of daylight left. The smiling faces of the soldiers of the 123rd New York, laughing and joking with quickened step northward, contrasted sharply with those they passed going south. "The Rebel soldiers from Lee's Army are scattering over the country for their homes," Sergeant-Major McLean noted.[517] It was a devastated land the Rebel soldiers were going back too, not just in property but in lives and culture. The South had been lifted up, inverted and shaken by a hydra of blue. Over the next few years reconstruction would attempt to remake the culture of the white south but after a decade of effort the North walked out. Jim Crow walked in.

The 20th Corps column marched as they did just weeks before when the war was a tempest lurking to harm them. Yet there were changes, the soldiers only had five cartridges per man and ranks were to be kept with no foraging allowed. "All were cautioned to conduct themselves as properly and in as friendly a manner as they would were they marching through Pennsylvania or New York," Sergeant Bull says.[518] Rations would be government issue or the soldiers would pay for anything from the locals. Pontoon trains were in line and called forward quite often to bridge the numerous streams and rivers the men had to cross. The number of waterways across their line of march still amazed the New Yorkers. Marching along the men observed many former Confederate soldiers breaking the spring sod with a mule or horse to get a crop in. Worried about famine, Grant had allowed Rebel soldiers to take their animals home and even issued some of the captured stock to the former enemy soldiers so crops could be planted.

Homeward miles were ticked off day by day: May 2nd twenty, May 3rd sixteen, May 4th twenty-two, May 5th twenty-three. "The boys really enjoyed this marching, but the only trouble was they did not march far enough each day. They wanted to march rapidly, for their great desire was to see home," Sergeant Morhous writes. For the Yankees it was easy to drop the war as they had been the victors. The inhabitants of the homes, towns and villages marched by would not readily accept the outcome. "The young ladies on our route would come out and sing Confederate songs and make fun of us as we passed. We think, and told them, that the laugh was on them now," Lt. Cruikshank noted, adding that bitterness was often encountered. "This feeling is general throughout the South, although I was given a good dinner by a Rebel Lieutenant. I spent two hours at his home and was well treated. The soldiers are not as bitter as those who stayed at home. The soldiers respect each other."[519]

Richmond was reached May 9th with the 123rd New York going into camp south of the James River. Many of the officers took the opportunity to visit the former Confederate capital. Visiting what stores remained in the city, Lieutenant Cruikshank finally found some black cloth for the mourning badge required to be worn for thirty days due to President Lincoln's death. Marching forward on May 11th the soldiers entered Richmond and passed in review before Generals Sherman and Halleck. Four days later the men were on the field of Chancellorsville, the march having been halted to give the veterans the chance to visit the battlefield.

"Walking over the field brought vividly to memory that terrible 3rd day of May, 1863," Sergeant Morhous writes. The 123rd soldiers "visited the line where so many of their comrades had fallen, and found that their dead bodies had been scarcely covered with earth by the Rebels who held possession of the field at the close of the fight."[520] Getting some shovels the men covered the remains and placed a wooden headboard at the spot carved with "123rd New York."

Sergeant Bull looked over the remains of the breastworks where the regiment made its stand. "I could locate the exact place when I had been wounded and the place by the little run in our rear where I had been carried. I went to the old log house around which hundreds of us wounded had been gathered after the retreat of our forces...I lived over again in memory and mind the awful eleven days there. I could truly feel a great sense of gratitude to God that I had not only survived that ordeal but that during the two years since that time I had escaped unscathed, and now could rejoice in the fact that I was alive and homeward bound."[521]

Although their time was short, at this moment many promotions came through for the officer ranks. Colonel James Rogers was promoted to Brevet Brigadier General as a slew of colonels made general, majors made colonel and captains made major. The term "brevet" can be defined as a commission giving higher honorary rank without higher pay. It was a way of granting recognition for good service.

On towards Washington on May 16th, the men covering sixteen miles. Morhous says the talk "was mostly about the eventful battle of Chancellorsville, the visit to the field having brought back fresh every little incident."[522] Another thirteen miles on the 17th under a steady rain and twenty miles the 18th brought them through Fairfax Station. The next day as evening fell the soldiers of the 123rd New

York stood by Fort Worth outside of Washington gazing at the U.S. Capital building. As camp was laid out and tents erected along the streets the men pondered their time in Maryland, Virginia, Pennsylvania, West Virginia, Ohio, Indiana, Kentucky, Tennessee, Alabama, Georgia, South Carolina and North Carolina. Their great desire now was to get to Upstate New York.

But first Washington County came to them. "Have had a good many of the Washington Co. people here to visit us," Sergeant-Major McLean wrote his mother. As early as May 21st civilians from home were in the camp of the 123rd New York making the rounds. Besides seeing their family or friends in uniform, many were there to see the Grand Review of the armies. On May 23rd the Army of the Potomac, under General Meade, passed through the streets of a Washington draped in American flags and red, white and blue bunting. People leaned out of windows, packed porches and lined the streets to watch the procession. It took about six hours for the 65,000 troops to march their route through the city and pass by the reviewing stand in front of the White House. While this was going on the 123rd New York sat in their camp polishing their rifles and cleaning their uniforms as best as possible. They also took the time to reflect and chat. "The men spent the day in writing home, talking of the past and their prospects for the future," Lt. Cruikshank says, "They had been associated together for three years and they knew the character of each other. They knew the weakness and strength of character, courage, power of endurance, cruelty or kindness of heart of every man with whom they had been associated. It had been a time to try men."[523]

At 2 o'clock the next morning the soldiers of Sherman's Army began marching into line. Forming the front ranks, the 123rd New York was leading the 1st Brigade, which was leading the 1st Division, which was leading the 20th Corps. The men had to stand and wait until nearly dawn while the rest of the Corps filed into order then the "forward, march" was given. "It would have paid you big to have been here at the recent reviews," Sergeant-Major McLean told his brother Henry. In his diary McLean wrote of the review, "All were disappointed in our appearance. They expected to see a set of guerillas, a sort of an organization mob, and were agreeably surprised to see instead a well disciplined and fine appearing army." Sergeant Bull says that "we leading the 20th Corps were accorded great applause by the hundred of thousands of spectators that for miles lined the streets of Washington for miles. We marched in company front the whole distance and I am sure our marching and appearance was fine...There were thousands of soldiers of the Army of the Potomac who had paraded the day before upon the streets viewing us as we marched, they shouted themselves hoarse in welcoming our return...It was a proud day for all of us, and the Review was a fitting ending of our long service."[524]

"Ending" was the key word. "We have seen parades & reviews enough & all we want is to get off the blue clothes as soon as possible," Sergeant-Major McLean told his sister Amanda a few days after the triumphant marches. To his mother McLean on June 1st wrote, "I think you are in to much of a hurry for us to get home. if we get there by the 4th of July we shall do well...We are in hopes of leaving here next week but it is uncertain."[525] Arriving at this time was the regimental baggage sent to the rear when the 123rd left Atlanta. McLean noted that all his items were properly returned from storage. By June 3rd Lt. Cruikshank had made the rounds of the regiment to see how the paperwork, muster and payroll, was coming for the regiment's discharge. Although the officers were working all day and into the evening hours it still looked like another few days would be needed. But by June 6th it was completed. Hand delivered to the War Department on the 7th the men were mustered out of United States service on June 8th, 1865. (The 123rd New York must have had some connections to get that quick a turn around.) The majority of the recruits, plus deserters returned to the regiment, were transferred into the 60th New York Infantry to serve out their remaining time.

Now it was the fast track for home. Leaving Washington on the 9th, the former soldiers went by rail to

New York City then by the steamer "John Taylor" up the Hudson River to Albany. Docking at Albany at sunrise June 11th, the men marched along the Troy Road to Fenton Barracks where they went into their final camp awaiting their discharge papers and pay. June 14th, 1865 it was all over. They were civilians once again. Welcomed home with receptions across the townships, the former soldiers began their return to families, farms and professions.

Buried about Washington County, and about the nation, were the dead of the 123rd New York Regiment. They had left 960 strong but out of those original volunteers, officers and enlisted, only 49%, 474, mustered out three years later. The most costly aspect to the men had been disease, killing 82 while combat took 71 (in action and from wounds). While disease control seems to have taken an effort to learn the officers and men absorbed combat lessons quickly. Their battle casualties were low for a New York regiment and to this can be attributed the constant entrenching the men did, plus the leadership shown by the officers. The largest cohort of loss for the original volunteers involved discharges and transfers for disabilities, totaling roughly 258 casualties. Many had been discharged during the war with their health broken. At the muster out in Albany a total of 522 men were given their papers, the additional soldiers recruits discharged with the regiment.[526]

As for desertions, the Washington County Regiment appears to have had 47 of the volunteers and 5 of the recruits go over the hill during the war. This total of 52 has to be taken with reservations as it is not clear as to who was arrested and returned to the regiment, nor if all desertions were properly listed on the records. "Ezra Dibble, the fellow that deserted with Sam Parker, they have been caught and brought back. What they will do with them is not known yet," Private Artemus Harrington (Co. G) noted in August, 1863.[527] Although the NYS Adjutant General Report lists Parker as a deserter, Dibble is not. No mention is made as to Parker's discharge but Dibble is listed as out with regiment. All that can be said is that desertions were low for the regiment compared to other New York regiments. Most of the 123rd losses occurred at two times: the initial month of service saw 10, then the disease laden camps of winter 1862/1863 saw 16 desert. Future deserters would leave randomly over the war and campaigns, whether to recover their health, flee their fears, or called by loved ones at home.

For Washington County as a whole, catharsis would come to souls as season after season saw sowing and reaping of crops, tending to births and the putting of flowers on graves. By January of 1868 "Rough & Ready Engine Co. No. 2" in Greenwich was ready to hold their first "Grand Fireman's Ball" with "Whitcomb's Full Band" playing the melodies. More events filled the evening air with music as year by year the war was left behind. The "First Grand Public of the Salem Social Club" was held in May of 1873. Their guest invitations stated, "On With The Dance, Let Joy Be Unconfined." Refreshments would be available and "Your Attendance with a Lady is Respectfully Solicited." The Salem Social Club would expand their dance dates to Thanksgiving ("The presence of Yourself and Ladies would add to our Pleasure") while in Greenwich the "Quickstep Association" started holding their "Grand Masquerade Ball" at Hill's Hall. By the mid-1870's dances were being held throughout the county during the winter and summer months. The Pond Valley Hotel in the Cambridge area held their "Harvest Home Open Air Dance" in late August of 1874. Dancers would have the opportunity to purchase sandwiches, ice cream, cake and lemonade as they made out their dance card. Each invitation had twenty-four spaces for dance partners as twenty-four dances would be played with a half-hour refreshment break every eight dances.[528] Starting promptly at 8 o'clock with a "Grand March" it was followed with melodies including quadrilles, polkas, Spanish waltz, gallop, Portland Fancy and-a tune that must have had the 123rd New York veterans flashing slight smiles to one another-a Virginia reel.

Appendix A: Muster Roll

The following listing is a composite from several sources. The basic building block was a copy of the 123rd New York muster roll from the Washington County Archive office. Officers and NCO's were listed in their order on the roll, privates were moved at times to arrange their names alphabetically. Names are per muster roll with additional spellings found in brackets. The roll was cross referenced with the New York Adjutant General's report of soldiers in the regiment, the Historical Data Systems' American Civil War Research Database website and Sergeant Henry Morhous' memoir. Aspects of an individual soldier's service has been added in the "Comments" section of the listing. Items within brackets, [and], are from the Adjutant General's report and/or information from the American Civil War Database website. Comments without brackets are from Sergeant Henry Morhous' book, *Reminiscences of the 123rd Regt. New York State Volunteers*. Where conflicts occur between Morhous and other sources I have gone with the American Civil War Database website or Adjutant General's information. Italicized words are wound locations from the *Salem Press* newspaper following battles. Age is given as listed on the muster roll. Under the "Discharged with Regiment" heading: Y = Yes; N = No; KIA = Killed in Action; DOW = Died of Wounds; D = Died; W = Wounded; POW = Prisoner of War; MIA = Missing in Action. When a "KIA," "DOW," or "W" is given the battle where the injury occurred is listed in the comment section. No claim is made as to this listing being perfectly accurate. It is presented here in the hopes it may help those interested in genealogical or historical research.

123rd New York Infantry

REGIMENTAL OFFICERS FIELD & STAFF	RANK	AGE	DISCHARGED WITH REGIMENT	COMMENTS
Archibald L. McDougall	Colonel	45	DOW	[5/25/64 New Hope Church; Right leg amputated; Died of wounds 6/23/64 Officers Hospital, Chattanooga, TN]
Frank Norton	Lt. Colonel	28	DOW	[5/1/63 Chancellorsville, *hip and body*; 5/12/63 Died of wounds Washington, D.C.; Former Captain 30th NY Militia & 77th NY, Co. I]
James C. Rogers	Major	22	Y	[Lt. Colonel 5/12/63; Colonel 11/19/64; Brig. General 3/13/65]
George H. Wallace	1st Lt. & Adjutant	26	N	[Captain Company C 5/12/63; Resigned 1/11/64 to enter U.S. Army 3rd Infantry]
John King	Quarter-master	39	N	[9/10/62 Commission; 10/25/62 Discharge]
John Moneypenny	Surgeon	37	N	[Discharged 3/17/63]
Lysander W. Kennedy	1st Assistant Surgeon	29	N	[Discharged for promotion 5/21/65, Surgeon 119th NY Inf.]
Richard S. Connolly [Connelly]	2nd Assistant Surgeon	31	Y	
Henry Gordon	Chaplain		N	[Discharged 4/18/63]
Walter F. Martin	Sergeant Major	20	Y, POW	[Enlisted Company D; Sergeant-Major 123rd NY; Promoted 2nd Lt. Co. F 2/11/63; POW Culp's Farm; Paroled; *Escaped*]
Charles D. Warner	Quarter-master Sergeant	22	Y	[Enlisted Company G; promoted Quartermaster Sergeant]
Clark Rice	Commissary Sergeant	20	Y	[Enlisted Company F; promoted Commissary Sergeant]
Edgar Wheelock	Principal Musician	20	N	[Enlisted Company H; Discharged 6/3/65 Louisville KY]

Name	Rank	Age	Discharged with Regiment	Comments
Lawrence M. Roy	Drum Major	18	Y	[Enlisted Company H]
Leonard Corning	Hospital Steward	26	Y	[Enlisted Company D]; promoted Hospital Steward
Andrew A. Buell	Clerk	21	N	[Enlisted Company C; Absent on detached service provost marshals office Troy, NY when regiment mustered out]
James Chapman	Surgeon	54	Y	[Mustered surgeon 5/7/63 with rank from 4/2/63; Prior service Assistant Sur. 90th NY Inf.]
Ambrose Stevens	Colonel	47	N	[Former Lt. Colonel 46th NY; Commission 123rd NY Colonel 7/1/64; Mustered out 2/19/65]
Myron White	Chaplain	49	Y	[Commission 4/7/64]

COMPANY "A"	GREENWICH & EASTON			
NAME	RANK	AGE	DISCHARGED WITH REGIMENT	COMMENTS
Reynolds, Abram	Captain	37	N	Resigned, Discharged July 18th, 1863
Mason, Alonzo T.	1st Lt.	23	Y	Promoted to captain July 18th 1863; aid-de-camp to General Williams at close of war
Shaw, James C.	2nd Lt.	23	Y	Promoted to captain of Company "B" on June 10th, 1863
Robinson, George	1st Sergt.	31	Y	Promoted to 1st Lt. July 18th, 1863; commanded unit while captain on staff duty; Promoted Captain March 13th, 1865
Harrison, William J.[H]	Sergeant	29	KIA	[Chancellorsville 5/3/83, *thigh*] Buried on field
Norton, Albert	Sergeant	26	Y	Detached with ambulance corps.
Cramer, George L.	Sergeant	40	N	Transferred to Veterans Reserve Corps [2/15/64]

Name	Rank	Age		Notes
Safford, Joseph	Sergeant	23	N, W, POW	[Chancellorsville; Discharge U.S. Hospital 6/9/65 Alexandria, Virginia]
Bosworth, Harvey N. [M.] [Besworth]	Corporal	19	Y	[Sergeant Jan. 1st, 1863;Promoted 2nd Lt. June 10th, 1863]; was aid-de-camp to Brig. General Selfridge commanding brigade
Cowan, Eugene	Corporal	20	Y, W	[Sergeant 1/1/63; 1st Sergeant 11/11/63; Wounded near Atlanta 7/29/64]
Dobbin, William H.	Corporal	22	D	[Died of remittent fever U.S. Hospital #1, Nashville, August 10th, 1864]
Richards, John W.	Corporal	22	Y	Promoted sergeant [11/11/63]
Jones, Roswell B. [Robert]	Corporal	30	D	Died at Stafford Court House March 5th, 1863
Cook, Albert M.	Corporal	19	Y	Promoted Sergeant [11/4/63], sick and sent to Nashville as Atlanta campaign commenced
Tanner, Albert W.	Corporal	18	Y	
Hyatt [Hyett], Aaron M.	Corporal	25	N	[Discharged 6/28/65 McDougall Hospital NY Harbor]
Young, Arnold A.	Musician	41	N	Discharged May 28, 1865 [5/27/65 NY, NY]
Clark, Palmer K. [Palon R.]	Musician	18	N, W	[Chancellorsville; Discharged due to wounds 12/24/63 Portsmouth Grove, RI]
Nilwarth, Alfred [Wilmarth]	Wagoner	26	N	Discharged for disability Feb. 1863 [2/21/63]
Allen, Albert	Private	33	D	Died Dec. 21st, 1863 at Murfreesboro of chronic diarrhea
Allen, Joshua	Private	23	Y, W	[Chancellorsville]
Baker, John	Private	20	N	Married a girl in Lincoln Co., TN, stayed behind when regiment left Elk River [Deserted 4/26/64 Elk River Railroad Bridge]

Name	Rank	Age		Notes
Bartlett, William	Private	40	KIA	Killed at Chancellorsville, lungs, buried on field [5/1/63]
Beaumus, Oscar [Baumes]	Private	18	KIA	Killed at Chancellorsville, buried on field [5/1/63]
Beaumus, John [Baumes]	Private	25	Y	
Bentley, Ansel	Private	36	N, W	[Chancellorsville; Discharged 5/19/65 Louisville, KY]
Booter, Ezra	Private	22	Y, W	[Chancellorsville]
Bowin, Fernando [Bourre, Ferdinand] (Bovrey, Bourri)	Private	19	Y	
Briggs, Leroy	Private	18	Y	
Brown, Adelbert	Private	20	Y	
Campbell, Charles	Private	28	Y	
Curtis, John	Private	24	Y	
Decker [Deeker], John	Private	30	N, POW	[Taken prisoner at Culp's Farm 6/22/64, Paroled 2/28/65; Discharged 6/29/65 NY, NY]
Dobbin, Alex.	Private	19	Y, POW	Taken prisoner at Chancellorsville; [Paroled]
Donahue, David	Private	35	N	[Discharged for disability 1/31/63]
Dorlhen, David	Private			[No Further Record]
Downing, Elisha	Private	38	Y	
Down [Don], John	Private	19	Y	
Durham [Darham], Richard H.	Private	23	N, POW	[Corporal 11/11/63, POW Culp's Farm; Paroled 2/22/65 North East Bridge, NC; Discharged 6/17/65 Camp Parole, Annapolis, MD]
Faxon, Cortland [Courtland]	Private	20	Y	
Fenton, William	Private	21	N, W	[Gettysburg 7/3/63; transferred to V.R.C. 3/16/64]
Fones, Sam'l L.	Private	38	Y	
Fowler, Charles A.	Private	33	Y	
Fuller, Benedict [Burdick]	Private	20	Y, W	[5/25/64 at Dallas, Georgia]
Galutia, Asel	Private	30	N	[Transferred 9/15/63 V.R.C.]
Galutia, Richard	Private	19	Y	

Name	Rank	Age		Notes
Giles, Thomas O.	Private	40	N	[Disability 1/31/63]
Gillson [Gilson], Charles	Private	24	Y	[Corporal 5/1/63]
Grooms, John	Private	20	N, POW	[POW 3/11/65 Fayetteville, NC; Paroled 3/29/65 Richmond, VA; Discharged 6/21/65 Albany, NY]
Hastings, Zachariah	Private	25	D	Died at Harper's Ferry Hospital Dec. 25th, 1862
Hay, Geo. H.	Private	18	N, W	Wounded at Chancellorsville, transferred to V.R.C. April 10th, 1864
Hempstreet [Hemstreet], Alex.	Private	19	N	[Transferred 3/11/64 V.R.C.]
Hillman, Jno. F	Private	22	N	[Discharged 6/8/65 Fairfax Seminary Hospital, VA]
Hornbrook [Hornibrook], John	Private	22	N	Discharged July 15th, 1864 for disability [7/8/64 Hospital NY, NY]
Hughes, John	Private	20	N	Deserted, returned under Lincoln's pardon proclamation, transferred to 60th N.Y.S.V. to serve remaining time
Hughs [Hughes], Thomas	Private	30	N, W	[Culp's Farm 6/22/64; Discharged 6/19/65 Hosp. Troy, NY]
Hyde, John H.	Private	19	KIA	[Chancellorsville]
Kernighan, Robert	Private	27	Y	
Knapp, Frank	Private	27	Y	
Knapp, Harry	Private	29	N	Scout for General Kane, discharged June 29th, 1863
Lambert, Alex.	Private	21	Y	
Lamphier, Nathan	Private	19	KIA	Killed Jan. 12th, 1864 [1/13/64] at Winchester Springs, TN, buried at Elk River Bridge
Lampman, Henry	Private	43	DOW	Died of Chancellorsville wounds at Acquia Creek Hospital [5/24/63]
LaPoint, Charles	Private	18	KIA	[Culp's Farm, 6/22/64 Marietta, GA]

Name	Rank	Age	Notes	Details
LaPoint, Joseph	Private	22	N, W	[Corporal 5/1/63; Peach Tree Creek; Deserted 8/16/64]
LaPoint, Vitel [Vitelle]	Private	35	Y	
Livingston, James	Private	40	Y	
Long, Lucius	Private	32	Y	
Manning, William H.	Private	19	Y, W	[Chancellorsville; Corporal 1/1/63]
Mitchell, Alex.	Private	33	D	Died of disease Aug. 16th, 1864 Chattanooga, TN [Absent, sick 7/23/64 Hospital]
Mosher, Edwin R.	Private	20	N	[Discharged 6/23/65 Albany, NY]
Orton, Wallace	Private	23	N, W	Wounded at Gettysburg, Discharged Philadelphia [Disability 4/5/65]
Parks, Daniel	Private	18	Y	
Pielling, James	Private	32	N, W	Wounded at Chancellorsville, transferred to V.R.C.; [V.R.C 1/1/64; Transferred back into 123rd 4/5/64; Mustered out 5/20/65 Hospital Murfreesboro, TN]
Potter, Albert	Private	28	KIA	Killed on skirmish line at Atlanta July 30, 1864, buried on field
Prire [Prive], John	Private	44	N	Discharged for disability April 17, 1865
Rice, Hiram	Private	20	Y	[Corporal 1/1/63]
Rice, Alonzo	Private	43	N	[Mustered out 6/6/65 U.S. Hospital Troy, NY]
Rodier [Rodire], Benjamin F.	Private	26	Y	
Rosebust [Rosebush], Adolphus	Private	24	Y	
Russell, George I. [J.]	Private	19	Y	
Sears, George W.	Private	26	Y	
Shearer [Sherer], Martin	Private	44	N, W	[Chancellorsville; Discharged for disability 6/15/64 Pine Hill, GA]
Sheffield, George	Private	41	Y	
Spencer, John A.	Private	21	Y	

Name	Rank	Age		Notes
Spencer, Wm. H.	Private	18	Y	
Spurhawk [Sparhawk], Oscar	Private	20	N, W, POW	Wounded & prisoner at Chancellorsville, discharged May, 1865 [5/16/65 Albany, NY]
Steeves [Steves], Jacob	Private	35	D	Died at Harpers Ferry Hospital Feb. 10, 1863
Stewart, Reuben	Private	22	Y	
Tefft, Caleb B.	Private	22	N, W	[Chancellorsville; Discharged 6/3/65 hospital Albany, NY]
Tefft, Charles	Private	25	Y, W	[Resaca]
Tefft, Hiram B.	Private	19	N	Transferred to the navy, April 1864 [5/18/64]
Tucker, Charles	Private	21	Y	[Corporal 11/14/63]
VanOrman, Benj.	Private	19	Y	
Waller, Munroe	Private	18	Y	
Whipple, David	Private	23	Y	
Wilcox, Albert C.	Private	19	D	[Died 8/31/63 Moreau, NY]
Williams, Erastus T.	Private	22	N	Discharged May 24, 1865 [Absent, hospital 1/10/63 Baltimore]
Wilson, John	Private	23	N	Discharged for disability March 1863 [3/12/63]
Wilson, Thos. W.	Private	44	Y	
Wright, Leroy	Private	21	W, KIA	[Wounded Chancellorsville, killed Peach Tree Creek 7/20/64]
Wright, Thomas D.	Private	42	Y	
Youngs, Hiram F. [J.]	Private	23	Y, W	[Chancellorsville]
	Enlisted Average Age	25.9		
RECRUITS				
Bennett, Albert	Private	18	D	[Enlisted 3/29/64; Transferred to Company C; Died of disease 5/3/64 Eruptive Hospital Louisville, KY]
Buck, George R.	Private	18	N	[Enlisted 9/13/64; Discharged 6/7/65 U.S. Hospital Troy, NY]

Name	Rank	Age	Discharged with Regiment	Comments
Cutter, John [Jr.]	Private	21	Y	[Enlisted 8/30/64]
Dixon, Phineas F.	Private	19	Y	[Enlisted 9/1/64]
Ferris, James K.	Private	18	N	[Enlisted 3/31/64; Discharged for disability 1/28/65 General Hospital, Louisville, KY]
Lampman, John	Private	18	Y	[Enlisted 9/1/64]
McCullough [McCollough], Thomas	Private	24	Y	Reenlisted from 22nd Regiment Aug. 29, 1864
McCollough, William	Private	31	Y	[Enlisted 8/29/64]
Potter, George W.	Private	19	Y	[Enlisted 8/25/64]
Scranton, William H.	Private	39	Y	[Enlisted 9/13/64]
Taylor, William H.	Private	23	Y	[Enlisted 8/29/64]
Weir, Archibald	Private	20	D	Recruit Aug. 1864, died in hospital Chattanooga typhoid, Jan. 1865 [1/8/65]
Whittaker [Whittiker], Leroy	Private	24	Y	Joined 9th NY June, 1863, sick, reenlisted Co. A 123rd fall 1864 [9/12/64]
Wolff, Michael J. [Wolf, John M.?]	Private	31	D	Enlisted 8/29/64 [Died of disease, inflammation of the lungs, 2/7/65 hospital, Jefferson, IN]
LESS THAN ONE MONTH IN REGIMENT OR DROPPED				
Dam, Tellas	Private			[Enlisted 4/15/65; Dropped from rolls April, 1865 claimed by 142nd Infantry]

COMPANY "B"	**KINGSBURY**			
NAME	RANK	AGE	DISCHARGED WITH REGIMENT	COMMENTS
Warren, George W.	Captain	30	N	[Resigned 6/10/63 Stafford Court House]
Warren, James C.	1st Lt.	32	N	Resigned January 28, 1863 [1/29/63]
Burton, Samuel C. [Barton]	2nd Lt.	33	N	Resigned January 7, 1863 [1/17/63 Stafford Court House]
Smith, George W.	1st Sergt.	20	Y	[2nd Lt. Co. B 1/17/63; 1st Lt. Co. K 1/12/65]

Name	Rank	Age	Status	Notes
Middleton, Joseph H.	Sergeant	18	Y, W	[1st Sergeant 6/10/63; Wounded, *wrist*,Peach Tree Creek]
Smith, Benjamin F.	Sergeant	31	Y, POW	[Culp's Farm 6/22/64; Escaped 1/6/65]
Heath, Levi	Sergeant	28	N	[Deserted 3/24/63]
Vaughn, Chas. A. [H.]	Sergeant	19	Y	
Hays [Hayes], Newton R.	Corporal	33	Y	[Sergeant 6/10/63]
Newton, Dan'l L.	Corporal	22	N	[Discharged for disability 7/15/63 Washington D.C.]
Warren, Joseph	Corporal	23	N	[Discharged hospital 6/6/65 Troy, NY]
Harris, Willard P.	Corporal	22	KIA	[Sergeant 6/10/63, Private 7/15/63, Sergeant 8/24/63; Resaca May 15, 1864]
Gleason, David T.	Corporal	31	N	[Discharged for disability 3/16/63 Harper's Ferry]
Harrington, Alonzo	Corporal	22	N	[Transferred 9/1/63 V.R.C.]
Harris, Orrin E.	Corporal	19	Y	[Private 6/25/63, Sergeant 5/20/64]
Gillman [Gilman], Ephraim T.	Fifer	23	Y	
Johnson, James	Drummer	18	Y	[Corporal 5/20/64]
Clarke [Clark], Francis	Wagoner	37	Y	
Carpenter [Carpentier], Leon	Wagoner	24	Y	
Akins, William D. [O.]	Private	23	DOW	[Peach Tree Creek 7/20/64; DOW 7/22/64]
Bailey, Norman L.	Private	25	N	[Discharged for Disability, 4/12/63 Baltimore]
Barber, Phineas	Private	22	N, POW	[Captured and Paroled no dates; Deserted near Chancellorsville 4/29/63]
Barber, William	Private	18	Y, W	[Dallas, 5/25/64]
Beach, John H.	Private	22	D	[Died of disease 1/16/63; Phthisis at Judiciary Square Hospital D.C.]
Bennett, Dennis	Private	24	N	[Deserted 1/15/63 Harper's Ferry hospital]
Bennett, Frank L.	Private	18		[No Further Record]
Bennett, James	Private	25	D	[Died disease 12/4/63 Hospital]

Name	Rank	Age	Status	Notes
Bennett, Lyman [Seymour]	Private	20	Y, W	Chancellorsville
Blake, A. [Andrew] J.	Private	22	Y	
Blakeman, Chas. F.	Private	19	N	[Discharged for Disability 3/16/63 Harper's Ferry]
Branch, Orvil [Orville]	Private	23	N, POW	[POW 3/19/65 Bentonville, NC; Paroled 4/2/65; Discharged Camp Parole, MD 6/19/65]
Briant, Roswell [Rossel O.]	Private	43	N	[Discharged for Disability, 4/12/63 Camp Williams, VA]
Buch [Buck], Lemuel	Private	26	Y	
Bullard, Arnold	Private	22	Y	
Burnett [Burnet, Bennett], Alexander	Private	20	D	[Died disease, typhoid, 1/16/63 Harper's Ferry]
Burton, Martin	Private	27	Y	[Corporal 6/25/63; Private, no date; Corporal 8/24/63]
Capron, Edward [Edmund]	Private	26	Y	[Corporal 8/24/63]
Carroll, Bernard [Barnard]	Private	35	Y, W	Wounded in hand [Near Dallas, GA 5/25/65]
Durkee, Ira	Private	22	N, W	[Wounded, *ankle severely*, Culp's Farm; Discharged for Disability 1/19/65 Hospital Madison, Ind.]
Fuller, Steenrod	Private	18		[No Further Record]
Fuller, Wm. M.	Private	18	Y	
Gile, Andrew	Private	38	Y	
Gleason, Reuben [Reubin L.]	Private	26	Y	
Green, Jabez	Private	44	N	[Discharged for Disability 3/16/63 Harper's Ferry]
Green, Jeremiah	Private	24	Y	
Green, Jerome	Private	22	N, W	[Wounded 7/30/64 Atlanta, GA] Discharge 5/31/65 McDougall General Hospital NY Harbor
Haight, Abram W.	Private	29	N	[Deserted 1/15/63 hospital Harper's Ferry]
Haines [Hanes], James	Private	18	N	Discharged 1862
Hale [Hall], William	Private	37	Y	
Hamilton, Jno. R.	Private	18	N, W	[Wounded 7/3/63 Gettysburg; Deserted 9/19/63]

Name	Rank	Age		Notes
Harrington, Geo. W.	Private	26	N, W	Wounded in hand at Peach Tree Creek [Transferred 1/2/65 V.R.C.]
Harrington, Harling	Private	25	N, W	Leg off at Pine Hill [Kenesaw Mtn., right leg amputated; Discharged wounds 10/4/65 Nashville, TN]
Harrington, Jonathan G.	Private	27	N	Hung himself since his return [Discharge 6/24/65 Hospital Albany, NY]
Harrington, Wm. F.	Private	21	N	[Absent, sick]
Harris, Horace	Private	43	N	[Discharged for Disability 3/28/63 Judicary Square Hospital, Washington]
Hazleton, Austin	Private	19	N, POW	[Chancellorsville; Paroled; Discharged 5/31/65 McDougall Hospital NY]
Hill, Henry	Private	24	Y	
Irish, Geo. W.	Private	27	N	[Discharge Disability 3/16/63 Harper's Ferry]
Knapp, Jno. H.	Private	18	N	[Transferred V.R.C. 8/23/63]
Lord, James	Private	38	Y	Accidentally wounded in hand at Bridgeport
Martindale, William	Private	18	Y	
McCloud, Thomas	Private	32	Y	
Mead, Elias	Private	35	N	Discharged 1863 [Disability 2/4/65 Harper's Ferry-This makes more sense if 1863 and not 1865 but 1865 reported]
Middleton, John H.	Private	20	D	[Died 1/16/63 Harper's Ferry Hospital; Died of phthisis]
Moore, Charles	Private	43	Y	
Morris, Thos. A.	Private	26	N	[Corporal 6/25/63; Private 7/15/63; Corporal 8/24/63; Discharged 6/15/65 U.S. Hospital Troy, NY]
Mosier [Mosher], Germand [Germond C.]	Private	19	Y	
Mosier [Mosher], Charles	Private	18	Y	
Norton, Edwin B.	Private	19	Y	[Corporal 6/25/63; Private 7/15/63; Corporal 8/24/63]
Ormsly [Ormsby], Ernest L.	Private	26	Y	

Name	Rank	Age	Status	Notes
Ormsly [Ormsby], John H.	Private	19	Y	[Corporal 6/25/63]
Ormsly [Ormsby], Silas A.	Private	21	Y, W	[Corporal 6/25/63] Slightly wounded Moccasin Creek
Parks, Ezekiel	Private	18	N	[Discharged for Disability 4/21/63 Stafford Court House]
Parl, James	Private	19		[No Further Record]
Pearson, Edwin [Edward C.]	Private	21	N, W	[Wounded Chancellorsville; wounded Culp's Farm; Transferred 12/30/64 V.R.C.]
Pelot [Pelott], Leander	Private	18	Y, POW	[Chancellorsville; Paroled]
Perry, Geo. M.	Private	32	N	[Discharge 6/6/65 Hospital Albany, NY]
Phair, Edward	Private	18	N, POW	[POW 11/18/64; Discharged 6/27/65 Camp Chase, OH]
Pixley, Wm. H.	Private	19	Y	
Ramsey, Robert	Private	28	N	[Deserted 12/13/62 Washington]
Ransom [Rawson], Chas. L.	Private	33	N	[Discharged Disability 10/10/63]
Stone, Dwight	Private	27	D	[Died at Bridgeport 11/27/63]
Stone, Walter	Private	21	N	[Discharged Disability 2/23/63 Stafford Court House]
Stover [Strover], George [E.]	Private	27	DOW	Wounded Chancellorsville, lockjaw [5/13/63]
Swears, Jonathan	Private	25	N	Deserted Cincinnati OH
Taylor, James [B.]	Private	18	N, W	[Peach Tree Creek, *arm*, Corporal 6/25/63; Private 7/15/63; Corporal 8/24/63; Discharge 5/24/65 McDougall Hospital NY Harbor]
Tucker, Lewis	Private	18	Y	
Van Vranken, Henry	Private	33	N	Discharged from hospital at close of war [6/26/65 Albany, NY]
Van Yea, Henry	Private	18	Y	[Corporal 6/25/63; Private 7/15/63; Corporal 8/24/63]
Wetmore, [Phileman] C.	Private	21	N	[Transferred 11/15/63 V.R.C.]

Name	Rank	Age		Notes
Wheeler, Munson	Private	25	D	[Disease, consumption, 5/22/64 Hospital #14 Murfreesboro, TN]
White, Joseph	Private	28	Y	
Yarker [Yaker], Jacob	Private	40	Y	Blacksmith
	Enlisted Average Age	**24.8**		
RECRUITS				
Ash, Joseph	Private	23	Y	[Enlisted 9/2/64 Troy, NY]
Ayatt, Alexander	Private		N	[Enlisted 2/18/64 Granville, NY transferred to 60th NY 6/8/65]
Batchelder, Isaac	Private	24	Y	[Enlisted 9/1/64]
Bruyet [Breyett], Moses	Private	24	Y	[Enlisted 9/1/64]
Carpenter, Eli	Private	22	Y	[Enlisted 9/1/64]
Chadwick, Almon	Private	33	Y	[Enlisted 8/31/64]
Chadwick, Milo	Private	35	Y	[Enlisted 8/31/64]
Flanaghan, Michael	Private		N	[Enlisted 2/26/64 Transferred 6/8/65]
Foley, James	Private	20	N	[Enlisted 1/6/65 Transferred 6/8/65]
Gates, Oliver	Private	18	Y	[Enlisted 9/4/64]
Grow, L. M.	Private		N	[Transferred 6/8/65 60th NY]
Hand, Hiram H.	Private	26	N	[Enlisted 4/10/65 Transferred 6/8/65]
Harris, Charles	Private	27	N	Enlisted Jan 6th 1865 transferred to 60th NY [Deserted 5/2/65 on march to Richmond VA]
Hartsby, Julius	Private		N	[Transferred 6/8/65]
King, John (Jr.?)	Private	21	N	[Enlisted 3/28/65 Transferred 6/8/65]
Lapham, Eli	Private	21	Y	[Enlisted 9/7/64]
Lyons, Daniel	Private	22	N, POW	[Enlisted 1/7/65; POW 4/1/65; Paroled 5/5/65; Discharge 7/12/65 NY, NY]
Moore, Joseph C.	Private	21	N	[Enlisted 9/7/64 Mustered out 5/21/65 Stewart Hospital, Richmond VA]
Nero, George H.	Private		N	[Enlisted 2/27/64 Transferred 6/8/65]

NAME	RANK	AGE	DISCHARGED WITH REGIMENT	COMMENTS
Potrin, William	Private	18	D	[Enlisted 9/7/64 Died disease 11/13/64 Hospital #2 Chattanooga TN]
Shelvin, James	Private		N	[Transferred 6/8/65]
Smith, George	Private	28	N	[Enlisted 1/23/65 Transferred 6/8/65]
Stevens, Earnest A.	Private		N	[Enlisted 2/27/64 Transferred 6/8/65]
Stuberfield, James	Private	23	N	[Enlisted 4/10/65 Transferred 6/8/65]
Thomas, Henry E.	Private	24	N	[Enlisted 3/24/64 Transferred 6/8/65]
VanYea, George	Private	18	Y	[Enlisted 9/1/64]
Williams, John	Private	40	N	[Enlisted 1/2/64; Deserted]
LESS THAN ONE MONTH IN REGIMENT OR DROPPED				
Simpson, Geo. H.	Corporal	28	N	[Deserted 9/23/62 Camp Chase]

COMPANY "C"	**WHITEHALL**			
NAME	RANK	AGE	DISCHARGED WITH REGIMENT	COMMENTS
Tanner, Adolphus H.	Captain	28	Y, W	[Promoted Major 5/12/63; Lt. Col. 11/19/64; Wounded Dallas 5/25/64]
Warner, Walter G.	1st Lt.		N	Resigned Feb. 11, 1863
Corbett, John C.	2nd Lt.	24	KIA	[Chancellorsville, *shot through heart*, 5/3/63]
Carrington, Luke H.	1st Sergt.	22	N	[Promoted 2nd Lt. 5/3/63; Military Railroad Conductor; Discharge 7/5/65 Albany NY]
Hillard, Nicholas	Sergeant	23	Y	[1st Sergeant 6/9/63]
Farrell, Richard W.	Sergeant	22	Y, W	[Chancellorsville, 5/3/63]
Morhous [Morehouse], H.C.	Sergeant	20	Y	
Wright, George	Corporal	44	KIA	[Chancellorsville, 5/3/63]
Gillott [Gillett], Leonidas S.	Corporal	20	KIA	[Sergeant, Chancellorsville, 5/3/63]
Penfield, Edward S.	Corporal	18	Y	

Name	Rank	Age		Notes
Wrangham, Thos. J.	Corporal	27	Y	[Sergeant 7/5/63]
Mosher, Abram	Corporal	26	N	[Disability, heart disease, 3/7/63 hospital Philadelphia PA]
Hollister, John C.	Corporal	24	Y	
Wells, George D.	Corporal	20	Y, W	[Chancellorsville]
Manville, Orville	Corporal	18	N, W	[Chancellorsville; Transferred to V.R.C. 5/1/64]
Whitney, Edson	Musician	31	D	Died in hospital at Harper's Ferry [Disease, commitent fever, 12/23/63]
Allen, Joseph W.	Private	26	Y	[Corporal 7/5/63]
Allen, Wm. H.	Private	21	W, DOW	[Wounded Culp's Farm 6/22/64; Peach Tree Creek, DOW 7/22/64]
Batey [Baty], Geo. H.	Private	23	Y	
Black, Geo. S. [T.]	Private	35	Y, W	[Chancellorsville; Absent, sick hospital 5/28/64]
Blanchard, Hiram T.	Private	44	N, W, POW	[Wounded, POW Chancellorsville; Paroled; Detached duty 4/11/64 U.S. Printing Office Nashville, TN]
Bogart, Joseph	Private	25	Y	
Bourdon, Mark	Private	32	N	Deserted at Fairfax Station [1/19/63]
Brannock, George	Private	26	Y	
Bryan, Thos.	Private	30	N	Discharged for Disability [Deserted 12/1/62]
Buell, Andrew A.	Private	21	N	[On detached duty Provost Marshals Office, Troy, NY when regiment out]
Butler, Winfield	Private	23	Y	
Carle, John	Private	21	Y, W	[Chancellorsville, 5/3/63]
Carroll, James	Private	25	N	Discharged for disability [1/1/63]
Clemens [Clemons], Henry	Private	32	N	Discharged for disability [Harper's Ferry 3/23/63]
Cook, Paschal [Parchal] L.	Private	19	Y, W	[Chancellorsville, 5/3/63]
Crawley, James	Private	26	Y, W	[Chancellorsville, 5/3/63]

Name	Rank	Age	Status	Notes
Crawley, Michael	Private	35	N, W	Gettysburg, discharged for disability [Deserted 7/2/63 Gettysburg]
Crow, Edward	Private	18	N, W	[Wounded, left leg, Culp's Farm 6/22/64; Discharged wounds 3/27/65]
Cull, Francis E.	Private	19	KIA	[Chancellorsville, 5/3/63]
Cull, Jed A.	Private	19	Y	[Corporal 7/5/63]
Day, Edward R. [B.]	Private	22	Y	[Corporal 5/1/64]
Dilts, Joseph H.	Private	28	D	Died in hospital at Harper's Ferry [Typhoid, 12/22/62]
Donahue, Charles	Private	21	D	Died in hospital at Atlanta [Died disease, Chronic Diarrhea, 12/22/64 hospital Chattanooga TN]
Douglass, John	Private	44	Y, W	[Chancellorsville]
Earl [Earls], James W., Jr. [No Junior]	Private	24	N, W	Supposed to have drowned in Ohio River returning from furlough [Wounded Chancellorsville 5/3/63; Deserted 8/30/63 hospital Philadelphia PA]
Forget, George	Private	24	N	Discharged for disability [5/27/63 Washington]
Foster, William	Private	19	Y	
Holt, Wm.	Private	19	KIA	[Chancellorsville, 5/3/63]
Horton, George	Private	21	Y, W	[Wounded Chancellorsville; Transferred 9/30/63 to V.R.C.; Transferred 11/1/64 back into Company C, 123rd]
Huntington, Wesley P.	Private	32	KIA	[Gettysburg, 7/3/63; National Cemetery, NY Plot E-30]
Hurlburt, James	Private	37	Y, POW	[Chancellorsville 5/3/63; Paroled]
Hutton, Wm., Jr.	Private	23	DOW	[Sergeant, 7/5/63]; wounded Peach Tree Creek carrying colors, died in hospital [7/22/64]
Johnson, Henry F.	Private	19	N, W, POW	[Chancellorsville; Discharged 6/16/65 Albany NY]
Kelly [Kelley], Thos.	Private	27	N	[Transferred 10/7/64 V.R.C.]

Name	Rank	Age		Notes
Killgallon [Kilgallin], James	Private	32	N, W	Wounded twice at Chancellorsville, discharged for disability [Transferred 8/1/63 V.R.C.]
King, Louis	Private	23	N	Deserted at Fairfax Station [1/19/63]
Kinny, Patrick	Private	22	Y	[Corporal]
Knowles, Geo. N.	Private	24	Y	
Lamb, Geo. W.	Private	21	Y	Teamster
Lamb, Wm. P.	Private	18	N, W	[Chancellorsville; Transferred V.R.C. 3/15/64]
Leonard, Geo. H.	Private	20	KIA	[Chancellorsville, 5/3/63]
Leonard, Nathan	Private	19	KIA	Supposed to have been killed at Chancellorsville [Deserted 5/3/63]
Manning, John W.	Private	26	Y	
McCarty [McCarthy], Thomas	Private	19	Y	
Meatt, Napoleon	Private	32	N	[Transferred V.R.C 7/1/63]
Moore [Moon], Franklin	Private	23	N, W	[Chancellorsville; Discharged wounds 5/13/63 hospital Philadelphia PA]
Mooris, Chas. W.	Private	18	Y	
Norton, Chas. H.	Private	18	N	[Discharged for Disability, 2/19/63 Alexandria VA]
O'Conner, Dan'l	Private	19	Y	
O'Reilley, Jas.	Private	18	Y	
Parde [Pardo], Horace	Private	19	Y	
Price, Joseph	Private	38	Y	
Rilley, James	Private	18	Y	[Corporal, 7/22/64]
Rose, Charles	Private	32	N	Deserted at Fairfax Station [1/19/63]
Sager, David H.	Private	25	KIA	[Chancellorsville, 5/3/63]
Scott, Richard	Private	43	Y	
Sears, John, Jr.	Private	18	D	Died in hospital at Savannah [4/6/64]
Sherman, Jas. J.	Private	21	Y, W	Wounded twice at Chancellorsville
Shields, Daniel	Private	33	N	[Discharged for Disability, 12/3/63]
Smith, John C.	Private	23	Y	[Corporal 7/5/63]
Tafft [Taft], Andrew	Private	23	Y, W	[Chancellorsville]

Name	Rank	Age		Notes
Tafft [Taft], Henry N.	Private	29	Y, W	[Chancellorsville]
Tafft [Taft], Hiram A.	Private	32	Y	
Tafft [Taft], Hiram Jr.	Private	28	Y, W	[Chancellorsville; Discharged for Disability 3/1/64]
Terrill, Richard	Private	44	Y	
Thompson, Nathan	Private	26	Y, W	[Chancellorsville]
Tighe, Michael	Private	39	N	[Discharged for Disability, 6/8/63]
Van Anden [Vanaden], John	Private	29	Y	[Corporal]
Whitten, Joseph	Private	23	N, POW	Taken prisoner while foraging [POW Goldsboro, NC 3/20/65; Paroled 3/30/65 Aikens Landing, VA]
Wilson, Andrew	Private	18	Y	
Winn, Geo. R.	Private	30	N, W	[Bentonville, 3/19/65]
	Enlisted Average Age	25.5		
RECRUITS				
Connely [Conley, Conely], James H.	Private	28	N	[Enlisted 12/28/63 Whitehall; Mustered out 6/7/65 Hospital Troy NY]
Cook, Alonson H.	Private	18	N	[Enlisted 12/15/63 Whitehall; Mustered out 5/31/65 McDougall General Hospital NY Harbor]
Gibbs, Henry G.	Private	25	Y	[Enlisted 8/25/64, Troy]
Johnson, Charles H.	Private	21	Y	[Enlisted 9/7/64, Troy]
Johnson, James W.	Private	26		[Enlisted Hebron, No Further Record]
Leet, Charles [M.]	Private	21	Y	[Enlisted 9/7/64, Whitehall]
Lyman, Warren E.	Private	25	Y	[Enlisted 9/5/64, Troy]
Neil, Calvin	Private	33	N	[Enlisted 9/2/64, Troy; Discharge 6/19/65 U.S. Hospital Troy NY]
Neil, James W.	Private	34	N	[Enlisted 12/21/63, Troy; 60th NY 6/8/65]
Neil, John	Private	37	N	[Enlisted 7/29/64 Troy; 60th NY 6/8/65]
Noble, Daniel	Private	45	N	[Enlisted 2/15/64, Granville; 60th NY 6/8/65]

Name	Rank	Age	Discharged with Regiment	Comments
O'Neil, Henry E.	Private	38	N	[Enlisted 12/21/63, Troy, 60th NY 6/8/65]
Rogers, John	Private	19		[Enlisted 8/30/64, Troy; No Further Record]
Smith [Chauncey S.]	Private	20	N	[Enlisted 12/15/63, Whitehall; Discharge 6/13/65 hospital Albany, NY]
LESS THAN ONE MONTH IN REGIMENT OR DROPPED				
Edgerly, George W.	Private	22	N	[Discharged at muster of regiment due to bleeding of the lungs]
Johnson, Michael	Sergeant	19	N	Deserted when regiment reached Washington [9/30/62]

COMPANY "D"	PUTNAM, DRESDEN, FORT ANN			
NAME	RANK	AGE	DISCHARGED WITH REGIMENT	COMMENTS
Barron, John	Captain	34	N	Dismissed for absence without leave Feb. 22nd, 1863
Anderson, Alex.	1st Lt.	30	Y	[Captain, 2/22/63]
Quinn, Edward P.	2nd Lt.	27	N, W	[1st Lt. 2/22/63; Culp's Farm 6/22/64; Discharged 5/1565 for Disability]
Swift, Willis [Jr.]	1st Sergeant	21	Y	[2nd Lt. 2/22/63]; Detailed to command pioneer and ambulance corps.
McLaughlin, Jno. A.	Sergeant	19	Y, W	Enlisted 44th NY 1861; enlisted 123rd July 30th, 1862; [1st Sergeant; Wounded Kenesaw Mtn. 6/19/64]

Name	Rank	Age	Status	Notes
Sartwell, Henry	Sergeant	23	N, W	Wounded at Chancellorsville-*Medal of Honor*-also wounded Culp's Farm [Kenesaw Mtn. 6/29/64; Discharge 5/27/65 hospital Albany NY]
Thompson, Alex. C.	Sergeant	30	D	Typhoid, Washington D.C. Feb. 12th, 1863 [U.S. Hospital Washington, 3/14/63 Diarrhea]
Commings [Cummings], James L.	Sergeant	24	DOW	[Dallas 5/25/64, DOW 5/27/64]
Nicholson, Albert	Corporal	21	Y, W, POW	Wounded Chancellorsville, taken prisoner in Georgia and held until close of war [POW 11/13/64 Madison, GA; Paroled 3/1/65]
Wright, George T.	Corporal	24	N	[Discharged disability 1/14/63]
Bull, Rice C.	Corporal	20	Y, W	[Chancellorsville; Sergeant 5/28/64]
Bartholemew, Jos.	Corporal	33	Y	[Sergeant]
Maxwell, Robert	Corporal	37	N	Discharged for disability January 13, 1863
Woodroof [Woodruff], Albert	Corporal	29	Y, W	[Cassville, 5/19/64]
Gourlie [Gourlee], [John] C.	Corporal	20	Y	[Sergeant 2/1/63]
Rich, Russel P.	Corporal	21	N	[Transferred 1/15/64 V.R.C.]
Nicholson, Chas.	Fifer	23	N	[Discharged for Disability, 8/22/63]
Van Wormel [VanWormer], Francis	Drummer	18	Y	
Backus, [Jairus] D.	Private	19	Y, W	[Wounded Culp's Farm 6/22/64]
Bartholemew, Chas.	Private	35	Y	
Batchelder, [Orestes] G.	Private	19	Y	Detailed as hospital steward
Belden, Levi A.	Private	18	Y	
Beldon [Beldin], Orrin J.	Private	19	Y	

Name	Rank	Age		Notes
Benson, Andrew E.	Private	18	Y	
Blair, G. W.	Private	20	D	Died of fever Feb. 26, 1863 Washington D.C. [Discharged for Disability 2/23/63]
Blanchard, Chas.	Private	24	Y	
Blanchard, Edw'd	Private	18	Y	
Brinor [Briner], Orson	Private	18	Y, W	[Dallas, 5/25/64]
Carter, Barrett	Private	26	N	[Discharged for Disablility, 12/26/62]
Chase, [George] W.	Private	23	Y	
Chase, Horace	Private	20	N	[Discharged for Disability, 11/9/62]
Chase, M.	Private	29	Y	
Clark, Wm. O.	Private	39	N	[Discharge Disability 2/4/63]
Condly [Connor], Daniel	Private	19	Y	
Congdon, Joseph H.	Private	24	Y	
Corbett [Corbet], Albert	Private	18	Y	Not old enough, joined at Salem, mustered in D.C.
Crowley, Timothy	Private	19	Y	
Cubb, T.	Private	19	Y	
Cummings, John S.	Private	22	Y	
Cummings, Robert I.	Private	30	N	Absent from regiment since July 17th, 1864 [Deserted]
Cunningham, James	Private	21	Y	
Dredrick [Dedrick], Henry O.	Private	20	D	Died of disease, July 25th, 1864 Madison, Ind. [Hospital]
Dona, F. [T.]	Private	35	N	[Discharge Disability 2/6/63]
Eastman, Seymour A.	Private	24	Y	
Eaton [Easton], Darwin	Private	22	D	Died of disease Stafford Court House March 1863 [3/20/63 Chronic Diarrhea]
Eaton, Levi	Private	40	Y	
Finch, Jerry	Private	21	KIA	[Chancellorsville, 5/1/63]
Fisher, Andrew J.	Private	33	Y	
Fisher, Ransom O.	Private	19	D	Accidentally killed with revolver Bridgeport, Ala. Dec. 1863 [12/8/63]
Fuller, John	Private	18	N	[Corporal; Transferred 7/1/63 V.R.C.]

Green, John	Private	37	N	[Absent, sick, 5/22/64 Hospital Louisville, KY]
Groat [Grout], Charles	Private	21	D	[Typhoid, Died Chattanooga Hospital 6/20/64]
Hall, John	Private	36	N, W	[Chancellorsville; Transferred 1/15/64 V.R.C.]
Harvey, Joel	Private	19	Y, W	[Peach Tree Creek, 7/20/64, *side*]
Haskin [Haskins], Peter L.	Private	38	N	Detailed as hospital steward [Discharged Hospital No. 2 Nashville 6/15/65]
Haynes, James H.	Private	18	D	Died of disease [Typhoid] Harper's Ferry Nov. 15th, 1862
Henderson, Wm.	Private	44	N	[Discharged for Disability 4/21/63]
Hiddleston, W. B.	Private	18	Y	
Hopkin [Hopkins], Oscar F.	Private	24	Y	
Kingsley, Freeland I. [J.]	Private	19	N	Corporal, discharged for disability 1863 [3/30/63]
Leigh, James D.	Private	18	N	[Discharged for Disability 2/23/63]
Lesson, John	Private	21	Y	
Loomis, James H.	Private	18	D	Died of disease Harper's Ferry 1863 [1/23/63 Chronic Diarrhea]
Loomis, William H.	Private	27	Y	
Martin, Reubin W. [S.]	Private	25	D	Died of disease 1862 [Fever, 12/21/62 Harper's Ferry]
Mattison, Albert	Private	27	N	[Discharged for Disability 4/21/63]
Mattison [Matison], Eli	Private	34	Y	Detailed as butcher
Mattison, Geo.	Private	25	D	Died of disease [5/23/63 Fort Ann NY]
Mattison, James M. [N.]	Private	36	N	[Discharged for Disability 4/24/63]

Name	Rank	Age	Status	Notes
McLaughlin, Alexander	Private	26	W, D	3rd Cavalry April, 1861; enlisted 123rd July 1862; died of disease at home on furlough Dec. 1st, 1863 [Wounded Chancellorsville; Died at Putnam NY]
McLaughlin, James	Private	22	Y	
McLaughlin, Wm.	Private	24	Y	[Corporal, 7/1/64]
McNutt, Issac	Private	27	DOW	Chancellorsville, died at Acquia May 15, 1863 [Died Douglas Hospital Washington 6/21/63]
Miller, A. K. [Kilburn]	Private	20	Y	
Moore, Wallace	Private	18	Y	
O'Conner, Daniel	Private		Y	
Pattison, Geo.	Private	20	Y, W	[Chancellorsville; Corporal]
Pettis, I. [Joseph]	Private	19	Y	
Plue, Allen	Private	19	Y	[Corporal 7/1/64]
Plue [Plew], Royal R. [B.]	Private	28	Y	
Rice, Edward E.	Private	21	D	Died of disease Alexandria, Va. December 1862 [Typhoid, 1/14/63 Lincoln Hospital Washington]
Rich, Seymour D.	Private	18	Y	
Rowell, N. S.	Private	21	Y	Corporal, served one year as scout
Rowell, Page [E. P.]	Private	18	N	[Discharged for Disability 1/30/63]
Shandley, B. [Bernard]	Private	25	DOW	[Peach Tree Creek, 7/20/64, *shoulder*; Died 8/4/64 Kingston GA]
Shelden [Sheldon], George	Private	21	Y, W	[Culp's Farm 6/22/64, *wrist*]
Smith, Oliver H.	Private	21	N, POW	[Culp's Farm; Paroled 4/28/65; Discharged 6/30/65 NY NY]
Spencer, Phineas M.	Private	18	N	[Discharged for Disability 11/20/63]
Swift, Julius	Private	18	Y	Detailed to ambulance corps.
Trowbridge, Byron	Private	18	N	[Deserted 7/15/63 hospital West Phil. PA]
Vaughn, James M.	Private	19	Y	

Name	Rank	Age		Notes
Vaughn, Job	Private	21	Y	[Corporal; Sergeant 7/1/64] Detailed to color guard
Wagender [Wagner], Daniel	Private	33	Y	
Walker, Amos	Private	28	Y, W	[Chancellorsville; Dallas]
Walker, Lewis	Private	17	N	[Discharged for Disability 12/30/63]
Wallace, James F.	Private	20	Y	
Ward, Asahel	Private	42	D	Died of fever Stafford Court House [2/26/63]
Welch, Chas.	Private	18	Y	Detailed to ambulance corps.
Whorter, Philip	Private	29	N	[Discharged for Disability 2/8/63]
Williams, Theodore	Private	25	Y	
Williamson, Daniel Ray	Private	30	Y, W	[Corporal, Peach Tree Creek, *face*]
Young, J	Private	41	Y	
	Enlisted Average Age	**24.1**		
RECRUITS				
Anderson, William, Jr.	Private	18	D	[Enlisted 3/26/64, Putnam; died of disease Chattanooga 11/13/64]
Brown, James T.	Private	22	N	[Enlisted 1/9/65, Troy; Transferred 6/8/65 60th NY]
Harvey, Edward F. [T.]	Private	40	N	[Enlisted 1/2/64, Whitehall; Transferred to 60th NY]
McCormack, James	Private	18	N	[Mustered 1/11/65, Troy; Transferred to 60th NY]
McLaughlin, Robert	Private	21	N, W	[Enlisted 3/26/64, Putnam; Culp's Farm; 60th NY]
McLaughlin, Wm. D.	Private	20	N	[Enlisted 3/1/64, Putnam; Transferred to 60th NY]
Raymow, Edward	Private	18	N	[Enlisted 2/10/64, Fort Ann; Transferred to 60th NY]
Smith, Alexander	Private	21	N, W	[Enlisted 3/29/64, Saratoga Springs; Atlanta 7/30/64; Transferred to 60th NY]
Smith, George	Private	21	N	[Enlisted 1/6/65, Troy; Discharged 5/10/65 Hart's Island NY Harbor]

COMPANY "E"	HARTFORD AND HEBRON				
NAME	RANK	AGE	DISCHARGED WITH REGIMENT	COMMENTS	
Weir [Weer], Norman F.	Captain	26	N, W, DOW	Wounded Chancellorsville, wounded Gettysburg & died; Company sent body home at their expense for burial; large funeral in the town [DOW 7/26/63 Gettysburg PA]	
Hale [Hall], George R.	1st Lt.	22	Y	[Captain, 7/26/63]	
Carey, Seth C. H.	2nd Lt.	24	Y, W	[Peach Tree Creek; 1st Lt. 7/26/63; Adjutant 3/15/64]	
Davey [Daicy], John H.	1st Sergeant	25	N, DOW	[2nd Lt. 7/26/63, 1st Lt. 3/29/64; Peach Tree Creek 7/20/64, Died 7/22/64]	
Reynolds, Harvey	Sergeant	20	N	[Discharged 5/26/65 McDougall Hospital NY Harbor]	
Potter, Douglas [Douglass]	Sergeant	22	Y	[1st Sergeant 11/11/63]	
Barker, Chas. H.	Sergeant	26	N	[Returned to ranks] Deserted in Loudon Valley, VA Dec.1st, 1862	
Bouche [Boushe], Peter	Sergeant	25	N, W	[Culp's Farm; Averasboro; Discharge 6/6/65 Albany NY]	
Hall, Duane M.	Corporal	24	Y	[Sergeant 12/1/62, Sergeant Major 1/14/64, 2nd Lt. Co. E 1/12/65]	
Weir [Weer], Sidney B.	Corporal	21	N, W	[Chancellorsville; Transferred to V.R.C. 2/15/64]	
Battie [Beattie], Wm.	Corporal	18	Y	[Sergeant 2/15/64]	
McMillen [McMillin], Wm.	Corporal	27	Y	[Sergeant 11/11/63]	
McEachron, Robt.	Corporal	23	N, W	[Peach Tree Creek; Discharged 6/13/65 Albany NY]	
McCarty, Thomas	Corporal	21	N	[Discharged for Promotion October 13th, 1863, Captain U.S.C.T. 7th Infantry]	

Name	Rank	Age	Status	Notes
Woodward [Woodard], Franklin	Corporal	20	N, W	[Dallas; Mustered out 6/10/65 Louisville KY]
Felleir [Tellier], Joseph	Corporal	21	N, W	[Chancellorsville; V.R.C. 4/19/64]
Whitlock, Arthur	Drummer	22	N, W	Wounded on picket near Stafford Court House [Transferred V.R.C. 11/15/63]
Chapman, Danl.	Musician	25	Y	
Vance, Edward [Edwin]	Wagoner	37	Y	
Adams, Albert	Private	19	Y	
Archambolt [Archambautt], Frank	Private	18	N, DOW	Culp's Farm, died on train enroute to Chattanooga, TN [6/29/64]
Armstrong, William [H.]	Private	24	Y	
Baker, Dennis	Private	21	Y, W	[Wounded Chancellorsville 5/3/63]
Barker, Abel M.	Private	21	Y	
Becock, Elliott	Private	21	Y, W	[Culp's Farm]
Bell, John	Private	18	KIA	[Gettysburg; Buried National Cemetery, NY Plot A-135]
Beverage [Beveridge, Jr.], Alexander	Private	30	D	[Died 12/18/62 Alexandria Hospital]
Briggs, Byron	Private	25	KIA	[Chancellorsville, *chest*, 5/3/63]
Brown, Darius	Private	22	Y, W	[Peach Tree Creek]
Burch, Eliot	Private	21	N, W	[Culp's Farm; V.R.C. 4/25/65]
Burke, William	Private	31	Y	
Chamberlin, Wm.	Private	20	N	On detached service [Mustered out 6/17/65 Albany NY]
Churchill, Chas. P.	Private	29	N	[Discharged for disability 4/13/65, Troy, NY]
Coy, Chauncey	Private	19	Y	
Crosier, James A.	Private	21	N	[Discharged Disability 2/19/63 Harper's Ferry]
Crosier, Wm. V.	Private	20	N	[Discharged Disability 5/13/63 Albany NY]

Name	Rank	Age	Status	Notes
Darling [Durling], Edward W.	Private	20	N, W	[Culp's Farm; Absent, hospital]
Dickerson [Dickenson], James	Private	25	Y	
Dolon [Dolan], Patrick	Private	26	Y	
Donally [Donley], Geo.	Private	25	KIA	[Peach Tree Creek, 7/20/64]
Forsyth, Edward	Private	23	N	[Discharged 6/22/65 hospital Albany NY]
Gilchrist, Wm.	Private	21	D	Died at Fairfax Station January 6th, 1863
Graham, John	Private	16	Y	[1865 Washington County Census shows John as discharged with regiment, 19 yrs. old, "Health very good"]
Graham, Wm.	Private	45	N, W	[Chancellorsville, V.R.C. 11/15/63]
Gray, Alvin	Private	19	Y, W	[Peach Tree Creek, 7/20/64]
Hatch, Adolphus	Private	22	Y	[Corporal 3/2/64]
Henry, James A.	Private	24	Y	[Corporal 3/2/64]
Hewitt, Smith	Private	18	D	Harper's Ferry December 18th, 1862 [Hospital]
Higley [Highley], Julius	Private	24	N	[Discharged for promotion, 6/30/64, 1st Lt. 109th U.S.C.T.]
Jefway, Adolphus	Private	20	D	Died at Atlanta September 18th, 1864 [Hospital, disease]
Johnson, James	Private	22	Y	
King, Andrew J.	Private	22	Y	
Lackey, Walter	Private	18	Y	
Lackey, Wm.	Private	21	Y	
Ladd, Wm. H.	Private	21	Y	[Corporal]
Latimer [Lattimer], George	Private	28	Y	
Liddle, Marcus	Private	21	Y	
Liddle, Marvin	Private	30	Y	
Loveland, Aaron	Private	20	N, W	[Chancellorsville 5/3/63; Discharged 6/8/65 U.S. Hospital Troy NY]
Mahaffy, Thomas	Private	27	Y	

Martin, Halen [Harlan] P.	Private	18	Y	
McEachron, James	Private	25	D	December 5th, 1862 died in camp Loudon Valley, VA
McGan, Mason	Private	20	Y	
McIntyre, Henry	Private	19	Y	
McKenna, Patrick	Private	28	N, W	[Averasboro, 3/16/65; Absent, hospital]
McMillen [McMillin], Andrew	Private	20	Y	
Miller, Henry C.	Private	23	N	[Discharged for promotion, 8/16/64, 1st Lt., 101st U.S.C.T.]
Moore, John	Private	20	Y, W	[Chancellorsville; Corporal 3/2/64]
Morris, Geo. T.	Private	25	Y	Detached service as blacksmith
Moro [Mow], Francis	Private	18	Y	
Munson, Ira	Private	26	D	Died of measles Feb. 16th, 1863; [Harper's Ferry]
Murphy, William	Private	23	Y, W	[Chancellorsville]
Murtha, Martin	Private	18	Y, W	[Culp's Farm]
Nelson, Oscar B.	Private	19	N	Discharged for disability July 13th, 1863 [Hospital Alexandria VA]
Norton, James A.	Private	29	KIA	[Corporal; Chancellorsville, *neck, 5/3/63*]
Park, Luther M.	Private	19	Y, W	[Culp's Farm, 6/22/64]
Patterson, John	Private	30	Y	
Pollack [Pollock], James	Private	28	Y	Brigade blacksmith
Qua, Ransom	Private	22	Y	[Corporal, 3/1/65]
Rasey, Wesley (Charles W.)	Private	20	Y	
Raymond [Rayment], Nathan	Private	21	D	Died at Stafford Court House Feb. 16th, 1863
Reynolds, Andrew	Private	22	Y	
Reynolds, James M.	Private	19	N	[Discharged 5/26/65 McDougall Hospital NY Harbor]
Rhoades, Amos	Private	20	Y, W	[Chancellorsville; Corporal 7/1/64]

Name	Rank	Age		Notes
Riley, John	Private	30	N	Deserted from Alexandria, Va hospital Feb. 16th, 1863
Scovill, Erastus	Private	18	N	[Hospital, Savannah 1/12/65]
Shevlin [Shelvin], James	Private	23	Y	
Smith, Philo	Private	18	D	Measles, April 24th, 1865 [Absent, sick Hospital New Bern, NC]
Smith, William M.	Private	24	Y	Driver ambulance corps.
Stiles, Samuel	Private	23	Y, W	[Peach Tree Creek, 7/20/64]
Tanner, Edward	Private	19	Y, W, POW	[Chancellorsville; Paroled]
Thomas, Hiram L.	Private	37	D	Died Harper's Ferry hospital November 30th, 1862
Thompson, Charles	Private	36	Y	
Wait [Waite], Harlon [Harlan] P.	Private	25	Y	[2nd Lt. 3/15/64; 1st Lt. 1/12/65]
Warner, Wm. H.	Private	22	N	Deserted January 22nd, 1863 [Dumfries VA]
Washburn, Philip	Private	28	Y	
Waugh, James	Private	25	N	[Discharged Disability 1/24/63]
Whitlock, Wm. J.	Private	26	Y, W	[Dallas, 5/25/64]
Whitney, Philander	Private	28	N	Discharged for disability April 9th, 1863 [Harper's Ferry]
Wiggins, James	Private	27		[No further record]
Wiles, Daniel	Private	21	N, W	[Chancellorsville; Transferred to V.R.C. 3/15/64]
Wood, Alba (Allen)	Private	24	N	[Discharged for Disability 3/19/63, Alexandria VA]
Wood, Mortimer	Private	18	N	[Discharged for Disability 3/25/63, Harper's Ferry]
Wood, Myron	Private	20	Y	
Wright, John	Private	27	W, POW, DOW	[Corporal; Wounded 5/25/64 Dallas; Wounded 6/22/64 Culp's Farm and POW] Died in prison hospital Atlanta July 3rd, 1864
	Enlisted Average Age	23.2		

RECRUITS				
Anderson, John	Private	23	N	[Enlisted 3/28/64, Whitehall; Transferred to 60th N.Y.]
Baker, Levi	Private	18	N	[Enlisted 2/15/64, Hartford; Transferred to 60th N.Y.]
Byrne [Burns], Charles	Private		N, POW	[145th NY; Transfer 1/12/64; POW 1/28/65; Paroled; Discharged 6/29/65 NY NY]
Clark, Thomas	Private	18	D	[Enlisted 2/8/64, Hartford; Died in hospital 3/22/64 in Albany, NY]
Donaldson, James H.	Private	18	N	[Enlisted 2/20/64, Hartford; Discharged 5/22/65 from U.S. Hospital in Philadelphia]
Dudley, John	Private	27	N	[Mustered 4/1/64, Troy; Transferred to 60th N.Y.]
Elliott [Elliot], William	Private	26	N	[Enlisted 2/29/64; Transferred to 60th N.Y.]
Feeney, Patrick	Private	26	D	[145th NY; Transfer 12/23/63; Died disease 1/28/65 U.S. Hospital Camp Dennison OH]
Holland, John O.	Private	18	N	[Enlisted 3/25/64, Hartford; Transferred to 60th N.Y.]
Law, Lawrence	Private	23	N	[Enlisted 3/28/64, Whitehall; Transferred to 60th N.Y.]
Orcutt, Joseph	Private	18	N	[Enlisted 2/15/64, Hartford; Discharged 5/27/65 NY, NY]
Patrick, John	Private	18	D	[Enlisted 9/1/64, Albany; Died 1/21/65 at hospital in Savannah]
Rison, Moses	Private	18	N	[Enlisted 3/30/65, Schenectady; Discharge 7/25/65 hospital Albany NY]
Stiles, Henry B.	Private	18	N	[Enlisted 1/30/64, Hartford; Transferred to 60th N.Y.]
VanGuilder, Burnam E.	Private	18	N, POW	[Enlisted 2/15/64; POW 3/7/65 Pee Dee River, SC; Released 4/2/65 Aikens Landing, VA; Mustered out 7/1/65 Annapolis MD]
White, Clarence	Private	18	Y	[Mustered 8/9/64, Albany]

ABSENT				
Daley, Dennis	Private	18	N	[145th NY; Transfer 1/12/64; Absent, sick in hospital as of 11/1/63] *Does not appear to have ever arrived at regiment*

COMPANY "F"	ARGYLE			
NAME	RANK	AGE	DISCHARGED WITH REGIMENT	COMMENTS
Robertson, Duncan	Captain	37	Y	
Reid, Donald	1st Lt.	24	Y	
Robinson, George	2nd Lt.	21	Y	[1st Lt. Co. C 11/11/63; Detached, Aide-De-Camp to General Williams 6/63 until muster out of regiment]
Crawford, Andrew L.	1st Sergeant	23	Y	[1st Lt. & Quartermaster 10/25/62]
Scott, George	Sergeant	24	N, POW	[1st Sergeant; Captured and Paroled no dates; Transferred to 16th U.S. Inf. 7/29/64]
Robinson, George L.	Sergeant	25	N	[Discharged for Disability 4/21/63 Stafford Court House] Died at Argyle July 1863
Rowan, James M.	Sergeant	21	DOW	[Culp's Farm 6/22/64, Died 6/24/64]
White, Dan'l M.	Sergeant	21	Y	[1st Sergeant]
Mickel, Jacob	Corporal	24	Y	
Williams, Jacob	Corporal	28	N, W	[Chancellorsville; Discharged for Disability 9/23/64 Cleveland OH] Died at Argyle December 1st, 1864
Stanly, Theodore	Corporal	24	N	[Discharged for Disability 3/28/63 Harper's Ferry]
McCollum, Wm. J.	Corporal	22	Y	[Sergeant 4/21/63]
McMurray, Sylvester	Corporal	24	Y	
Robinson, Alexander	Corporal	24	N	[Discharged for Disability 12/1/62] Died at Argyle July 4th, 1863
Schermerhorn, James	Corporal	32	N	[Transferred to V.R.C. 5/20/63]

French, John	Corporal	23	Y		[Sergeant]
Rexstraw, Jno. E.	Musician	22	Y		
Armstrong, Wm. J.	Wagoner	28	N		[Discharged for Disability 1/4/64, Nashville, TN]
Bain, Geo. K.	Private	20	N		[Discharged for Disability 11/30/62, Harper's Ferry] Died at Argyle January 7th, 1863
Bain, John	Private	25	Y		
Baker, Garner	Private	43	POW, DOW		[Chancellorsville, 5/3/63; POW 5/3/63; Died of wounds]
Beattie [Battey], Orlando D.	Private	27	Y		
Brady, Wm.	Private	24	Y, W		[Chancellorsville]
Campbell, Wm. R.	Private	18	Y, W		[Dallas, 5/25/64]
Carter, Charles	Private	18	Y, W		[Chancellorsville]
Cartwright [Carthwright], Joseph	Private	37	D		[Died 4/21/65, chronic diarrhea]
Conklin, James H.	Private	25	N		[Discharged for Disability 4/21/63 Stafford Court House]
Copland [Copeland], Wm. J.	Private	21	Y		
Crawford, Jas. H.	Private	26	Y		
Cronk, Robert J.	Private	40	N, W		[Gettysburg, V.R.C. 2/15/64]
Curnus [Curns], James	Private	30	Y		
Curtis, Clark	Private	18	N		[Mustered out 7/7/65 Fairfax Seminary Hospital]
Curtis, Simon D.	Private	23	N		[Discharged for Disability 6/13/63 Washington]
Dennison [Denison], Thomas	Private	18	Y		
Dings, Charles	Private	20	N, POW		[POW Fayetteville, NC 3/9/65; Paroled 5/5/65; Discharged 6/29/65 NY NY]
Dobbin, James S.	Private	39	N, W		[Chancellorsville; Absent, sick in hospital NYC as of 3/12/65]
Durkee, Schuyler	Private	25	Y		[Corporal 7/27/64]
Ellsworth, Stokes	Private	26	Y		
Emmerson, Wm. H.	Private	21	D		[Died 2/10/63, measles, Stafford Court House]

Name	Rank	Age	Status	Notes
Fullerton, Russell	Private	24	N, W	[Corporal; Wounded Chancellorsville; wounded Peach Tree Creek, *body*; wounded 3/14/65 Carolina; Discharged for wounds 4/2/65 Columbus OH]
Haggard [Haggart], Theodore	Private	25	D	[Died, typhus, 1/8/63 Harper's Ferry]
Hay, James	Private	33	N, W	[Resaca; Discharge 7/14/65 Albany NY]
Hopkins, Henry G. [C.]	Private	24	N	[Discharged Disability 8/26/63 Long Bridge VA]
Hopkins, Taylor A.	Private	21	KIA	[Peach Tree Creek, 7/20/64]
Hutchins, Henry G.	Private	23	D	[Died, typhus, 1/15/63 Fairfax, VA]
Irwin, David	Private	24	Y, W	[Near Goldsboro 4/10/65]
Irwin, Henry	Private	23	N	[Transferred to V.R.C. 8/15/63]
Johnson, Samuel	Private	23	D	Died while in the army [Disease Chattanooga TN]
Kilmer [Killmer], Archibald	Private	27	N	[Discharged 8/2/65 Louisville KY]
Kinney, Ebenezer	Private	22	N, W	[Peach Tree Creek, *right arm amputated*; absent, hospital NYC at muster out]
Knickerbocker, Wm. S.	Private	22	N, W	[Dallas, 5/25/64; hospital, Cleveland, OH]
Lackey [Leckey], Wm.	Private	26	N, W	[Chancellorsville, *left knee*; Absent, hospital]
Lant [Laut], Wm. A.	Private	38	N	[Discharged for Disability 3/16/63, Harper's Ferry]
Laport, Joseph	Private	18	N	[Discharged for Disability 3/27/63; Reenlisted Co. F 12/22/63; Transferred to 60th NY 6/3/65]
Malone, Patrick	Private	35	N, POW, D	[POW Culp's Farm; Died Disease Andersonville 9/21/64; *Died of fever; Andersonville Gravesite # 9457*]
Martin, John	Private	22	N, W	[Corporal; Culp's Farm 6/22/64; *Severe wound right leg, amputated*; Hospital New York; Discharged 7/19/65 NY NY]

Name	Rank	Age		Notes
McCandless, Matthew	Private	19	N	[Discharged for Disability 6/9/63 NY NY]
McClosky [McCloskey], John	Private	37	Y	
McDougall, Alex. J.	Private	21	N	[Discharged for Disability 8/17/63 Convalescent Camp VA]
McDougall, Duncan R.	Private	21	Y, W	[Corporal; Chancellorsville, *right shoulder*]
McKibbon [McCibin], George	Private	37	N, W, POW, D	[Chancellorsville, DOW]
McLellan [McClellan], Dan'l M.	Private	21	Y, W	[Chancellorsville; Corporal 8/1/63]
McMillan, Jno. R.	Private	22	N, W	[Corporal; Sergeant; Peach Tree Creek, *arm*; Discharge 5/24/65 U.S. Hospital #1 Nashville]
McMurray, Jos. M.	Private	20	N, W	[Peach Tree Creek, *severe wound left shoulder*, 7/20/64; Discharge 2/16/65 Troy NY]
McNeil, Moses S. [L.]	Private	43	Y	
McWhirter [McWhorter], And. H.	Private	23	N, W	[Corporal; Peach Tree Creek, *right arm amputated*; Discharged for wounds 6/18/65]
Mickel, George	Private	18	Y, W	[Culp's Farm, *left knee*]
Morrish, Joseph	Private	39	D	[Died of dropsey 10/28/64 hospital Atlanta]
Morrison, W. H.	Private	21	Y	
Murray, John	Private	33	N, POW	[Chancellorsville; Deserted 8/12/63 Camp Parole MD]
Nelson, William J.	Private	26	Y, W	[Goldsboro, *slight wound ear*]
Pendergrass, Robert A.	Private	21	Y	
Perry, James E.	Private	21	Y	
Peterson, Duncan A.	Private	18	Y, W, POW	[Chancellorsville; Paroled]
Reid, Alexander	Private	21	Y	
Reid, Charles E.	Private	23	Y	
Reid, Harvey M.	Private	18	D	[Died Disease 2/26/63, typhus, Stafford Court House]
Robbins, Peter	Private	24	N, W	[Chancellorsville; Discharged Disability 3/26/64 Albany NY]

Name	Rank	Age		Notes
Robinson, George H.	Private	24	N, W	[Peach Tree Creek; *right arm amputated*; Discharged 6/15/65 wounds NY NY]
Robinson, Orville C.	Private	19	Y	
Robinson, Zenus [Zenas] S.	Private	44	N	[Discharged 1/26/63; Disability, Harper's Ferry]
Rogers, Thos.	Private	24	N, W	[Dallas 5/25/64; Discharged 5/22/65 Hospital, Murfreesboro TN]
Scott, Abner	Private	18	Y	[Transferred 5/20/63 V.R.C.; Mustered out with regiment 6/8/65 Washington]
Scott, John	Private	20	Y, W	[Culp's Farm, *leg*]
Scott, William H.	Private	19	Y	
Selfridge, John T.	Private	41	Y	
Sheffield, Wm.	Private	35	N	[Absent, sick 4/27/64 Hospital, NY, NY]
Skellie, William C.	Private	23	N, W	[Chancellorsville; Discharge 7/12/65 Finley Hospital D.C.]
Smith, Robert	Private	24	Y	[Corporal 7/4/63]
Smith, Russel C.	Private	18	Y	
Smith, William H.	Private	19	N, W	[Chancellorsville, *hip*, 5/3/63; Peach Tree Creek, *face*, 7/20/64; Discharged 5/23/65 NY NY]
Stow, James	Private	22	N, W	[Peach Tree Creek, *arm and breast*, Discharged for Disability 1/20/65 NY NY]
Stuart [Stewart], David G.	Private	21	KIA	[Culp's Farm]
Taylor, George L.	Private	21	KIA	[Chancellorsville]
Taylor, James W.	Private	19	Y	
Tucker, Simon	Private	31	Y	
Williams, John D.	Private	26	Y	
Williams, Robert	Private	22	Y, POW	[Chancellorsville; Paroled]
Wilson, Christopher	Private	24	Y	
Wood, William J.	Private	21	KIA	[Chancellorsville, 5/3/63]
	Enlisted Average Age	**25.0**		
RECRUITS				
Bearheau [Bourbean], Charles	Private	22	N	[Enlisted 12/22/63 Schenectady; 60th NY]

Name	Rank	Age	Discharged with Regiment	Comments
Byrne [Burns], John	Private	18	N, W	[145th NY 12/23/63; Peach Tree Creek, left arm amputated; Discharged as John Burns January 19th, 1865]
Carter, Henry C. [J.]	Private	22	N, POW	[Enlisted 8/4/64 Troy; POW 1/28/65; Paroled; Discharge 5/22/65 NY NY]
Clark, Philip S.	Private		Y	[145th NY 12/23/63]
Coffin, John B.	Private	34	Y	[Enlisted 8/31/64 Kingsbury]
Damels [Daniels], Harry C.	Private	18	N, POW	[145th NY 12/23/63; POW 3/9/65 Fayetteville, NC; Paroled 5/5/65]
Delmore [Denmore], John	Private	18	N, POW	[145th NY 12/23/63; POW Fayetteville, NC; Paroled 5/5/65; Discharged 6/29/65 NY NY]
Dempsy, William H.	Private	21	Y	[145th NY 12/23/63]
Dugard, Seth W.		19	Y	[145th NY 12/23/63]
Farrel, James	Private	18	N	[Mustered 3/26/64 Brooklyn; 6/8/65 60th NY]
Fox, Barney	Private	23	N	[145th NY 12/23/63; 60th NY 6/8/65]
Godfery, John Y.	Private	21	Y	[145th NY 12/23/63]
Mickle, John	Private	22	N	[Enlisted 4/1/64 Troy; 60th NY 6/8/65]

COMPANY "G"	WHITECREEK & JACKSON			
NAME	RANK	AGE	DISCHARGED WITH REGIMENT	COMMENTS
Gray, Henry C.	Captain	19	Y, W	[Wounded 7/30/64 Atlanta; Major 11/19/64]
Hill, James	1st Lt.	24	Y	[Captain 11/19/64]
Archer, Charles	2nd Lt.	23	N	[Discharged 2/17/63]
Rice, Jerome B.	1st Sergeant	21	N, W, POW	[2nd Lt. 2/17/63; Chancellorsville; Paroled] Transferred Signal Corps. [Mustered out 6/27/65 Albany NY]

Name	Rank	Age		Notes
Warner [Jr.], William S.	Sergeant	22	Y	[1st Sergeant 6/2/62; 1st Lt. 11/19/64]
Edgerton, Ebenezer S.	Sergeant	34	N	[Discharged for promotion 10/9/63; 1st Lt. Company H, 7th U.S.C.T.]
Wilcox, Robert	Sergeant	18	Y	[1st Sergeant 4/1/65]
Warren [Warner], Sylvester R.	Sergeant	21	Y, POW	[Chancellorsville 5/3/63; Paroled]
Eldridge [Eldredge], Dewitt F.	Corporal	18	Y	[Sergeant 12/15/63]
Colter [Coulter], Clarence	Corporal	24	DOW	[Chancellorsville, *head wound*; Died at hospital 10/2/63 Alexandria Va.]
Stevenson, John A.	Corporal	19	Y, W	[Chancellorsville; Sergeant 12/15/63]
Wells, George H.	Corporal	18	Y, POW	[Chancellorsville; Paroled]
Wood, Henry C.	Corporal	22	Y	
Brown, Hiram W.	Corporal	33	Y, W, POW	[Chancellorsville; Paroled]
Gilbert, Joseph	Corporal	19	Y	
McLean, William C.	Corporal	19	Y	[Promoted Sergeant Major March 27th 1865]
Esmann, James S.	Drummer	18	Y	
Shaler, Andrew	Musician	18	Y	
Alexander, Robert	Private	22	Y	[Corporal 4/1/65]
Arnold, Charles W.	Private	18	Y	
Arnold, Henry L.	Private	25	Y, W	[Corporal; Peach Tree Creek]
Bailey, John W.	Private	19	N	Transferred Hospital Steward [Discharged for promotion to hospital steward 2/27/64 U.S. Army]
Baldwin, Dyer	Private	19	D	[Died 12/4/63, small pox, Hospital, Baltimore]
Bennett, Ferner (Phineas)	Private	18	Y	
Bennett, James	Private	27	Y	
Bennett, Martin	Private	21	N, W	[Wounded 7/20/64 Peach Tree Creek, *arm*, Discharged 7/11/65 Albany NY]
Bennett, Romaine [Romain]	Private	19	Y	

Name	Rank	Age		Notes
Carter, Joseph	Private	24	Y	
Castello [Costolo], Michael	Private	24	N, W	[Transferred V.R.C. 3/2/64]
Cavanah [Cavanaugh], John	Private	22	Y	
Clark, George	Private	23	N, W	[Corporal; Dallas 5/25/64; Discharged for wounds, 12/9/64]
Clary [Cleary], James H.	Private	23	N	[Deserted 1/23/63 hospital Harper's Ferry]
Colter [Coulter], Henry	Private	28	Y, W	[Peach Tree Creek, *arm*]
Coon, Andrew J.	Private	26	D	Died of disease Stafford Court House Feb. 19th, 1863
Coon, Layton	Private	31	Y	
Cornell, Flavius J.	Private	30	Y	[Corporal 12/1/63]
Cowen, Peter	Private	28	Y, W	[Peach Tree Creek, *arm*]
Crombie, Peter	Private	18	DOW	[Dallas 5/25/64; Died 6/6/64; *right arm amputated*]
Decker, Charles W. [H.]	Private	21	Y	
Dibbie [Dibble], Ezra	Private	23	Y	
Ellis, Alexander	Private	33	N, W	[Chancellorsville, Discharged for wounds 11/2/63, Albany; Reenlisted Feb. 27th, 1865 Company D, 123rd NY, mustered out 6/23/65 Harewood Hospital Washington]
Fenton, George S.	Private	21	Y	
Ferris, James H.	Private	44	D	[Died of chronic disease 1/13/63 hospital Harper's Ferry]
Foster, John	Private	18	D	[Died disease, peritonitis, 6/2/63 Stafford Court House]
Fowler, John S.	Private	20	N	[Deserted from hospital, Washington]
Fuller, John M. [N.]	Private	20	Y	
Gamber [Gamby], Rolland M. [Rollin H.]	Private	18	Y	
Graves, Philander	Private	33	N, W	[Wounded, no date, V.R.C. 8/1/63]

Gray [Gay], Hiram T.	Private	27	Y	
Harrington, Artemas C.	Private	25	Y	
Harrington, William S.	Private	18	Y	
Hart [Hartt], Manville [Montravill]	Private	23	Y, W	[Resaca, 5/15/64]
Hatch, Jonathan	Private	23	Y	
Henry, Peter	Private	23	Y	
Hiland [Highland], Thomas	Private	22	Y	
Hoffman, Charles	Private	18	N	[Deserted 7/19/63 Harper's Ferry]
Howe, Lucian [Duncan]	Private	20	N	[Discharged for Disability 2/23/63]
King, Hiram	Private	22	N	[Discharged for Disability 1/23/64]
Lamb [Lambert], David C.	Private	23	N, POW	[POW 6/22/64 Culp's Farm, Andersonville, Savannah, Exchanged 12/10/64; Discharge 7/6/65 Hospital, York PA]
Lambert, George W. [N.]	Private	21	N, W, POW	[Chancellorsville; Discharged for wounds 9/25/63]
Larrabee [Larabee], LeRoy	Private	30	Y	
Lawton, Clark H.	Private	23	Y, W	[Peach Tree Creek, *head*]
Luddy, John	Private	26	N, POW	[Culp's Farm; Andersonville; Paroled 2/15/65; Mustered out 8/25/65]
Marshall, John L.	Private	24	Y	
Martain [Martin], William	Private	20	W, KIA	[Chancellorsville; Killed 5/15/64 Resaca GA]
Mattison, Isaiah	Private	20	Y	
Maxwell, Robert	Private	21	Y	
McComber [McCumber], John	Private	26	KIA	[Chancellorsville; Listed as Absent]
Monnegan [Monneghan], Matthew	Private	25	Y, POW	Culp's Farm; Andersonville Dec. 1864; returned to regiment April 1865 [POW 6/22/64 near Kenesaw Mtn.; Paroled 12/16/64]
Moore, James H.	Private	18	Y, POW	[Chancellorsville, Paroled]

Name	Rank	Age		Notes
Moore, William	Private	27	Y	[Corporal 4/1/65]
Morrissey, James	Private	23	Y, POW	[Culp's Farm 6/22/64; Paroled]
Palmer, John E.	Private	42	N	[Transferred V.R.C. 8/1/63]
Parker, Chauncey C.	Private	18	D	[Died of Peritonitis 2/7/63, Stafford Court House]
Parker, George W.	Private	22	Y	[Corporal 1/5/65]
Parker, Samuel [William S.]	Private	41	N	[Deserted 10/27/62 Pleasant Valley MD]
Petteys [Peters], John	Private	18	N	[Transferred V.R.C. 4/17/63]
Pratt, Dennis	Private	18	Y	
Pratt, Sylvester	Private	23	N	[Discharged 6/23/65 Albany NY]
Qua, William C.	Private	23	N	[Discharged for Disability 10/2/63]
Rogers, Albert	Private	21	N	[Discharged for Disability 3/27/63]
Ross, Ebenezer	Private	44	N	[Discharged for Disability 4/21/63]
Scrimger, James	Private	18	N	[Deserted 7/17/63 Harper's Ferry]
Scrimger, John S.	Private	25	N	[Transferred V.R.C. 1/9/65]
Small, Thomas B.	Private	20	Y	
Smith, Wm. J.	Private	18	Y	
Welch, Chas. [S.]	Private	18	N, W	[Wounded, no date; Mustered out 6/14/65 Camp Dennison OH]
Welch, Henry	Private	23	KIA	[Peach Tree Creek 7/20/64]
Whittaker [Whitaker], Caleb [Clark]	Private	23	D	[Died disease, Phthisis, 9/19/63 Hospital Alexandria VA]
	Enlisted Average Age	**23.3**		
RECRUITS				
Bartholomew, Francis	Private	18	N	[Enlisted 2/6/65, Troy; Transferred 60th NY]
Bell, Lewis	Private	30	N	[Enlisted 2/4/65, Troy; Transferred to 60th NY
Black [Block], George	Private	29	N	[Enlisted 1/15/65, Albany; Transferred to 60th NY]
Cone, Andrew [Alanson] B.	Private	42	N	[Enlisted 12/30/63, Cambridge; Transferred to 60th NY]

Name	Rank	Age		Notes
Connell, Stephen	Private	29		[Enlisted 9/7/64, Albany; No Further Record]
Crofut [Crofut], Henry D. [S.]	Private	38	N	[Enlisted 3/3/65, NYC; Transferred to 60th NY]
Crowley [Cowen], Nathan C.	Private	22	N	[Enlisted 1/10/65, Troy; mustered out Harts Island, NY 5/8/65]
Dupie, Emile	Private	28	N	[Enlisted 1/23/64, Troy; Transferred 6/8/65 60th NY]
Duterne, Edward	Private	29	N	[Enlisted 1/23/64, Troy; Transferred 6/8/65 60th NY]
Fenton, Joseph	Private	44	N	[Enlisted 2/6/65, Troy; Transferred to 60th NY]
Fowler, Henry C. [P.]	Private	20	Y	[Enlisted 8/29/64, Troy]
Gurney, Andrew	Private	21	Y	[Enlisted 9/10/64, Troy]
Hanes, Charles	Private	27	N	[Enlisted 1/6/65 Troy; Transferred 6/8/65 60th NY]
Herrington [Harrington], William M.	Private	20	D	[Enlisted 8/13/64 Cambridge; Died of typhoid at Atlanta hospital 10/3/64]
Johns, David I. [S.]	Private	19	N	[Mustered 2/13/65 NYC; Transferred to 60th NY]
Legnard, Francis	Private	22	N	[Enlisted 1/9/65 Troy; Discharge 7/19/65 Harewood Hospital D.C.]
McGrath, Edward	Private	25	Y	[Enlisted 9/2/64 Troy]
Miller, Robert	Private	18	N	[Enlisted 9/13/64 Troy; Discharged 5/27/65 hospital Albany NY]
Mulligan, Thomas	Private	24	N, POW	[Enlisted 1/6/65 Troy, Co. B, transferred to Co. G; POW 4/1/65; Paroled 6/5/65; Discharge 7/7/65 NY, NY]
Nelson, John	Private	44	N	[Enlisted 8/31/64 Troy; Discharge 6/24/65 U.S. Hospital Troy NY]
Sullivan, Martin	Private	18	Y	[Enlisted 9/12/64 Troy]
LESS THAN ONE MONTH IN REGIMENT OR DROPPED				
Clark, George	Private	23	N	[Enlisted 9/15/64; Unassigned; No further record]

Name	Rank	Age			Comments
Lawton, Albert	Private	18		N	[Enlisted 8/6/62] Transferred to 93rd NY due to prior enlistment
Orcutt, George	Private	19		N	[Enlisted 7/28/62; Transferred 93rd NY]

COMPANY "H"	SALEM				
NAME	RANK	AGE	HEIGHT INCHES	OUT WITH REGT.	COMMENTS
Crary, John S.	Captain	34		N	Resigned July 28th 1863 [Discharged 7/27/63]
Elliott, Benjamin	1st Lt.			N	Resigned February 5th 1863 [Discharged 2/4/63]
Culver, Josiah W.	2nd Lt.	20		Y	Promoted 1st Lt. Feb 20th 1863; promoted Captain Oct 21st 1863; detached service Hart's Island N.Y. July 25th Aug 18th 1864
Cruikshank, Robert	1st Sergeant	26	70	Y	[2nd Lt. 2/4/63; 1st Lt. 7/27/63]
Beattie, [Robert] B.	Sergeant	19	70.5	Y	Promoted 2nd Lt. Oct 21st 1863 [7/27/63]; detached service Hart's Island N.Y. July 25th 1863 to May 15th 1864
Dennison [Denison], William H.	Sergeant	26	69	Y, W, POW	[Chancellorsville, *abdomen*; 1st Sergeant 4/11/63]
Ross, Daniel R.	Sergeant	21	69	Y, POW	[Culp's Farm; Returned 5/3/65]
Amidon [Ameden, Anderson], Larned S.	Sergeant	38	70	N, W	Transferred from Co. E August 22nd 1862; Wounded Dallas; discharged May 19th 1865 U.S. Hospital near Troy
McFarland, Frank	Corporal	20	69.5	Y, W	[Culp's Farm, *left leg*]
Cowan, James H.	Corporal	20	67	D	In hospital Nov. 1st; Died from disease Harper's Ferry December 2nd 1862 [12/5/62]
Gray, James C.	Corporal	20	70	D	[Sergeant; Died of disease 3/21/65 Salem NY]
Stewart, William H.	Corporal	22	68	DOW	Chancellorsville, *shell tore off arm below elbow*; Died 5/12/63]

Name	Rank	Age	Height	Status	Notes
Briggs, Garrett [Garriet] W.	Corporal	23	64	Y, W	[Chancellorsville, *slight wound thigh from ball;*Sergeant 3/6/65]
Creighton, William A.	Corporal	22	70	N	Sick, sent to hospital August 19th 1864 discharged from Keokuk, Iowa hospital at close of war [Mustered out 6/2/65 Hospital Albany NY]
Williamson, Frederick J.	Corporal	23	65.5	D	Sergeant; sick Jan 17th 1865 died of disease Savannah March 6th 1865 [Hospital] Chronic Diarrhea
Sherman, Charles R.	Corporal	20	68	Y	Ambulance Corps duty Oct. 28th, 1862 [Sergeant 6/21/64]
Danforth, Philip H.	Musician	20	68.5	Y	
Dunlap, Martin P.	Bugler	34	67.5	D	Died of disease in camp Stafford Court House February 25th, 1863
Edie, George H.	Musician	23	68	Y	[Private, reduced to ranks]
Hopkins, John	Wagoner	21	68	Y	Ambulance Corps duty Oct. 28th, 1862; Detailed to Ambulance Corps August 8th, 1864
Allen, John	Private	18	68.5	Y	Transferred from Company E to H Aug. 22nd, 1862
Atwood, Samuel (Dave)	Private	22	64	N	[Discharged 6/5/65 U.S. Hospital Albany NY]
Baker, Elijah	Private	44		N	[Discharged for Disability 5/21/64 Chestnut Hill Hospital Philadelphia PA]
Barry, John	Private	40	64	N	Transferred from Company A to H Aug. 22nd, 1862 [Discharged 1/4/63 Harper's Ferry Hospital]
Beattie, James L.	Private	22	69	KIA	Killed on picket line Atlanta, August 18th, 1864
Beebe, George	Private	36		Y	[Corporal 3/6/65]
Billings, Charles	Private	20	71	D	[Died of disease 12/14/62 at Loudon Valley, Va.]

Blowers, David	Private	36	70	N	Transferred from Company E to H Aug. 22nd, 1862 [Discharged 3/27/63 Convalescent Camp Alexandria, VA]
Brown, Milo H.	Private	20	66.5	D	[Died of disease 11/27/62 at Loudon Valley, Va.]
Burns, Patrick	Private	18	68.5	N	[Transferred V.R.C. 10/1/64]
Burtis, Evander	Private	25	72	D	[Died at Philadelphia 9/7/62; cholera]
Chase, Lewis D.	Private	39	69	Y	
Cleveland, Henry J.	Private	25	65	Y, W	[Wounded 6/16/64 Pine Mountain; Corporal 7/15/64]
Creighton, George M.	Private	19	69	N	[Absent, sick Chattanooga Hospital at muster out of regiment]
Cruikshank, William	Private	23	72	N, W	[Corporal, Chancellorsville, *ball through both thighs,* discharged due to wounds 3/15/64 Washington]
Danforth, Henry	Private	21	66.5	DOW	[Peach Tree Creek 7/20/64; Died 7/29/64 hospital Kingston, Georgia; *Left leg amputated*]
Deuel, Benjamin Austin	Private	27	69	POW, MIA	[Corporal 2/1/63]; Morhous: "Taken prisoner Culp's Farm, never heard from"
Dickinson [Dickenson], Thomas	Private	36	66	D	[Died of disease at Atlanta field hospital 9/10/64]
Divine, Michael	Private	44	68	N	Transfer from Company A; Deserted at Frederick October 1st, 1862
Doig, John	Private	18	66.5	Y, W, POW	[Chancellorsville, *ball through face*; Paroled]
Donehue [Donohue], Peter	Private	25		Y	
Foster, Daniel A.	Private	25	68	Y	
Gleason, Edward	Private	19	65	Y, W	[Chancellorsville, *finger of right hand*; Corporal 2/2/65]
Graves, Edward [Edmund]	Private	36	68.5	N	[Discharged 4/21/63]
Gray, Levi H.	Private	18	72	Y	[Corporal 7/15/64; Sergeant 3/21/65]

Name	Rank				Notes
Harwood, Newell L.	Private	33	71	N	Discharged Baltimore hospital [12/15/62]
Hever [Hover], Jacob	Private	44	65	N	Missing while on march June 27th, 1863; [Deserted 6/25/63 Leesburg VA]
Holbrook, Jeremiah	Private	21	68	N	Transferred from Co. E August 22nd, 1862; deserted November 24th, 1862 Loudon Valley; [*Arrested 5/14/64 and returned to unit*; Transferred 60th NY at 123rd muster out]
Hopkins, Albert	Private	18	69	Y	[Corporal 7/15/64]
Hopkins, Silas	Private	28	69	N	Discharged Harper's Ferry Hospital November 16th, 1863; Discharged at Albany August 25th, 1864
Johnson, Archibald	Private	18	70	DOW	[Chancellorsville, *shell wounds side and arm;* Died 5/6/63]
Kearsing, Joseph	Private	18	55	W, POW, DOW	[Culp's Farm; Died 6/29/64 in Confederate hospital Atlanta GA]
Mahaffy, Samuel	Private	28	72	Y	[Corporal 11/15/63]
Mains, John A.	Private	21	68	KIA	Chancellorsville [Absent, missing] (See Sergeant Robert Cruikshank letter May 8, 1863)
Marshall, Charles	Private	26	66	KIA	Chancellorsville, *ball in thigh shattered bone left on field;* [Absent, missing] (See Sergeant Robert Cruikshank letter May 8, 1863)
Matthews [Mathews], Horace P.	Private	21	68	Y	
McFarland, Mitchell	Private	20	73	N, W	[Chancellorsville, *neck,* Transferred 11/1/63 V.R.C.]
McMurry [McMurray], James	Private	29	69	POW, MIA	Transfer from Co. E Aug. 22nd 1862; POW Chancellorsville "never heard from" [Deserted 5/3/63 Chancellorsville]
McNassor, Peter	Private	18	64	KIA	[Culp's Farm 6/22/64]

Name	Rank	Age	Height	Status	Notes
Nelson, David E.	Private	29	69	N	Transfer from Co. E Aug. 22nd 1862; discharged April 21st, 1863
Orcutt, Chester	Private	28	65	Y, W	Transfer from Company E; [Peach Tree Creek]
Orcutt, William	Private	21	67	D	[Died of disease 1/26/64 Elk River Bridge, TN]
Parker, Calvin I. [J.]	Private	18	72	Y	[Corporal 5/12/63]
Perkins, John A.	Private	19	71	Y, W, POW	[Chancellorsville, *ball through left thigh*; Paroled]
Pierce, William	Private	27	66	Y, W	[Resaca 5/15/64]
Pratt, Alex.	Private	18	68	Y	
Rich, William L.	Private	26	68	KIA	[Chancellorsville, *ball through chest;* Died of wounds 5/4/63]
Schneider, John (Snyder)	Private	39	70	Y	
Sheppard, Chas. A.	Private	26	65	N	[Deserted 5/2/63 Chancellorsville]
Stover, Theodore	Private	18	64	Y	Transferred from Co. A Aug. 22nd 1862
Streeter, Alvah	Private	36	67	N, W	[Chancellorsville, *ball through right arm, amputated below elbow*; Discharged for disability Springfield, Illinois 6/6/64]
Sweet, George	Private	24	70	D	[Died of disease in camp Stafford Court House 2/26/63]
Sweet, Henry G.	Private	18	65	D	[Died of disease Harper's Ferry hospital 12/26/62]
Torrence, Owen [Orren]	Private	44	68	N	[Discharged 6/5/65 U.S. Hospital Camp Dennison OH]
Warner, David H.	Private	24	66	D	[Died of small pox 4/26/65 Hospital Willet's Point NY]
Warner, William	Private	19	65	Y	
Wells, Alex. H.	Private	20	68	N	[Transferred 6/15/63 V.R.C.]
West, Richard	Private	33	68	D	Missing from camp Loudon Valley Dec. 6th, 1862; found with throat cut Dec. 13th, 1862; "committed suicide" [Died 12/7/62] (Suicide: See Sergeant Robert Cruikshank letter December 13, 1862)

Name	Rank	Age	Height	Y/N	Notes
Whitney, Edward D.	Private	25	70	Y	[Corporal 3/21/65]
Wood, Charles E.	Private	26	69	Y, W, POW	Transfer from Co. E Aug. 22nd 1862; [Chancellorsville, *ball through face entering nose and coming out under chin*; Paroled]
Wright, James H.	Private	30	68.5	N	[Discharged Baltimore hospital 12/15/62]
	Enlisted Average Age	**25.4**	**68.0**	Enlisted Average Height	
RECRUITS					
Ackerson, James T.	Private			Y	[145th NY 12/26/63]
Boseman, Patrick	Private	18		Y	[145th NY 12/26/63]
Brennan, Francis	Private			DOW	[145th NY 12/23/63; Peach Tree Creek, *head*; Died of wounds 7/25/64 hospital Vining Station GA]
Brower, William W.	Private			N	[145th NY 12/26/63; Discharged 6/19/65 hospital Fairfax Seminary VA]
Butler, William H.	Private	20		Y	[145th NY 12/26/63]
Coles, John F.	Private	42		Y	[145th NY 12/26/63]
Consedine, Peter	Private	31	67	N	[145th NY 12/23/63; Discharge disability 12/27/64 Carver Hospital Washington]
Conway, James	Private			Y	[145th NY 12/26/63]
Conway, William	Private	29		N, W	[145th NY Transfer; Culp's Farm, *hand*; Mustered out 5/31/65 McDougall Hospital NY Harbor]
Cusick, James	Private	33	66	N	[3rd MD Transfer 11/27/63; 6/8/65 60th NY]
Dupont, Eugene	Private	18		Y	[145th NY 12/26/63]
Farnum, Harlan	Private	18	64	N, POW	[145th NY 12/26/63; POW 2/8/65; Andersonville Prison; Paroled 4/28/65; Mustered out 5/16/65 NY NY]
Fergerson, John	Private			Y	[Joined regiment 4/9/64]
Fitzgerald, William	Private	20		Y	[145th NY 12/26/63]

Name	Rank	Age			Service
Flynn, Patrick	Private	32	62.5	N, W	[145th NY 12/26/63; Culp's Farm 6/22/64, *left leg*; Absent, hospital, muster out]
Haley, Mathew	Private			Y	[145th NY 12/26/63]
Heiley, Michael	Private	33		KIA	[145th NY 12/23/63; Peach Tree Creek 7/20/64]
Holz, William	Private	18		Y	[145th NY 12/26/63]
Johnson, Crandall	Private	19		N, W	[145th NY 12/26/63; Culp's Farm; Discharged 5/29/65 Louisville KY]
King, Hugh	Private	38	68	Y	[145th NY 12/26/63; Corporal 2/28/65]
McCabe, Bernard	Private	36	66	N	[Mustered 7/21/64, Troy; Transferred 6/8/65 60th NY]
Miller, William E.	Private	21		Y	[145th NY 12/26/63]
Murphy, Patrick	Private	18		Y	[145th NY 12/26/63]
Nelson, Robert D.	Private	18		Y	[Enlisted 8/31/64, Troy]
Penderghast, Philip	Private	19		Y	[Enlisted 8/16/64, Troy]
Raal, Patrick	Private	18		Y	[145th NY 12/26/63]
Ransom, Benjamin	Private	38		N	[145th NY; Transferred 1/15/64 V.R.C.]
Ross, John D.	Private	18		Y	[Enlisted 9/1/64, Salem]
Smith, William	Sergeant	19	68	N, POW	[145th NY 12/26/63; 123rd NY Sergeant on transfer; POW 2/24/65; Paroled; Discharged 6/21/65 Annapolis MD]
Steevens, John C.	Private	28	68	N	[145th NY 12/26/63; Absent, sick, hospital at muster out]
Sweeney, John	Private	44		Y	[145th NY 12/26/63]
Walsh, Joseph [Welsh]	Private	19		N	[145th NY 12/9/63]
Welch, William H.	Private	18		N	[145th NY 12/26/63; Mustered out 6/24/65 Jarvis Hospital Baltimore MD]
Willan, Thomas	Private	43		N	[145th NY 12/26/63; 4/1/65 V.R.C.; Absent, sick, Baltimore]
Zimmerman, William	Private	18		Y	[145th NY 12/26/63]

LESS THAN ONE MONTH IN REGIMENT OR DROPPED					
Hendrahan, Michael	Private	22	69	N	Deserted at Salem August 23rd, 1862
Pattridge, William C.	Private				Left sick at Salem
Sweeny [Sweeney], John	Private	22	69	N	Deserted at Salem August 20th, 1862 [8/28/62]

COMPANY "I"	CAMBRIDGE AND EASTON			
NAME	RANK	AGE	DISCHARGED WITH REGIMENT	COMMENTS
Hall, Orrin S.	Captain	47	Y	
Beadle, Marcus	1st Lt.	28	Y, W, POW	[Wounded Chancellorsville, *back*; POW 7/2/63 Gettysburg; Escaped 2/14/65 Winnsboro SC; Prior service as Provost U.S. Army 1st Infantry]
Shiland, Albert	2nd Lt.	21	. N, W	[Chancellorsville, *ankle*; Discharged Disability 9/14/63]
Aldrich, Elias H.	1st Sergeant	24	N	[Discharged for promotion 7/1/64, 2nd Lt. 100th U.S.C.T.]
Darron [Darrow], Clark	Sergeant	21	D	[Died Heart disease & diarrhea, 1/14/65 Savannah GA]
Beatty, Arthur W.	Sergeant	31	Y	
Fairchild [Fairchilds], George	Sergeant	32	N, W	[Culp's Farm, *hand*; Discharged 6/23/65 Albany NY]
Clapp, George	Sergeant	29	N	[Deserted 2/28/63]
Dennis, George L.	Corporal	20	Y, POW	[Chancellorsville; Sergeant 3/4/63; 1st Sergeant 2/28/65]
Fisher, William G.	Corporal	18	Y	[Sergeant 7/1/64]
Skeller [Skellie], John	Corporal	23	Y, W	[Culp's Farm, *right side*; Sergeant 2/28/65]

Name	Rank	Age	Status	Notes
Starbuck, Chas. A.	Corporal	21	N	[Discharged for promotion, 1st Lt. 8th U.S.C.T.]
Dyer, J. Gardner	Corporal	21	Y	
Slocum, Fred. A.	Corporal	22	N, W	[Peach Tree Creek, *breast*; Discharged 6/28/65 Albany NY]
Hines, Jno. Jr.	Corporal	24	Y	[Sergeant 2/28/65]
Skinner, Lemuel T. [S.]	Corporal	21	N, W	[Chancellorsville, *side*; Discharged 6/26/65 Louisville KY]
Larmon, Jno. A.	Musician	23	Y, POW	[Chancellorsville; Paroled]
Miller, William B.	Musician	18	N	Discharged for disability January 7th, 1863 [Fort Barnard VA]
Bartlett, Horace	Wagoner	23	Y	[Wagoner]
Ames, Frank L. [I.]	Private	18	Y, W	[Wounded 6/14/64 Pine Mtn. and 6/16/64 Lost Mtn.]
Baker, Charles H.	Private	18	Y	
Bassett, Jas. A.	Private	27	N, W	[Chancellorsville; Mustered out 5/13/65 Nashville TN]
Beadle, Joseph R.	Private	32	D	Died in hospital Acquia Creek May 23rd, 1863
Bennett, Jno. W.	Private	23	N	[Transferred 9/5/63 to V.R.C.]
Bentley, Hiram F.	Private	18	N, W	[Dallas, 6/2/64; Transferred 2/1/65 V.R.C.; Mustered out 7/2/65 Camp Douglas Chicago IL]
Bentley, John H.	Private	18	Y	[Corporal 5/1/65]
Bishop, Roswell K.	Private	20	KIA	[Chancellorsville]
Bratt, David H.	Private	25	Y	
Cobb, John H.	Private	28	Y, POW, W	[Chancellorsville, *foot*; Paroled; Wounded 6/14/64 Pine Mtn.; Wounded 6/16/64 Lost Mtn.]
Conner, John	Private	32	Y	Also had enlisted in Company E 123rd NY
Darrow, Peter H.	Private	25	N	[Discharged for Disability 1/10/63 Fort Barnard VA]
Dennis, Chas. H.	Private	25	N	[Discharged for promotion 3/21/64 1st Lt. 39th U.S.C.T.]
Derby, Theodore A.	Private	20	Y	

Name	Rank	Age		Notes
Eldridge [Eldredge], Leroy [Deroy W.]	Private	21	Y	[Corporal 2/28/65]
Ferrie [Ferris], Nelson	Private	40	N	Deserted Fairfax Station January 20th, 1863
Fletcher, Josiah	Private	32	N, W	[Chancellorsville, *head*; Discharged 5/31/65 McDougall Hospital NY Harbor]
Galloway [Gallaway], Rufus [P.]	Private	29	N, W	[Chancellorsville; Transferred to V.R.C. 1/1/65]
Gifford, Alanson	Private	27	Y	[Corporal 5/1/65]
Goodwin, Alonzo	Private	24	Y	
Goodwin, Charles C.	Private	21	Y	
Gorham, Augustus O.	Private	18	N	Transferred to 93rd NY December 3rd, 1862
Hagerty, William	Private	29	N, W	[Chancellorsville, *back*; Deserted on expiration of furlough while home from hospital 7/15/63]
Hayner, Robert O. W.	Private	23	N	[Discharged for disability 1/15/63 Fort Barnard VA]
Hennelly, Richard	Private	20	D	[Died 10/15/63 Lincoln Hospital Washington]
Hennelly, Thomas	Private	20	Y, W, POW	[Chancellorsville; POW, Paroled; wounded Peach Tree Creek, *arm*]
Herman, Jacob	Private	27	N, W, DOW	[Corporal; Wounded Peach Tree Creek, *head*, 7/20/64; Died 5/6/65 wounds hospital Albany, NY]
Higby, George	Private	18	Y, W	[Peach Tree Creek, *face*]
Hill, Hugh	Private	20	N	[Discharged for Disability 1/21/63 Fort Barnard VA]
Hodge, Havony [Harvey] A.	Private	30	N	[Discharged for Disability 1/13/63 Fort Barnard VA]
Hoover [Hover], Anderson D.	Private	25	Y	
Hoover [Hover], John	Private	27	Y, POW, W	[POW Chancellorsville; Paroled; Culp's Farm, *left side*]
Jenkins, Charles	Private	18	Y	
Jenkins, John	Private	21	Y	
Kelly [Kelley], John	Private	28	Y	

Name	Rank	Age	Status	Notes
Ketcham, George	Private	22	Y	
Ketcham, John	Private	22	N, W	[Chancellorsville, *side*; Discharged wounds, no date]
King, Albert	Private	30	D	[Died disease in Louisville hospital 9/13/64]
King, Ira	Private	19	Y	
Knopf, Edward	Private	20	Y	
Latimer, Joseph B.	Private	22	Y	
Link, William H.	Private	24	Y	
Lunday, James	Private	23	Y	
McConnell, William	Private	28	N	[Discharged for Disability 1/9/63 Fort Barnard VA]
Minor [Miner], John	Private	42	N	[Discharged for Disability 7/24/63 U.S. hospital Baltimore]
Minor [Miner], Oliver	Private	25	Y	
Morehouse, Alonzo	Private	18	D	[Died disease, fever & diarrhea 12/5/62 Loudon Valley VA]
Neil, William E.	Private	21	Y, POW	[Chancellorsville; Paroled]
Obern, John	Private	21	Y, W	[New Hope Church 5/25/64]
Oliver, James	Private	25	N, W	Wounded March 23rd, 1863 Harper's Ferry; also wounded Loudon Heights; [Discharged for Disability Harper's Ferry Hospital 3/23/63]
Pecott, Joseph	Private	28	Y	
Phelps, Lewis H.	Private	30	Y, W	[Chancellorsville, *back*]
Phelps, William H.	Private	20	W, D	[Wounded Chancellorsville; Died Hospital Savannah 4/1/65]
Russell, George H.	Private	18	Y	
Scott, William I. [J.]	Private	24	D	[Died 2/22/63 at Stafford Court House]
Searls, Benj. F.	Private	23	Y	
Shaw, Harmon	Private	32	N	[Discharged for Disability 4/14/63 Fort Barnard VA]
Sherman, James [D.]	Private	21	N	[Discharged for Disability 11/25/63 Albany NY]
Skellie, John L.	Private	22	N	[Discharged for Disability 4/23/63 Stafford Court House]

Name	Rank	Age	Status	Notes
Skellie, Robert W.	Private	20	W, KIA	[Wounded Chancellorsville, *thigh*; killed New Hope Church, 5/25/64]
Skellie, William	Private	23	D	[Died at Pleasant Valley 10/31/62; Disease, diarrhea]
Spring [Springer], James S.	Private	20	Y, POW	[Chancellorsville; Paroled]
Starks, Chas. H.	Private	18	N, POW	[POW Goldsboro, NC; Paroled 5/5/65; Mustered out 6/23/65 Albany, NY]
Stiles, Issac	Private	21	N	[Discharged 5/25/64 McDougall Hospital NY Harbor]
Thomas, Inman	Private	33	Y	
Thompson, Daniel W. [M.]	Private	29	Y	[Corporal 8/31/64]
Tripp, Lewis S.	Private	24	N, W	[New Hope Church 5/25/64; Absent, hospital Nashville]
Weatherwax [Wetherwax], Wm. C.	Private	25	Y	
Weir, Thos. A.	Private	20	N	[Discharge 6/23/65 Albany NY]
White, John F.	Private	38	Y	[Corporal 8/31/64]
Wicks [Wickes], Elihu	Private	23	N	[Discharged for Disability 6/24/63 Hospital Fairfax Seminary VA]
Wicks [Wickes], James P.	Private	31	N, W	[Chancellorsville, *back*; 1/1/65 Discharge wounds Albany NY]
Wood, Jesse P.	Private	20	D	[Died 2/15/63 at Stafford Court House]
	Enlisted Average Age	**24.1**		
RECRUITS				
Barrett, Isaac	Private	32	N	[Enlisted 2/29/64, Kingsbury; Transferred 9/12/64 from Co. I to Co. C; 6/8/65 transferred to 60th NY]
Bentley, Gardner [Gardiner] C.	Private	18	N	[Enlisted 12/29/63 White Creek; 60th NY]
Bruns, Frederick	Private	38	Y	[Enlisted 9/14/64, Troy]
Burdick, George	Private	27	N	[Enlisted 12/29/63, White Creek; 60th NY]

Name	Rank	Age		Notes
Burdick, Halet [Hallett]	Private	20	N	[Enlisted 12/29/63, Cambridge; 60th NY]
Chapman, Henry	Private	24	KIA	[Enlisted 4/5/64, Granville; killed Peach Tree Creek]
Corey [Cory], Charles [H.]	Private	43	N	[Enlisted 2/15/64, New Lebaron; 60th NY]
Cozzens, John	Private	35	N	[Enlisted 2/22/64, Whitehall; 60th NY]
Hall, Dennis	Private	18	N	[Enlisted 2/29/64, Cambridge; 60th NY]
Hillis [Hellis], Michael	Private	20	Y	[Enlisted 9/5/64, Troy]
Hodge, Charles W. [H.]	Private	18	N	[Enlisted 12/29/63, White Creek; 60th NY]
Jenkins, John Sr.	Private	42	N	[Enlisted 12/31/63, Cambridge; Discharge 7/6/65 hospital Troy NY]
Mickle, John	Private	22	N	[Enlisted 4/_/64, Troy; 60th NY]
Platt, James W.	Private	19	N	[Enlisted 3/25/64, Dresden; 60th NY]
Robinson, Almon	Private	36	N	[Enlisted 3/22/64, Kingsbury; 60th NY]
Robinson, William	Private	22	N	[Enlisted 3/22/64, Kingsbury; 50th NY]
Spanable, William	Private	23	N	[Enlisted 7/15/64, Troy] Deserted Sept. 8th, 1864 Martinsburg, VA area on way to command
Stevenson, William	Private	24	N	[Enlisted 2/12/64, Troy; 60th NY]
LESS THAN ONE MONTH IN REGIMENT OR DROPPED				
Bleecker, Thomas S.	Private			[According to NYS Ad. Gen: Private Company B, 7th Artillery; 2nd Lt. 10/21/63 for 123rd NY but commission declined] *Not on muster roll nor Morhous listing*
Marley, Patrick	Private	28	N	Deserted September 8th, 1863; [From train to Baltimore MD]

COMPANY "K"	GRANVILLE AND HAMPTON			
NAME	RANK	AGE	DISCHARGED WITH REGIMENT	COMMENTS
Wiley, Henry O.	Captain	31	KIA	[Peach Tree Creek 7/20/64]
Warren, Hiram O.	1st Lt.	26	Y	[Captain Co. C 1/12/64]
Baker, George W. (S.)	2nd Lt.	31	Y	[1st Lt. 1/12/64; Captain 8/8/64]
Brown, William W.	1st Sergeant	21	Y	
Howard, Horace E.	Sergeant	23	DOW	[1st Sergeant 1/28/63; Chancellorsville, *thigh*; Died Acquia Creek Hospital 5/28/63]
Coy, Lorenzo R.	Sergeant	30	Y	
Austin, Judson H.	Sergeant	26	Y	[1st Sergt. 10/1/64; 2nd Lt. 1/12/65]
Hall [Hale], Fayette	Sergeant	29	N, W	[1st Serg. 6/1/63; Wounded 6/22/64 Culp's Farm, *right ankle*; Discharged 5/15/65 Hospital #19 Nashville TN]
Barnard [Barnards], Leroy L.	Corporal	21	N	[Transferred to 93rd NY 12/5/62]
Cowan, Chas. D.	Corporal	23	Y, W	[Resaca, *arm & side*; Sergeant 1/28/63; 1st Sergeant 3/28/65]
Allen, Henry E.	Corporal	25	Y	[Sergeant 6/1/63]
Guilford, Chauncey, I. [L.]	Corporal	25	Y, W	[Peach Tree Creek, *arm & side*] Color Guard Member
Rasey, Edward B.	Corporal	28	N	[Mustered out 5/22/65 Louisville KY]
Donahue[Donohue], Michael	Corporal	21	Y	[Sergeant 4/30/65]
Lahue, John Jr.	Corporal	19	N	Two years with regiment, transferred into US Navy, sailed on U.S. Winnebago
Thompson [Thomson], Warren	Fifer	37	Y	
Hays [Hayes], Michael	Musician	17	N	[Deserted Stafford Court House 2/18/63]

Name	Rank	Age	Status	Notes
Allard, William C.	Private	18	D	[Died of disease, Washington Hospital, 3/20/63; Buried Military Asylum, D.C.]
Bedell, Nathaniel	Private	39	Y	
Blossom, Joseph S.	Private	43	Y	[Corporal 1/1/63]
Bondein [Baudoin], Xiste [Xiston]	Private	35	D	[Died 5/18/64 Hospital Chattanooga, Tennessee; Chronic Diarrhea]
Bowker, Martin	Private	23	Y	
Burdett [Baudett], Joseph	Private	18	Y	
Butler, Martin V.	Private	18	Y	
Carmody, Daniel	Private	21	D	[Died Stafford Court House 3/9/63]
Cook, [Altidore] W.	Private	23	N, W	[Chancellorsville, *right shoulder & foot*; Discharged for Disability 1/9/64]
Cook, Franklin	Private	18	Y	
Costello, Richard	Private	26	Y	
Cowan, George H.	Private	20	Y, POW	Chancellorsville, clerk at brigade hqts.
Doane, [Albert] W.	Private	18	KIA	Chancellorsville, leg shot off, last seen tieing gun strap around limb to stop blood loss; [*Leg shot off by shell;*Died of wounds 5/10/63]
Donohue, Thomas	Private	18	N, W	[Peach Tree Creek, *severe wound left shoulder* 7/20/64; Discharged wounds 7/12/65]
Dowd, Horace	Private	21	W, D	[Corporal 6/1/63; Culp's Farm, *right elbow*; Died chronic diarrhea, hospital Nashville 9/13/64]
Dushen [Dushon], Edward	Private	26	N	[Discharged for Disability 5/25/63]; Reenlisted with 16th Artillery December 1863
Ford, [James] H.	Private	18	N	[Discharged for Disability 8/28/63]
Gerden [Gordon], James	Private	35	D	[Died at Harper's Ferry Hospital 1/19/63]

Name	Rank	Age		Notes
Hale [Hall], [Ralph] R. E.	Private	18	D	[Died 1/13/63 hospital Harper's Ferry VA]
Harris, Andrew	Private	18	Y	[Corporal 4/30/65]
Harris, Morris	Private	20	Y	[Transfer from Co. G 9/4/62]; Detailed Ambulance Corps
Hill, [Noah] G.	Private	19	Y	
Hill, Wm. M.	Private	20	Y	
Hills, [William] R.	Private	32	N	[Discharged 6/6/65 hospital Albany NY]
Humphrey, David J.	Private	21	Y, W	[Chancellorsville, *foot*]
Huntington, Thos.	Private	39	N	[Discharged for Disability 2/11/63]
Knapp, M. H.	Private	22	Y	Shell struck knapsack Chancellorsville knocking him down, Corporal
License [Licence], [Thomas] J.	Private	23	Y	
McCoy, John	Private	35	N	[Discharged Disability 1/26/63]
Mitchell [Jr.], William	Private	32	N	[Mustered out 6/16/65 Slough Hospital Alexandria VA]
Mosier, Henry	Private	35	N, W	Wounded on picket Stafford Court House[2/7/63]; [Transferred V.R.C. 3/15/64]
Mounts, Abel J. [F.]	Private	23	N	Disabled, Discharged [Deserted 7/6/63]
Murphy, James	Private	39	Y	
Murphy, John	Private	18	Y	
Norton, William	Private	21	N, W	Lost arm at Gettysburg, discharged Baltimore [10/17/63]
O'Brien, James	Private	27		[No further record]
Osborn, [Alpheus] C.	Private	24	KIA	Killed on picket Atlanta [8/9/64]
Osborn, George	Private	35	N, W, D	Wounded Resaca, died of disease in North Carolina [Died 2/28/65 Hanging Rock SC]
Ostrander, Lawrence	Private	37	Y	[Corporal 1/28/63]
Pellerin, Ugillo [Urzule]	Private	22	Y	Detailed to Ambulance Corps

Name	Rank	Age	Status	Notes
Pitts, [Benjamin] F.	Private	23	Y, W	[Wounded Gettysburg; Wounded *left leg* Dallas 5/25/64; Discharged wounds 4/3/65]
Pitts, John	Private	18	DOW	[Resaca 5/15/64; Died 5/20/64]
Pitts, Russell [Basile] (Bassel)	Private	43	N	[Discharged 6/16/65 hospital Albany NY]
Potter, [Amos] C.	Private	20	N, W	[Resaca, *left shoulder*; Discharge 7/13/65 hospital Albany NY]
Potter, Lemuel	Private	28	Y	
Potter, Philip	Private	38	Y	
Potter, [Stacy] H. [K.]	Private	22	Y	[Corporal]; Detailed clerk at brigade headquarters
Rearden [Reardon], William	Private	46	D	Died at Hilton Head October 1864 [Transferred V.R.C. 10/1/64]
Rogers, David	Private	26	Y	[2nd Lt. Company I 1/12/64]
Roynes [Rodney], Brazie [Bazile]	Private	28	N, W	[Chancellorsville, *finger*; Transferred 10/1/64 V.R.C.]
Shaw, Milo	Private	39	KIA	Supposed killed at Chancellorsville [Absent 6/8/65 POW]
Sherman, John	Private	36	N, W	[Wounded 3/16/65 Averysboro, NC; Deserted U.S. Hospital 5/25/65 Troy NY]
Stiles, Samuel	Private	19	Y	
Tanner, Edward	Private	26	KIA	[Chancellorsville, *leg shot off by shell*]
Thayer, [Nelson] A.	Private	22	KIA	[Gettysburg 7/2/63]
Thompson, [Edwin]	Private	21	N	[Discharge 6/28/65 Portsmouth Grove RI]
Tooley, Horace	Private	26	DOW	[New Hope Church; Died 6/8/64 near Dallas GA]
Tooley, William	Private	21	POW, KIA	[Chancellorsville, Paroled; KIA 4/10/65, skirmish, Mocassin Creek NC]
Waite, B. F.	Private	24	Y	
Walker, Thes. [Thomas]	Private	27	Y	

Name	Rank	Age		Notes
Warner, Edmund	Private	35	N	Deserted near Dumfries [1/22/63]
Welch, Henry	Private	18	N, W	[Corporal; Peach Tree Creek, *two fingers shot off left hand*; Discharged April 21st, 1865]
Wescott [Westcott], Charles [C.]	Private	24	N	[Discharged for Disability 6/1/63]
Wilbur, Fayette	Private	22	N, W, POW	[Chancellorsville, *hand*; Transferred V.R.C. 1/1/64]
Wilkins, Henry	Private	18	Y, W	[Culp's Farm 6/22/64, *right hip*]
Williams, Ellis	Private	21	Y	
Williams, [John] P.	Private	24	N, POW	[Chancellorsville; Deserted Camp Parole Annapolis MD]
Williams, William R.	Private	32	N	Home on sick leave, did not return [6/8/65 Absent, sick]
Willis, Edwin	Private	31	N	[Discharged for Disability 4/23/63]
Willis, Peter M.	Private	20	N	[Discharged for Disability 3/20/63]
Wright, [Benjamin] F.	Private	35	D	Supposed died hospital Nashville, TN [Absent, sick at regiment muster out]
Wright, Isaiah [Isiah]	Private	18	N	[Transferred 1/1/65 V.R.C.]
Wright, James A.	Private	29	Y, W	[Culp's Farm 6/22/64, *right ankle*; Peach Tree Creek 7/20/64]
Wright, James H.	Private	20	Y	[Wounded Nose's Creek, GA 6/19/64]
Wright, Samuel	Private	23	N, W	[Chancellorsville, *hand*; Transferred V.R.C.]
Wyman, [Benjamin] F.	Private	21	Y	
	Enlisted Average Age	**25.6**		
RECRUITS				
Adams, William	Private	23	N	[Enlisted 3/31/64 Hartford; 60th NY]
Cary [Carey], Peter	Private	39	N	[Enlisted 4/5/64, Albany; Mustered out 9/5/65 NY, NY]
Fowler, George	Private	25	N	[Enlisted 3/31/64, Hartford; 60th NY]
Godphrey, Eleazer	Private	18	N	[Enlisted 4/15/64, Gilboa; 60th NY]

Hall, Ira	Private	18	N		Mustered 12/31/62; [Deserted 7/6/63]; Claims sent home by proper authority, subsequent service 93rd NY
Hammond, Jerry	Private	29	N		[Enlisted 12/14/63, Whitehall; 60th NY]
Harris, James	Private	44	Y		[Enlisted 9/12/64, Troy]
Hill, John F.	Private	18	Y		[Enlisted 9/7/64, Albany]
Lone, Patrick	Private	26	N		[Enlisted 4/15/64, Troy; 60th NY]
McHugh, Charles H.	Private	21	Y		[Enlisted 9/7/64, Albany]
Newton, Charles G.	Private	29	N		[Enlisted 8/4/64, Whitehall; Discharged 5/10/65 Hart's Island NY Harbor]
Rich [Rock], Edward	Private	43	N		[Enlisted 2/19/64, New Lebanon; 60th NY]
Stacy, Ira	Private	36	D		[Enlisted 8/31/64, Troy; Died "disease of the heart" 2/24/65 Lancaster SC]
Van Guilder, Frederick	Private	21	N		[Enlisted 9/5/62, Granville]; Mustered 12/31/62; Served nine months but omitted from muster roll so not paid, left and joined a Vermont regiment [Deserted 7/6/63]
VanGuilder, John J.	Private	19	N		[Enlisted 2/22/64, Granville; 60th NY]
VanGuilder, Rufus	Private	20	N		[Enlisted 2/19/64, Granville; 60th NY]
VanGuilder, Sawyer	Private	18	N		[Enlisted 2/22/64, Granville; 60th NY]
VanGuilder, William	Private	18	N		[Enlisted 2/17/64, Granville; 60th NY]
Waite [Wait], Cassius J. [G.]	Private	18	Y, W		[Enlisted 9/29/62, Granville; Wounded New Hope Church]
Wait [Waite], Clark H.	Private	18	D		[Enlisted 3/26/64, Hartford; Intraregimental transfer Company E to K; Died of disease 12/11/64 U.S. Hospital Jefferson IN]
Waters, John H.	Private	18	Y		[Enlisted 9/17/64, Troy]
Waters, Merritt J.	Private	19	N		[Enlisted 3/25/64, Dresden; 60th NY]

Name	Rank	Age		Notes
Waters, William	Private	25	DOW	[Enlisted 3/25/64, Dresden; Resaca, *legs amputated*; Died of wounds 5/15/64]
Wilder, John S.	Private	21	Y	[Enlisted 9/13/64, Troy]
Wilson, Christopher	Private	33	N	[Enlisted 2/22/64, Whitehall; 60th NY]
Wilson, Eugene	Private	18	N	[Enlisted 3/22/64, Putnam; 60th NY]
LESS THAN ONE MONTH IN REGIMENT OR DROPPED				
Barker, David M.	Private	19	N	Minor, not mustered in. [19 years old, discharged for minority]
Dickinson, Joseph	Private	21	N	[Deserted 9/9/62]
Hayes [Hays], Edmund [Edmond]	Private	23	N	[Deserted 9/5/62]
Hindly [Hendley], Wm. S.	Private	22	N	[Deserted 9/8/62]
Potter, Jonathan W.	Corporal	26	N	[Deserted 9/8/62]
Ryan, John	Private	24	N	[Deserted 9/5/62]
Balermo, U; Flood, Daniel; Haley, Andrew; Heath, George; Rasey, J.W.			Unknown	All Unknowns not listed on NYS Ad. General Report or muster roll but Morhous lists at end of company names and Wash. Co. Historians' bounty list has them.

Appendix B: Personnel Totals

The following totals for companies and regiment were gleaned from the muster rolls above, numbers are approximate:

123RD NEW YORK INFANTRY ORIGINAL MUSTER TOTALS, RETURN TOTALS AND CASUALTIES							
COMPANY	IN SEPT. 1862	OUT JUNE 1865	PERCENTAGE RETURNED	KIA	DOW	DOD	POW
FIELD & STAFF	15	7	46.6%	0	2	0	1
A	103	51	49.5%	8	1	7	6
B	93	40	43.0%	1	2	6	6
C	87	45	51.7%	9	2	4	4
D	102	57	55.8%	1	3	12	2
E	105	56	53.3%	4	4	9	2
F	100	46	46.0%	4	3	8	8
G	89	51	57.3%	3	2	6	10
H	81	33	40.7%	5	4	12	8
I	92	46	50%	2	1	9	9
K	93	42	45.1%	7	3	9	4
TOTALS	**960**	**474**	**49.3%**	**44**	**27**	**82**	**60**

RECRUITS & TRANSFERS	TOTAL FOR COMPANY	OUT OR TRANSFERRED JUNE 1865	PERCENTAGE RETURNED	KIA	DOW	DOD	POW
A	14	9	64.2%	0	0	3	0
B	27	22	81.4%	0	0	1	1
C	14	8	57.1%	0	0	0	0
D	9	7	77.7%	0	0	1	0
E	16	7	43.7%	0	0	3	2
F	13	9	69.2%	0	0	0	3
G	21	14	66.7%	0	0	1	1
H	35	21	60.0%	1	1	0	2
I	18	15	83.3%	1	0	0	0
K	26	19	73.0%	0	1	2	0
TOTALS	**193**	**131**	**67.8%**	**2**	**2**	**11**	**9**
TOTALS 1862 MUSTER AND RECRUITS	**1153**	**605**	**52.4%**	**46**	**29**	**93**	**69**

ABOVE DOES NOT INCLUDE PERSONNEL WITH LESS THAN ONE MONTH IN REGIMENT, UNKNOWN, OR DROPPED FROM ROLLS

Appendix C: Prices for Clothing and Weapons

ADJUTANT GENERAL'S PRICE LIST FOR CLOTHING: INFANTRY				
Enlisted Volunteer's Monthly Clothing Allowance $3.50 or $42 per Annum Throughout War				
	January 1st 1863	January 7th 1865	Percent Increase	1865 Value in 2007 Dollars
Forage Cap	$0.56	$1.00	78.6%	$13.37
Flannel Shirt	$1.46	$2.32	58.9%	$31.03
Flannel Drawers	$0.95	$1.60	68.4%	$21.40
Trousers	$3.55	$4.75	33.8%	$63.53
Bootees	$2.05	$2.70	31.7%	$36.11
Great Coat	$9.50	$12.00	26.3%	$160.49
Wool Blanket	$3.60	$7.00	94.4%	$93.62
Rubber Blanket	$2.55	$4.40	72.5%	$58.85
Knapsack	$2.14	$3.10	44.9%	$41.46
January 1st 1863 Weapon Prices:			1863 Value in 2007 Dollars	
Carbines:	Smith's	$29.00	$482.18	
	Burnside	$30.00	$498.81	
	Gallager's	$30.00	$498.81	
Pistols:	Colt Army	$25.00	$415.68	
	Remington Army	$16.00	$266.03	
Rifles:	Springfield with Bayonet	$19.25	$320.07	
	Foreign Enfield with Bayonet	$18.00	$299.29	

Prices from original listing at the Washington County Historian's Office, Fort Edward, New York. Dollar value for 2007 computed from website information of the Federal Reserve Bank of Minneapolis on Consumer Price Index.

Bibliography

New York State Library, Manuscripts and Special Collections, Albany, NY
  McDougall File #21033; Eaton Family Papers #SC17395; McLean Family Papers #SC20811.

United States Army Military History Institute, Carlisle, PA
Civil War Miscellaneous Collection
  John Gourlee Letters; Tooley Brothers 123rd NY; Noah G. Hill Co. K 123rd NY; William R. Hills Co. K 123rd NY; Smith Hewitt Co. E 123rd NY; William T. Shimp Co. A 46th PA; Henry Welch Papers.

Gettysburg National Military Park Library, Gettysburg, PA
  V6-NY123a, Albert Cook; V6-NY123b, Sgt. Lorenzo Coy; V6-NY123, 2nd Lt. Seth Carey; V6-NY123IN Clark. McLean; Coco Collection, Box B-18A, James Peifer 46th PA; 6-MD3, 3rd MD.

Washington County Archives, Fort Edward, NY
  123rd NewYork muster roll; Microfilm rolls #1287 & #1288, *Salem Press* 1862-1865.

Washington County Historian's Office, Fort Edward, NY
  Robert Cruikshank Papers; Argyle, Box 2, Folder 23, Orville Robinson Letters, also Sylvester McMurry; Hartford, Box 1, Folder 7; Putnam, Folder 9; Salem, Box 7, Folder 2; Record #459, Folder: Civil War Letters, S McMurry letter; Record #43, 123rd Reg. Co. H Muster Out Rolls; Record #43, Box F; Box B, Civil War Misc.; Kingsbury, Box 1, Folder 83.

Washington County Historical Society, Fort Edward, NY
  Artemas Harrington Letters; Oscar Fisher Letters.

Rensselaer County Historical Society, Troy, NY
  Rice Bull Papers.

Adirondack Community College Library, Queensbury, NY
  Hill Collection.

Hartford Enlistment Center Museum, Hartford, NY
  Dickinson Letter Collection.

Pember Library, Granville, NY
 Box 16, Folder #20, Wiley letters; Box 19, *Granville Register.*
Cambridge Public Library, Cambridge, NY
 Microfilm, *Washington County Post* years 1854, 1859.

WEBSITES

Henry Welch Letters can be found at Hamilton College Library website:
http://library.hamilton.edu/collections/about/index.php?page_id=welch

Robert Cruikshank Letters can be found at Ohio State University eHistory website:
http://ehistory.osu.edu/osu/sources/letters/cruikshank/index.cfm

For data on personnel, regiments and battle statistics: Historical Data Systems' American Civil War Research Database at www.civilwardata.com.

BOOKS

The War of the Rebellion: A Compilation of the Official Records of the Union and Confederate Armies. 128 Vols. Washington: Government Printing Office, 1880-1901.

New York State Adjutant General's Report. State of New York, Division of Military and Naval Affairs. Annual Report for the year 1903, V5, pp. 351-499.

Adams, George. *Doctors in Blue.* Baton Rouge: Louisiana State University Press, 1996.

Bailey, Anne. *War and Ruin, William T. Sherman and the Savannah Campaign.* Wilmington, DE: Scholarly Resources Inc., 2003.

Barrett, John. *Sherman's March Through the Carolinas.* Chapel Hill: University of North Carolina Press, 1956.

Bauer, Jack, editor. *Soldiering, The Civil War Diary of Rice C. Bull.* San Rafael, CA: Presidio Press, 1977.

Calarco, Tom. *The Underground Railroad Conductor.* Schenectady, NY: Travels Thru History, 2003.

Coggins, Jack. *Arms and Equipment of the Civil War.* Wilmington, NC: Broadfoot Publishing, 1962.

Cole, Philip. *Civil War Artillery at Gettysburg.* Cambridge, MA: DaCapo Press, Perseus Books Group, 2002.

Davis, George, and Perry, Leslie, and Kirkley, Joseph. *The Official Military Atlas of the Civil War.* NY: Barnes & Noble, 2003.

Esposito, Vincent, editor. *The West Point Atlas of American Wars, Volume I, 1689-1900.* NY: Henry Holt Co., 1995.

Fox, William. *Regimental Losses in the American Civil War 1861-1865.* Albany, NY: Albany Pub. Company, 1889.

Gara, Larry. *The Liberty Line, The Legend of the Underground Railroad.* Lexington: University of Kentucky Press, 1961.

Gates, Paul W. *The Farmer's Age: Agriculture 1815-1860.* Holt, Rinehart and Winston, 1960.

Gibbon, John. *The Artillerist's Manual.*

Grant, Ulysses. *Personal Memoirs of U.S. Grant.* NY: J.J. Little & Company, 1885.

Griffith, Paddy. *Battle in the Civil War.* Surrey, England: Fieldbooks, 1986.

Kramer, Samuel. *Maryland and the Glorious Old Third in the War for the Union.* Wash.: T.J. Brashears Printer, 1882.

Lacour-Gayet, Robert. *Everyday Life in the United States before the Civil War 1830-1860.* NY: Frederick Ungar Publishing, 1969.

Luvaas, Jay, and Nelson, Harold. *U.S. Army War College Guide to the Battle of Gettysburg.* Philadelphia: Harper & Row, 1987.

McPherson, James. *The Atlas of the Civil War.* NY: Macmillan, 1994.

McPherson, James. *Battle Cry of Freedom.* NY: Random House, 1988.

Medical and Surgical History of the Civil War. Wilmington, NC: Broadfoot Publishing Company, 1992.

Moore, Mark. *The Battle of Bentonville.* DaCapo Press, 1997.

Morhous, Henry. *Reminiscences of the 123rd Regiment, N.Y.S.V.* Fort Edward, NY: Washington County Historical Society, 1995.

Northup, Solomon. *Twelve Years a Slave.* Mineola, NY: Dover Publications, 1970.

Parkerson, Donald H. *The Agricultural Transition in New York State.* Ames, Iowa: Iowa State University Press, 1995.

Perry, Kenneth, editor. *We Are in a Fight Today, The Civil War Diaries of Horace P. Mathews & King S. Hammond.* Bowie, MD: Heritage Books, 2000.

Pfanz, Harry. *Gettysburg – Culp's Hill & Cemetery Hill.* Chapel Hill, NC: Un. of North Carolina Press, 1993.

Sears, Stephen. *The Civil War Papers of George B. McClellan.* NY: Ticknor & Fields, 1989.

Shelden, Michael. *Orwell, The Authorised Biography.* London: Minerva Press, 1992.

Siebert, Wilbur. *Vermont's Anti-Slavery and Underground Railroad Record.* New York: Negro University Press, 1937, reprinted 1969.

The Tribune Almanac and Political Register. New York, The Tribune Association: Years 1857, 1861, 1865.

U.S. War Department. *The 1863 U.S. Infantry Tactics.* Mechanicsburg, PA: Stackpole Books, 2002.

Washington County Planning Department. *An Introduction to Historical Resources In Washington County, New York.* Granville, NY: Grastorf Press, 1976.

MAPS

O'Reilly, Frank, and Mink, Eric, and Dove, John. *Battle of Chancellorsville.* Series of twelve maps. 1998.

Desjardin, Thomas, and Friends of the National Parks at Gettysburg. *The Battlefield of Gettysburg.* Series of three maps, July 1st, July 2nd and July 3rd, 1863. Gettysburg: Friends of the National Parks at Gettysburg, 1998.

Kelly, Dennis, and Bearss, Edwin. *The Battlefields of Kennesaw Mountain and Kolb's Farm, Georgia 1864.* Series of two maps. Kennesaw Mountain Historical Association, 1994.

Kennedy, Frances, editor. *A Guide to the Atlanta Campaign, May – September, 1864.* Dalton-Whitfield Chamber of Commerce, 2000.

Notes

ABBREVIATIONS IN NOTES

NYSL	New York State Library, Albany, New York
USAMHI	U.S. Army Military History Institute, Carlisle, PA
O.R..	*The War of the Rebellion: A Compilation of the Official Records of the Union and Confederate Armies.* 128 Vols. Washington: Government Printing Office, 1880-1901.
HWL	Henry Welch Letters, Hamilton College Library, Clinton, NY
GNMPL	Gettysburg National Military Park Library, Gettysburg, PA
RCHS	Rensselaer County Historical Society, Troy, NY
RCL	Robert Cruikshank Letters, History Department, Ohio State University
WCA	Washington County Archives, Fort Edward, NY
WCH	Washington County Historian's Office, Fort Edward, NY
WCHS	Washington County Historical Society, Fort Edward, NY

[1] Lacour-Gayet, *Everyday Life in the United States before the Civil War 1830-1860*, p. 28.

[2] Federal Census of 1850, Washington County, New York; "Intellectual Life, Education," *The Greenwood Encyclopedia of Daily Life, 19th Century*, p. 165, 166.

[3] Federal Census of 1850, Washington County, New York; *Proceedings of the Board of Supervisors of Washington County* for the years 1856, 1857 and 1858, Hill Collection, Adirondack Community College.

[4] Washington County Planning Department, *An Introduction to Historic Resources In Washington Count, New York*, p. 45, 49, 50, 56, 64.

[5] Lacour-Gayet, p. 27, 41, 42, 44.

[6] Parkerson, *The Agricultural Transition in New York State*, p. 3.

[7] Author's study, random numbers generated for 50 samples per township in the 1850 and 1860 Federal Census and total property values present compared; Parkerson, p. 112.

[8] Parkerson, p. 7, 9.

[9] Parkerson, p. 10, 11, 64; Gates, *Farmer's Age of Agriculture*, p.277.

[10] Gates, p. 204, 207, 223, 309, 310.

[11] Parkerson, p. 14, 94, 89; Gates, p. 291, 282.

[12] Gates, p. 213.

[13] Gates, p. 242, 244.

[14] Parkerson, p. 62.

[15] U.S. Census website,
www.census.gov/population/documentation/twps0056/tabA-20.xls
www.census.gov/population/documentation/twps0056/tabA-19.xls
[16] *The New York State Freedom Trail Commission Report,*
www.oce.nysed.gov/freedom%20trail/ftchrono2 p. 2.
[17] Calarco, *The Underground Railroad Conductor*, pp. 47-56; *An Introduction to Historic Resources In Washington County*, p. 60.
[18] Gara, *The Liberty Line*, p. 44.
[19] *Tribune Almanac and Political Register for 1857*, p. 46.
[20] *Washington County Post*, Cambridge Public Library.
[21] *Tribune Almanac and Political Register for 1857*, p. 46.
[22] U.S. Census website,
www.census.gov/population/documentation/twps0056/tabA-20.xls
www.census.gov/population/documentation/twps0056/tabA-19.xls
[23] Wikipedia website, United States Presidential Election, 1860
http://en.wikipedia.org/wiki/United_States_presidential_election%2C_1860.
[24] *Tribune Almanac and Political Register for 1861*, p. 46.
[25] *Washington County Post*, Cambridge Public Library.
[26] NYSL, McLean Family Papers, Box 3, April 11th & May 15th, 1862 diary.
[27] NYSL, McLean Family Papers, Box 3, July 7th, 1862 diary.
[28] NYSL, McLean Family Papers, Box 3, July 22nd, diary.
[29] NYSL, McLean Family Papers, Box 3, July 23rd & 24th, 1862 diary.
[30] WCA, *Salem Press* August 19th 1862, p. 2
[31] NYSL, McLean Family Papers, Box 3, Aug. 4th & 7th, 1862 diary.
[32] RCL, Introduction
[33] Author interview with Rush Benson, descendant
[34] WCH, Record 43, Box F, Company H enlistment forms.
[35] WCH, Record 43, Box F.
[36] RCHS, Rice Bull Papers, Box 1, Original Manuscript, p.3.
[37] *Ibid.*
[38] *Ibid.*, p. 5, p. 6.
[39] *Tribune Almanac and Political Register for 1861*, pp. 30-31.
[40] *Ibid.*, p. 36
[41] Website: http://www.civil-war.net/pages/mississippi_declaration.asp
[42] Morhous, *Reminiscences of the 123rd Regiment, N.Y.S.V.*, p. 8.; RCL, Introduction; RCHS, Bull Papers, pp. 7 & 8.
[43] RCHS, Bull manuscript, p. 8.
[44] RCL, September 11th, 1862
[45] RCHS, Bull manuscript, p. 12.
[46] *Ibid.*, p. 13.
[47] RCL, September 16th, 1862
[48] RCHS, Bull manuscript, p.14.
[49] Morhous, p. 12.

[50] RCHS, Bull manuscript, p. 18.
[51] RCL, September 21st, 1862.
[52] RCHS, Bull manuscript, p. 18, p. 13, p. 18.5.
[53] RCHS, Rice Bull, Box 2, Sept. 21st & Oct. 5th, 1862 letters.
[54] NYSL, McLean Family Papers, Box 1, Oct. 19th, 1862 letter.
[55] RCHS, Bull manuscript, p. 17.
[56] RCL, September, 21st, 1862.
[57] HWL, October 11th, 1862.
[58] USAMHI, Smith Hewitt file, Co. E, 123rd NY, Civil War Miscellaneous Collection.
[59] RCL, September 23rd, 1862; WCH, Argyle, Box 2, Folder 23, Sept. 21st, 1862 letter; USAMHI, William R. Hills, Co. K, 123rd NY, Civil War Miscellaneous Collection.
[60] NYSL, McLean Family Papers, Box 3, Sept. 29th, 1862 diary entry.
[61] RCL, October 9th, 1862; October 23rd, 1862.
[62] HWL, October 11th, 1862; October 26th, 1862.
[63] USAMHI, Noah G. Hill, CO. K, 123rd NY, Civil War Miscellaneous Collection.
[64] WCH, Argyle Box 2, Folder 23, O. Robinson letter Oct. 26th, 1862.
[65] RCHS, Rice Bull Papers, Box 2, October 21st, 1862 letter.
[66] WCH, Argyle Box 2, Folder 23, O. Robinson letter Oct. 26th, 1862.
[67] HWL, Oct. 11th, 1862; USAMHI, Tooley Brothers, 123rd NY, Box 103 Civil War Miscellaneous Collection, Horace letter Oct. 28th, 1862; WCH, Argyle Box 2, Folder 23, O. Robinson letter Oct. 26th, 1862; NYSL, McLean Family Papers, Box 3, Oct. 18th, 1862 diary entry.
[68] HWL, Oct. 11th, 1862; RCHS, Rice Bull Papers, Box 2, Oct. 5th, 1862 letter.
[69] NYSL, McLean Family Papers, Box 3, Oct. 7th, 1862 diary entry; HWL, Oct. 26th, 1862.
[70] USAMHI, Noah G. Hill, CO. K, 123rd NY, Civil War Miscellaneous Collection.
[71] USAMHI, John Gourlee Letters, Civil War Miscellaneous Collection.
[72] RCL, November 6th, 1862.
[73] USAMHI, Smith Hewitt file, Civil War Miscellaneous Collection, Nov. 18th, 1862 letter; NYSL, McLean Family Papers, Jan. 4th, 1863 diary entry; RCHS, Rice Bull Papers, Box 2, Jan. 11th, 1863 letter.
[74] RCL, Nov. 8th, 1862.
[75] RCL, Nov. 15th, 1862; USAMHI, John Gourlee Letters, Civil War Miscellaneous Collection.
[76] HWL, Nov. 16th, 1862.
[77] NYSL, McLean Family Papers, Nov. 7th, 1862 diary entry.
[78] NYSL, McLean Family Papers, Nov. 27th, 1862 diary entry.
[79] NYSL, McLean Family Papers, Box 1, Dec. 2nd, 1862 letter; RCL, Dec. 13th, 1862; WCA, *Salem Press* Dec. 23rd, 1862, p. 2.
[80] RCHS, Rice Bull Papers, Nov. 20th 1862 letter.

[81] RCHS, Bull manuscript, p.8.
[82] RCL, Dec. 3rd, 1862; Dec. 21st, 1862; Jan. 21st, 1863.
[83] RCL, Jan. 11th, 1863; Dec. 21st, 1862; Dec. 3rd, 1862.
[84] RCHS, Rice Bull Papers, Dec. 7th, 1862 letter.
[85] WCH, Dillon Collection, Nov. 1st to Dec. 31st 1862 Co. H muster.
[86] HWL, Dec. 21st, 1862; RCHS, Rice Bull Papers, Dec. 19th, 1862.
[87] RCHS, Rice Bull Papers, Dec. 25th, 1862.
[88] NYSL, McLean Family Papers, Box 1, Dec. 30th, 1862 letter.
[89] RCHS, Bull manuscript, p. 16.
[90] RCHS, Bull manuscript, pp. 16-17; NYSL, McLean Family Papers, Box 1, Jan. 28th, 1863.
[91] McPherson, *Battle Cry of Freedom*, p. 584; RCHS, Bull manuscript, p. 17; McLean Family Papers, Box 1, Jan. 28th, 1863.
[92] Perry, *We Are In a Fight Today*, p. 8; USAMHI, John Gourlee Letters, December 19th, 1862 letter, Civil War Miscellaneous Collection.
[93] NYSL, McDougall File, Jan. 26th, 1863 letter.
[94] *Ibid.*
[95] NYSL, McLean Family Papers, Box 3, October 9th, 1862 entry.
[96] Perry, p. 8; Morhous, p. 21.
[97] NYSL, Eaton Family Papers, Feb. 9th, 1863 letter.
[98] RCHS, Bull manuscript, p. 21; NYSL, McLean Family Papers, March 9th, 1863 letter.
[99] RCHS, Rice Bull Papers, Feb. 6th, 1863 letter.
[100] HWL, Jan. 25th, 1863.
[101] McPherson, *Battle Cry of Freedom*, p. 585.
[102] RCL, April 25th & April 22nd, 1863; NYSL, McLean Family Papers, Box 1, April 10th, 1863 letter.
[103] WCH, Argyle, Box 2, Folder 23, April 12th, 1863 letter.
[104] NYSL, McLean Family Papers, Box 1, April 10th, 1863 letter.
[105] RCHS, Rice Bull Papers, April 5th, 1863 letter.
[106] NYSL, McLean Family Papers, April 17th, 1863 diary entry.
[107] HWL, April 16th, 1863; RCHS, Bull manuscript, p. 25; NYSL, McLean Family Papers, Box 1, April 26th, 1863 letter.
[108] WCH, Argyle, Box 2, Folder 23, April 12th, 1863 letter.
[109] Esposito, *The West Point Atlas of American Wars, Volume I,* Map 84.
[110] GNMPL, File V6-NY123a, Albert Cook letter May 8th, 1863.
[111] Information on all units can be found on Historical Data Systems' American Civil War Research Database at www.civilwardata.com.
[112] RCHS, Bull manuscript, p. 31; Morhous, p. 26.
[113] RCHS, Bull manuscript, p. 33.
[114] RCHS, Bull manuscript, p. 33; Morhous, p. 26.
[115] RCHS, Bull manuscript, p. 34.
[116] RCHS, Bull manuscript, p. 35.
[117] Esposito, Map 85.
[118] RCHS, Bull manuscript, p. 37; HWL, May 10th, 1863.

[119] RCHS, Rice Bull Papers, May 17th, 1863 letter; RCL, May 8th, 1863; RCHS, Bull manuscript, p. 37.
[120] *O.R.*, Series 1, Vol. 25, Part 1, p. 697.
[121] Esposito, Map 87.
[122] RCHS, Bull manuscript, p. 40.
[123] *Ibid.*
[124] *Ibid.*, p. 41.
[125] *Ibid.*, p. 42.
[126] O'Reilly, Mink and Dove, Battle of Chancellorsville map series, Map 6 of 12, May 2nd, 1863, 9 p.m. to 11 p.m.
[127] RCL, May 8th, 1863; RCHS, Bull manuscript, p. 47.
[128] RCHS, Bull manuscript, p. 47.5; HWL, May 10th, 1863; RCL, May 8th, 1863; Morhous, p. 33; GNMPL, File V6-NY123a; RCHS, Bull manuscript, p. 47.5; RCL, May 8th, 1863.
[129] GNMPL, File V6-NY123a, Albert Cook letter May 8th, 1863.
[130] Esposito, Map 88; O'Reilly, Mink and Dove, Battle of Chancellorsville map series, Map 11 of 12, May 3rd, 1863, 8 a.m. to 9 a.m.; Fox, *Regimental Losses in the American Civil War*, p. 568 and *O.R.* Series 1, Vol. 25, Part 1, p. 807, for total loss of 805; For percentage of 33rd NC, Fox, p.558.
[131] Esposito, Map 88; *O.R.*, Series 1, Vol. 25, Part 1, p. 671.
[132] RCL, May 8th, 1863.
[133] *O.R.*, Series 1, Vol. 25, Part 1, p. 688.
[134] RCL, May 8th, 1863.
[135] NYSL, McDougall File, letter.
[136] *O.R.*, Series 1, Vol. 25, Part 1, p. 709; *O.R.*, Series 1, Vol. 25, Part 1, p. 705.
[137] RCL, May 3rd, 1863.
[138] *Ibid.*
[139] Morhous, p. 32, 33, no name is stated by Morhous; *O.R.*, Series 1, Vol. 25, Part 1, p. 445, for report on 123rd Colors by General Carr.
[140] Citation from U.S. Army website, www.army.mil/cmh-pg/mohciv2.htm; Morhous, p. 35.
[141] RCHS, Bull manuscript, pp. 51-52.
[142] RCHS, Bull manuscript, pp. 53-54.
[143] RCHS, Bull manuscript, p. 54.
[144] Esposito, Map 90; Fox, p. 550, p. 544; WCA, *Salem Press*, May 26, 1863, p.2.
[145] Casualty numbers from Historical Data Systems' American Civil War Database, www.civilwardata.com used.
[146] *O.R.*, Series 1, Vol. 25, Part 1, p. 445; *O.R.*, Series 1, Vol. 25, Part 1, p. 391.
[147] Desertion numbers from Historical Data Systems' American Civil War Database, www.civilwardata.com; USAMHI, Kramer, *Maryland and the Glorious Old Third in the War for the Union*, p. 25.

[148] Historical Data Systems' American Civil War Database, www.civilwardata.com.
[149] RCHS, Bull manuscript, p. 55; Morhous, p. 31; O.R., Series 1, Vol. 25, Part 1, p. 450; author's study of company casualties.
[150] RCHS, Bull manuscript, p. 57.
[151] HWL, May 10th, 1863.
[152] NYSL, McLean Family Papers, May 10th, 1863 letter.
[153] NYSL, Eaton Family Papers, Letter dated March 10th, 1863 but should be May 10th, 1863.
[154] WCHS, Oscar Fisher letters, May 7th, 1863.
[155] GNMPL, Albert M. Cook May 8th, 1863 letter.
[156] Shelden, *Orwell, The Authorized Biography*, p. 293.
[157] Adams, *Doctors In Blue*, pp. 113-115.
[158] RCHS, Bull manuscript, pp. 92-94.
[159] RCHS, Bull manuscript, p. 97.
[160] WCH, Argyle, Box 2, Folder 23, May 16, 1863 letter.
[161] Casualty numbers from Historical Data Systems' American Civil War Database, www.civilwardata.com used, 123rd figures adjusted per research; varying casualty numbers can be found also in *O.R.*, Series 1, Vol. 25, Part 1, p. 184; also Morhous, pp. 33-35; also NYSL, McLean Family Papers, May 7th, 1863 letter. Adams, p. 114.
[162] Historical Data Systems' American Civil War Database, www.civilwardata.com; New York State *Report of the Adjutant-General*.
[163] RCL, May 14th, 1863; HWL, May 24th, 1863; GNMPL, Albert M. Cook May 8th, 1863 letter; WCH, Argyle, Box 2, Folder 23, May 16th, 1863 letter.
[164] WCH, Argyle, Box 2, Folder 23, May 16th, letter.
[165] WCH, Record #459, Folder: Civil War Letter, June 5th, 1863 letter.
[166] RCL, April 7th, 1863 and May 12th, 1863 letters.
[167] HWL, June 12th, 1863.
[168] NYSL, McDougall File, June 11th, 1863 letter.
[169] NYSL, McDougall File, June 21st, 1863 letter.
[170] RCL, Cruikshank describes the picket posting in letters from May 24th, 1863 and May 28th, 1863; HWL, June 12th, 1863.
[171] RCL, June 5th, 1863; Morhous, p. 39.
[172] *O.R.*, Series 1, Vol. 27, Part 3, p. 881, June 10th, 1863 Letter.
[173] NYSL, McLean Family Papers, Box 1, May 22nd, 1863 letter; NYSL, McDougall File, June 7th, 1863 letter.
[174] *O.R.*, Series 1, Vol. 27, Part 1, p. 35; *Ibid* p. 36.
[175] Morhous, p. 41.
[176] RCL, June 13th, 1863; Hartford Enlistment Center Museum, Letter "J" June 22nd, 1863; GNMPL, June 25, 1863 letter, File 6-123-NY-INF.
[177] Morhous, p. 43; GNMPL, File V6-NY123, June 23rd, 1863 diary entry; WCH, Argyle, Box 2, Folder 23, June 23rd, 1863 letter.
[178] GNMPL, File 6-PA46, June 25th, 1863 letter; HWL, August 2nd, 1863.

[179] RCL, June 20th, 1863.
[180] RCL, June 24th, 1863.
[181] WCH, Argyle, Box 2, Folder 23, June 23rd, 1863 letter.
[182] RCL, June 26th, 1863.
[183] GNMPL, File V6-NY123, June 28th, 1863 diary entry.
[184] *O.R.*, Series 1, Vol. 27, p. 60.
[185] Esposito, Map 94, Map 95.
[186] *O.R.*, Series 1, Vol. 27, p. 788.
[187] NYSL, McDougall File, June 23rd, 1863 letter.
[188] Esposito, Map 95.
[189] *O.R.*, Series 1, Vol. 27, p. 65.
[190] Esposito, Map 97.
[191] RCL, June 30th, 1863; Morhous, p. 46.
[192] GNMPL, File V6-NY123, July 1st, 1863 Cook diary entry; GNMPL, File 6-NY123b, July 2nd, 1863 Coy letter.
[193] GNMPL, File 6-NY123b, July 2nd, 1863 Coy letter.
[194] Morhous, p. 47; RCL, July 2nd, 1863; GNMPL, File 6-NY123b, July 2nd, 1863 Coy letter.
[195] *O.R.*, Series 1, Vol. 27, Part 1, p. 287.
[196] RCL, July 2nd, 1863.
[197] *Ibid.*; *O.R.*, Series 1, Vol. 27, Part 1, p. 783; HWL, July 18th, 1863.
[198] Pfanz, *Gettysburg – Culp's Hill & Cemetery Hill*, p. 287.
[199] *Ibid*, p. 288, p. 291.
[200] Pfanz, p. 292; *O.R.*, Series 1, Vol. 27, Part 3, p. 498.
[201] *O.R.*, Series 1, Vol. 27, Part 1, pp. 793-794.
[202] RCL, July 3rd, 1863; *O.R.*, Series 1, Vol. 27, Part 1, pp. 784-785.
[203] Pfanz, Map 17.1, pp.319-320.
[204] RCL, July 3rd, 1863; Casualty figures calculated from historical markers at Gettysburg National Military Park.
[205] GNMPL, File V6-123NYa, July 9th, 1863 letter; *O.R.*, Series 1, Vol. 27, Part 1, p. 831.
[206] *O.R.*, Series 1, Vol. 27, Part 1, p. 238.
[207] Morhous, pp. 50-51; GNMPL, File 6-NY145, July 9th, 1863 letter; *O.R.*, Series 1, Vol. 27, Part 1, p. 831.
[208] Coggins, *Arms and Equipment of the Civil War*, p. 82; *O.R.*, Series 1, Vol. 27, Part 1, p. 784 for McDougall, p. 893 for Edgell.
[209] *O.R.*, Series 1, Vol. 27, Part 2, p. 456.
[210] Shot distances found in Gibbon, *The Artillerist's Manual*, p. 455-456; Cole, *Civil War Artillery at Gettysburg*, p. 161.
[211] Confederate artillery locations from "The Battlefield at Gettysburg" Map, July 3rd, 1863-Day Three by Desjardin; Actual types of artillery in units from historical markers at Gettysburg National Military Park; *O.R.*, Series 1, Vol. 27, Part 2, p. 379.
[212] *O.R.*, Series 1, Vol. 27, Part 1, p. 417; *Ibid*, p. 898.
[213] RCL, July 3rd, 1863.

214 RCL, July 3rd, 1863; GNMPL, File 6-123NY, July 6th, 1863 letter; *O.R.*, Series 1, Vol. 27, Part 1, p. 798, p. 785.
215 GNMPL, File 6-123NY, July 30th, 1863 letter.
216 GNMPL, File 6-NY123b, July 6th, 1863 letter; RCL, July 4th, 1863; GNMPL, File V6-NY123IN, July 4th, 1863 diary; Morhous, pp. 52-53; GNMPL, File V6-NY123, July 4th, 1863 diary entry.
217 HWL, July 18th, 1863; GNMPL, V6-NY123a, July 9th, 1863 letter; GNMPL, V6-NY123, July 5th, 1863 letter.
218 Causalty figures from Historical Data Systems' American Civil War Database, www.civilwardata.com.
219 *Ibid.*
220 RCL, July 5th, 1863, July 6th, 1863.
221 GNMPL, V6-NY123IN, July 12th, 1863 letter.
222 RCL, July 7th, 1863; Morhous, p. 54; GNMPL, V6-NY123IN, July 9th, 1863 letter and July 12th, 1863 letter.
223 RCL, July 8th, 1863; GNMPL, V6-NY123IN, July 12th, 1863 letter; GNMPL, V6-NY123a, July 8th, 1863 diary entry.
224 RCL, July 9th, 1863.
225 RCL, July 11th, 1863; Morhous, p. 56.
226 GNMPL, V6-NY123IN, July 12th, 1863 letter; RCL, July 14th, 1863; GNMPL, V6-NY123IN, July 17th, 1863 letter.
227 GNMPL, V6-NY123IN, July 17th, 1863 letter.
228 RCL, July 17th, 1863.
229 WCH, Robert Cruikshank Papers.
230 *O.R.*, Series 1, Vol. 27, Part 2, p. 880.
231 GNMPL, File V6-NY123IN, July 17th, 1863 letter; GNMPL, File V6-NY123a, July 29th, 1863.
232 GNMPL, File V6-Ny123IN, July 23rd, 1863 diary entry.
233 RCL, July 24th, 1863.
234 RCL, July 25th, 1863, July 26th, 1863.
235 RCL, August 2nd, 1863.
236 GNMPL, File V6-NY123IN, July 17th, 1863 let.; Morhous, pp. 60, 61.
237 HWL, August 2nd, 1863, August 23rd, 1863.
238 HWL, August 2nd, 1863.
239 USAMHI, William T. Shimp letters, probably August, 1863.
240 NYSL, McLean Family Papers, Box 1, August 29th, 1863 letter; Morhous, pp. 61-62.
241 WCH, Putnam, Folder 9.
242 HWL, September 5th, 1863, August 16th, 1863.
243 WCH, Argyle, Box 2, Folder 23, September 1st, 1863 letter.
244 WCH, Robert Cruikshank Papers, September 1st, 1863 order.
245 NYSL, Eaton Family Papers, September 9th, 1863 letter; USAMHI, John Gourlee Letters, September 13th, 1863.
246 HWL, September 10th, 1863.
247 *O.R.*, Series 1, Vol. 29, Part 2, p. 203

[248] HWL, September 19th, 1863.
[249] *O.R.*, Series 1, Vol. 30, Part 1, pp. 142-143.
[250] *O.R.*, Series 1, Vol. 30, Part 1, p. 146, p. 148; *O.R.*, Series 1, Vol. 29, Part 1, p. 150, p. 147, p. 147, p.152, p. 147, p. 148, p. 148, p. 149.
[251] *O.R.*, Series 1, Vol. 29, Part 1, p. 150.
[252] *O.R.,* Series 1, Vol. 29, Part 1, pp. 158, 170-171.
[253] *O.R.,* Series 1, Vol. 29, Part 1, pp. 173, 184.
[254] *O.R.,* Series 1, Vol. 30, Part 4, p. 38.
[255] Morhous, p. 67; NYSL, McLean Family Papers, Sept. 28th, 1863 diary entry.
[256] GNMPL, Coco Collection, Box B-18A, *North Carolina Historical Review*, Vol. XXXII, Number 4, p. 552.
[257] Morhous, p. 68; Perry, p. 15; NYSL, McLean Family Papers, Oct. 2nd, 1863 diary entry.
[258] *O.R.*, Series 1, Vol. 29, Part 1, pp. 182-183.
[259] Morhous, p. 68.
[260] *O.R.,* Series 1, Vol. 31, Part 1, p. 693.
[261] USAMHI, John Gourlee Letters, November 8th, 1863.
[262] *O.R.,* Series 1, Vol. 31, Part 1, p. 73.
[263] RCL, October 14th, 1863.
[264] NYSL, McDougall File, October 12th, 1863 letter.
[265] USAMHI, John Gourlee Letters, December 18th, 1863.
[266] GNMPL, Coco Collection, Box B-18A, *North Carolina Historical Review*, Vol. XXXII, Number 4, p. 553.
[267] Historical Marker, Old Jail Museum, Winchester, TN.
[268] NYSL, Eaton Family Papers, November 1st, 1863 letter; NYSL, McLean Family Papers, Box 1, October 28th, 1863 letter.
[269] Morhous, p. 73.
[270] Hartford Enlistment Center Museum, Dickinson Letter Collection, Letter M, October 6th, 1863; USAMHI, Tooley Brothers 123rd New York, December 24th, 1863 letter; USAMHI, John Gourlee Letters, December 18th, 1863; HWL, October 29th, 1863.
[271] RCHS, Bull manuscript, p. 108, p. 232.
[272] RCL, December 2nd, 1863.
[273] HWL, December, 1st, 1863; USAMHI, John Gourlee Letters, Dcember 10th, 1863.
[274] USAMHI, John Gourlee letters, December 10th, 1863.
[275] USAMHI, Tooley Brothers 123rd New York, Horace letters December 18th and 24th, 1863.
[276] USAMHI, Tooley Brothers 123rd New York, William letter December 25th, 1863.
[277] USAMHI, Tooley Brothers 123rd New York, William letters August 2nd, 1863 and August 6th, 1863.
[278] HWL, December 18th, 1863.
[279] WCH, Record #43, 123rd Reg. Co. H Muster Out Rolls.

[280] See Perry, Appendix E, pp. 157-165 for discussion of 145th New York, also pp. 166-167 for listing of transfers into 123rd New York; *O.R.*, Series 1, Vol. 30, Part 4, p. 293; *O.R.*, Series 1, Vol. 32, Part 1, p. 27.
[281] RCL, In a Jan. 12th, 1864 letter to his wife Robert states he has 29 men from the 145th transferred in and present.
[282] WCH, Robert Cruikshank Papers.
[283] NYSL, McLean Family Papers, Jan. 26th, 1864 diary entry and March 31st, 1864 diary entry.
[284] NYSL, McLean Family Papers, Jan. 28th, 1864 diary entry; NYSL, McLean Family Papers, Box 1, Dec. 25th, 1863 letter; USAMHI, Tooley Brothers 123rd New York, Horace letters both Dec. 18th, 1863.
[285] RCL, December 26th, 1863, caterer mentioned in Dec. 5th, 1863 letter.
[286] NYSL, McLean Family Papers, Box 1, letter is dated January 1st, 1863 but should be January 1st, 1864, stationary has "Bridgeport, Ala." printed on upper right corner.
[287] RCL, Nov. 19th, 1863 and Nov. 29th, 1863.
[288] HWL, December 1st, 1863, the letter is dated Dec. 1st, 1862 but is from Bridgeport, Ala. and discusses activities in Tennessee.
[289] Morhous, pp. 74-75.
[290] RCL, January 2nd, 1864.
[291] HWL, Nov. 20th, 1863; NYSL, McLean Family Papers, Nov. 12th, 1863 diary entry.
[292] NYSL, McLean Family Papers, Jan. 7th, 1864 diary entry.
[293] NYSL, McLean Family Papers, Jan. 9th, 1864 diary entry; HWL, Jan. 14th, 1864; NYSL, McLean Family Papers, Jan. 19th and 22nd, 1864 diary entry.
[294] RCL, Jan. 15th, 1864; NYSL, McLean Family Papers, Jan. 14th, 1864 diary entry.
[295] HWL, Jan. 15th, 1864.
[296] NYSL, McLean Family Papers, Box 1, No date on letter to parents, letter from Elk River Bridge, TN.
[297] USAMHI, Tooley Brothers 123rd New York, William Jan. 28th, 1864 letter.
[298] RCL, Feb. 2nd, 1864 letter with notations through February 12th.
[299] *Ibid.*
[300] *Ibid.*
[301] RCL, Feb. 13th, 1864 letter with notations through the 21st in letter; USAMHI, Tooley Brothers 123rd New York, William Feb. 21st, 1864 letter.
[302] RCL, Feb. 13th, 1864 letter with notations through the 21st in letter.
[303] RCl, Feb. 26th, 1864.
[304] *Ibid.*
[305] RCl, Feb. 22nd, 1864 and March 5th, 1864.
[306] *O.R.*, Series 1, Vol. 32, Part 1, pp. 499-501; see also: RCL, March 24th, 1864; Morhous, pp. 82-83.

307 HWL, March 23rd, 1864.
308 RCL, March 20th, 1864.
309 RCL, March 13th, 1864.
310 NYSL, McLean Family Papers, 1864 Diary entries for March 1st, April 22nd, March 13th, March 23rd, April 5th.
311 WCH, Robert Cruikshank Papers
312 NYSL, McLean Family Papers, March 30th, 1864 diary entry; GNMPL, V6-NY123b, Diary of Sgt. Lorenzo Coy, April 12th, 1864 entry.
313 NYSL, McLean Family Papers, Box 1, April 27th, 1864 letter.
314 HWL, April, 22nd, 1864.
315 WCHS, Artemus Harrington, June 28th, 1864 letter; USAMHI, William Tooley letter, Jan. 11th, 1865 (letter dated 1864 but from Savannah).
316 USAMHI, Tooley Brothers 123rd New York, April 23rd, 1864 letter.
317 GNMPL, V6-NY123b, Diary of Sgt. Lorenzo Coy, March 27th, 1864.
318 USAMHI, Tooley Brothers 123rd New York, April 19th, 1864 letter.
319 GNMPL, V6-NY123b, Diary of Sgt. Lorenzo Coy, April 8th, 1864 entry.
320 GNMPL, V6-NY123b, Coy letter No. 12, possibly March 11, 1864.
321 WCA, *Salem Press,* Nov. 11th, 1862; Pember Library, Box 19, *Granville Register* Oct. 16th, 1863; HWL, March 25th, 1864.
322 NYSL, McLean Family Papers, April 4th, 1864 entry.
323 Fox, pp. 546-547: Wilderness 17,666; Spotsylvania 18,399; North Anna 1,293; Cold Harbor 12,737; Petersburg Assault 11,386; Total 61,481.
324 RCL, April 5th, 1864; April 19th, 1864; March 29th, 1864.
325 WCA, *Salem Press*, May 24th, 1864.
326 RCL, April 27th, 1864; *O.R.*, Series 1, Vol. 38, Part 4, p. 17.
327 USAMHI, Tooley Brothers 123rd New York, May 6th, 1864 letter.
328 RCL, May 10th, 1864.
329 RCL, May 14th, 1864.
330 USAMHI, Tooley Brothers 123rd New York, May 17th, 1864 letter; injuries listed by William Tooley in letter, Robert Cruikshank letter of May 15th, 1864, Coy diary entry May 15th, 1864, also referenced with Historical Data Systems' American Civil War Database, www.civilwardata.com.
331 HWL, June 9th, 1864; RCL, May 15th, 1864; Morhous, p. 86.
332 USAMHI, Tooley Brothers 123rd New York, May letter; *The Medical and Surgical History of the Civil War*, Vol. 11, p. 135 for Waters operation, p. 160 fatality of hip operations; casualties from Historical Data Systems' American Civil War Database, www.civilwardata.com; HWL, June 9th, 1864.
333 RCHS, Bull manuscript, p. 257.

[334] GNMPL, V6-123b, Coy diary entry May 16th, 1864; HWL, May 20th, 1864.
[335] RCL, May 19th, 1864; McPherson, *The Atlas of the Civil War*, pp. 172-173, also Esposito, Map 145.
[336] USAMHI, Tooley Brothers 123rd New York, William, May, 1864 letter.
[337] GNMPL, V6-NY123b, Coy diary May 16th, 1864; Morhous, pp. 92-93; GNMPL, V6-NY123b, Coy diary May 20th, 1864.
[338] Morhous, pp.92-93.
[339] Morhous, p. 94.
[340] USAMHI, John Gourlee Letters, June 8th, 1864.
[341] *Ibid.*
[342] RCL, May 25th, 1864.
[343] *Ibid.*; USAMHI, John Gourlee Letters, May 29th, 1864.
[344] RCL, May 25th, 1864.
[345] Morhous, p. 95; RCL, May 25th, 1864.
[346] Casualty list for 123rd NY derived from Historical Data Systems' American Civil War Database, www.civilwardata.com; USAMHI, John Gourlee Letters, June 28th, 1864.
[347] USAMHI, Tooley Brothers 123rd New York, William June 1st, 1864 letter.
[348] *The Medical and Surgical History of the Civil War*, Vol. 11, p. 263 for McDougall operation; WCA, *Salem Press*, July 5th, 1864/July 12th, 1864/August 9th, 1864 issues; O.R., Series 1, Vol. 38, Part 2, p. 30; NYSL, McLean Family Papers, Box 1, July 19th, 1864 letter.
[349] GNMPL, V6-NY123b, Coy diary, May 28th and May 31st, 1864 entry.
[350] USAMHI, Tooley Brothers 123rd New York, William June 7th, 1864 letter; GNMPL, V6-123b, Coy diary entry June 4th, 1864.
[351] USAMHI, Tooley Brothers 123rd New York, William June 7th, 1864.
[352] GNMPL, V6-123b, Coy diary entry June 6th, 1864; USAMHI, Tooley Brothers 123rd New York, William June 7th, 1864; HWL, June 9th, 1864.
[353] O.R., Series 1, Vol. 38, Part 4, p. 455.
[354] GNMPL, V6-123b, Coy diary June 12th and June 13th, 1864.
[355] GNMPL, V6-123b, Coy diary June 13th, 1864; RCL, June 13th, 1864 and June 14th, 1864.
[356] GNMPL, V6-123b, Coy diary June 15th, 1864.
[357] RCL, June 19th, 1864; NYSL, McLean Family Papers, Box 1, June 18th, 1864 letter.
[358] GNMPL, V6-123b, Coy diary June 18th and 20th, 1864.
[359] RCHS, Bull manuscript, p. 160.
[360] RCHS, Bull manuscript, p. 164.
[361] RCL, June 22nd, 1864.
[362] NYSL, Eaton Family Papers, July 13th, 1864 letter (letter dated July 13th, 1863 but discusses Culp's Farm battle); RCL, June 22nd, 1864.
[363] GNMPL, V6-123b, Coy June 22nd, 1864 diary entry.

[364] RCL, June 22nd, 1864.
[365] GNMPL, V6-123b, Coy June 22nd, 1864 diary entry; NYSL, Eaton Family Papers, July 13th, 1864 letter (letter dated July 13th, 1863 but discusses Culp's Farm battle).
[366] Casualty list for 123rd NY derived from Historical Data Systems' American Civil War Database, www.civilwardata.com; also cross referenced with listing by Morhous, pp. 104-105; also Clark McLean listing, NYSL, McLean Family Papers, Box 1; also NYS Adjutant Gen.
[367] *O.R.*, Series 1, Vol. 38, Part 1, p. 68.
[368] RCL, June 23rd, 1864 and July 11th, 1864; NYSL, McLean Family Papers, August 28th, 1864 diary entry; HWL, July 2nd, 1864.
[369] NYSL, McLean Family Papers, Box 1, June 23rd, 1864 letter.
[370] GNMPL, V6-123b, Coy June 27th, 1864 diary entry.
[371] GNMPL, V6-123b, Coy July 3rd, 1864 diary entry; NYSL, McLean Family Papers, Box 1, diary entries June 23rd and July 6th, 1864.
[372] NYSL, McLean Family Papers, July 9th & July 18th & July 19th, 1864 letters.
[373] USAMHI, John Gourlee Letters, July 12th, 1864; NYSL, McLean Family Papers, July 18th, 1864 letter.
[374] USAMHI, John Gourlee Letters, July 12th, 1864; USAMHI, Tooley Brothers 123rd New York, William July 10th, 1864 letter.
[375] *O.R.*, Series 1, Vol. 38, Part 5, pp. 149-150 for telegrams between Grant, Halleck and Sherman.
[376] RCL, July 20th, 1864; USAMHI, Tooley Brothers 123rd New York, William July 24th, 1864 letter; USAMHI, John Gourlee Letters, July 26th, 1864.
[377] USAMHI, John Gourlee Letters, July 26th, 1864.
[378] Morhous, p. 111; USAMHI, John Gourlee Letters, July 26th, 1864.
[379] RCL, July 20th, 1864.
[380] USAMHI, Tooley Brothers 123rd New York, July 24th, 1864 letter; RCL, July 20th, 1864.
[381] RCL, July 20th, 1864.
[382] GNMPL, V6-123b, Coy July 20th, 1864 diary entry; RCHS, Bull manuscript, p. 194; Casualties from Historical Data Systems' American Civil War Database, www.civilwardata.com.
[383] Brigade casualty totals from regimental losses given by Historical Data Systems' American Civil War Database, www.civilwardata.com (detachment of 3rd MD not included).
[384] RCHS, Bull manuscript, p. 195.
[385] USAMHI, John Gourlee Letters, July 26th, 1864.
[386] RCL, July 21st, 1864.
[387] HWL, July 29th, 1864.
[388] RCL, July 21st, 1864.
[389] NYSL, McLean Family Papers, July 21st, 1864 diary entry; GNMPL, V6-123b, Coy diary entry July 21st, 1864.

[390] Pember Library, Box 16, No. 20, July 23rd, 1864 Rogers letter, Sept. 13th, 1864 Rogers letter, Sept. 29th, 1864 Baker letter.
[391] RCL, July 22nd, 1864.
[392] NYSL, McLean Family Papers, July 25th, 1864 diary entry; USAMHI, Tooley Brothers 123rd New York, William July 24th, 1864 letter.
[393] USAMHI, John Gourlee Letters, Aug. 3rd, 1864; RCL, July 28, 1864.
[394] GNMPL, V6-123b, Coy Aug. 4th & 5th, 1864 diary entries.
[395] GNMPL, V6-123b, Coy Aug. 8th, 1864 diary; RCL, Aug. 16th, 18th, 20th.
[396] NYSL, McLean Family Papers, July 29th, 1864 diary entry; USAMHI, John Gourlee Letters, July 19th & July 26th, 1864.
[397] RCL, August 26th, 1864.
[398] NYSL, McLean Family Papers, Box 1, August 29th, 1864 letter.
[399] USAMHI, Tooley Brothers 123rd New York, Aug, 29th, 1864 letter.
[400] GNMPL, V6-123b, Coy Aug. 26th, 1864 diary entry; NYSL, McLean Family Papers, Box 1, August 29th, 1864 letter.
[401] NYSL, McLean Family Papers, August 2nd, 1864 diary entry; WCA, *Salem Press*, September, 13th, 1864.
[402] RCL, Aug. 31st & Sept. 1st, 1864.
[403] USAMHI, John Gourlee Letters, September 15th, 1864.
[404] RCL, Sept. 2nd, 1864; USAMHI, John Gourlee Letters, September 15th, 1864; NYSL, Eaton Family Papers, September 4th, 1864 letter.
[405] NYSL, McLean Family Papers, Box 1, Sept. 3rd, 1864 letter.
[406] RCL, September 3rd & 5th, 1864.
[407] Eaton Family Papers, September 4th, 1864 letter; McLean Family Papers, Box 1, Sept. 3rd, 1864 letter.
[408] NYSL, McLean Family Papers, Sept. 6th, 1864 diary entry.
[409] USAMHI, William T. Shimp, August 20th, 1864 letter.
[410] RCL, Sept. 5th, 1864; USAMHI, John Gourlee Letters, Sept. 15th, 1864; Morhous, p. 127; NYSL, McLean Family Papers, Oct. 14th, 1864.
[411] WCH, Robert Cruikshank Papers.
[412] *Ibid.*
[413] USAMHI, John Gourlee Letters, Sept. 22nd, 1864; RCHS, Bull manuscript, p. 255; Morhous, p. 130.
[414] USAMHI, Tooley Brothers 123rd New York, Sept. 26th, 1864; NYSL, McLean Family Papers, Oct. 14th, 1864.
[415] WCH, Record 43, Box F also Box B Civil War Misc.
[416] WCH, Kingsbury, Box 1, Folder 83.
[417] NYSL, Eaton Family Papers, Oct. 25th, 1864 letter; Hartford Enlistment Center Museum, Letter "U" August 10th, 1864; National 1864 election totals Wikipedia website; McClellan and the army vote, Sears, pp. 588-589; 123rd NY voting: RCL, Oct. 20th, 1864 also Morhous, p. 131 (McLean in an Oct. 20th, 1864 letter gives 344 Lincoln, 30 McClellen. As he was working as a regimental clerk the additional eight votes might be staff officers.); 46th PA voting from regimental report in

Historical Data Systems' American Civil War Database, www.civilwardata.com; Washington Co. results Tribune Almanac for 1865, p. 48.

[418] O.R., Series 1, Vol. 44, Part 1, p. 228.
[419] RCL, October 20th, 1864.
[420] Ibid.
[421] USAMHI, John Gourlee Letters, Nov. 7th, 1864; USAMHI, Tooley Brothers, September 26th, 1864 letter.
[422] USAMHI, John Gourlee, Sept. 23rd and Nov. 3rd, 1864 letters.
[423] NYSL, McLean Family Papers, September 29th, 1864 entry.
[424] O.R., Series 1, Vol. 44, Part 1, p. 230 for 123rd NY effectives, p. 16 Corps, p. 220 Division, p. 226 Brigade, p. 23 regimental commanders.
[425] RCHS, Bull manuscript, p. 264.
[426] NYSL, McLean Family Papers, Nov. 15th, 1864 entry; RCHS, Bull manuscript, p. 269.
[427] O.R., Series 1, Vol. 44, Part 1, p. 8.
[428] RCHS, Bull manuscript, pp. 276-277.
[429] RCHS, Bull manuscript, p. 275.
[430] Morhous, pp. 134-135.
[431] O.R., Series 1, Vol. 44, Part 1, p. 211.
[432] O.R., Series 1, Vol. 44, Part 1, p. 223.
[433] Morhous, p. 138; O.R., Series 1, Vol. 44, Part 1, p. 223; Bull, p. 184; USAMHI, Tooley Brothers 123rd NY, Jan. 11th, 1865 letter (letter dated 1864 but from Savannah, GA and discusses March to the Sea).
[434] RCHS, Bull manuscript, pp. 286-287.
[435] Battle casualties Historical Data Systems' American Civil War Database, www.civilwardata.com; Destruction of village, Bailey, *War and Ruin*, pp. 72-74.
[436] Bailey, pp. 69-70.
[437] O.R., Series 1, Vol. 44, Part 1, p. 224.
[438] Morhous, p. 139.
[439] NYSL, McLean Family Papers, Nov. 27th, 1864 entry; O.R., Series 1, Vol. 44, Part 1, p. 224; Morhous, p. 140.
[440] O.R., Series 1, Vol. 44, Part 1, p. 44.
[441] Morhous, p. 142.
[442] Morhous, p. 144.
[443] Morhous, p. 145.
[444] Morhous, p. 146; O.R., Series 1, Vol. 44, Part 1, p. 224.
[445] NYSL, McLean Family Papers, Dec. 15th, 1864 entry; RCL, Dec. 17th, 1864; NYSL, McLean Family Papers, Dec. 19th, 1864 entry.
[446] McLean Family Papers, Dec. 22nd, 1864 diary entry.
[447] O.R., Series 1, Vol. 44, Part 1, p. 210.
[448] USAMHI, John Gourlee Letters, Dec. 19th, 1864.
[449] USAMHI, Tooley Brothers 123rd NY, Jan. 11th & 15th letters.
[450] McLean Family Papers, Dec. 17th, 1864 letter.

[451] USAMHI, John Gourlee Letters, Dec. 19th, 1864.
[452] HWL, December 18th, 1864.
[453] O.R., Series 1, Vol. 44, Part 1, pp. 229-230 for 123rd, pp. 225-226 for brigade, p. 219 for division.
[454] O.R., Series 1, Vol. 44, Part 1, pp. 210-211.
[455] O.R., Series 1, Vol. 44, Part 1, p. 13; 2007 dollar value derived from Consumer Price Index for 1864 from Federal Reserve Bank of Minneapolis website.
[456] McPherson, *The Atlas of the Civil War*, p. 198.
[457] USAMHI, William T. Shimp, Jan. 3rd & 26th, 1865 letters.
[458] USAMHI, Tooley Brothers, Jan. 15th, 1865 letter; Perry, p.29; Morhous, pp. 150-151.
[459] NYSL, McLean Family Papers, Box 3, Jan. 1st, 1865 diary entry.
[460] NYSL, McLean Family Papers, Jan. 9th, 1865 diary entry, also Jan. 9th, 1865 letter to father.
[461] Morhous, p. 153; RCHS, Bull manuscript, p. 2.5; NYSL, McLean Family Papers, Jan. 17th, 1865 diary entry.
[462] O.R., Series 1, Vol. 47, Part 1, p. 608; *Ibid.,* p. 619; McLean Family Papers, Jan. 26th, 1865 diary entry.
[463] McLean Family Papers, Feb. 1st, 1865 letter.
[464] Morhous, p. 155; McLean Family Papers, Feb. 6th, 1865 diary entry; O.R., Series 1, Vol. 47, Part 1, p. 620; RCL, Feb. 3rd & 9th, 1865.
[465] Morhous, p. 156.
[466] RCL, Feb. 10th & 16th, 1865.
[467] Morhous, pp. 157-158.
[468] RCHS, Bull manuscript, p. 300.
[469] Morhous, p. 158.
[470] For destruction of Columbia see Barrett, *Sherman's March Through the Carolinas,* pp. 63-91; O.R., Series 1, Vol. 47, Part 1, p. 22.
[471] Morhous, pp. 158-159.
[472] Morhous, p. 162; RCL, Feb. 22nd, 1865; RCHS, Bull manuscript, p. 9.5.
[473] RCHS, Bull manuscript, p. 17.
[474] RCHS, Bull manuscript, p. 13.
[475] RCL, March 2nd, 1865.
[476] RCHS, Bull manuscript, p. 13.
[477] RCHS, Bull manuscript, pp. 13-14; NYSL, McLean Family Papers, March 9th, 1865 diary.
[478] Morhous, p. 166; RCL, March 11th, 1865.
[479] RCHS, Bull manuscript, p. 17; RCL, March 10th, 1865.
[480] For Fayetteville destruction see Barrett, pp. 140-146.
[481] USAMHI, Tooley Brothers, March 12th, 1865 letter; USAMHI, John Gourlee, March 28th, 1865 letter.
[482] RCL, March 13th, 1865.

[483] For battle description and maps see Moore, *The Battle of Bentonville*, pp. 7-15; Rogers battle report and quote, *O.R.*, Series 1, Vol. 47, Part 1, p. 623.
[484] Battle casualties Historical Data Systems' American Civil War Database, www.civilwardata.com.
[485] RCL, March 16th, 1865; Morhous, p. 169; *O.R.*, Series 1, Vol. 47, Part 1, p. 623; NYS Adjutant General Report for year 1903, V5, p. 351-499.
[486] For battle see Moore, pp. 16-70.
[487] *O.R.*, Series 1, Vol. 47, Part 1, p. 624.
[488] *Ibid.*, Morhous, p. 171.
[489] Total casualties from Fox, p. 548, p. 551; Corps casualties, Moore, pp. 74-75; Regimental losses from Historical Data Systems' American Civil War Database, www.civilwardata.com.
[490] RCHS, Bull manuscript, p. 26.
[491] RCHS, Bull manuscript, pp. 27-28.
[492] NYSL, McLean Family Papers, March 23rd, 1865 diary entry; Fox, p. 533.
[493] HWL, February 10th, 1865.
[494] Regimental losses from Historical Data Systems' American Civil War Database, www.civilwardata.com.
[495] *O.R.*, Series 1, Vol. 47, Part 1, Regiment p. 625, Brigade p. 612-613.
[496] USAMHI, Tooley Brothers, April 1st, 1865; WCH, Robert Cruikshank Papers, equipment inspections for April 13th, 1864 & April 6th, 1865.
[497] NYSL, McLean Family Papers, April 2nd, 1865 letter.
[498] NYSL, McLean Family Papers, April 7th, 1865 diary entry.
[499] NYSL, McLean Family Papers, April 2nd & 4th diary entries, April 2nd, 1865 letter.
[500] USAMHI, Tooley Brothers, April 1st, 1865 letter.
[501] Morhous, p. 174-175; *O.R.*, Series 1, Vol. 47, Part 1, p. 627; NYSL, McLean Family Papers, April 14th, 1865 letter.
[502] *O.R.*, Series 1, Vol. 47, Part 1, pp. 614-615.
[503] *O.R.*, Series 1, Vol. 47, Part 1, p. 603.
[504] RCL, April 15th, 1865.
[505] Morhous, p. 176.
[506] RCL, April 12th, 1865 narrative; NYSL, McLean Family Papers, April letter; RCL, *Ibid.*
[507] RCHS, Bull manuscript, pp. 8-9; RCL, April 15th, 1865 letter.
[508] NYSL, McLean Family Papers, April 14th, 1865 letter.
[509] NYSL, McLean Family Papers, April 17th, 1865 letter.
[510] RCL, April 17th, 1865.
[511] NYSL, McLean Family Papers, April 20th & 25th, 1865 letters.
[512] RCHS, Bull manuscript, p. 9; Morhous, pp. 178-179.
[513] RCL, April 24th, 1865.
[514] NYSL, McLean Family Papers, April 24th, 1865 diary entry; Morhous, p. 180.

[515] *O.R.*, Series 1, Vol. 47, Part 3, p. 532, pp. 482-483.
[516] NYSL, McLean Family Papers, April 25th, 1865 letter.
[517] Morhous, p. 181; NYSL, McLean Family Papers, April 20th, 1865 letter.
[518] RCHS, Bull, manuscript chapter The Homeward March, p. 1.
[519] Morhous, p. 181; RCL, May 10th, 1865.
[520] Morhous, p. 186.
[521] RCHS, Bull manuscript, pp. 4-5.
[522] Morhous, p. 187.
[523] NYSL, McLean Family Papers, June 1st, 1865 letter; RCL, narrative, May 23rd, 1865.
[524] NYSL, McLean Family Papers, May 26th, 1865 letter, May 25th, 1865 diary entry; RCHS, Bull manuscript, p. 8.
[525] NYSL, McLean Family Papers, June 1st & June 2nd, 1865 letters.
[526] Numbers approximate and arrived at by a review of Appendix A muster roll; WCA, Return total of 522 found in June 13th, 1865 *Salem Press*.
[527] WCHS, Civil War Letters of Artemus Harrington, August 27th, 1863.
[528] WCH, Salem, Box 7, Folder 2, "Old Dance Programs."